I0008589

DISCOVERY AND EXPLORATION
OF AUSTRALIA.

A HISTORY

OF THE

DISCOVERY AND EXPLORATION

OF

AUSTRALIA;

OR,

AN ACCOUNT OF THE PROGRESS OF GEOGRAPHICAL DISCOVERY
IN THAT CONTINENT, FROM THE EARLIEST PERIOD TO
THE PRESENT DAY.

BY THE

Rev. JULIAN E. TENISON WOODS,

FELLOW OF THE ROYAL GEOGRAPHICAL SOCIETY; OF THE GEOLOGICAL SOCIETY;
OF THE LINNÆAN SOCIETY; OF THE ROYAL SOCIETY OF VICTORIA;
HON. MEM. GAW. AND V. P. PENOLA INSTITUTES, ETC.
AUTHOR OF "GEOLOGICAL OBSERVATIONS IN SOUTH AUSTRALIA,"
"NORTH AUSTRALIA," "NOT QUITE SO OLD AS THE HILLS,"
ETC. ETC.

IN TWO VOLUMES.—VOL II.

LONDON:
SAMPSON LOW, SON, AND MARSTON,
14, LUDGATE HILL.
MELBOURNE: H. T. DWIGHT.
1865.

[The right of Translation is reserved.]

NEW YORK
PUBLIC

THE NEW YORK
PUBLIC LIBRARY
98014
ASTOR, LENOX AND
TILDEN FOUNDATIONS.
1898

CONTENTS.

CHAPTER I.

EYRE OVERLAND TO WESTERN AUSTRALIA.

CHAPTER II.

FROME AND HORROCKS.

CHAPTER VII.

WESTERN AUSTRALIA.

CHAPTER VIII.

MITCHELL ON THE UPPER BAROOO.

CHAPTER IX.

KENNEDY'S FIRST JOURNEY AND LEICHHARDT'S LAST.

CHAPTER X.

ANOTHER DISASTROUS EXPEDITION.

CHAPTER XI.

ROE, GREGORY, AND FITZGERALD IN WESTERN AUSTRALIA.

CHAPTER XII.

LAKE TORRENS AGAIN, AND A SEARCH FOR LEICHHARDT.

CHAPTER XIII.

AUSTIN IN WESTERN AUSTRALIA.

CHAPTER XIV.

GREGORY TRACES UP THE VICTORIA RIVER.

CHAPTER XV.

LAKE TORRENS AGAIN.

CHAPTER XVI.

THE DISCOVERIES OF BABBAGE, WARBURTON, AND F. GREGORY.

CHAPTER XVII.

A. C. GREGORY EXPLORES THE BAROOO.

CHAPTER XVIII.

STUART'S FIRST JOURNEYS.

CHAPTER XIX.

STUART AT THE CENTRE OF AUSTRALIA.

CHAPTER XXVIII.

LANDSBOROUGH'S DISCOVERIES.

CHAPTER XXIX.

M'KINLAY'S JOURNEY ACROSS THE CONTINENT.

CHAPTER XXX.

HOWITT'S JOURNEYS.

CHAPTER XXXI.

STUART'S LAST JOURNEY—CONCLUSION.

DISCOVERY AND EXPLORATION OF AUSTRALIA.

CHAPTER I.

EYRE OVERLAND TO WESTERN AUSTRALIA.

Eyre's expedition to the centre of Australia—Crystal Brook—Lake Torrens—Termination of the Flinders Range—The Mundy and Frome—Eyre stopped at Lake Torrens—Returns to Port Lincoln—Starts for King George's Sound—Unsuccessful attempt to reach the head of the Australian Bight—Second attempt—Starts finally to the westward—First stage—Five days without water—Sufferings of the men and horses—Second stage—Seven days without water—Third stage—Desertion of the native boys — They return — Murder of the overseer — Horrible situation of Mr. Eyre—Rapid advance—Another seven days without water — Better country — Wylie's meal — Rest in good pasturage —A vessel in sight—Providential assistance—Last stage, and arrival at King George's Sound.

THE explorations described in the preceding volume have an interest very different from the rest of this history. They owed their novelty principally to the countries passed through, whose richness and fertility might give a theme to a new race of poets in the south. It is true there were hair-breadth escapes and exciting adventures in these early expeditions, but they were not very important. The explorers suffered, but as yet no part of the Australian desert had been unfolded to the view, and the horrors of journeys amid its wastes had not been fully experienced. We now leave the classical ground of Australian discovery. The old-fashioned officers, with large retinues of convicts dragging an absurd amount of baggage into the interior—the naval officers and the marine surveys slowly fade

from view. A new race of explorers comes now upon
the field—a band of heroes, such as Eyre, who crossed
the Australian Bight with a single companion; such as
Stuart, who almost crossed the continent with two
men and a few horses; or like Burke and Wills, who
did their work like men, and nobly laid down their lives
in the task. And these feats, the deeds of such men,
are now to come before the reader. It is unnecessary
to bespeak his attention. No history of travel and
adventure ever contained so much exciting interest as
the explorations now to be recorded. It is marvellous,
indeed, how they are so little known. In other times,
they would have been treasured up like the deeds of the
classical heroes of old; in our own they are not heard
much beyond the shores of Australia. It would be a
satisfaction to think that this was because heroism was
now common, and every man a hero.

At any rate, we have had many in Australia. Foremost among them stands the fame of Mr. Eyre, whose
name has already occurred in the preceding volume.
Once having tasted the pleasures of discovery, it seemed
as if he would not rest unless he were treading unknown
lands. In 1840 he was astir again. People were talking in South Australia of exploring a route to King
George's Sound, and thus putting the colonies in communication. Meetings were held and committees formed,
but nothing was positively decided upon. During this
state of hesitation, Mr. Eyre returned from Western
Australia. He was keenly desirous of an exploration
of some kind, but did not think much of the proposed
scheme. He pointed out that it was useless to expect
to get an available road in the desired direction; and
even if it could be traversed by man, its barrenness
would make it quite impassable for cattle and sheep.
Instead of this, he proposed another plan. This was to
conduct an expedition to the north; one-third of the
expenses of which he undertook to bear. This offer
was readily acceded to by the Government, and a sum
was raised by subscription to meet the expenditure of
the outfit. The party was soon equipped. It consisted
of Mr. Eyre, Mr. E. B. Scott, four men, and two native

boys. They were provided with thirteen horses, forty sheep, besides stores for three months, and they were to have a further supply sent by sea to the head of Spencer's Gulf.

On the 18th June the party were entertained at Government House, by the governor, Colonel Gawler, and a silk union-jack was presented with much ceremony to Mr. Eyre, with directions to plant it in the centre of Australia. After the breakfast, the whole party accompanied Mr. Eyre on the first part of his journey; and so little was the country settled at that time, that they did not bid him farewell until they reached the open bush on the Gawler Town Road.

Eyre's plan was to follow up the Flinders Range until it led him to the centre of the continent. He suspected that Lake Torrens, or the low ground he had seen from Mount Eyre, might prevent him penetrating very far to the westward, but he had little doubt that the Flinders Range would continue to the north. With this view, he kept upon his former track until the 27th, when he reached a more westerly portion of the Rocky River, which ran through a deep and picturesque gorge. Next day, in emerging from the hills, they came upon a pretty pebbly stream of clear and rippling water, which was named Crystal Brook. These were the only new features found upon their journey, and on the 3rd July they reached Mount Brown, and camped while waiting for the supply vessel *Waterwitch.*

They had not long to wait. Two days afterwards she was seen at anchor. Leaving the overseer (John Baxter) to superintend the landing of the stores, Eyre, with one of the black boys, started for a preliminary examination beyond Mount Eyre. This they reached next day (the 7th), and then struck to the north-west, to examine Lake Torrens. They crossed immense plains for the first day and a half, and they had to toil over heavy red sand ridges, with plains between. There was no watercourse in the whole extent, and all they had to supply their wants was the precarious remains of a chance shower, which had left puddles here and here. At last they reached the lake. Eyre says he found it to be

B 2

completely girt by a steep sandy ridge, exactly like
those surrounding the sea-shore. No rocks nor stones
were visible anywhere, but many saline crusts appeared on the outer edge. Upon descending into its
basin he found the bed dry, and coated completely over
with a crust of salt, forming one unbroken pure white
sheet, which glittered brilliantly in the sun. The crust
yielded to the foot, as he stepped upon it, and a dark
soft mud oozed out. He tried to walk a little distance,
but was obliged to return.

In truth, it was a desolate place. The cold wintry
glare of the white salt rendered it almost impossible to
say whether there were water in the bed or not. But
there was, at any rate, moisture in the atmosphere, for
the refraction of the air made the distance as hopeful in
appearance as it was cheerless in reality. Eyre, however, was almost certain that there was no water in the
lake, at least for five miles from where he stood. At
this distance the depression was about twenty miles wide,
with what looked like high land on the west; but this
may have been refraction. Northward, the vast area
was interminable as far as the eye could reach—an
immense plague-spot of sterility, which was equalled,
in barrenness and perhaps surpassed, by the bleak wilderness which lined the bank.

Eyre determined to steer to the northward. It was
evident he could not cross the lake, and there was no
sustenance for men or horses on its banks. His only
chance was to keep the range as far as it might lead
him. The furthest point of the hills visible was Mount
Deception, to the north-west. In crossing the immediate
plains towards it, they relied for water on the puddles.
Besides these, there was little to vary the scene, except
sundry ridges, stunted pines, and straggling bushes.
There were the marks of some few watercourses from
the hills; dry, of course, and not easily followed. Some
of them contained crusts of salt, which showed what the
character of the water would have been had any remained.
Added to this, the salt-water tea tree began to make its
appearance—a shrub which is never seen except where
the soil is saline and the water too brackish for use.

This was not a pleasant prospect for Mr. Eyre. Whichever way he turned difficulties met his view. In one direction was an impracticable lake; in another, a barren desert; and in a third, a range of inhospitable rocks. He spent many days in examining the country north of the depôt, but its character seldom varied. Barren sandy plains formed the lower level, and the hills were of quartz and ironstone. Even they were gradually becoming less elevated as they went northward. The valleys between them were stony, and the whole country became more barren, while springs along the hill sides, which had hitherto been numerous, were few in number, difficult to find, and very far in among the ranges. Long and anxiously he searched for a good large spring, and not liking to return without accomplishing his object, he reduced his rations until they were barely sufficient to support life. At last he was successful. At a place about one hundred and fifteen miles north of Mount Arden he found a supply sufficient for his immediate wants, and then returned to the depôt, after an absence of fifteen days.

His first care was to send back the *Waterwitch*, with the news of his proceedings hitherto, and then to move off with his party towards Depôt Pool. They arrived there on the 30th July; and when they were established, Eyre again started in advance. He steered for the most western part of Mount Deception, which he called Termination. The intermediate country was like what he encountered before—that is, barren stony plains and dry watercourses. From the summit of the hill, Lake Torrens bore to the south of west, but the view was shut out by sand ridges. He did not venture further towards the west, but descended amid the hills to search for water. A long journey was repaid at length by finding some pools in a watercourse, named the Scott, and to this he removed his party; but the supply of water was so scanty that they could not hope to remain there long.

Meanwhile, as they advanced, the hills were found to turn eastward, and to decrease in elevation very rapidly. In lat. 29° 30' they ceased altogether, and Eyre found himself in a low level country of alternating

plains of stones and sand. These had evidently been
lately flooded, but in spite of this were destitute of
grass, water, and timber of any kind, except a small
salsolaceous plant. The surface was as smooth as if
washed and scoured quite recently.

Throughout this open tract many small flat-topped
hills were interspersed. None of them were more than
a hundred feet high, and their banks were precipitous.
They would have formed an agreeable break to the prospect but for their sides, which were white and chalky,
covered over with stones, and not a scrap of vegetation.
They seemed to Eyre like the relics of tableland washed
to pieces and swept away.

These plains did not look encouraging; but Eyre
determined to try and force his way through them. He
steered north-west, and soon found himself stopped by
a salt marsh, like Lake Torrens. Twice again he essayed
the passage, each time more to the eastward, and each
time again was stopped by Lake Torrens, or what he
thought to be the lake. It is known now that if he
had continued to the northward he might have passed
between the lakes, for there are several salt basins in
this locality. But by a singular mischance he came
every time upon a separate lake, and he concluded that
the low country round the Flinders Range was completely surrounded by Lake Torrens, which, commencing
not very far from Spencer's Gulf, takes a circuitous
course of nearly four hundred miles, with a breadth of
from twenty to thirty, following the sweep of the Flinders Range, in the form of an immense horse-shoe. This
error still disfigures the majority of Australian maps in
the present day.

One very high summit in the range he named Mount
Serle, in lat. 30° 30', long. 139° 10'. This was the first
point from which he got a view of Lake Torrens, as he
thought, to the eastward. He naturally concluded that
he was hemmed in by an impassable barrier.

The refraction from these lakes was most extraordinary and deceptive. When away from the bed a vast
body of water seemed to intervene between them and
the ranges; and when away from the ranges, mock

water seemed to be laving their bases and reflecting the outlines of their rugged summits. The whole scene, says Eyre, partook more of the nature of enchantment than reality; and as the eye wandered over the unbroken crust of pure white salt, lit up by the glaring sun, the glittering effect was brilliant beyond description. Certainly, all is not gold which glitters here.

Two watercourses, the Mundy and the Frome, were seen by Eyre, but they seldom contained any water. The latter emanated from the south side of Mount Serle, and then ran under its westerly aspect with an abundance of clear water; but at twenty-three miles from its source it became as salt as the sea. The discovery of this fact effectually crushed Eyre's few remaining hopes. He at once sent the party back to Mount Arden, while he continued a final examination of this dreadful country. A conspicuous hill on the Flinders Range was named Mount Distance; and beyond this there were only the table-topped hills already described, with one remarkable peaked hill to the north-east.

To this he steered through thirty-five miles of most arid country. The view from it confirmed his cheerless anticipations. He was now past all the ranges, and for three-quarters of the compass the view was one unbroken level, except where the fragments of the tableland or the ridges of the lake interrupted its uniformity. The sight was a sickening disappointment to Eyre. He named the hill Mount Hopeless, and then reluctantly followed his party to Mount Arden.

Many natives were seen about this upper part of the range. They were generally hostile and treacherous, shunning communication with the explorers. Once, however, the latter had come upon a camp, and the owners had quitted it in such haste and fright, that two children were left behind. They seemed very much frightened, so Eyre tied a red handkerchief round the neck of one, and left the place. On revisiting it next morning, the parents had not returned to take away their children. Some days afterwards the camp was again revisited. The children were now gone. The red handkerchief had been carefully taken off and hung upon a tree, while all around the plains were strewed with green boughs, as if to propitiate the supernatural beings who had thus come mysteriously among them.

In describing these explorations, it has not been stated how much Mr. Eyre suffered from hunger, fatigue, and, above all, thirst. He was often days without water, and seldom had any other bed than the naked earth. This, of course, was followed by frequent attacks of illness, but he still went through the most laborious portions of the duty himself, and seemed not to consider his own sufferings. All these incidents he narrates with singular modesty, while giving the greatest share of praise to his companion, Mr. E. B. Scott.

Early in September, the party reached Mount Arden. It was not now Mr. Eyre's intention to make the overland journey to King George's Sound, as first proposed. He could not get to the northward, and, therefore, west from Port Lincoln seemed the only course open. But it was necessary to get fresh supplies, because he had now but three months' provisions left. With this view he intended to proceed overland to Port Lincoln, and despatch some boat from the settlement there to Adelaide, for an additional stock of rations.

On September 13th, they left the depôt, and came at twelve miles to the head of Spencer's Gulf, where they crossed the channel connecting it with Lake Torrens. Next day, in travelling through open plains, with loose gravelly stones upon the surface, they passed to the south of a table-topped hill which they had seen from Mount Arden. It resembled the hills at the end of the Flinders Range, but was larger, and composed of slate instead of chalk. Here they rested until the 17th. Eyre now sent two men with one native boy with the drays, and sheep, and seven horses, on to Streaky Bay, on their track of last year, while he and Mr. Scott, one man and the black boy, went with five horses and the dray to Port Lincoln for supplies.

The latter road was unknown, and, therefore, forty gallons of water were provided, and fourteen days' provisions. The country was not worth exploring, however. It was a dense scrub, with no water, and yet abounding in natives. They kept down Baxter's Range, but found no watercourses, and on the second day were obliged to send back their dray for a fresh supply. While it was absent, the natives came down to Eyre's camp, and stole a great number of his instruments. But he never saw them, for the scrub was very thick around him. They kept him sleepless for the whole night, but beyond this did no great harm. His companions returned meanwhile, and dragged the dray through the dense scrub with the utmost difficulty, and but for some pools of water found in some granite rocks (named Refuge Rocks), they would have had to return. They managed, however, to keep their course, subsisting on pools, and on the 1st October, reached a cattle station, then kept by a Mr. C. Dutton, who, in 1842, perished in making the same journey which Eyre had just successfully accomplished. *

Mr. Eyre was again disappointed when he reached Port Lincoln. Provisions were not to be obtained. All he could do was to hire a little open boat, and to send Mr. Scott into Adelaide, asking for assistance. This journey of Mr. Scott was not the least of the courageous feats performed on this expedition. To go in an open boat, over an exposed and almost unknown sea, as far as from the Land's End to the Bay of Biscay, was an exploit which is worth remembering.

On the 22nd, Mr. Scott returned on board the *Waterwitch*, with an abundant supply of stores and provisions, sent by the governor. He had also placed the cutter at Mr. Eyre's disposal to co-operate with him along the coast to the westward. They brought also two more men and some kangaroo dogs.

The *Waterwitch* was now sent round to Streaky Bay, while the rest of the party proceeded overland on the route described in Eyre's former expedition. They all arrived there by the 3rd of November, and found the party sent from the head of Spencer's Gulf safe and well, but in a great state of excitement about the long delay of their companions at Port Lincoln.

* His body was not found until twenty years after; and then some bones, with a whip and gloves near them, were found at the crossing-place, near the head of Spencer's Gulf.

From his previous experience, Eyre knew that after leaving Streaky Bay he would have terrible difficulties to contend with; but they surpassed his expectations when he came to encounter them. The country was fearfully sandy and arid; there was scarcely any grass, and the scrub was so dense, that they had frequently to cut their way through it. But still the party advanced courageously. Eyre directed the captain to take the cutter to Fowler's Bay, landing water at Smoky Bay as he passed. Thus, with the help of water from the ship from time to time, the whole party were after much labour again united at Fowler's Bay.

Here the stores were landed, and as the anchorage was insecure, the *Waterwitch* was sent back to Denial Bay, with orders to return on the 11th December. During the intermediate time, Eyre hoped to be able to see enough of the country ahead to send back despatches of his prospects, for he knew that once he had reached the high cliffs of the Australian Bight, it would be dangerous to detain the vessel near him. He then set out. For three days he toiled through the terrible sand around him, but finding no water he was obliged to return to the camp. He started again, having previously sent on water in a dray. This enabled him to advance much further. At twenty-seven miles from his depôt camp, he dug a well, and luckily struck water.

The next stage was twenty-two miles. No water was found at that distance, and the horses were knocked up. Worse than this, they were surrounded by a party of natives, whose suspicious movements very much harassed them. The horses were so much jaded that it was useless to attempt to take the dray and stores any further, and their only hope of saving them was by burying the baggage, and driving the horses before them as rapidly as possible back to the water. But to bury stores in the presence of natives, was to ensure their destruction. While they remained, therefore, it was useless to do anything, so they sat down and waited patiently for them to go. This the perverse savages would not do. Hour after hour they sat watching the explorers, who could only look on at their horses droop-

ing rapidly, without being able to make an effort to
save them. At last the natives slowly moved away.
As soon as the last was out of sight, the stores were
hurriedly buried, and the horses driven back as fast as
they could go. But it was too late. Three fell down
upon the road, and before proper assistance could be
sent they were dead.

Altogether, Eyre was engaged for twenty-four days
unsuccessfully attempting to round the head of the
Bight. He returned to the depôt camp on the 15th
December; but the journeys had rendered both men and
horses so weak, that a long rest must be given previous
to another attempt. Their proceedings hitherto were
not very encouraging. The furthest point reached was
within twelve miles of the head of the Bight. The
country passed through was of the worst kind: low, flat
lands, or a succession of sandy ridges, densely covered
with scrub (*Eucalyptus dumosæ*), salt-water tea tree,
and other shrubs; whilst here and there appeared a few
patches of open grassy plains. The surface rock was
limestone, full of very recent fossils.

Eyre now determined to lessen his party. The
death of four horses made it impossible to carry through
enough provisions for all; and even if he could, the
scanty supply of water made a division more desirable.
He, therefore, sent back all but the overseer, one man,
two native boys, and Mr. Scott. In his despatches he
requested more assistance. He intended to remain six
weeks in the depôt, and asked the Government to send
some oats and bran before he started.

When the cutter was gone, Eyre made another
attempt to round the head of the Bight. This time he
was successful. He even advanced about fifty miles
beyond, and reached the line of remarkable cliffs described by Flinders. The country was still a succession
of sand ridges with scrub, and for sixty miles, at least,
there was not a drop of water to be found. The country
was impracticable for drays, that was certain, and probably almost so for horses. There were natives, however, at the head of the Bight, who showed him some
grass and water, and they made him understand that

there was no more for at least a hundred miles, or
where the first break occurs in the limestone cliffs.

The country did not change when the cliffs were
reached. These were precipitous sides to a perfectly
level country. They were about 300 or 400 feet high,
and the full swell of the southern ocean was under-
mining them. The upper crust was an oolitic limestone,
and below this was a concrete of sand, small pebbles, and
shells. Beneath this appeared immense masses of a coarse
greyish limestone, of which by far the greater portion
of the cliffs was composed, and immediately below, a
narrow bed of cream-coloured limestone, which the impracticable nature of the cliffs prevented Eyre from
examining closely. Immediately along their summits,
and for a few hundred yards back, very numerous pieces
of flint were lying loosely scattered upon the limestone.
Back from the sea, and as far as the eye could reach, the
country was level, and generally open, with some low
prickly bushes and salsolaceous plants, and here and
there gum scrubs and grassy openings.

The facts thus ascertained were purchased by the
severe sufferings of the horses. It was only by burying
water that they were able to penetrate so far. When
the cutter returned, Eyre resolved to reduce his party
still further, and to take no baggage which the horses
could not carry. To his great regret he sent back Mr.
Scott and another of his men, retaining only his overseer, Baxter, and three native boys. The number of the
latter was now raised to three, because the cutter had
brought back a native of King George's Sound, named
Wylie, whom Mr. Eyre had taken to Adelaide the preceding May.

On the last day of January, 1841, the cutter left the
small party to pursue their labours in this desert. Eyre
knew that there was a fearful task before him, and
he resolved to remain in the camp until the horses had
consumed all the oats and bran lately received. While
waiting, he tried to explore the north of Fowler's Bay.
The weather was scorchingly hot, but he succeeded in
penetrating about twenty miles. The first ten was a
dense, heavy scrub of mallee and tea tree. Emerging

from this, he entered an open, pretty-looking country, consisting of grassy plains; but when he turned back he felt convinced he was approaching a country very like that between Flinders' Range and Lake Torrens.

On the 23rd February, the small party prepared for a start. They buried their surplus stores, and burnt their rockets, to the great amusement of the natives, who had kept near the depôt more or less during the whole time of their encampment. Just as they were preparing to start, the cutter was again seen. Mr. Scott landed in haste, and was delighted to find that Eyre was not yet gone. He brought letters from the governor, requesting his return to Adelaide, as every-one regarded the attempt to penetrate further westward as sheer madness. His Excellency assured him that he was perfectly satisfied with what had been done, and that if he would only return he would assist him in any attempts he might wish to make round Lake Torrens, or to explore the northern interior. He, however, implored him to push his daring and hardihood no further.

To all this Eyre gave a refusal. He had made up his mind to go westward, and thither he must go. He therefore sent Mr. Scott back, and the devoted little band moved off on the 23rd February. It would have been better for Eyre had he done otherwise. His attempt was rash, and could result in nothing very important; and the sequel will show that it entailed loss of life, and a fearful amount of suffering. One is at a loss to understand why he so easily gave up his northern project. If he found Lake Torrens an obstacle, why not go round it and start for the north at the head of the gulf? Had he done so, Stuart's discoveries might have been anticipated by twenty years.

Eyre, as we have said, buried his stores at the depôt, in case he should have to fall back. * They moved on slowly, as they had fourteen sheep to drive before them. They had taken the precaution to bury water and

---

* Twenty years afterwards these stores were found; they were in a good state of preservation, and nearly dry.

provisions in advance. Some of these casks had been disturbed by the natives; but only a little water was taken, for the natives drink but little. On March 3, they arrived at the head of the Bight. In this journey the sand was the worst evil they had to contend with. It blew about them so as to almost bury them and their provisions, besides nearly blinding them, and rendering their food almost uneatable. They also suffered great inconvenience from a large kind of horse-fly, which abounded here, and was able to inflict a very severe bite.

They had now reached the furthest water with which they were acquainted, and relied only upon the vague directions of the natives for the next they hoped to find. Eyre set off on the 7th March with the youngest of the native boys and the sheep, hoping that by travelling slowly they might accomplish their journey better. He was also anxious to have more time to look for water, and thus keep the horses which remained behind a smaller time without it. The overseer was to follow with the pack horses.

The first stage was twenty-four miles, and the next twenty-six, through a level open country, without grass or water. These plains continued into the interior, with only occasional patches of scrub. The effect of the refraction upon them was singular. More than once Eyre turned aside to examine what looked like large timber, and proved to be bushes; and what they thought with certainty were two natives, turned out to be crows. The next day there was the same country along with the interminable cliffs, but no grass and no water. The sheep were failing. Eyre thought it looked likely to rain, and sat up nearly all night, hoping to catch a few drops, but none fell. This day they accomplished twenty-five miles. At night they hurried on by moonlight. After ten miles their hearts bounded with joyous expectation, for they found native tracks. They followed them down to a native well, but it brought no relief; they turned from its dry bed with sickening disappointment. Downright exhaustion made them camp at eight miles further. At five next morning they were again upon their journey. They gazed anxiously along the cliffs, hoping to see some break in them, but the rocks continued in the distance, with a uniformity which made the explorers almost despair. Yet their massy and unbroken battlements or buttresses had an aspect of beauty even for the bloodshot, haggard eyes of the beings who then gazed at them.

At noon they were one hundred and ten miles from the last water, and the sheep could go no further. Mr. Eyre now left them in a yard, with a note to the overseer to hurry on with the horses, while he made a hasty advance. Struggling for the lives of all, he quickened his steps. Still the same cliffs and the same country. At ten miles the native paths were again met, and led to the same horrible disappointment.* Five miles further again, the same paths and the same destruction to the temporary hopes raised by them. Eyre and his companion tried to keep the high ground, but scrub appeared on their path. Still they kept steadily onwards, leading the horses, and forcing their way as best they could; but they made very little advance, and fatigue at last compelled them to desist. Eyre tried to sleep, but could not; and the sufferings of the horses, which had now been several days without water, were most pitiable. Early on the 11th they moved on, and reached the edge of the cliffs. They now noticed some hillocks of sand which they had passed in the scrub unseen. Perhaps, thought Eyre. the water alluded to by the blacks was there. The hills were miles behind now, and the suspense whether to advance or recede was maddening. At last he resolved to proceed. At seven miles further he came to a break in the cliffs, with sand drifts between, in which, by scraping and digging, water was found in abundance. One breathes freely at coming to the climax of such a recital.

Here was relief, but there was no time for rest. The first care was to return to the overseer with water.

---

* Major Warburton has proved that these tracks were made by rats, and not natives; in fact, from circumstances discovered by the major in his expedition, it may be doubted whether any natives are to be found here.

He was met at no great distance behind with all the
sheep and the horses. The animals had got through
the journey better than they could have anticipated;
but some of their loads were lightened by burying
stores. These were easily recovered. The whole
journey through the desert country was one hundred
and thirty-five miles, which had taken five days to
accomplish; thus they had got over the first stage.
Memorable indeed, but only the commencement. At
the place of their encampment the cliffs receded about
ten miles from the sea, but still ran parallel with the
coast. Eyre examined them now for the first time, and
found that they were full of fossils. There were many
traces of natives about.

They rested six days at the water, and on the 18th
they again proceeded. At first they tried the beach,
but it was too sandy, and so they again travelled behind
the shore ridge, amid low scrubby undulations. They
dug for water this day, but what they obtained was
quite salt. Next day they made a long stage, and
reached a place where there was abundance of dry
grass, but no water. They had counted on obtaining
some before this, and as the animals were quite unfit to
make another long stage, they buried their stores, and
hurried back forty miles to the water. Eyre remained
with the baggage, sheep, and the stock of water, which
amounted to six pints. The sheep were not hard to
manage, for they were only three, and all that remained
of their flour was one hundred and forty-two pounds,
and this was to supply five persons for the rest of their
journey. If they could have ridden, their prospects
would not have been so bad; but the horses were too
weak to carry them, and they were obliged to walk.
Under these circumstances, there was no possibility of
having provisions enough to last the journey, and yet
Eyre resolved to proceed.

On the 25th, the overseer returned with the horses,
and a fresh supply of water, and they started again
next day—not, however, before they had thrown away
every article which they could possibly dispense with,
retaining only one suit of clothes and a blanket each.

To encourage them in their undertaking, a sheep was killed before starting. They wanted such assistance, for every one of the party bore on his face the wan traces of exhaustion and starvation.

It will be needless to recount the daily sufferings of this stage; they were an aggravated repetition of the last. The cliffs had receded from the coast and disappeared, and they travelled as well as they could along the coast, when not impeded by the seaweed and sand. The latter and the horse-flies were terrible sources of suffering to them. They went on toiling, and hoping that each day would bring them to another watercourse; but each day only renewed the bitter disappointment of the last. Two days after starting, one of the horses lay down from exhaustion. With difficulty he was raised to his feet, and was only then got along by distributing his load among the others. Six miles further a Timor pony fell, and was abandoned. For five days they had gone without water, and now they followed the men about like dogs, making the most imploring signs.

The overseer now began to despond, and requested Mr. Eyre to return to the *cache* at Fowler's Bay. He seemed to have a presentiment of his fate. But Eyre was still deaf to all entreaties. He consented, however, to leave all the baggage, and make a push to save the lives of the horses. Thus they advanced a little quicker; but in the afternoon a mare dropped behind. Shortly afterwards they had to tie a horse up to a tree, in the hope of saving him, should water be reached that night. Of this there was some hope, for a few high sandy cones were seen in advance. They did not reach them that day, as the tide obliged them to encamp. They were one hundred and thirty-six miles from the last water, and hope was still deferred. The sand-hills were reached, and were as dry and barren as any part of their journey.

Another day of suffering took them through the same barren and cheerless country. That night they experienced a little relief. A heavy dew fell, and about a quart of water was obtained by a sponge. The

horses still advanced in a surprising manner. It is true
they were failing, but the wonder was, how they had
held out so long. On the 30th, some sand ridges were
seen in advance; but the horses were scarcely able to
crawl towards them. Eyre left them, and hurried on
with the overseer. No water was found in the ridges.
Almost frantic with despair, they dug down in what
seemed a favourable hollow. Who shall tell their joy
when, at five feet, fresh water rapidly trickled out from
the sand! Thus they obtained relief on the seventh
day, during which they had come one hundred and
sixty miles without water. They would never have
done it but for the moisture of the sea air, and how
they did it even then is a mystery. This was the second
stage.

This saved the animals' lives, though they were
scarcely able to crawl. The labours of the party had
been very great in keeping them from the sea-water,
which they made frantic efforts to reach. Now their
exertions were as great to prevent them drinking too
much. They then killed one of the two remaining
sheep; and when a little recruited, the overseer was
sent back with one native to bring back the stores
buried about forty-seven miles away. The party began
to suffer extremely from the cold, for there was no wood
to make large fires at night. Worse than all, they ran
out of shot; and though Eyre succeeded in shooting a
fine wallaby* with ball, yet their prospect now of
obtaining supplies by shooting became very slender.
The overseer was absent about ten days, and Eyre
became very anxious about him. When he returned,
at last, the cause of his delay was easily explained.
He had had to abandon one horse, with his load, only
thirteen miles from where the stores were buried. Two
others, abandoned five miles from the camp, were easily
recovered. He had on his way dug for water five
times; on four occasions he had reached salt water,
and once was stopped by a rock, so their finding fresh
water in the place where they did was most providen-

* A small kind of kangaroo, inhabiting the scrub.

tial. Eyre went back thirty-four miles, and recovered the load of the dead horse, and they were ready to recommence a new portion of this terrible journey.

They were now six hundred and fifty miles from King George's Sound, and their provisions were barely enough to last three weeks, and yet they were obliged to rest a few days, because the horses could do no more just then. The overseer again begged Mr. Eyre to return, but he would not. Yet he was suffering perhaps more than the others; he was very ill from living upon some unwholesome fish they had caught, and his chances of life seemed very small, if he persisted in his undertaking. But go on he would. He consented to kill a horse for food; it was one which was so ill that his life could not be saved in any case, and the consequence of such unwholesome diet was that they were all ill again. Bad as it was, the native boys thought they had not had enough of it, so during the night they stole a large quantity. Mr. Eyre detected this act of dishonesty, and to punish the two eldest of them, deducted a third portion of their usual share of rations. They resented this by leaving the party, and endeavouring to make their way by themselves; but as they had been very much disaffected ever since the rations were reduced, Eyre was not surprised at their conduct.

The last sheep was now killed, as a preparation for another journey. The overseer then went to examine the country in advance. The news brought back was not encouraging; the road lay along even more thick and scrubby land than before. It seemed threatening rain, so the start was delayed. Anxiously they watched each darkening cloud, praying earnestly for some few drops of water; but the clouds cleared off, and the night was clear and cold. Just as they were turning in for the evening, the native boys came back; they could not exist upon their own resources, and were sadly famished before they submitted to the humiliation of returning. Eyre took them back, believing them to be sincere, and little suspected the treachery they meditated. Again, on the 26th and

c 2

27th, it seemed wild and stormy, and threatening rain, but none fell.

On the latter date they started, again leaving behind them everything except the provisions, their arms, ammunition, and clothes. They only advanced fifteen miles the first day. The next stage was, however, eighteen, through a thick scrub, and along the top of the limestone cliffs, which had reappeared, but were now not more than three hundred feet high. On the 29th they made nineteen miles; but the day was so windy that they could scarcely stagger along the tops of the cliffs. In the evening the horses were all hobbled, and turned out to feed, and the stores were piled under an oilskin, while every one was obliged to make break-winds of boughs to protect them during the night. Mr. Eyre on this eventful evening took the first watch, from six to eleven. The night was bitterly cold, and the wind was blowing hard from the south-west. The horses fed well, but rambled a good deal. At half-past ten Mr. Eyre went to fetch them back. He found them at a short distance, and was picking his way, in the dark, among the bushes, when he was suddenly startled by a gunshot. It was from the camp, and of course he hurried there immediately. About one hundred yards from it he met Wylie, the King George's Sound native, running, and crying out, " Oh, massa! oh, massa! come, look here !" He reached the camp, and there before him lay his overseer in the agonies of death, with a wound in his chest, from which the blood was flowing rapidly.

A glance around explained the whole scene. The two younger natives were gone, whilst the scattered fragments of the baggage which had been piled under the oilskin told the reason why. The overseer was beyond human aid, for he expired immediately after Eyre's arrival. It was a horrible scene, and the feelings of the survivor were shocked as well by the crushing weight of the disaster as its suddenness. Eyre describes it with a reality that none but a witness could do justice to. He says: " The horrors of my situation glanced upon me. I was alone in the desert.

The frightful, appalling truth glared upon me in such startling reality as almost to paralyze my mind. At the dead hour of night, with the fierce wind raging around me, in one of the most inhospitable wastes of Australia, I was left alone with one native boy. I could not rely upon his fidelity, for he was perhaps in league with the other two, who might be waiting to kill me. Three days had passed since we had found water, and it was very doubtful when we should find more. Six hundred miles of country had to be traversed before I could hope to obtain the slightest help or assistance, whilst I knew that not a drop of water or an ounce of flour had been left by the murderers."

The guns were gone, and only a rifle and a pair of pistols left. The former was useless, as a ball was jammed in the barrel; and the latter had no cartridges to fit them. Obtaining possession of all the remaining arms, useless as they were, he went with the native to look for the horses. After a long search, he found them; and when he brought them back to the camp, he sat down to watch. He passed a bitter night. Every moment, he tells us, seemed to him an age, and he thought the morning would never come. The night was frosty. He had nothing on but a shirt and trousers, and to mental anguish was now added intense bodily pain. He tells us that suffering and distress nearly overwhelmed him, and life seemed scarcely worth the effort to prolong it. Ages could never efface the horrors of that single night; nor would all the world, he says, ever tempt him to go through similar ones again. Truly, the position was horrible in the extreme. To have to pass the night by the corpse of his only companion, who lay with glazed and staring eyes in the position in which he fell; and this, in the midst of an awful desert, surpasses almost any of the terrors of which, unfortunately, exploring expeditions are so full.

But things were then at their worst. When morning dawned, about forty pounds of flour, four gallons of water, besides tea and sugar, were found still left to them. Fortunately, too, in trying to clean the rifle, it went off, and though the ball whistled close to Eyre's head, yet, to his immense relief, he felt he could now protect himself. His plans were soon arranged. He wrapped the body of the overseer in a blanket, and covered it with leaves, for the ground about was all rock. He then moved quickly away, leaving everything behind, except the horses, arms, and provisions.

He was very suspicious of his companion at first, but probably without reason. The truth seems to have been that the whole three natives agreed to rob the explorers, and decamp. While they were doing so, the overseer awoke, and one of the boys shot him. This was a crime for which Wylie was totally unprepared, and so drew back. There is no doubt that he was now truly alarmed, and afraid of his former companions. The other boys were of a different tribe, and spoke a different language. He knew well they would as readily shoot him as the overseer, so he had every reason to be faithful to Mr. Eyre. He, however, denied all previous knowledge of the robbery.

They advanced ten miles that day (April 30), and then camped until the cool of the evening. Eyre made sure that the murderers had returned to the *cache* in Fowler's Bay; but in this he was mistaken. Soon after they had camped, Wylie called his attention to two white objects which were stealing through the bushes ; these, covered with their blankets, were advancing with their guns in rest toward Eyre. The latter was now truly alarmed, for he knew that by following him they might easily surprise his camp. He advanced towards them, and they retreated. He then dropped his arms, and tried to get near them, hoping to get an opportunity to rush on the eldest, and wrest his gun from him. The blacks were not to be surprised, and would hear of no parley. They begged and implored Wylie to go with them, and he only turned a deaf ear to their entreaties. Finding that they wanted nothing else, Eyre determined to push on too rapidly for them to follow, and thus avoid having to shoot the elder of the boys. When they saw Wylie going away with Mr. Eyre, they uttered most plaintive cries, and moved after them as well as they could. When night closed in, they were lost to view; they were never heard of afterwards. Like all the natives, they were improvident, and utterly thoughtless of the morrow, and so very probably they consumed their provisions the very first day, and then slowly perished. It does not appear possible that they could ever have reached Fowler's Bay.

Mr. Eyre made all the haste he could over the scrubby, stony ground of the country upon which he was, not only to get free from his murderous followers, but also to reach water, for this was the fifth day that the animals had been without a drink. They advanced twenty-eight miles on the 1st May, still along the cliffs, whilst the inland country increased in elevation. But the horses were giving way; it seemed impossible that they could endure it much longer, yet they managed to crawl twenty-one miles next day. The country now improved, and there were many traces of natives, but still no water. At four and a half miles the day following, they reached some sand-drifts. The wretched horses could scarcely move over them. Whilst persevering in their efforts to get them along, they found a native well. To attempt to describe their feelings at the sight of water would be vain. This was the end of their third stage. It was seven days since they had left their last depôt, and they had meanwhile crossed one hundred and fifty miles of desert, or rather rocky, barren, and scrubby tableland. Probably the horses suffered less in this than the former stages, but in no other part of Australia could they have survived so long.

They made a long rest at this portion of their journey. Water was too necessary to them to be passed hurriedly by. While they were refreshing themselves they killed and jerked one of the horses. Every day they looked out anxiously for the tracks of the native boys, but no signs of them were seen. It was evident they had perished, and Eyre and Wylie were now the only survivors of this ill-fated expedition; but even they were so emaciated and exhausted that it seemed quite a chance if they would ever reach the settled districts.   Yet Eyre was as confident of success as ever.

They started away again upon the 10th May, but now a great part of their sufferings were mitigated. The country became hilly, and water was easily obtained. New difficulties now arose.   On the 12th Eyre was too ill to leave the camp. He rallied a little next day, but on the two following days they were again unable to proceed.   Both were very ill, principally because of the diseased horse-flesh which they were obliged to feed upon.

On the 16th and 17th they managed to crawl along as fast as their pitiable state would allow them.   On the latter day a native dog stole fourteen pounds of their meat, which, bad as it was, could not be spared in their famished condition: they were again reduced to short rations in consequence.   They got along but slowly now, for in proportion as the country became well watered it also became soft, and the horses were ready to lie down wherever the passage was difficult. On the 18th they arrived at a nice green grassy spot, on which they were fortunate enough to kill a young kangaroo. Wylie was delighted at this. " Massa, you see me *pta* (eat) all night," was what he used to say to Eyre whenever any butchering left offal for him to masticate. He generally kept his word. On this occasion his supper is worth recording. He commenced by eating a pound and a half of horse-flesh with a little bread. He then disposed of the entrails, paunch, liver, lights, tail, and two hind-legs of the young kangaroo, which was not a very great deal.   But next a penguin, which he had found dead upon the beach, and upon this he forced down the hide of the kangaroo after singeing the hair off. He wound up the meal by swallowing the tough skin of the penguin; then he made a small fire, and slept after all his exertions. However marvellous this may appear, none who know the gormandizing powers of the natives will doubt the story.

On the 19th they only advanced four miles, for they then reached such excellent grass and water (inside Point Malcolm), besides abundance of kangaroo, that Eyre determined to rest here six days to recruit the horses. They accordingly rested, and were able to procure a good many kangaroo, besides plenty of fish and crabs. The stay was very beneficial to them. Wholesome food in abundance had a wonderful effect upon their health. Albeit, Wylie still swallowed the skin of every kangaroo which was shot except one, which, to his ineffable disgust, the native dogs stole. The horses, too, were much improved, strong enough, indeed, to carry Eyre occasionally, and this was a great matter.

On the 26th they started again, making direct for Cape Arid, and thus cutting off Cape Pasley. They made eighteen miles this day, and when they camped were in sight of some high, bluff, craggy hills in the interior. Eyre named the range after Lord John, now Earl Russell. These mountains constitute the first break in the character of the scenery for many hundred miles. From thence until 30th May their journey was through a country pretty well grassed, with salt-water creeks; but on the date just named they met a fine fresh-water lake, of moderate size, six miles from a small stream. By this time their provisions had nearly run out, and their sufferings again commenced. They were not so fortunate either with their guns, and so they were reduced each day to a few spoonfuls of flour and water. Two days more were spent in crossing many fresh-water streams towards Lucky Bay, where an addition to the food was obtained in the roots of a kind of reed which grew there plentifully. At best, however, it was a precarious subsistence; but they had now set aside all delicacy, and lived like savages, on whatever they could find. Fortunately, a most unexpected relief was at hand, or it may be doubted whether they would have ever reached King George's Sound.

On the 2nd June, as their stock of flour was exhausted, they commenced their journey without breakfast. They soon reached the sea-side, and they could scarcely believe their eyes when they saw some boats at a short distance from the land. Their joy was, however, mingled with the most intense anxiety. Every effort was made to attract attention by firing guns and waving their clothes, but in vain. Bitterly despairing at last of being able to receive the help which was so near, they sat down upon the ground and sullenly watched them. Help was nearer than they thought. As they cast their eyes around a new joy was in store for them. There, beneath them, lay at anchor the ship from whence the boats proceeded, and which in their eagerness they had not noticed before. Words cannot describe the frantic joy with which they galloped down upon the beach and hailed the stranger. A boat was soon put ashore, and, as much to the astonishment of one as the other, they were taken on board. Mutual explanations soon told all, and Eyre was most kindly and hospitably received by Captain Rossiter, of the French whaler *Mississippi*.

To this providential aid Eyre undoubtedly owed his life. One cannot help admiring the extraordinary luck which attended him in this journey. Few men have ever survived to tell such a tale as his. He remained on board the ship until the 14th June, and then, being thoroughly restored, and supplied with fresh provisions, he renewed his journey. The country was well watered, and, equipped as he was, Eyre could now arrange his stages as he wished, besides being more indifferent about his camp, as he had now a good supply of warm clothing.

At first their journey was through well-grassed marshy country, but it soon became arid, with stony hills to cross, and salt lakes to go round. On the 21st June they found a fine hole of fresh water, with no grass, and a little beyond were two chains of salt water ponds trending towards the sea. On the 22nd they passed another and a large salt-water lake, and then a salt-water river fully 100 yards wide. This latter obliged them to trace it up two miles to find a crossing place, and then succeeded undulating sandy country.

The above forms a good specimen of the monotony of their diary. It will not be necessary to particularize further. They were not very far from the coast, and therefore almost on the track of other explorers, but whether or not there was little of interest in the remainder of their journey. The main features need only be indicated. The country up to Flinders' Cape Barren was of the most sterile description. It took them twelve days to reach this point, but they had no scarcity of water, as it rained heavily nearly every day. When they were 150 miles from Rossiter Bay (where they had obtained relief), they saw a good many traces of natives about. From Cape Barren, he tried to pass between Mount Barren Ranges and the sea, but finding this impossible, he kept over the hills, through a worthless country with dense scrub. The rocks were all quartz, granite, sandstone, grit, and ironstone.

On the evening of the 30th June they saw the hills behind King George's Sound. Wylie's joy knew no bounds, but he was not so near home as he thought. It took four days more to get through the intervening scrub, marshes, and watercourses; and just as they thought they had arrived at the close of their labours a large salt-water inlet stopped their further progress. As they went round it, the rain set in heavily; and when not clambering through deep rocky ravines, they had to wade through the flat country. On the 6th July they came upon the Candiup, a large stream with many deep reaches, emptying itself into a wide and deep arm of the sea. From the heavy rains which had fallen they had great trouble in crossing many of the smaller torrents. Difficulties seemed to increase as they advanced, but with home so near it is easy to understand how they would be overcome. Nothing could stop them now. Mr. Eyre had to wade through the Candiup seven times before he got the horses over; and then, four miles beyond, they reached the King's River, which is a large salt arm of Oyster Harbour. The horses could not be got across this, and therefore, instead of sleeping at Albury, as they had expected, they were obliged to encamp with the river before them. Next morning they abandoned everything except the charts, and pushed on as fast as their exhausted condition would allow. As the day advanced, they got fairly into the town, and though it was but a miserable village, the sight of so much civilization brought tears of joy and gratitude into the eyes of Mr. Eyre.

Thus he brought his expedition to a close. Foolish and rash as it was, a man of Eyre's noble character might be excused for undertaking what to others might seem impossible. As a man he was courageous and daring ; as an explorer he would probably have been unequalled had his fate conducted him to a better field. His account of his travels is written in a manner worthy of the subject, and should be considered a classic in Australian literature.

In conclusion, it may be mentioned that his arrival in Albury created the greatest astonishment. Had a dead man risen from the grave he could not have been regarded with more wonder and astonishment. His friends were almost out of mourning for him, as he had been considered as dead long ago.*

* Many readers will be curious to know of Mr. Eyre's subsequent fate, as he occupies no further place in this history. As a slight recognition of his services, he was made a Lieutenant-Governor in New Zealand, and afterwards received various colonial appointments. He has since been knighted, and is now Governor of Jamaica.

CHAPTER II.

FROME AND HORROCKS.

Russell upon the East Coast—Frome to the north—The Passmore River—The Lucas—Loss of one of the party—Mount Bryan—Horrocks—The early settlers north of Adelaide—Horrocks starts for the interior—Gulnare Plains — Mount Remarkable—Horrocks' Pass — Excursion towards the lake—Accident—Death of Horrocks.

NOT to interrupt explorations connected with the same locality, it has been thought better to insert here some discoveries by Messrs. Russell upon the Darling Downs. In October, 1841, they went in search of a run, and in sixty miles from a station on the downs came upon a beautiful reach of the river Condamine. For five days they followed the river for 100 miles to the north-west, until it emptied itself into a flat covered with scrub. In returning, two of the party attempted to reach Wide Bay, across the Eastern Range, but a thick scrub prevented them.

Another expedition was made in November, 1841, to discover where the Condamine re-appeared after losing itself in a lagoon which had no visible outlet. After one day's journey along the lake they came to a small gully, which widened to a deep rocky river-bed with fine grazing country on both banks. The direction of the river was northerly, only running in floods, but having long deep reaches and large lagoons. All around the country was undulating and rich, with plenty of timber, and no scrub. Thus was discovered the extensive pastoral tract known in Queensland as Cecil Plains.

In April, 1842, circumstances took Mr. Russell to Moreton Bay, where he formed a party to explore the country round Wide Bay. The party consisted of four, with a crew of seven convicts for the boat. Much trouble was expected from the natives, as they had murdered the crew of the *Stirling Castle*, wrecked there some years before. On the 9th of April, after some difficulty from the surf, they landed at the bottom of Wide Bay, which is twenty-five miles from the entrance. The natives received them kindly, and directed them to where they would find a river named Monobocolo. They pulled up this river on the 12th for fifty miles, though after the first thirty the tide ceased, and it became very small. Its banks were lined by a thick scrub. At their camp in the evening numbers of natives joined, and amongst them was an escaped convict, who had been fourteen years with the blacks. His name was Davis. He was delighted to see the faces of civilized men again, and, notwithstanding that the gaol was still a probable home for him on his return, he joined the party, and told them there were three other rivers falling into Wide Bay, and a very large one going into the sea to the northward. Mr. Russell, however, was not able to visit them then, and he returned to Moreton Bay.

On the 24th November, 1842, he started again, calling at Wide Bay. From thence he took a westerly course inland. The first part of his journey was through a very scrubby country. It gradually became more open, and then he reached the Boyne, which flows into Port Curtis. Upon this river he returned south-west, and explored all the intervening tract to the Condamine.

In the year following, the same gentleman explored back again to the Boyne from the Condamine, but to the west of his former course. The land was generally undulating, thickly timbered, and well grassed. There were occasional ridges of granite and patches of scrub, and small streams running down from the great range. Crossing a bend of this they came to a small creek which led northward, and at less than fifty miles from the Darling Downs reached the Boyne. They followed this river for 300 miles, passing one large tri-

butary from the eastward named the Stuart. The country round both rivers was of a fine description, more
adapted, however, for the growth of sugar and coffee
than wool.

Immediately after the publication of Eyre's despatches, Captain Frome, the Surveyor-General of South
Australia, was sent with a party to Lake Torrens, to
extend the observations made during the last expedition. The Government thought on the subject much as
we do now. It seemed hardly possible to the South
Australians then, as it does to us, that the lake could
extend in a complete horseshoe, without any outlet at all to the northward. Even supposing that it did,
it was very important to find out what was the southern
boundary of its eastern arm. This was the primary
object of Frome's expedition.

He went out in 1842 and 1843. In the first year
the most northern place which he reached contained
water. This was a deep ravine near Black Rock Hill,
in lat. 32° 45'. At this point the dray and party were
left, while Frome proceeded with a light cart, equipped
with provisions for a month and water for three days.
His object was to ascertain the extent of the lake eastward, and in this direction he travelled. The first
course was north-east, in order to try to reach Mount
Lyell, which Mitchell had seen from the Darling, bearing to the westward of his track. Frome experienced
very much the same kind of ground which Eyre had
found on the west side of Flinders' Range, but there
was more moisture. It had rained a good deal on the
lower part of the plains, so that there was a great deal
of surface water. This, however, disappeared as they
went east, and at last the only supply found was a small
quantity in what was named Rowe's Creek. From
this point the country declined to the north-east, and
the range began to disappear. Whatever watercourses
they met showed that the country was subject to violent
floods. The rains seemed to be heavy and short : the
Lucas, for instance, has a bed whose section nearly
equalled the bed of the Murray. The Passmore, further
north, which was still running, had flood-marks twenty

feet above the stream, and yet at a short distance from
its source it was not only dry, but its channel was
scarcely traceable. By this time the horizon all round,
except on the side of the ranges, was unbounded.

Captain Frome was obliged to continue his course to
the northwards for some distance further, because of the
water. At lat. 30° 59' the lake was visible, and distant
only fifteen or sixteen miles. It appeared covered with
water, studded with islands, and backed by a bold and
rocky shore. These appearances were, however, all due
to refraction. There was no moisture in the bed when it
came to be examined, but a thin crust of salt covered
the whole surface. The scenery now became terrible in
its aridity. The soil was sandy. As Frome advanced
it became loose and drifting, and was now without a
blade of grass or vegetation. The lake was at last
reached, but much sooner than they had expected. The
shore was thirty miles to the west of its position on
Eyre's charts. To be sure of his own correctness, Frome
thought it best to make for Mount Serle, and from its
height compare Eyre's map with the country thus displayed; but he was disappointed in his efforts to
reach the summit. On the east side the mount terminated in almost perpendicular cliffs, and so he was
obliged to return without effecting his object. Lake
Torrens and the edge were found to be 300 feet above
the sea level, but its true bed, which was evidently much
lower, could not be reached.

Captain Frome was thus forced to return to the
Passmore River, as the nearest point from which he
could cross to the eastern low hills which lay south of
Lake Torrens. From thence he sent back two men
and three horses to the depôt. His party now consisted of Messrs. Henderson and Hawker, with
one trooper in charge of the light cart. He started
across the plains amid the usual scenery of low, flat,
sterile plains. The second evening he reached the
most northern of the elevations. There was no water
to be found upon any of them. While they were
searching for it, they unfortunately, lost the trooper,
who had crossed in front of the dray, and become

entangled in a dense scrub. Of course, all thought of
further exploration had to be abandoned while they
searched for their comrade. This detained them three
days, and they were unsuccessful. The delay made such
inroads upon the provisions and water that they were
obliged to return to the depôt without reaching Mount
Lyell, as they desired. At the depôt they learned
that the trooper had made his way back, after being
five days without food or water. From where Frome
turned back he could see about sixty miles from
Mount Serle. The view only confirmed Eyre's report.
The country was absolutely sterile. He therefore
moved southwards.

He returned, first to Mount Bryan, a mountain
whose name and discovery were connected with the fate
of the unfortunate man of that name, as recorded in the
preceding volume. From this point Frome again
started to the north-east, hoping, with the aid of a recent
heavy fall of rain, to see a good deal of the country.
But as he advanced the land was very dry. Though the
hills had an elevation of nearly 1,500 feet, there was no
evidence of rain having fallen there since the deluge.
This prevented Frome from going very far, but he
says, that from the summit of a hill named Mount
Porcupine, he had an extensive view over one of the
most sterile prospects that could be imagined. On
returning to Mount Bryan the horses got bogged only
fifty miles from a locality where rain appeared never to
have fallen.

Previous to this journey, and indeed before even
the second of Eyre, a great deal of the country to the
north of Adelaide had been explored by Mr. J. Ains-
worth Horrocks. He arrived in the colony in March,
1839, and soon after started into the interior to find a
home in the unknown bush. He settled on the Hutt
River, about a hundred miles to the north of Adelaide,
where he introduced both sheep and cattle. For the
first fifteen months after his establishment, he had no
nearer European neighbours than those living in the
town of Gawler, seventy miles distant. But he had
plenty of black ones, and all these dishonest, treacher-

ous and hostile. In spite of these difficulties, Mr. Horrocks managed to make a good many excursions into the country about Eyre's track. In any other direction there were no discoveries to be made. As long as the range was kept, new views of fertile valleys and rocky streams might continually be seen; but as soon as a divergence to right or left was made, it brought the explorer into the mallee scrub or the sterile salinas of Lake Torrens.

In one of these excursions a very extensive tract of available country was found beyond the Broughton River. Horrocks was accompanied by three others on the journey, and they were at one time much distressed for want of food. Before reaching the Rocky River, they came to some immense plains, named Gulnare Plains, after a dog of Mr. Horrocks, which supplied the party with so many emu, that they were in no want of food while on this open ground. The plains were soon afterwards taken up as a sheep station by Mr. J. B. Hughes. Various other portions of these ranges were settled upon by different persons, who each in their way added to the general knowledge of the country around. It may be interesting to the colonists to know who these men were, especially as some have since taken a leading part in the subsequent history of the colony. First among them was Mr. G. Hawker, for many years Speaker of the House of Assembly; and besides Mr. Hughes, just mentioned, who, according to his ability, mingled in the politics of South Australia, there were Messrs. E. B. Gleeson, Campbell, Pine, John Jacob, Eardley, Heywood, and W. Robinson. It is, moreover, a singular and exceptional fact, that the majority of these gentlemen resided, until very lately, on the stations which had been the scenes of their early struggles.

The last expedition made by Horrocks resulted in some small discoveries, but what gives it a greater and melancholy interest, is its connection with the fate of of the unfortunate explorer himself. In 1846, he organized an exploring party to take up the place which had been missed by Eyre. That was to cross the head of Spencer's Gulf, and then to travel north-

west from the further side of Lake Torrens. He hoped
at least to be able to reach Swan River.

The first part of his plan was most feasible, and had
he lived to carry it out, no doubt a great deal of the
explorations of Warburton and Stuart would have been
anticipated. He started on the 27th July, 1846, and
travelled at first over the country into which so many
of his former explorations had led him. On the 7th
August, he reached Wild Dog Creek, a stream which
runs down from the slopes of Mount Remarkable. It
need hardly be said that it runs but seldom, though on
its course there are valuable waterholes, which supply
the wants of the settlers near. This creek Horrocks
followed down to Mount Remarkable, from whence it
was his intention to cross the ranges of Spencer's Gulf.
The mount is worth describing. In travelling north it
is first seen from Gulnare Plains, where a red soil and
low stony undulations of sterile aspect fade off in the
distance to gloomy, rounded hills. Among them, in the
north, is suddenly seen the faint outline of a high, sharp-
peaked hill. It is so much higher than the rest, and has
such a steep appearance, and is apparently so isolated from
the others that at first one is apt to conclude its origin
to have been volcanic. But the isolation is only apparent.
From its north-western side, the continuation of the
Flinders range proceeds, and though its steepness
justifies the view from a distance, a closer inspection
gives it a much more pleasing aspect. The country
around it is most fertile. This throws a charm of contrast over the scenery one has to pass before reaching the
mount. Its flowery dales and grassy slopes are nearly
always verdant, even in seasons when the barren red
plains further away boast of no other sign of vegetation
than a scanty crop of parched and whitened grass, as
wintry-looking as anything could be in such a temperature.

It should have been mentioned that in two respects
Horrocks was rather better equipped than any which
had preceded him. He had a camel, and went determined to rely for fresh provisions principally on a flock
of goats. The camel was the only one then in the

colony, perhaps also in Australia. The experiment of exploring with such an animal was watched with interest by all those who knew that the interior of the country was so similar to the native haunts of the animal. It reflected great credit on Horrocks, that he was the first to put the interesting question to the proof, and makes one regret all the more the disaster which terminated the expedition. The goats, too, were a decided improvement, and it is a great pity that no other explorer has since tried them. It has already been related in Gray's expedition, that the goats were the only animals which did not seem to suffer much in that disastrous journey. Not only do they travel well, but they can subsist in the most barren soil, and yield abundance of nourishing milk in the most arid region. A Mr. Whitehorn made explorations at Cape Colony, in regions as inhospitable as the central desert, and relied principally on goats—not only as food, but as his beasts of burden. One cannot help feeling, therefore, that equipped as Horrocks was, his success would have been very great had his life been spared.

At Mount Remarkable, Horrocks heard from the natives that a very practicable pass across the range to Spencer's Gulf could be found. This was the direction in which he intended to proceed. On the 17th August, he started very early with one dray and four horses, and reached the top of the range in safety. While the other dray was being brought up, Horrocks put a load of provisions on the camel, and took him down a narrow valley. This was the first time he had ever carried a load, and he did not cause any sanguine expectations as to his future performance. He got enraged at one time, and bit large holes in two bags of flour ; and at another, he playfully scattered his load all down the pass. The whole journey was, however, accomplished much better than could be expected down such very steep hills. Certainly, the drays were upset, but only once ; and the main damage done was the destruction of the artificial horizon.

The greatest difficulty in this pass was a creek which ran down the centre of it. By cutting and

digging into the bank on either side a passage for the
carts was easily made. By the 20th, they had got over
the main obstacles, and then proceeded towards Mr.
Eyre's Depôt Creek.   Their course was over a desolate
plain, filled with watercourses, stony, and covered with
salsolaceous plants.   No water could however be found.
In searching for it, one of the party came upon two
natives, and endeavoured to make them understand
what they wanted, but they fled away in great alarm.
There was a good reason for their doing so just then.
They had been hunted down very much by troopers and
hostile tribes which the Government had employed to pursue them for murdering two of Mr. Tennant's shepherds,
and carrying off about nine hundred of the sheep.
    On the 22nd, Eyre's old camp upon Depôt Creek
was reached.   The party remained here a few days to
recruit, while Horrocks and his companion Mr. Gill
made excursions towards the hills which lay in the
direction of Lake Torrens.   They crossed the creek
from the lake at nine miles, and another one mile
beyond.   The ground at both places was tolerably firm,
but sandy, and producing little grass.   Eight miles
beyond, the land became very stony and desolate, and
though it was undulating, yet neither in the valley
nor on the hills did it support any growth except
stunted salt bush.   In passing between the sand
undulations and the range, they saw two native men
and one woman with a child.   They rode up to the
woman while the men made off.   She was dreadfully
frightened at first, but by degrees Horrocks pacified
her, and induced her to go with them to the water.
On their way they passed five native children, but none
of them would approach.
    At two miles over very stony ground, she brought
them to a gully running south, where were several
more natives, to whom the lubra shouted and motioned
away.   Mr. Gill led Mr. Horrocks' horse, and he
advanced, making signs of peace.   Two men, armed
with spears, came out to meet him.   They sent away
the women and children, and were very sulky, refusing
to show the water.   They appeared alarmed at the

horses. The water was at length shown. It was only a puddle, and would very soon dry up. As soon as they had drunk, the natives retired with violent gesticulations, and Mr. Horrocks then left Mr. Gill to mind the horses, while he ascended a hill near. The view was pretty extensive. About sixty or seventy miles to the N.W. were two small rises on a tableland. Between them and for many miles around was a large plain, apparently supporting nothing but salt bush growing amid small sand rises.

This view convinced Horrocks that the country was impassable in that direction, and at anyrate so late in the season, so he determined to return to the camp and proceed westward, until the country to the north should show some signs of improvement. In returning, they saw many natives, who threatened and gesticulated a good deal; but as they seemed afraid to approach, Horrocks took no notice of them. But as he proceeded they grew more bold, and about six advanced upon them with their spears in rest. Horrocks and his companion halted, and when the savages were within two hundred yards, fired three shots. This stopped them for a time, but their rage was as great as ever; neither did they seem to understand what a gun was. They however, retreated about fifty yards and set the scrub on fire. In the meantime, the explorers reloaded, not however without considerable trouble, for the cartridges were undone, and most of the bullets were too large. They then advanced about eighty yards. Mr. Gill fired one shot, at which the blacks only laughed, as they thought when the balls missed them that it was because the bushes were a sufficient protection. But the next discharge was more effective, for Horrocks, in in his journal,* significantly adds,. that they beat a

---

* This journal has never been published before; and amid the brilliant exploits of other explorers the efforts of this brave young man have been quite forgotten. I am glad to be the first to rescue them in some degree from oblivion, and trust that I shall in some measure repay Mr. Arthur Horrocks for letting me have the use of his late brother's MS. The original journal is the merest outline of each day's proceedings, of course intended to be filled up and revised subsequently. The sense, however, is generally pretty clear, and proves Horrocks to have been a keen and accurate observer.

rapid retreat as soon as the guns were fired. From many signs about the camp it was concluded that these were the very natives who had recently murdered the shepherds. What made this more probable, was the indifference displayed as to the effect of fire-arms. The shepherds they had killed were provided with guns, but they would not go off, and this the savages concluded was the case with all.

This last adventure of Horrocks was also the concluding exploration of the journey. As soon as he returned to camp, he made preparations to continue his advance westward with the whole party, first going with the camels to some hills to the north-east, which he was determined to explore. This was on the 25th. As he was loading the camel next day, an accident happened which stopped all further proceedings. His gun, which was carelessly slung, went off by some mischance, and discharged its contents full into his face. The wound was seen at once by his companions to be mortal, and so they rapidly returned with him to his station. Five days after his return he died. He was then but twenty-eight years of age, and one cannot help thinking that if one so energetic had lived, such zeal, vigour and ability as he had displayed in his early days must eventually have raised him to the highest position among Australian explorers.

CHAPTER III.

LEICHHARDT'S EXPEDITION.

Early settlement at Port Victoria—Leichhardt starts overland to establish
communication between Moreton Bay and the North Coast—Dense scrubs
along the Condamine—Acacia Creek—Dogwood Creek—Dawson River—
Expedition Range—The Boyd—Ruined Castle Creek—Zamia Creek—
The Mackenzie—Peak Range—The Isaacs—The Suttor or Belyando.

THE north coast, as we have seen in a previous chapter,
had been given up as hopeless, by the colonists who had
settled upon it.   Melville Island and Raffles Bay had
been tried in succession, but had only convinced the
Government that the northern shores were utterly unfit
for occupation by civilized beings.   And yet it soon
became evident that some establishment was necessary
there, if not for the colonists, at least for the safety of
the vessels making the voyage through Torres Straits.
In consequence of the wreck of the *Charles Eaton*, upon
the north coast, which resulted in the most cruel sufferings to all the survivors, the home authorities determined to try the experiment of a military establishment
at Arnhem's Land, and to maintain that at least at all
risks.   Port Essington, though abandoned the first of
all (in 1823), was selected this time; and in 1831 Sir
Gordon Bremer had erected a town at a part of the
bay named Port Victoria.

The success at first was much better than was
expected, and it was thought that if an overland route
could be formed between the new colony and Moreton
Bay, Port Victoria would become an important trade
depôt on the high road between Sydney, Melbourne,
Adelaide, and the East Indies.   In order, therefore, to
bring the newly established settlement into this imme-

diate connection, an overland expedition was much
desired by the colonists generally. The sum of a
thousand pounds was recommended by the Legislative
Council to be appropriated for the purpose, which,
aided by other sums subscribed, was soon enough to
defray the expenses of such an expedition.

In August, 1844, the party was fitted out, and the
command of it given to Dr. Leichhardt, who had already
distinguished himself as a scientific man, and by many
excursions into the bush, amid the outlying districts
beyond the Darling. The party consisted of ten indi-
viduals (two natives), and they were provided with
sixteen head of cattle, seventeen horses, two hundred
pounds of sugar, eighty pounds of tea, twenty pounds
of gelatine, and twelve hundred pounds of flour. The
stores were carried by the horses and bullocks, upon
pack-saddles, and at first the amount of baggage was so
great that the men had all to walk. For animal food
they intended to rely upon their cattle and shooting,
for which purpose thirty pounds of powder and eight
bags of shot were provided. Mr. Gilbert, who was
collecting for Mr. Gould, the Australian naturalist,
volunteered as naturalist, and Dr. Leichhardt himself
was an able botanist, geologist, and astronomer, and
thus the scientific requirements of the expedition were
provided for. The rendezvous was Moreton Bay.

Owing to preparations, and many other delays, it
was not until the 1st October that they were on the
edge of the unexplored districts This was on the
western slope of the coast range, whence many streams
descend into the Condamine River, and thence into the
Darling. The Condamine rises in this range, and passing through the tableland of the tract called New
England, receives the whole drainage of the range,
and then finally joins the Darling through the rivers
Balonne and Culgoa, subsequently discovered by Sir
Thomas Mitchell. The Condamine is for a great
distance the separation between the western sandstone
and the eastern basaltic plains.[*]

* On the latter the fossil remains of many gigantic Marsupiata have been
found.

And now, before commencing the record of Leichhardt's journey, let me warn my readers that it is not
one of the most interesting with which we have here to
deal. For upwards of eighteen months he was struggling through unexplored tracts, and therefore the
daily journeys must possess more or less of monotony.
It is difficult to abridge the narrative, and not make
it more tedious, unless an abridgement is made which
would prevent this history conveying to readers the
main features of every new country discovered. Without having had the advantage of seeing the same
scenery, it is difficult to enlarge upon the meagre
details left by Leichhardt, and, in truth, if one subtracts
the valuable botanical information contained in his
travels, very little of the real exploring narrative will
remain. Readers will kindly, therefore, forget the
aridity of the description, and remember only the fertile
character of the country through which this expedition
passed.

Crossing Jimba Creek and Waterloo Plains in a
north-west direction, the first camp was made at a chain
of ponds eight miles from the starting-place. Nothing
remarkable was visible except the high ranges behind.
The next day was spent in arranging the pack-saddles,
and the day following only took them to the edge of a
dense Myall scrub, which was skirted by a chain of
waterholes. This Myall, be it remembered, is the
Acacia pendula discovered first by Oxley, which has a
long, drooping appearance, like a weeping willow, and
only grows in marshy places.

The scrub was for a time a great obstacle to their
advancement in the direction they wished to go, for
they could not attempt to penetrate it. But it soon
became more open, and covered with permanent lagoons
of water. They still skirted this on a west-by-south
course, though the country on the right was now rich
and well grassed; the banks of the lagoons full of
shell-fish (*Unio*), and the *Gristes Peelii*, better known as
the Murray cod. The 6th was spent in repairing
pack-saddles, and the next day, in following the chains
of lagoons, they came upon the Condamine, flowing to

the north of west. The stream was sluggish and muddy, besides being full of reeds, and the banks were thickly timbered and scrubby. Besides this, they were often cut in by gullies running down from the higher land, which, together with the scrub, very much impeded the explorers. The banks on the other side were open and well grassed. There appeared to be a great many natives about, for the trees were much marked by their axes in extracting the honey from the wild bees' nests.

On the eighth they only advanced between eight and nine miles, in consequence of the dense scrubs of of Myall and Brigalow, with which the banks of the stream were lined. They were in consequence frequently obliged to travel along the bed of the river. There was a peculiarity in the banks which is well known in various other places in this district. The stiff clay soil was often washed into pits, or deep depressions, which the settlers distinguish by the name of melon holes.

Finding that the Condamine flowed too much to the westward, they left it, and kept their north-west course. At first the country was beautifully undulating, but the party was soon stopped by a dense Brigalow scrub, which turned them to the south-west again. In this direction they soon found themselves almost surrounded by many others, of awful appearance, while the water was so scarce that it was with difficulty they found enough to encamp near. Not the slightest channel was visible to indicate the flow of water, but the ground was rotten and swampy, as if never drained at all. Yet, at two miles from the camp, they came to a creek, Harley's Creek, and soon after a chain of lagoons, lined with scrub. In spite, however, of the scrub, the valley was extremely picturesque, and further on the country opened, and though covered with flint pebbles, had many scattered tufts of grass. The chain of lagoons soon disappeared, and the country became extremely flat. Little by little, scrubs appeared before them, until a very vast thicket opposed them. From this point they tried to penetrate north-west, but at the end of two days were obliged to return to the little lagoon. This, however, was not all. They had very much damaged their pack-saddles and provisions, and had lost a tent, besides, what was still worse, one hundred and forty-three pounds of flour.

By the time they had extricated themselves from the scrub, the rain commenced falling in torrents, and the ground became so boggy that they were forced to remain in camp, in spite of themselves. Their progress was entirely stopped for ten days. In the meantime an occasional excursion was made. Thus a creek was discovered, and named Hodgson's Creek, which, like the whole country about, seemed to drain into the Condamine. The monotony of the weather had been varied also by one or two camp incidents, such as the loss of two of the party for two days, and the insubordination of the black fellows, who were banished from camp, and only received back after expressing great contrition.

Leaving Kent's Lagoon, where they had camped, they crossed Hodgson's Creek, and kept their north-west course. The country was at first a *Casuarina* thicket, but soon opened out into a forest, through which a good many creeks drained southward, from the high land, into the Condamine. The first was named Acacia Creek, and the second Dogwood Creek, which was so wide and boggy that it had to be followed a few miles before a crossing place could be found. It is easy to understand the nature of this country, if it is remembered that the party were now crossing below the northern watershed of the Condamine, and thus traversed the heads of a good many of its tributary creeks. The country on their banks was generally well grassed, but timbered more thickly than the explorers cared to see. The valleys were in fact scrubby, becoming more and more precipitous, until one was reached with flat topped sides, and a precipitous descent of more than a hundred feet in places. It took them no less than three days to head them all, and then they had only made a very few miles in a direct line As they penetrated the open forest lining the tableland distant ranges were visible to the north-west.

It now became evident that the provisions supplied
to the expedition would not suffice for the party travelling at such a slow rate. It was necessary to reduce
the numbers, because it was too early to commence
reducing the rations. Leichhardt therefore prepared
despatches, relating his progress hitherto, and then
sent two men back to the settled districts. The
remaining members of the expedition were delayed in
camp for some days longer, while they made their first
experiment in drying the meat of a newly slaughtered
steer.

They were then upon the tableland from which the
waters of the Condamine were derived, and it was
hoped that it would prove a dividing range to waters
which would lead them to the northward. The land
was first a dead level, with no signs of drainage in any
direction. In the commencement of their journey it
was scrubby, but this gradually changed to an ironbark
(*Eucalyptus resinifera*), and cypress pine forest, as the
country declined to the northward. By-and-by, the
level was broken into spurs of the tableland, with
creeks running between them, and as the country got
lower and more undulating, they came upon a fine
creek, flowing to the north-west. They had not gone
ten miles along this before they became convinced that
it was a river, and it was named the Dawson. It was
a pretty stream. Fine boxflats, plains, and lagoons
lined the sides. It looked like a secluded glen, because
of the dense Brigalow scrubs, which in the distance
bounded the horizon. A good deal of sandstone was
found in the bed of the river, in which impressions of
fossil plants were found.*

Until the 14th, they travelled down the Dawson,
but the scrub and thickets made their progress slow.
Water and game were abundant, for though the stream
was not running, it possessed fine reaches, covered with
fowl. In lat. 25° 37' the channel took so decided a
turn towards the east, that Leichhardt thought it best

---

* These fossils have been determined as belonging to the sandstones and
shales of the Australian coal deposits, whose age has been disputed, but which
are very probably of Palæozoic origin.

to follow it no longer, so he crossed it, and again tried
to penetrate the unknown country to the north-west.
In searching for an available route, a fine creek and
another river were found to join the Dawson, and then
succeeded a dense scrub, which forced them back to the
river.

A lengthened examination was now made of the
surrounding features, before proceeding further The
country opened a little to the north-west, and in that
direction Leichhardt penetrated alone to find a passage
for his companions. He soon reached a fine open
country, and a creek fringed with corypha palms, a
plant whose picturesque aspect fringed every one of
the rocky gullies which were seen.   The main creek
was found after crossing the Gilbert's Ranges, with a
valley of luxuriant tropical vegetation, extending about
nineteen miles from east to west. The hills on each
side were evidently part of the coast range, those on
the north being named after Mr. Gilbert, and the
southern ones Lynd's Range. The watershed between
it and the Dawson was Middle Range, but the latter
river had been followed too far, because they now supposed they were upon the coast side of the Dividing
Range, and all the streams they met with flowed to the
westward. Though this was correct, inasmuch as all
the creeks of this locality have an exit on the west
coast, yet, singularly enough, they all do so by the
Dawson River, making a sweep round from the intervening land.

They followed up one of the creeks until the 25th.
This was Robinson's Creek, and led through some open
country, which was hilly, with rocky and steep banks.
High mountains were visible in the north-west. At
the end of this creek they came at last upon a dividing
range. Every time they turned to the westward they
came upon tremendous gullies, with perpendicular walls,
while to the east the descent was easy and sloping.
With difficulty they climbed the acclivities, and when
they reached the top there was a still higher range,
rising at the right of Robinson's Creek. This was called
Expedition Range.

On the 27th they ascended it.   From its extremity
they saw a vast opening prospect of mountains, with
sharp peaks and precipitous sides, in beautiful and wild
variety.   Two of the highest peaks were named Mounts
Nicholson and Aldis, after gentlemen in Sydney, and
though the prospect of traversing these ranges would
have deterred other men, Leichhardt looked forward to
them with undisguised joy, as containing new rivers and
a fertile and picturesque country upon their slopes.

From Expedition Range they descended into a broad
valley, with a watercourse and well-grassed banks, but
steep and almost impassable.   It soon joined a river,
named the Boyd, which was broad and flowing, but,
unfortunately, in the wrong direction.   They were on
the side of the southern waters.   Leichhardt again
ascended the mountains of the range, and found that
altogether it consisted of five parallel ridges; the three
easterly ones draining to the east, and the others into
the Boyd.   North of the latter river, there was a
mountain barrier, extending east and west.   The fossil
plants in the sandstone still continued, and the vegetation did not differ much from that of Moreton Bay,
with the exception of the tropical aspect given by the
palm trees.

The rocky barrier to the north now occupied several
days in crossing.   As often as they tried to ascend it,
they were driven back by the steep, impassable gullies.
Two days were occupied by Leichhardt in trying to
find a passage for the bullocks, but all in vain.   The
sandstone was worn into cliffs and precipices, pillars
and arches, of grand and picturesque appearance to any
but those who had to peer amid the stony forest in
search of a passage for the cattle.   At last, an open
country was discovered to the north-west.   They moved
the cattle slowly towards it.   It was a difficult and
laborious march.   They passed through a system of
creeks and glens, called Ruined Castle Creek, because
of the appearance of the sandstone which lay about
like ruined castles.   This was indeed penetrating the
mysteries of an unknown land, whose hidden beau-
ties were as fertile as they were picturesque, and which

gave a home to abundance of game and a harmless
multitude of natives. In keeping north-west, too,
another beautiful change soon took place in the flora.
The arborescent *Zamia* was soon very abundant, with
its crown of fan-shaped leaves and its gracefully scarred
stem. In latitude 25° 5′ a creek was found, which was
perfectly lined with them, and hence the name of a
stream, which has since become a memorable portion of
Leichhardt's discoveries.

On the 5th December, they reached the creek at six
miles journey. It was very winding and scrubby, and
several hills approached it; the largest of which was
called Bigge's Mountain. The creek was dry, but had
water-holes here and there. It led into very level
country, across which they struck upon their old course,
over ridges and extensive plains, whose soil and vegetation were exactly like the Darling Downs. In crossing
these plains, they passed two creeks on the 9th, the
second of which they followed up to the north-east.
This brought them to ranges whence others, flat-
topped, well grassed, and lightly timbered, were seen
beyond.

Crossing the range, they came upon gullies going
to the north-west, and from the head of one, which was
very rocky, a most splendid view was obtained. There
was a fine valley, with plains and isolated hills here
and there, making the diversity of the vale almost
charming. Beyond these, isolated long hills and rough
ranges faded into the distance, the highest being east
and west. These were called Christmas Ranges. The
gully was so very rugged that the valley of promise was
only reached with difficulty. It was not well watered,
as far as streams were concerned, but they had no difficulty in finding sufficient for a camping ground. The
first camp was near a water-hole at the edge of a dense
scrub. Entering this on the 15th, they came to a dry
watercourse, with ponds, and this was followed about
twelve miles by Leichhardt himself. In the meantime,
others of the party had found a dry creek, which led to
an open country to the westward, and in nearing this,
fine lagoons were found, to which the whole party were

moved. These were named Brown's Lagoons, and
the explorers remained at them until the 22nd, while
another bullock was killed and dried. The country
around was good, but evidently liable to inundation,
and though many traces of natives were seen, none made
their appearance.

On the 22nd they travelled a good deal to the north
of their usual course, through a flat country. First they
went along a fine lagoon, and as this diverged into a
regular channel, they followed it until it was totally
enveloped in scrub. All of a sudden, however, it
disappeared for four or five miles, and then it was
joined by many watercourses from the Christmas
Ranges. Further on it was joined by the watercourse
which Leichhardt had followed for twelve miles on the
15th, and again by a tributary, which made it now a
fine sheet of water. The country became open, and
two small creeks having joined the main stream, the
whole, to the great surprise of Leichhardt, almost
entirely disappeared. Soon afterwards they came to
another creek, which also strangely disappeared ; then
lagoons succeeded, then scrub, and, finally, ridges of
basaltic formation.

These facts were ascertained by Leichhardt, his companions having meanwhile been moved back to Brown's
Lagoons. In returning, the doctor lost his way, and
was a long time consequently without food. It was by
keeping too much to the east that he got astray ; and
thus he passed an extensive Myall forest, with hilly
undulating country round it. The box flat near the
strangely disappearing creek was named Albinia Downs.
To the north-west was a hummock mountain, and near
it a creek, with tributaries running to the south and west.
It was named Comet Creek, from the circumstance of
the large comet of 1844 having been first seen there.

Following the creek down, they came upon other
watercourses. In lat. 24° 25' they crossed it, still continuing in the immense flats of Albinia Downs, though
at the foot of a small range, which fringed the north
side of Comet Creek. Natives were seen here, but no
communication could be established with them. They

VOL. II.   E

fled away in the greatest alarm whenever they saw any of the explorers, yet they had evidently seen whites before, because many of the trees were marked by toma-hawks, and the savages sent the alarm from one to another by calling out " White fellow." The party were detained for many days amid the fine flats and basaltic ridges of Comet Creek. The country about it was often very rich, and though the water was scarce, enough was always found for the wants of the party. By the 9th January, the channel had become very broad, and was certainly one of the main drains of the hills in this neighbourhood. Natives were again seen, but this time they did not seem at all frightened, but readily communicated with the explorers.

On the 10th, the creek was found to sweep to the eastward, round a high basaltic plain of rich black soil, though sandstone cropped out here and there. The vegetation was rich and luxuriant, but the slopes from the plain to the creek were steep, and torn by deep gullies. The creek seemed now a puzzle to the ex-plorers. It had taken so many directions that it was most annoying to follow it, and yet the main stream, to which it must be a tributary, seemed as far off as ever. On this day their anxiety terminated, for the creek turned suddenly round to the westward and joined a fine broad river.

It was not running, and its course was slightly to the east of north, but there were very fine reaches of water in the bed, sometimes eight miles long and one hundred and fifty yards broad. The valley was deep and winding; the land on each side was high, level, and sometimes scrubby, and so were all the numerous gullies which ran down to the stream. This was at the head of the river. As it was followed down, it became open forest land, varied with tracts of impervious scrub. Tracks of natives were very numerous; but what was not very pleasant to explorers who wanted to penetrate into the unknown interior, they could distinctly feel the sea breeze in the evening. The stream was called the Mackenzie, and where they came upon it a high range was visible to the north-west.

On the 14th, during their second day's journey along the river in a north-east direction, they crossed a creek, and on the Mackenzie taking a sudden turn to the westward, a large stream from the north joined it at almost right angles. The junction exposed a fine section of underlying rock, which showed layers of sandstone with seams of coal shale among them. The further course of the Mackenzie was evidently too much to the eastward for the purposes of the explorers, as it could be seen running in that direction through scrub and open country, with the banks often interrupted by basaltic dykes. In lat. 33° 18', Leichhardt resolved to leave it and keep his north-west course.

While the party were killing and drying another of their cattle, their leader made a journey on their intended course. After passing the river gullies, he came to sandstone ridges covered with scrub. Crossing these and an open Brigalow scrub, he passed a tributary of the Mackenzie, and then another creek. Despatching his black companion to bring up the party to this point, he proceeded to Mount Stewart to see the nature of the country before him. The view was very extensive, and not very encouraging. The only level plain was in the north-east, where he did not want to go. In every other direction were terraces of flat-topped ranges, and on the route of his north-west course peaked hills were seen rising in the distance. Towards these he rode. He went over undulating country until he reached a creek, and having satisfied himself that he could bring his party up thus far, prepared to return to the camp. But this was not very easy. He lost his way, and after great exhaustion and suffering only succeeded in reaching his companions upon the fourth day. Then the rainy season set in, and the country soon became so altered in appearance that the difficulty of recognising any place was only exceeded by the labour of getting along. Besides this inconvenience, terrible thunderstorms visited the explorers every afternoon.

On the 25th January, they were encamped about thirty-four miles north-west of the Mackenzie. The country generally afforded the party but very little

E 2

assistance to their scanty supply of food, but here many nests of the wild bee were found, and as these were full of delicious and aromatic honey, it formed an agreeable addition to their supplies. As they moved beyond the creek discovered by Leichhardt, they passed many other watercourses, which were tributaries to the first stream. This now flowed through a wide valley, and when they had left it, and crossed several fine open ridges, they descended to another channel, with numerous muddy waterholes. The creeks were all alike, that is, well grassed and openly timbered, on boggy ground, but fringed by dense scrubs. All of them flowed to the south-east. Having ascended next day to the head of the main, or Newman's Creek, they found themselves upon the tableland out of which arose the peaks already mentioned, and in front of them were well-grassed, lightly timbered plains, with silex and fossil wood cropping out of the rich black soil. The range was named Peak Range, and the three conspicuous hills were called respectively Roper's, Scott's, and M'Arthur's Peaks. They were fine conspicuous mountains, composed of domite, surrounded by sandstone covered by a low scrub. Leichhardt had reason subsequently to remember this range, for it was near it, in a subsequent expedition, that his whole party were laid up by fever, and obliged to give up a most promising exploration. As they now advanced into the plain, the number of peaks in view increased. All were conical mountains, and gave a most striking aspect to the scene. Attractive and pleasing as they were, they did not form a very agreeable sojourn to the explorers. Leichhardt searched in vain among their valleys for water. Hour after hour he rode on, expecting in each vale to find what he sought, while he and his poor horse suffered extremely. The camp had been moved up, meanwhile, to some waterholes found on the plains, and here it was kept while the search was made. While waiting for Leichhardt, Mr. Gilbert found that the plains extended far to the westward, and that beyond them a range existed higher than the one before them.

It was not until the 2nd February that the camp

could be moved, and then only to a glen between Scott's and Roper's Peaks, where a little water had been found. They then moved northward, over well-grassed basaltic ridges, or sandstone scrubs, with small creeks. Just as they became seriously uneasy about their progress, because of the scarcity of water, they came upon a stream, which was running; and, what was better, exactly in the direction they wished to go. After following this a little way, it turned east into a plain and joined another. Near the junction was a very conspicuous hill, with many water-holes. Here they camped while Leichhardt ascended the peak. He had from this a fine view of the range he had quitted, with some new elevations visible to the west. From one of these, named Phillips's Mountain, a stream seemed to rise.

Proceeding north-north-east, over several water-courses and a sandstone range, they came to a sandstone, and the creek from Phillips's Mountain, which contained water. The course they followed took them over the spurs from the Peak Range, between which, of course, were many mountain streams. None of them were large enough to follow until they arrived at one named Hugh's Creek, which seemed likely to lead to some main channel flowing to the north. In following it down they came to another, which had cut a course amid the large square blocks of sandstone, and made the valley look like a cemetery. It was called, in consequence, Tombstone Creek. There were numerous natives found about here.

The 12th and 13th were occupied by Leichhardt in an unsuccessful search for water to the northward, because he did not wish to follow the westerly direction of the present stream. A dry river was seen, and Mr. Gilbert found that it was joined by Hugh's Creek, and several others. A little further on large lagoons were found in the bed, and to these the party were moved. The lat. was 22° 20'. The river seemed to come from the east, apparently from a range named Coxen's Range. It was called the Isaacs. Leichhardt went to the top of the range and had an extensive view. East, the country was level, with distant hills, while to

the west were the Peak Ranges, still swelling with
distant elevations beyond, while to the north there was
nothing but a heaving outline of innumerable mountains, affording the greatest contrast to the unbroken
horizon which bounded them on the south.   Returning
to camp, another long delay ensued while a bullock was
killed and dried, so that, on the 23rd, they were only
in lat. 22° 6'.   Still keeping the course of the stream,
they looked anxiously for the junction of some better
watered channel.   Water had become very scarce, and
some native wells were barely sufficient to supply the
wants of the party.   The stream seemed to keep a
north-west course, and they travelled along its banks,
over dry watercourses, by passing from waterhole to
waterhole, until the 28th, when a beautiful country
opened before them.   Natives were numerous here, but
very amicable, so that they had a great many com-
munications with them.   Every evening a severe
thunder-storm passed over them, generally with copious
rain.

In the commencement of the beautiful country the
river divided into two branches; one coming from the
east, and the other from the north.   Mr. Gilbert traced
up the rest of the stream, and soon came to the head
of the Isaacs and of another system of waters which
collected in a creek flowing to the westward.   The
party were moved to this watershed, and after a very
short journey, found themselves at the head of another
creek, which from its promise was named the Suttor
River.

Thus far, Leichhardt had progressed very well in his
journey.   He had kept very near the coast; but not
so near as to prevent him learning a great deal of the
nature of the intervening country, and certainly near
enough to carry onwards, slowly and surely, the object
of his explorations.   Three important rivers had already
conducted him very successfully along his route, and
several important ranges and fertile tracts of country
more than requited the trouble attending the exploration.   Probably the first part of the journey was the
most difficult, and at any rate it has the least interest for

the reader. The country into which we shall follow
him in the next chapter possesses a little more interest,
but it is only fair to warn readers not to form too high
anticipations of the narrative, even though it deals with
more varied scenery.

CHAPTER IV.

LEICHHARDT'S JOURNEY (continued).

The Suttor—The Burdekin—Robey's and Thacker's Ranges—The Clarke—
The Perry—Separation Creeks—The Lynd—The Mitchell—Murderous
attack on the party by natives—Carpentaria and its various rivers—The
watershed of Carpentaria—The Roper—Its watershed—South Alligator
River—East Alligator River—Arrival at Port Essington—Rewards of the
Government and people of New South Wales.

The course of the Suttor at first was scrubby and open,
with many dry watercourses joining. But it soon
became evident, that though now completely dry, at
times it contained a large body of water. It was not,
however, so dry that the party could not obtain
sufficient supplies for their small wants. On the 13th
of March, they found that its course was south-south-
west; but still they followed it down though they
would have to retrace their steps subsequently. The
whole country to the westward was a flat through
which the Suttor appeared at times to run. The banks
were very scrubby.

On the 17th, Leichhardt discovered a fine lake in the
channel, and the country now became very open. From
this point, as they went down, the channel became
wider and wider, often winding round large islands
which were the only very scrubby lands in the neighbourhood. But these promising appearances did not last
long. On the 21st, all at once, the water suddenly disappeared, and with the exception of a small pool every
two miles, the deepest holes were dry. This continued
for thirteen miles, and then it resumed its old character, with fine lagoons and box flats. Natives were
numerous; but it was impossible to approach them, as

they were timid and shy. On the 23rd, the party moved ten miles north-east to the junction of a large creek. After passing one or two more tributaries the river ran almost due north: it also changed its character and became a broad running river in a level country between flat-topped ridges, from the summits of which no other elevations could be seen. This country was lightly timbered.

When in lat. 20° 49′, the Suttor was joined by a stream as large as itself, and then turned its course to the north-east. The new stream was named the Cape, and was probably one of the streams subsequently discovered by Mitchell. They travelled down the river to lat. 20° 41′ over well-grassed, lightly timbered flat or hilly country. They encamped on the 28th, near a fine mountain to the north-east, which was named Mount McConnel. The Suttor wound round its western base, and at four or five miles beyond joined a river, the bed of which at the junction was fully a mile broad; yet the stream was not quite so large: and though it was running, it was scarcely ten yards wide, and the greater part of the bed was full of belts of trees, which now and then were replaced by extensive sheets of water occupying the whole channel. The new stream was named the Burdekin. Its direction was very little west of north, so that after stopping to kill another bullock, they commenced travelling up along its course. The road was not an easy one: the banks were hilly and mountainous, besides being intersected by deep gullies and creeks. The latter became at last such an impediment that the explorers had to cross to the west side. It was, however, for all the difficulty, such a new and exhilarating scene to the men, that the toil occupied the smallest share of their attention. Here they found themselves in very different scenes from the usual Australian character. A broad shining sheet of water, fringed with palm trees and lined with tropical vegetation, was really a novelty; but when the water was so extensive that only the densely wooded summits of the ranges on the further side could be seen, while the gullies and watercourses around spoke of immense falls of

water in rainy seasons, the prospect was truly different
in every way from anything the travellers had seen before. And yet it was an almost silent land. There
was a little game; but Leichhardt looked in vain amid
the bamboos and palm trees for the naked form of the
dusky savage, whose figure would have been so much
in keeping with the scene. The lonely sources of the
tributary creeks looked as if they had never been
awakened before by human echoes.

As they went up, ranges appeared along the edge
of the stream close enough to bear a portion of the drift
brought down in times of flood. In lat. 20° 14' they
passed a small river from the north-east in a most
beautiful and well-grassed country, amid which multi-
tudes of creeks meandered. A large trap dyke called
the attention of the explorers to the rocks around,
which were found to be limestone abounding with fossil
corals. On the 14th, they had reached lat. 19° 45',
travelling over many basaltic ridges and fording the
river, now almost unapproachable from high stiff grass.
Again the banks became difficult to travel along, and
though the country around was open, they saw before
them rugged ranges and inaccessible hills, which told
how difficult it would be to trace the river up to its
source. On the 18th of April, they came to the commencement of the ranges. At first, the hills were
conical but rounded. North of this was a valley, and
again beyond were rugged mountains. They continued their journey in the old north-west direction.
To avoid the river gullies, they kept near to the range,
and soon met another river fully as large as the Burdekin, and coming from the east.

This was not the only tributary. As the banks became more mountainous, the number of rivers increased.
First, there was the Clarke (named after the Rev. W.
B. Clarke); and then, in lat. 19° 1', the Perry. By the
end of the month, they had only advanced as far as lat.
18° 59', for they were much delayed in having to cross
the ranges which now lined the river on either side;
but at last they crossed. They were still far from the
head of the stream, which now ran through very level

country, where the water cut deep into the light sandy
loam. It was hoped therefore that the Burdekin would
lead very far towards the Gulf of Carpentaria; but this
hope was soon destroyed. On the 3rd of May, the
banks became hilly and much cut by deep gullies.
These ceased for a time, and fine plains succeeded.
Suddenly, however, the river turned eastward, into a
field of broken lava, where the wild disorder of the
scattered boulders made it impossible to follow it further. The volcanic rock formed part of a tableland,
which extended to the westward, and it was evident
that they had now arrived at the head of the Burdekin,
and probably at the watershed between it and more
northern waters.

The party slowly ascended the tableland. The
country was beautiful and well watered; but no plain
could be more difficult to travel over. It was a long
time before a passage could be found to the west, at
least, one that cattle could travel over, for the ground
was terribly rough. At last, a passage was discovered.
The aspect of the scenery was now very tropical, and
they saw an unmistakable sign of the approach to the
north coast in the gigantic ant-hills which dotted the
ground here and there. This gave the name to Big
Ant-hill Creek, and a watercourse which ran in the
division between the lava and sandstone was called
Separation Creek. The latter they reached on the
20th of May, in lat. 18° 2'. It led, unfortunately, in
the wrong direction; and as Leichhardt knew that he
was now upon the watershed, he spent some days
searching for some watercourse which might lead him
to the north and westward. For a long time he sought
in vain. Valley after valley was tried; but they
all turned to the east after a time. At last, a valley
was found trending to the westward. This was followed with great anxiety, and the watercourse which
went down it watched with interest. It was dry for a
long time; but a small pool was discovered at length.
This was soon followed by another, and then another,
until a chain of ponds was reached, which was evidently
the head of a large river flowing to the north-west.

This was an immense relief to Leichhardt, for he now felt almost certain that this stream must lead into the Gulf of Carpentaria; and thus the most formidable portion of his journey was got over. The river was called the Lynd. The progress down it was at first very slow, because the land about the head was rocky beyond conception. But, by the 27th, their labours almost terminated. At that date, in lat. 17° 54', they passed through a gap, leading into large flats of open, sandy soil. The gap also gave them a view of the surrounding country, which was not cheering, though very little of its nature could be seen, except that it was both rugged and rocky in the extreme.

At the gap they were detained in slaying another of their cattle, and the difficulties they had to contend with in doing so are worth recording. This part of the north coast abounds with a species of kite (*Milvus isiurus*), which is distinguished as much by its singular boldness, as by its ravenous propensities. They mustered in hundreds around Leichhardt; and it was nothing extraordinary to see one swoop down and take the meat from off the fork of a man as he was eating. Another instance of the same kind of thing will be recorded in Sturt's journey.

Until the 3rd of June, the party found the sides of the river pleasant travelling; for though the tributary creeks to cross were very numerous, the banks were level and the country smooth. But on the above date, porphyry ranges approach the stream, and formed precipices on each side, so that there was nothing left but to climb them. Both men and cattle were tired and footsore, and this addition to their labours was a severe trial. It must be admitted, that time had now elapsed sufficient to weary all the party of the expedition; and as their rations were low and their clothing very insufficient to protect them, the grumblings and murmuring at each new labour were anything but pleasant for the leader to hear. Many things in the narrative indicate this; and Leichhardt states that his followers kept repeating—continually repeating, that they would never reach the north coast. Still they kept down the Lynd.

It was as yet still only a chain of water-holes; but the channel was broad, and joined by many tributary creeks. In lat. 17° 30', the banks became again so rocky, and the country so difficult, that they had to quit the stream, and venture on to higher ground. When they rejoined the channel, it was a running stream, and this made the fourth flowing river they had discovered on their journey.

From thence, to lat. 16° 30', the, country passed through was a series of box flats, only once interrupted by a sandstone range. It then joined a fine broad river, evidently much liable to floods at times; but now with only a small stream running in it. It was named after Sir Thomas Mitchell. The explorers kept down, over a very level well-grassed country; passing from lagoon to lagoon in the channel. On the 25th, they were in lat. 15° 51'. Here it was evident that they had passed the head of Carpentaria, as well as the latitude of the mouths of the Van Diemen, Staten, and Nassau rivers of the Dutch charts; so that it was useless to follow the stream any further. Leichhardt therefore now, for the first time, turned to the westward. The Mitchell, when last seen, was very broad, and lined with palm trees. It was a fine river; but as so little water was found in it near the mouth, it could never be of service as a navigable channel.

The journey to the west was different from their course hitherto, and would entail new difficulties. Up to this time they had managed to travel along the banks of streams; but here their route lay across the course of all they could hope to meet, flowing down into the Gulf of Carpentaria. The reader need hardly be reminded of the aspect of the country they had now to pass through. The low shores, the mud flats, the mangrove swamps, and the salt-water inlets, must be fresh in memory. The land party had to test the accuracy of Flinders' observations from a different point, and under circumstances of greater risk. One cannot help sympathizing with the devoted little band. If it was desolate to gaze from the deck of Flinders' ship, at the low muddy shores, with glaring soil and

scorching sky, how much more must the scenes have
been gloomy to these men walking through it, with an
army of natives, hostile and savage, in ambush all
around them? At first, however, the journey was far
from disagreeable. They travelled over well-grassed
plains, with hills of timber, and here and there a creek
with a thicket of trees. In one of these thickets
the explorers encamped, on the 28th, amid some
beautiful plains; because the shelter saved them from
trouble in erecting protection from the wind, and they
considered themselves safer from the natives. They
could not have made a more fatal mistake. The imprudence of this kind of camp in a strange country, amid
hostile and treacherous natives, cannot be too much
blamed; more especially as the character of the natives
on this part of the coast was so well known. Not even
a night-watch was kept, and this evening a sad lesson
was given to Leichhardt. Just after nightfall, as the
explorers were quietly disposing themselves to rest,
thinking of nothing but the adventures of the day and
the labours of the morrow, savages were stealing into
the brush. They conducted their approach so stealthily
that no suspicion of danger occupied the minds of the
party, who chatted or dropped to sleep, or mended their
weapons and clothes. Yet the natives had been all day
upon their tracks, and now only waited for the night
to pounce upon their quarry. Suddenly, the onslaught
was made. Mr. Gilbert, the naturalist, was immediately killed by a spear, and Messrs. Roper and Calvert
dangerously wounded by spears and waddies. It was
but the work of a moment, and had the camp been compact, not one would have been left to tell the tale.
Fortunately, the tents were scattered, and after the
first alarm, a shot or two dispersed the assailants before
more mischief was done.

This sad disaster seemed to threaten the safety of
the whole party. With such a diminution of their
numbers it did not appear that they could manage to
find labour enough to secure the baggage, animals, and
stores. It was certainly a critical position, and Leichhardt now displayed a presence of mind which would

have been better employed in avoiding the danger. He left the camp at once, carrying his wounded companions on horseback, and making the stages as rapidly as he could. Of course, the wounded men suffered extremely; and their cries at being moved were pitiable to hear; but there can be no doubt that Leichhardt was right in travelling on, and trying to terminate their journey as soon as possible.

Their course was now south-west, in order to trend round the Gulf of Carpentaria. They soon entered upon a series of plains, which extended to the west as far as the eye could reach, but interrupted occasionally by small strips of forest. Crossing these plains they came to broad sheets of sand, scrubby, and incrusted with salt. Beyond the sand they saw a dense line of mangroves on a salt creek, which they headed, and thus at last came in sight of the sea. Now, for the first time, they unravelled the mystery of the rivers marked by the Dutch, as running in the gulf. It will be remembered that neither Flinders nor Stokes could find them subsequently, even though they were better provided than the Dutch with the means of discovery. On the 7th, they crossed a large salt-water river, which they supposed was the Staten. The usual box flats continued until the 9th, when the Van Diemen was crossed. Little creeks were passed in the interim, and belts of timber, but nothing to vary the country in any important particular. Natives very numerous, but of course the party were not anxious to communicate with them. The kites were also still plentiful, and much more daring and troublesome than they had ever been before.

All the meat for killing, except one steer, was now expended. It is true they had the bullocks, but these they did not wish to touch for the present. The drying operations of their last steer occupied them until the 12th; and then they passed over eight miles of a most beautiful country, crossing a river which was named the Gilbert, after their late unfortunate companion. Five miles further, they came to a creek, where they camped. The next few days were a similar record of plains, much open forest land, and creeks; but there was considerable difficulty in procuring water. The land was good, and in some places even rich, and at any rate they were quite done with scrubs, and the country was moderately well grassed. Their progress was not very rapid. Mr. Roper suffered so much from his wounds, that they were obliged to rest on his account; but there seemed a very good prospect of his ultimate recovery.

On the 17th, they crossed the dry bed of the Caron River or Comet Inlet, and then passed on to a chain of lagoons. From this place creeks became more frequent, and the plains were interrupted with tea-tree thickets and grassy swamps, with plenty of fresh water. But all the creeks were not fresh. They were too near the sea for that, and whenever a large river was met, it was always full of salt water. By degrees, too, the aspect of the country changed. Except in the neighbourhood of the streams, there was no rich soil, and the prevailing rock was a sandstone, which sometimes formed undulating hills. The want of water caused Mr. Roper to suffer extremely, but still he was improving, and Mr. Calvert might almost be considered convalescent. In the meantime, the shifts made by the party to vary the monotony of their diet were most amusing. Every tree which had berries, every new plant which boasted of anything like fruit, was immediately stripped of its fructification, and tried as an aliment, or roasted to make coffee. Sometimes this mode of experimental cooking was attended with very unpleasant results. The journal frequently records sickness and various other painful visitations, caused by some new plant whose medicinal qualities were now experienced for the first time. The pandanus was the most obstinate fruit which was met, and with a patience, such as only a starving man could give to the work, Leichhardt made many mournful experiments in cooking before he found a way of eating the fruit with impunity.

Box flats, plains, and hills of forest, succeeded as they journeyed on, until the 24th. On that day another salt-water river was passed, and the next day many inlets from the sea. The party were thus much distressed for fresh water, and the search for it not only took them out of their course, but made them retrace their steps. Thus it was that they could not be said fairly to continue their journey until the 30th. The scenery did not vary. The whole prospect, as they camped at the end of each day's route, was an immense plain, with here and there a belt of trees, or a solitary palm. Natives were numerous, but not very communicative. The explorers had now somewhat recovered from their panic, and would gladly have got some information from the savages as to the route before them. But they never had a chance. As soon as the natives saw them, they ran away as fast as they could, and were easily concealed in the thickets. After journeying through the same monotonous succession of box flats, plains, scrubby ridges, with an occasional creek, they reached, on the 6th August, at what Leichhardt thought was the Albert River of Stokes.* It was a fine broad river; too broad indeed, for they had to travel up it some distance before it could be forded. The stream itself was salt, though fresh water was abundant in the neighbourhood. Leichhardt saw the plains on the upper part, which he thought were Stokes's Plains of Promise; but he was certainly not struck with their appearance of fertility; on the contrary, he questioned if they were so rich as many of the box flats he had passed already. These were not, of course, the Plains of Promise; but it is amusing to remark that such a mistake was made on a locality which had little pretensions to being called plains, and none whatever to richness and fertility.

They did not clear these plains, or whatever they were, until the 18th. On that day they met another salt-water river, with well-grassed banks. More plains succeeded, and at five miles, another brook, named Beame's Brook, and, at two miles, a small river,

---

* He was mistaken, however. This river was never discovered before, and was afterwards named the Leichhardt by Gregory.

named the Nicholson. After this the scenery changed, and they were not troubled any more with brooks. The land was covered with scrubs, which were rarely open, and in which water could not easily be found. It delayed them very much to search for it. Many reconnoitring journeys, as fatiguing as they were disappointing, were entailed upon Leichhardt and his men, but without advancing them an inch upon their route. There were plenty of creeks, and no great scarcity of waterholes; but they were all dry, nor was there any prospect of their being filled until the rainy reason. The country still remained scrubby; it took a good many days to get through seventy miles of it—a journey which could never have been made, but that they found a few water-holes, with scanty supplies in them. A small river was passed, named the Marlow, and a large salt-water creek, with many tributaries, named Turner's Creek.

On the 4th September, the country became more open, and the latter part of their journey lay through a fine box flat, with a creek named after Mr. Wentworth, of Sydney. Next day they travelled about twenty-two miles, over open forest land, reaching a fine river, in lat. 16° 41'. It was nearly dry where they crossed, though still running, and was supposed to be the Van Alphen River of the Dutch. Again another scrub ensued. For nineteen miles they kept through it on their old north-west course, and this brought them to another river, named the Calvert. Near it the sandstone of the north coast began to occur. The whole territory round the gulf was generally well grassed, even in the scrub; but the feed, like that of all the Australian coast, was dry and coarse. This was a more cheering view of the locality than that given by Flinders and Stokes; but, certainly, their experience of the mud flats, the mangroves, and the shallow bay, which never gave them many opportunities of a near view, was not the sort of scenery to impress them favourably at a glance. By the 9th September, the party began to experience the difficulties of the sandstone tableland. They came to

steep and rocky ridges, with higher ranges to the westward still before them. They were soon entangled in
the hills, and were obliged to keep to the north. This
brought them to another broad salt-water river, with a
fresh-water creek joining. This was in lat. 16° 28', and
was thought to be the Abel Tasman River. Twelve miles
beyond it they camped upon a fine fresh-water creek.

It is useless to particularize the daily journeys for
upwards of a hundred miles further, because the records
of one day are so extremely like those of another. It
will be quite sufficient to give a brief description of
the country passed through. It was generally composed of sandstone scrubs and stringy bark forest, with
occasionally a few, and those very few, box-wood flats.
Some creeks and salt-water rivers were seen, most of
them broad and important, but as they were passed
very near their mouths, nothing certain could be
inferred as to their size. The principal rivers were
named Seven Emu, Cycas, Robinson, and Macarthur
Rivers. Natives were very numerous, but they did not
communicate, except in one instance, when the explorers
were able to hunt one up into a tree. This did not
put him exactly in a state of mind to give information, so they were obliged to let him go without any
advantage to themselves, except amusement.

The labours of the party were very great, and their
provisions much reduced; but their health kept up,
except when disturbed by some culinary novelty in the
way of fruit. Mr. Roper was now convalescent, and,
with the exception of the loss of Mr. Gilbert, they had
nearly recovered from the effects of the disaster their
imprudent confidence had caused. Their greatest
want now was clothes. Their stock was quite exhausted, and they were travelling half naked, or in a
pitiable condition of rags and tatters. There was not
such a thing as a whole boot among them. This was
their worst privation, and even the best dressed had his
garments so patched and stitched that the most enterprising dealer in old clothes would not have given six-
pence for the whole suit. Truly, it was a very different display to their triumphal exit from Brisbane

F 2

a year previously; and though they looked confidently towards the successful termination of their journey, it was a matter of speculation as to who would be best able sufficiently to smother his feelings of decency on their arrival, and enter Port Essington, to tell the inhabitants that a band of naked explorers were outside the town. Latterly, their cattle were much reduced in number, and consequently their means of transport. This was a great mortification to Leichhardt, who, much to his regret, was obliged now to abandon nearly half of his botanical and mineralogical collection. It was all the more distressing, because they were now amid an almost entirely different flora. The only tree still to be recognised was the honeysuckle or *Banksia,* which has a range right across the continent. The other trees besides the palm were known to the men by colonial appellations, such as the bloodwood and the raspberry jam. The origin of the latter name, let me inform my readers, has no connection whatever with any produce from the tree.

On the 13th October, after passing through some wretchedly sterile and sandy country, with salt creeks, it became more open at the Limmen Bight River, which had large sandy plains extending along its banks. The stream itself was too wide for them to cross, and they had to prolong their journey very much by travelling up it, and heading many large salt-water creeks. The travelling, also, was none of the easiest, because high, stony, sandstone hills often approached close to the stream, though flats occurred between them. The ranges were flat topped, and four remarkable ones, which were close together, were named the Four Archers. The river was forded in lat. 15° 13', on the 14th. The party then moved ten miles north-west, over stony ridges and open box flats, at the end of which was another river, named the Wickham, seven hundred yards wide, but, fortunately, nearly dry. Next day, travelling over box flats, brought them to a system of parallel ranges, steep, and of white colour, with box flats between; and a long succession of similar ranges were seen in the north-west. The eastern slopes were very steep, but the north-western sides very gentle. With every care in selecting a route, the greatest possible difficulty was experienced in crossing. On the 16th and 17th, they travelled twenty miles, over an undulating country of scrub, tea tree, and box flats, spending the second night near some small water-holes, which contained scarcely sufficient for their wants.

The heat of the days was most oppressive. On the 26th, the men could scarcely crawl along, and their only remaining dog died. This was a great loss to them, as he had been of much service in catching game, of which they had now a good supply. That is to say, good in the sense in which the term game was understood, for it included, besides kangaroo and emu, pelicans, hawks, crows, and lizards. The country was, however, fine enough to support anything. Leichhardt says that it was surpassingly beautiful, and a great deal more worthy of the name of Plains of Promise. The fact is, he had unconsciously passed the proper locality of these plains. It seemed natural to expect a large river in such a place, and they soon came upon one. It was fresh, and from five hundred to eight hundred yards broad; but what was better still, it ran to the south-east, so that they could keep along its banks, and continue their course. The right of the stream was a fine open box country, and on the left was a range of hills, giving origin to small creeks which joined the channel from time to time. Beautiful as it was, it proved rather unfortunate to the explorers. Four of the horses were drowned in it, and, consequently, some more of the baggage had to be abandoned. The animals perished in trying to drink at the steep banks. Three fell in the first time they tried to get at the water, and one (Leichhardt's favourite horse) some days after.

The river was called the Roper, and it preserved its important character up to lat. 14° 45', where it was joined by a creek named the Wilton. On the 24th it began to change its appearance. A waterfall was passed, and the northern banks were bounded by isolated hills and chains of rocky ranges. It is true that grassy plats intervened between these mountains and

the stream; but the ground was so stony that the party
might as well have been amid the ranges. Other
mountains ran along the river, approaching the bed in
lofty cliffs, and precipices of sandstone and argillaceous
slate. The scenery became wild and romantic. The
valley of the river was blocked up by boulders of
sandstone and large sombre *Casuarina* trees. The
aspect again changed in lat. 14° 40'. The ranges still
continued, and well-grassed plains extended along their
sides; but a range now appeared running east and west,
which told the party that the channel was near its
source. Natives were seen here, who seemed peaceable, as the explorers thought; but afraid of the whites.
Afraid they certainly were not, for they made a treacherous attempt to surprise the camp, which, but for
the lesson Leichhardt had already received, would have
succeeded. On the 28th, they had reached the head of
the Roper, which was a bubbling spring.

They now tried to keep their course without the
help of any river. They found at first a good sized
creek, with one solitary water-hole, in an undulating
tea-tree forest. This forest continued seven miles further, and then succeeded an immense lightly timbered
flat, with high formidable ranges all round. The
ranges were basalt, which was the first time this rock
had been met since leaving the head of the Lynd.
This was very interesting to men in other circumstances, but to the explorers it was rather discouraging,
because no water was to be found in the soil. On the
30th, they travelled only about four miles along a
rocky range, and came to a valley going to the north-
west, but bounded by high cliffs. Following this
for seven miles, they were delighted by meeting a
rivulet coming from the north-west. This was satisfactory in every respect except one, and that was, that
they knew from it that as yet they had not crossed the
watershed of Carpentaria.

In their camp by this stream, another of their horses
died suddenly and mysteriously, either from the bite of
a snake, or from eating some poisonous herb. The
latter cause seemed the most probable, and was con-

firmed to some extent by Gregory's experience in the
same place twelve years after. This unfortunate accident caused another delay. The creek was called
Flying Fox Creek, from the number of large bats
which they killed, and which formed a welcome addition to their rations. They had eaten them before
without difficulty, but strange to say, now that they
were far too famished to be particular, they found them
"rather strong" in flavour. Leichhardt mentions the
fact in his journal, and adds, rather naïvely, "In our
messes at night it was rather difficult to find the cause
of any particular taste, as the cook in his hurry was not
over nice in cleaning the *game*."

On the 1st November, the ranges approached so
near to the creek that the explorers had to cross them.
On the east side tea-tree flats extended, and the country
was well grassed and lightly timbered. The creek
was joined by others, and though hills were seen to the
north and south, the aspect of the country was like
that of a large park. Soon another large creek was
seen, but it was evident they were still among the
waters which belonged to the Roper. They followed
the last creek until the 4th of November, but as its
course was too much to the westward, Leichhardt left
it, and with much difficulty ascended the ranges to the
northward. From this he saw two high sandstone
ranges, which extended exactly in the direction he
wished to go. It was with reluctance, therefore, he
continued to follow a creek in the valley. Yet even
that terminated next day, and the sandstone plateau
stood before them as they emerged from a forest at the
foot. But it was useless to try to ascend it there.
They were flanked by bluff escarpments, precipices,
and chasms, which defied the efforts of the explorers to
climb, attended as they were with cattle. At first they
knew not which way to turn, and it was with very
great reluctance they at last decided on travelling to
the south. This course brought them over a sandy
tableland, with a valley, which led them at last to
western waters. But their troubles were very far from
being over yet. The creek did not give them much

satisfaction. It led too much to the south, and they were obliged, unfortunately, to leave it. Though they soon found another stream, after passing over some forest and rocky soil, it did not seem to promise an extrication from their difficulties any more than the first. The view from it was most disheartening to the northwest, being over a high, rocky sandstone country, which seemed, in the words of Leichhardt, to be "hashed into blocks of stone." They wound round the creek for a time, but that course was soon found to be impracticable. The bed was flanked at last by precipices, which jammed it into a narrow gorge. Following up a tributary, they came to a river, but, sad to say, running even to the south of west. Rendered dogged almost by repeated disappointment, they crossed it on the 13th, and proceeded to the north-west, passing over sandy forest and creeks, with stony ground, and finally winding up with a most distressing journey over the ranges.

If readers bear in mind the description of the country found by King upon the north coast, and that in which Grey made his preliminary and disastrous exploration, they will understand what Leichhardt had to endure amid the gorges, chasms, and defiles of the same sandstone tableland.   When it is remembered how this soft ferruginous rock becomes fissured, one cannot help wondering that Leichhardt got through it at all. He might have come upon a place like the gorges of the Blue Mountains, which stopped the colonists for so long, and even had the ranges been accessible in places, it might have exhausted his provisions and the last strength of his party before he succeeded in finding them.

So, then, unfortunate as he was, wearisome as these fissures were, these climbings, and staggerings over broken rocks, might have been much worse. At any rate, the worst was over now. On the 17th they came to the further edge of the tableland. After travelling along a Banksia and tea-tree forest, with numerous small creeks, suddenly a magnificent valley opened before them, and lay beneath their feet. But their last difficulty was the greatest. They were separated from the valley by a precipice nearly eighteen hundred feet in height, and could look down with longing eyes upon a large river, which seemed to meander away in silvery wavings until it was lost in a hazy distance of rich and fertile plains.

They turned aside with reluctance from such a view, and again faced the rocks, in the hope of finding a means of easy descent. For many days they were baffled in every attempt to reach the valley. Every creek they descended, and every slope, terminated in a precipice which shut them from it. A most tantalizing land of promise lay before them, upon which they could only gaze with longing eyes. Their provisions meanwhile were getting very low, and the whole party nearly famished by the straits to which they were reduced. They ate anything now. First of all, they had found an appetite for every portion of the intestines of the slaughtered animals; now their gaunt and ragged figures might be seen crowding eagerly round their daily ration of boiled green hide. Worst of all, their shot was completely expended, so that now even " game" failed them. Their only dependence was upon a few bullocks kept in case of unforeseen delay.

At last they were extricated from the tableland. On the 22nd they got down upon the valley, and Leichhardt then found that he was upon the South Alligator River. They travelled down it with joyous alacrity, for they now began to foresee the end of their journey. The banks were scrubby and sandy at first, but soon became wet and marshy. On the 29th November they left it, and travelled more to the westward, over creeks amid densely wooded sandstone ridges. Here they met many natives, who were very friendly, and had evidently seen white men before. They vociferated many words to the explorers, which not until the savages left did Leichhardt know were badly pronounced English words. It is fortunate, perhaps, that the men did not understand them, for they would have fancied themselves much nearer the settlement than they really were. It cheers one, however, to think that the termination of their labours and sufferings were now very near at hand.

More creeks and abundance of water abounded each
day, until they reached a pretty level country, and finally
emerged into an immense plain. This was bounded by
open forest land and a salt creek. Another party of
natives was now met, not only speaking English words,
but very friendly to the whites. They showed them
water and got food for them, and then sent one of their
tribe to act as a guide to the explorers. With their
guide, they moved across a plain, on the 3rd December,
and then reached a broad salt-water river bounded by a
low range. This was the East Alligator River. It
was, however, an obstacle instead of an assistance, and
they had to steer round it, as it was much too wide for
them to cross. They again met with natives, who, like
the others, treated them very hospitably. The explorers
needed such assistance badly, and their state of destitu-
tion was now far below that of the savages. Their
pitiable condition may be guessed from the sad dis-
closures of the annexed quotation :—" I went up to
meet them" (it is Leichhardt who is speaking), "and they
gave me the roasted (singed ?) leg of a goose, which
they were pleased to see me eat with avidity. I asked
for allamurr (a grass root), and they seemed sorry at
not having any left, but offered to get some next day, if
we would stay. None of these natives would taste our
green hide ; they took it, but could not overcome their
repugnance, and tried to drop it unseen. Poor fellows,
they did not know how gladly we would have received
it back !"

Leichhardt was obliged to keep to the southward —
amid some lagoons—so that he did not cross the head of
the river until the 6th December. They now again
turned to the north. In their hurry, every moment
seemed a year's delay. The large plain which lay before
them, lined on each side with ranges, and dotted with
palm trees, seemed as if it would never be crossed ; and
when it was, their impatience was increased, for it led
into rocky ground, with forests of tropical luxuriance,
almost as difficult to traverse as the scrubs. On the
15th May they came in sight of Mounts Bedwell and
Roe, which were both in the neighbourhood of Port

Essington. In their joy, they went a little too fast, and thus kept to the north of the settlement, which they ought to have reached on the 16th. At last, however, their long, wearisome journey terminated. On the 17th December, nearly famished and naked, their last bullock nearly eaten, and with no stores left, nor any animals except the horses upon which they rode, they reached the settlement.

Thus terminated this expedition, which, with the loss of only one man, Mr. Gilbert, had crossed the continent, a distance of over three thousand miles, in one year and three months. Certainly this was a very long time ; but in comparing it with subsequent expeditions, it should be remembered how little of the nature of the interior was known at that date. The party had suffered great privations, but, considering their equipment, were rather fortunate in not having to suffer more. The natives in the latter part of their journey had been very kind to them, especially when they were near to the settlement, and but for this the destruction of the party was inevitable just as their labours were completed.

After a month's stay at the port, the whole party returned by sea to Port Jackson. The people of Sydney were overjoyed at seeing them safe again. It was considered quite certain that they had perished, and a party sent out in search of them had returned with no other tidings than that they had gone away to the north-west. Rewards were voted to them by the Legislative Council, and the people also subscribed the sum of £1,400 as a recompense for labours which were intended to benefit the colony at large. Unfortunately, they did not ; except in leading to the knowledge of the available country on the Dawson, Suttor, Mackenzie, and Burdekin. All that country is now occupied by squatters, but the colony of Port Essington is abandoned. Even if it did exist, better routes have been since discovered than the one traversed by Leichhardt.

In order not to interrupt the rest of the narrative, it is better at once to describe the further vicissitudes of the settlement upon the north coast. No young colony had ever greater difficulties to struggle against. The

climate was very unhealthy, and owing to either the
heat or the nature of the soil, very little could be grown
by the settlement for its own use.   Most of the produce
was imported from Sydney.   These disadvantages were
bad enough, but occasional visitations made the town
almost like a cemetery.   First, there was the regular
fever and ague in the rainy season, and then periodical
hurricanes not only destroyed the shipping, but once
left scarcely a house standing in the town.   Twice
the settlement was also nearly destroyed by earth-
quakes.   These might certainly not recur, but the
soldiers still continued to die.   With such difficulties,
no wonder the Government directed the place to be
abandoned.   A faint effort was made to get the colony
removed to Cape York, but peremptory orders were
reiterated to relinquish the idea of any settlement whatever.   So in 1850 the whole north coast was again
abandoned.

CHAPTER V.

STURT AND THE DESERT.

A plan to explore the centre of Australia—Sturt starts with a party for the Darling—Laidley's Ponds—The Barrier Ranges—Rocky Glen Creek—Lake Torrens—Flood's Creek—Grey Ranges—Stokes's Range—Awful heat—Depôt Pool—Sturt's retreat cut off.

WHILE Leichhardt was toiling on his weary journey to Port Essington, another expedition was undergoing more perils and sufferings, with less success, in another part of the Australian continent. This was the party under the command of Sturt. Since his successful journey down the Murray he had been appointed surveyor-general of the colony of South Australia, and in that capacity still planned and pondered over the exploration of the continent as the one darling project of his life. In 1843 he wrote to Lord Stanley, then Secretary for the Colonies, tendering his services to conduct a party into the interior of the Australian continent. He stated in his letter that he was confident that a good country would be found a little beyond the tropics, and that if a line were drawn due north from Mount Arden, on the Flinders Range, and another north-west from lat. 29° 30', long. 146° E., they would meet in a spot where he would guarantee that good land existed. He did not state in his letter what were his reasons for this belief; and though it had no better foundation than the observations founded on the migration of birds, still recent explorations have shown that his conjecture was not very far from the truth. The letter was referred to the celebrated Sir J. Barrow, and as that officer reported favourably of the scheme, Lord Stanley sent out instructions to the governor of South Australia to

equip the party. The governor complied with alacrity,
for the administration of the colony was then in the
hands of Sir George Grey, the explorer (subsequently
also governor of Cape Town), whose journey forms so
important a part of the preceding volume.

Sturt was directed in his instructions to proceed due
north from Mount Arden, and try to make the centre of
the continent, but on no account to risk the safety of
the party by trying to cross it. There was not much
danger of this, if the directions of the home Government were to be followed. Proceeding northwards
to the tropics from Mount Arden was a simple impossibility, according to the state of geographical knowledge
at that time. It would have brought the party right
into the middle of the great horseshoe bend of Lake
Torrens, and it was considered proved by Eyre that any
attempt to turn the flank of the lake eastward or westward was utterly impracticable. Of course, colonial
secretaries cannot know everything, but considering
that human life often hangs on the course of expeditions
such as this of Sturt, it would have been better either to
have studied the geography of the country or not to
have made the instructions too precise.

Naturally, Sturt did not see the utility of trying to
cross the lake, so he resolved upon another plan. He
intended to start from the Darling, at the point from
which Mitchell had turned back in 1833. Here it will
be remembered that Mitchell, after tracing the river
downwards from its sources, had been deterred from
proceeding by the hostility of the natives. The place
was called Laidley's Ponds, and Mitchell understood
that the Darling was there joined by a stream which
came from distant mountains, barely visible to the
north-west. This range had been seen by Frome, from
the west side, when he explored the east arm of Lake
Torrens, and from its size it was thought to give rise to
some considerable streams. Now, as the country between the river and the ranges was an open plain, Sturt
hoped to cross it by the aid of the streams; and once the
ranges were gained, he had no doubt of being able to
proceed to the centre by the aid of the watercourses he

should see among the hills. He was, as the sequel will
show, miserably deceived in the most of these anticipations. In the foregoing pages the reader has seen a
good many specimens of disastrous expeditions, as rash,
foolhardy, and impracticable as any that ever led men
to destruction; but here one meets with a record of
suffering, disaster, and failure resulting from as feasible
a plan and as plausible a theory as ever was conceived
by explorers.

On the 24th September, 1844, the whole party were
assembled at the Darling, ready for a start. It numbered, besides the leader, Mr. Poole, assistant-surveyor;
Mr. J. H. Browne, surgeon; Mr. John M'Dougall
Stuart, as draughtsman; and twelve men. The animals
were eleven horses, thirty bullocks, one boat and boat-
carriage, three bullock-drays, one-horse dray, a spring-
cart, two hundred sheep, and six dogs. The provisions
were calculated to last eighteen months.

From the junction of the Murray and Darling, up
to Laidley's Ponds, they explored the small remainder
of the river which was still unknown. It was found to
wind very much, and the bed contained so small a
stream that it could be crossed in most places without
wetting the feet. From the appearance of the channel
it seemed seldom very deep; but while the party were
encamped upon its banks, a fresh came down, which
caused it to rise nine feet in a single night. The
scenery on its banks was picturesque and cheerful,
with very grassy flats contiguous to the water; and
yet, though the flats were green, at times they were
occasionally so parched as not to possess a blade of
grass. Mr. Eyre had previously found them so, near
the junction of the Murray, and from thence to the
ponds, a distance of one hundred miles; the natives
gave precisely the same accounts.

However, it was pleasant travelling for Sturt; and
on the 8th October the party reached Laidley's Ponds,
or, as the natives called them, Williorara. The sight
of the place wofully disappointed him. Instead of
finding a creek from the hills, which could be seen
dimly looming in the north-west, there was nothing

but a watercourse, leading to two lakes, into which the
floods of the Darling were then flowing. This was in
lat. 32° 25', long. 142° 5' E. There was no grass in
the locality, and it looked cheerless and inhospitable.
Mr. Poole was despatched to one of the lakes, named
Cawndilla, to report on the state of the feed, and,
failing in finding it, to proceed to the north-west, and
try to reach the ranges. He returned in four days.
He had found the lake, but no feed; he had then gone
to the ranges, whence he saw many hills to the north,
and some ranges to the south-west, in which direction
there was also a lake. With this exception, he had
found no water in the hills. This was not a very
encouraging or hopeful beginning.

The party left the Darling on the 17th, by which
time the floods had reached Cawndilla. After completing his surveys up to this point, Sturt started on
the 21st, with Dr. Browne and some men, and the
light cart, to make a preliminary exploration in the
ranges. At a quarter of a mile they crossed a sand-
hill separating the two lakes, Cawndilla and Minan-
dichi, and then succeeded the level of the great plains
between them and the ranges. The soil was either a
barren sand or clay, with patches of brushwood widely
distributed, besides grass tufts, and a few, very few
trees. They steered across this bleak tract about
north-west for a hill, which the natives called Coonbaralba, fourteen miles to the east of Mr. Poole's
explorations. At twenty-six miles they reached a sand-
hill, and then a dry creek, with a course parallel to
their own. In travelling up it they met with small
native wells, from time to time, which satisfied their
immediate wants. On the second day their guide led
them to the westward, away from the creek, for the
sake of finding water. This he did in a small watercourse, still coming from the hills; and in following up
this, came upon a long and beautiful serpentine pond.

From this point Sturt struck north-west to the
ranges. From the first rise he crossed a valley, and
then ascended at once to the top of the range. The
view was not extensive, for many hills were beyond

them, but separated by an inaccessible valley. There was nothing cheering in the prospect : the hills raised their bare, rocky summits, as if they had never been moistened by the dews of heaven ; and the distant prospect was cold, cheerless, and unfertile. A south course brought them to another valley, and from the range on the further side they saw a desolate extent of forest tableland, surrounded by hills, but without a creek or sign of water of any kind to lead them to the north-west. They now returned to the gap in the ranges from whence the serpentine sheet of water issued.

On the 24th they made another attempt to explore. They journeyed up the creek to the gap, and having passed it, found themselves at the entrance of a large plain. The hills they had ascended the day before were trending north, and there was a small, detached range upon their right, which ran east and west. They then left the creek, and proceeded north-west along the foot of the northern range, which consisted of large masses of ironstone. Sturt traced the range as far as a gap, which was too tortuous for him to attempt to go through, and then he returned to Cawndilla. This kind of proceeding seems to have been the fault of Sturt in this exploration. Instead of doing like Leich- hardt, who sent back a companion to bring up the party directly he had reached water, Sturt used to continue his investigations, and then have to ride back to camp. Apart from the double fatigue to the animals, this proceeding caused immense delay.

On the 1st November the whole party were moved up to the serpentine water-hole, which the natives called Parnari. On the 6th, Sturt again journeyed to the north-west, with three men and the horse-cart, with a tank of water. They soon crossed the whole of the ranges, which here were of granite, and reached the western base : they found a pool of water around some sandstone gullies. The country on the western side was an unbroken level as far as the eye could reach, perfectly barren and useless. This was in lat. 31° 22'. Fortunately, they found an easy road to the north-west, and soon reached a fine creek, coming from a rocky gorge in the ranges. This did not serve them for long, but when it failed they took a supply in the tank, and went on the 11th towards some low hills, which were just visible in the distant west. The first five miles was over barren but firm clay, but after this the ground became covered, or rather macadamized, with broken, angular fragments of quartz on an undulating plain. Luckily, there was not much of this; and thenceforth, until they turned back on the evening of the 12th, it was merely a succession of sand ridges, looking more sombre because of the pine trees (*Callitris*) which clothed them. The west was still the same unbroken level plain.

As they ascended the ranges on their return, a thunderstorm overtook them, and on looking back Sturt could see the plains covered by fine sheets of water. With the help of these he could have penetrated much further than he had; but as soon as he returned to the camp, Mr. Poole was despatched in the same direction, while the party was moved slowly up to the creek on the western gorge of the range. It now received the name of the Stanley or Barrier Range. Sturt hoped that Mr. Poole would be able to reach the north-east angle of Lake Torrens, and probably, some water-course, which might carry him on his desired course to the north-west.

Mr. Poole left on the 20th November, and returned on the 2nd December to the camp, which was now established in advance of the rocky glen before mentioned. He had travelled west and a little north through a most barren country, until he had seen Mount Serle, on the Flinders Range—a mountain already mentioned in connection with the explorations of Frome and Eyre. Soon after sighting this mount, the country became a mere series of barren sand-hills, until they reached low, marshy lakes, apparently unbounded to the north and south. They were slightly brackish, and probably connected with Lake Torrens. Thus a westerly course was closed upon Sturt, and he had now no resource left but to try to procure water in striking along the ranges to the north.

On the 4th he sent Flood, one of his best men, to
proceed about sixty miles to the north in search of
water, because they could not remain long where they
were. The heat was intolerable, often rising to 125° in
the shade; and what little water there was became
every day alarmingly lower in consequence. When
Flood returned, he reported having found water about
forty miles in advance. It was situate in a beautiful
creek. This was cheering news, though considerably
damped by the report that the range was rapidly de-
clining at that distance, and could not continue much
further to the north. On the 10th, the whole party
reached Flood's Creek. Sturt meanwhile had ascended
the ranges, from whence he saw Mitchell's Mounts
Lyell and Babbage. The aspect of the country was
most discouraging. Even the few natives that were
seen were woefully emaciated, as if the land could
support no life of any kind. From Flood's Creek two
of the party, Messrs. Poole and Browne, were again
sent out to search for water to the north-west, while
Sturt made a journey to Mount Lyell. His course was
through dense scrubby ranges, until he came within
five miles of the hill. He found it to be two thousand
feet high, and of a most barren, sterile character; but
the country towards the Darling seemed even worse.
The curse of a desolate wilderness seemed to meet
Sturt whichever way he went.

Messrs. Poole and Browne did not return until the
25th, after having reached the 28th parallel of latitude,
and having found abundance of what appeared to be
permanent water. But the nearest part of it was forty
miles away, and it seemed to be very doubtful if the
cattle could be got to make so long a journey in such
weather. The heat during all the time was frightful.
The thermometer ranged daily from 100° to 120° in the
shade, and the cattle did nothing but remain under the
trees during the whole day. This was making them
very poor. Even the nights were insupportably warm,
for the hills were on fire, and it seemed dreadful to
contemplate being without water for only a single
night. Messrs. Browne and Poole had found that the

G 2

Barrier Range soon terminated. But after an open space to the north had been passed, another range succeeded, which seemed of more importance than the one they had left. It was rugged, and composed of indurated quartz, and there was a quantity of gypsum scattered upon the slopes of the hill. It was perfectly flat at the top. Fifteen miles from this they found a fine creek, and proceeding along it to the north-west found about twenty or thirty fine water-holes. This led them to an open tableland, on which the creek trended to the west. Poole, therefore, left it, and at two miles further crossed a branch creek, with water and grass; at seven and a half miles another; at twelve miles over open plains, another, muddy, and trending east; finally, at ten miles more, over stony plains, which made the horses suffer extremely, they passed another creek, and then they returned. They got a view of the country to the north-west from one of the ranges, and saw that it extended before them as a vast impenetrable scrub, hopelessly thick and level.

Though Sturt was very timid of advancing by water which might fail, and thus have his retreat cut off, yet he left Flood's Creek with many misgivings on the 28th. Before doing so, he ascended one of the hills of the Barrier Range, the view from which he thus describes: "We stood, as it were, in the centre of barrenness. I feel it impossible, indeed, to describe the scene, familiar as it was to me. The dark, broken line of the Barrier Range stood behind us to the south-eastward, the horizon was bounded by the hills I had lately visited, and from the south-west, round to the east, the whole face of the country was covered with a gloomy scrub, that extended like a sea to the distant horizon."

On the 30th, they reached the first creek discovered by Messrs. Poole and Browne. Both horses and bullocks were so much exhausted by the journey that some had fallen down dead from thirst. A few of the men who were left behind with the tanks and drays were, by the negligence of one of the advance party, left without relief, and they also suffered extremely. It

was not until the day after New Year's Day, 1844, that
all the party were brought up to the creek. The heat
they endured seemed scarcely credible: the ground
became so hot that the bullocks pawed it to get a cool
bottom; the men's shoes were scorched, as if by fire;
and some, who had stripped to the heat, were blistered
and severely burnt. The comet of 1844 had been
visible to the party, and it will be remembered that the
heat of the subsequent summer was very much felt in
England.

A hill near the camp was named Mount Arrowsmith. The rock was specular iron and highly magnetic. The stream was named Browne Creek. Up to this
time the party had been travelling upon the western
side of the Stanley Range, and consequently all the
creeks crossed had a westerly flow. Now, however,
they were on the east side of the new range, and the
flow of all the waters was to the eastward, The range
was distinguished by the name of Sir G. Grey, governor
of the colony.

They now moved slowly along the range, from
creek to creek, over stony plains. Wherever one of
them was followed it was found to terminate, after a
short course, in plains or reedy lagoons. The journey
on the 10th was much impeded by scrub, so that they
had to encamp without water; but they soon passed
through the scrub next day, and then traversed open
plains, sandy in places, and often thickly covered with
small fragments of quartz. Keeping a little to the
eastward, to avoid the spurs of the ranges they camped
upon a nice grassy place, with a fine sheet of water
before them. Unfortunately, this was very shallow and
rapidly drying up. It was impossible to stop there
long, and another camp must be looked for as soon as
possible, though it seemed hard to say where to search.

On the 14th, Sturt and some of the party made a
journey to the north-west. Their first care was to
trace up the creek they were upon; but finding no
water, they left a red hill, named Mount Poole, and
proceeded upon their course. Most of the water-
holes Messrs. Poole and Browne had discovered were

now dried up completely. They were two days searching these watercourses, and then Poole was sent back
with directions to make every search for water on his
way home. Sturt continued his surveys among the
hills. They were nearly all flat-topped, and composed
almost exclusively of indurated quartz or metamorphic
sandstone. It was not a range, but a series of isolated
table-hills, with occasionally small pools of bad water
at their bases. They diminished gradually to the
northward, becoming insignificant hills; and on the
18th, Sturt had reached a place where they had ceased
altogether. The plains beyond them were densely
clothed with scrub, with one or two little creeks, containing a small quantity of stagnant water : and yet,
for all their barrenness, there were many signs of
natives, as though this was one of their favourite
residences. Sturt entered the scrub. Abandoning one
of the creeks, he struck to the north-west. He was
soon on a perfect desert. Sandy flats and barren sand
ridges succeeded each other, like waves of the sea. In
the evening some hills were reached, with dry watercourses, showing the fall of waters to be still to the
east. The top of a barren rock of quartz and oxide of
iron, was only five hundred and seventy feet above the
level of the sea. As for the view, it would have appalled
more hopeful hearts than Sturt's. A dark sea of scrub
met the gaze all round. Sickened with so many dis-
appointments, Sturt abandoned all hope of proceeding
further in that direction. He now resolved to try the
nature of the country north-east of the Grey Range.
The hills he left were named after Captain Stokes.
They formed an important part of the route made by
Howitt in his track from the Darling to Cooper's Creek
in his search for Burke and Wills.

Amid a suffocating heat, Sturt returned to the creek
in the scrub. He found that his camp had been very
close to a native village, which was now completely
deserted. The position was in lat. 29° 14', long.
141° 14' E. He turned up the creek. The channel
was, as usual, soon lost in the plains. He would have
gone further, but the intolerable heat compelled him to

camp. The thermometer reached the incredible height of 131°, rendering any exertion quite out of the question. Thus the journey to the north-east was as unsuccessful as the north and westerly ones; and at length, after eleven days' absence, Sturt returned to the camp. He found that the water-hole where he had left the party was nearly exhausted, but that Mr. Poole had, upon his return, passed to the westward of a small range, where he had found water extending in a long sheet in the bed of a creek. Likewise, on crossing the head of the channel, he had entered a rocky glen, where there were successive pools in rocky basins, which contained an inexhaustible supply of water. It was a great relief to Sturt's mind to hear this news. He lost no time in moving his party to the glen and forming a depôt there. He knew that he might have to remain near these basins for some time, but he little suspected how long. For six months the party continued at this spot: they were in ignorance that the other waters had failed upon every side, and that all advance and retreat were alike cut off.

The camp was situate about three and a half miles south-south-east of Mount Poole. Stony plains lay between, which extended behind to a slightly hilly country. On the west was the low range, through which the creek came. The situation was very little above the level of the sea. The country was dry and parched beyond description, and the thermometer ranged daily from 100° to 117° in the shade. The only living things which seemed to brave this heat were kites (*Milvus affinis*), which abounded. They were similar to those which proved so troublesome to Leichhardt at Carpentaria, and quite as bold. They would fly within a foot of the men, and then suddenly turn back, flapping their wings, and pushing out their talons into their faces. Indeed, this camp must have been a cheerless spot.

Sturt was not satisfied with the result of the last journeys to the northward, and he determined on making another attempt. He set out with one lad, with a horse and cart, and a tank of water, determined

to reach the 27th parallel. It is needless to particularize
the details of the journey. He found a little water on
the ranges; but once he had reached the plains he was
met by the same uninterrupted scrub and desert. Still
he manfully pushed on until his horse was nearly dead,
and he and his companion almost spent with exhaustion.
The journey was, of course, fruitless. No change in
the country appeared at his furthest camp; yet if he
had only known it, his turning-point was only thirty
miles from the western bend of Cooper's Creek. But
he retraced his steps without seeing any hopeful indications. His latitude from where he turned back was
only 28° 9'.

On his return from the north, Sturt had intended to
try an easterly course; but the total failure of water in
that direction obliged him to go just the opposite way.
On the 17th February he went to the creek near the native
camp, and followed it down. As it proceeded through
the flat valley, bounded by sand-hills, it increased in
size. At fifteen miles it joined another from the south,
containing a scanty supply of water. This was hopeful,
especially as at twenty-one miles it turned to the west
of north, and the country became more level and open,
with numerous traces of natives. But the hopes did
not last long. At twenty-nine miles the creek was lost
on an immense plain, surrounded by sand-hills. Sturt
turned to the north. At two miles he found the creek
again, and in a fertile little valley, evidently very liable
to floods. This brought him to sand-hills similar to
those bounding Lake Torrens. But there was no sign
of the lake, even from the highest of the sand-hills; and
as the heat was too intense to pursue the inquiry further,
Sturt reluctantly returned. On the 21st he reached
the camp. The temperature was so high that the men
were all suffering very much in consequence. It was
quite impossible to work, and writing, drawing, or
mapping the country was out of the question, for the
ink and colours dried up as fast as the pens or brushes
could be replenished. To obviate this, Sturt ordered
an underground room to be sunk. This, when it was
finished, was their only source of comfort in their

lonely, desolate position. They watched the days going
by in gloomy inaction, with nothing to encourage them
in the aspect of the desert all round, except that
the weather became a little cooler. The last days of
February were a little chilly, and the birds near them
then migrated northwards.

CHAPTER VI.

STURT'S CENTRAL EXPEDITION (*continued*).

Journey to the eastward—Evelyn Plains—Extraordinary dryness of the atmosphere—Journey to the westward—Scurvy makes its appearance—Rain
at last—Death of Mr. Poole—Fort Grey—Lake Torrens—Strzelecki's
Creek — Other creeks — Red Sand-hills — Stony Desert — Sand ridges
again—Eyre Creek—The Central Desert—Cooper's Creek—Another
attempt to the north—Explores Cooper's Creek—Return to the Darling.

ON the 13th March, Sturt and a small party started
again to the eastward. Water had been found lower
down in the Depôt Creek, and with the assistance of
this, it was hoped a considerable distance could be got
over. After passing wide plains, they found the creek
with plenty of water in it, the channel being between
high banks of rich soil. They crossed it, and continued
to ride eastward over lands liable to occasional inundation, and somewhat sandy. They were, however,
covered with grass, large heaps of which had been
threshed out by the natives, and piled like haycocks.
This singular custom had been noticed by Mitchell in
coming down the Darling, and to this day the object of
it is not understood. At about two and a half miles
from the creek they saw a small hill, and south of this
a channel was found again, but quite dry. The plains
were named Evelyn Plains, and the same prefix was
given to the creek, in another reach of which, and little
further down, the party fortunately found water. On
the 15th, they again pursued their south course over
flooded plains, and again lost the stream. On turning a
little more to the east, they were soon met by scrub,
and as the creek had now completely disappeared, they
returned to their last camp. They made another journey
to the east, but very little information was collected

on this excursion. The furthest point was still a hundred and thirty-eight miles from the Darling, and ninety-seven from the depôt. The scrub was very thick, but they could see beyond them a fine range about thirty miles away, where the country seemed to improve. The ranges were high and clear of scrub, and the whole of the intermediate country looked as if liable to inundations. They returned to the camp on the 21st, and from thence to the end of the month nothing further was done.*

The month of April set in without any notable change of weather. It appeared, says Sturt, as if the flood-gates of heaven were closed upon them for ever. From day to day they watched the clouds gathering, and listened with eagerness to the distant thunder; but no rain came. The wind used to shift and blow in gusts, until their hopes were almost assured by the approach of a storm; but still no rain. The atmosphere was so dry that the drays almost fell to pieces; every screw in their various boxes was drawn, and the horn handles of their instruments and combs were split into fine laminæ. The lead dropped from the pencils; their *hair*, and the *wool* upon the sheep, *ceased to grow*; and the finger-nails became as brittle as glass. It was a fearful season in a fearful place. But all these miseries were not the worst. Many of the party were soon laid up with scurvy. Sturt was slightly affected, and Dr. Browne more severely; but Mr. Poole was in a short time the greatest invalid of all.

On the 18th, they noticed heavy clouds over the bearing of Mount Serle, and Sturt, hoping that it had rained in that direction, made a journey of more than seventy miles to the westward. No water was found. A few hollows, in the bed of a dry creek, contained a little moist mud, but this was all. So poor Sturt was obliged to return. The country he passed through was in general barren, with a few grassy flats and box-wood, and many sand ridges. This was the last attempt made for a time by Sturt. All April, May, and June,

* The ranges seen to the eastward were about the line of route crossed by Burke and Wills on their journey to Cooper's Creek, in 1860.

the barometer kept high, and no rain visited the poor prisoners. Their only living visitor was a native, and he came in a starving condition seeking food, even, as he believed, at the risk of death. Mr. Poole became daily worse, and could now scarely bear being shifted in his bed. Though no others were confined, yet Sturt and Browne were so crushed and overwhelmed by their cruel position that they rarely left their tents. The water in the depôt was failing. It was now only two feet deep, and there seemed but little probability of its holding out much longer. The provisions were likewise getting low.

Sturt had almost resigned all expectation of getting much further into the interior, but he hoped if the rain came, to send back half the party with Mr. Poole, whose only chance of life now lay in his speedy removal to the settled districts. This diminution would eke out the stores for a longer period. With this view, a return party was told off, and their provisions weighed out, and held in readiness for the long-desired wet weather. It came at last. On the 12th July, a gentle rain commenced falling, which continued all night, and then other wet days succeeded until the creek rose bank-high. But it was too late to save Mr. Poole. He was sent off as rapidly as possible; but the return party had only left a few hours when one came back to say that Mr. Poole was dead. They buried him near the depôt, and cut his initials on a tree that stood hard by. His grave is in the desert, not very far from that of Burke and Wills.

On the morning of the 18th, the remainder of the party pushed on to the north-west. They kept out from the range across swampy and stony plains, in which, now at least, there was no scarcity of water. Their progress was slow. On the 26th, they were only in latitude 29°, or sixty-one miles from the depôt. East of this, Sturt chose a grassy and well-watered creek as a depôt, to which the whole party were conducted. This was called the Park, or Fort Grey, situate upon Frome Creek. While these arrangements were being made, Mr. Stuart was directed to chain in a west-south-

west line, direct for Lake Torrens, about the latitude of
Mount Hopeless, in order to connect Sir T. Mitchell's
survey with those of Frome and Eyre. Stuart's journey
is easily described. For one hundred miles from Depôt
Creek he met with nothing but barren sand-hills, among
which there was now a little surface water. Then he
met with a small creek. The country was exactly like
a low barren sea-coast. Shortly after passing the creek,
he saw ranges to the west, and then a dry lagoon, the
surface of which was white with salt. This was part of
the arm of Lake Torrens. Beyond the lagoon there
was an immense shallow basin, ten or twelve miles
broad, with sheets of water in patches as blue as indigo,
and as salt as brine. This was what is now known to
be Lake Frome. There was a gradual descent of about
a mile and a half to the margin of the basin, and the
intervening ground was covered with low scrub.
Stuart tried to cross it, but it was an immense quagmire
utterly impassable. Whichever way he examined it,
north or south, the character was still the same. This
was in lat. 29° 14', long. 139° 12'. The distant ranges
were, respectively, sixty-five and thirty-three miles
away. The boiling point of water, if correct, showed the
lake to be considerably lower than the level of the sea.

Sturt now made preparations to continue his journey
to the northward. He thought it advisable not to risk
the safety of his party by taking all with him, so he
left it in charge of Mr. Stuart, and took three men with
Dr. Browne. He had provisions with him to last
fifteen weeks. On the 14th August, the small party
left the camp. Their course for four days was over
sand ridges and grassy flats, rather but not much better
than the country passed over in going to Lake Torrens.
The only water was the surface pools left by the rains,
so that if this country continued much further, their
retreat would be cut off in a few days. On the 18th,
however, they came to a fine creek with large reaches
of water, and many huts of natives. This channel
evidently contained constant supplies, for there were
large mussel-shells in it like those found on the Lachlan
and Darling. They called it Strzelecki's Creek.

It disappeared a little distance to the east of where they came upon it, so they left it and continued upon their old bearing. From the creek the plains had almost the appearance of lagoons bounded by sand ridges, and apparently often liable to inundation. They stopped that night at a dry creek, named after Leichhardt, and when, next day, another creek was passed, immense plains succeeded, with a soil very similar to the flats of the Darling; the few trees seen were box and polygonum; both being of a kind only found in flooded ground. Other creeks succeeded, as they journeyed on; all with more or less water in them, and very fine gum trees growing in their beds. The traces of natives round the water-holes were numerous, and this was accounted for by the quantities of fish to be found in them. Beyond the creek an immense plain extended, but with water-courses and lagoons in them; some containing only salt water.

So far the journey was very satisfactory. The country was not bad, and there was plenty of water. There seemed, indeed, a probability now of reaching the centre of the continent, as the scenery slowly improved. On the 24th August, it became much better than usual for about eight miles; and just as they thought they were coming at last to a favourable change, a hill of red sand rose before them. This looked ominous, but Sturt did not then understand its terrible import so well as he did subsequently, when better experience had taught him the nature of those fiery looking hills. The first was soon succeeded by another, and then another, and then a series. For twenty miles they toiled through these distressing ridges, whose glaring red colour was in keeping with their aridity. Some salt lagoons were passed; then the country improved slightly, but only very slightly. They camped without water; but that evening they found, in a dark-looking valley to the north-west, a beautiful pool, to which they all moved next day. They rested here. Sturt during the day strolled to a sand-hill, about two miles away, which shut out the view of their course. From the summit of this hill he saw what destroyed all his hopes. An immense plain met his gaze, occupying about half the horizon. It was perfectly level, of a dark purple colour, without a tree, a blade of grass, or the faintest trace of vegetation—a stony desert, in fine, on to which the sand-hills abutted like cliffs upon the ocean.

Terrible as it looked, Sturt determined to try to cross it. On leaving the camp on the 26th, a more abundant supply of water was found, and they then set out to traverse the desert. It was a weary, trying journey; for the ground was as thickly as possible strewn with rounded fragments of quartz and sandstone. It was in fact just like a shingle beach. With no other view but the stones all round them, they camped in the middle of the plain without a drop of water. Next day they continued onwards. At ten miles there was a sensible fall of some few feet from the level of the Stony Desert, and they descended into a belt of polygonums, about two miles wide. Anyone familiar with the dark wiry appearance of this leafless shrub will understand how this solitary piece of vegetation added to the cheerless character of the scene. Beyond the polygonum was another feature in the desert of great extent. This was an earthy plain, without vegetation, resembling a boundless flat on which floods had settled and dried. In this there were many channels making to the north-east. Towards evening some hills appeared to the westward, and in travelling towards them, they came to some water. There was, however, not a blade of grass for the horses, and this was their second day without food.

In making for the hills next morning, they found a watercourse with plenty of water, but not a scrap of vegetation. The hills were reached, but there was no relief in them. Sand ridges rose up in terrible array before their eyes. There were flats beyond, and by these Sturt was as much dismayed as the sand, for they were evidently little better than a quaking bog in wet weather. The slightest rain upon them would, he considered, effectually cut off his retreat. How just this opinion was, M'Kinlay subsequently experienced, when he found this country deluged with water, and the ground a perfect morass. Keeping along the sand ridges, which ran north-west, they came upon a box forest, but still no grass. About an hour before sunset they arrived on the banks of a large creek, which was quite dry, except in a small native well which barely contained enough for their wants. Near this was a deserted native village, and natives were seen near. The horses were quite exhausted, and one of them became so bad, that he was turned loose. He was not found afterwards.

The next day's journey was over the interminable sand ridges, and then succeeded plains so cracked and fissured that the horses could with difficulty be induced to pass over the wide rents, often fifteen feet deep. They camped without searching for water; for it was useless to look for it on such ground. It was hard to say what the horses lived upon meanwhile, but they used to gnaw the bark off the trees, and pick about amid the rushes and dead leaves. On the 1st September, in travelling due north, they came upon some puddles which satisfied the cravings of the animals. During the day, also, they found a little grass, so Sturt did not leave this spot until the 3rd September. As they went on, the country improved; but they were risking a good deal in their advancing without leaving water behind them in case of a retreat. They reached a fine creek next day, with splendid reaches of water in it, and good grass. This was called Eyre Creek. It was a great godsend to them in any case; but the best thing about it was that its course was in the direction they wished to proceed. And so for two days they travelled along it, amid such pleasant scenes that they almost forgot the difficulties of their position.

But on the 6th a change came. The creek terminated in a salt lagoon, and beyond this the water entirely failed. The grassy woodland continued for several miles, evidently liable to floods, but suddenly it ceased. They entered then upon plains supporting nothing but samphire and polygonum, and bounded by sand-hills. The ground was almost incrusted with salt. Where they halted the view was most cheerless. To the west were heavy sand-hills, almost impracticable for the horses; to the north and north-east were dark green samphire plains, through which the glittering white of dried salt lagoons shone in the far distance. Dr. Browne was sent to the westward, to look for the creek. He found it indeed, but its bed was glittering with salt. Sturt then tried to continue through the sand-hills, but it was useless: the further they travelled the higher the ridges became, until from the summit of one they saw them extending northwards in parallel lines beyond the range of vision.

It was a hopeless task to attempt to proceed further. Sturt was by this time thoroughly dispirited. He says in his journal : " Halted at sunset in a country such as, I believe, has no parallel upon the earth's surface, and one which was terrible in its aspect. Not a blade of grass. From the top of one of the ridges the view extended 15° or 20° to the north. No ray of hope. Sandy ridges on each side. At this particular spot, the furthest to which we had penetrated, I computed that we were about fifty miles from the creek which had so suddenly and unaccountably failed us. We stopped near a few Acacia bushes, almost without food since we left the creek on the 6th, and now on the second evening without water."*

This was Sturt's furthest point. It was little more than a degree from the tropics, and scarcely a hundred and fifty miles from the centre of the continent, and yet he was obliged to turn back. It was heart-breaking for him to do so. An eyewitness has related how he sat for more than an hour on the top of the sand-hill with his face buried in his hands, evidently quite crushed by this final disappointment. Had it not been for his companions he would certainly have gone on, and as certainly perished. As it was, they had been too long without water, and did not know if a retreat was still open to them. Sturt

* Downs, or sand-hills, form a prominent feature of the Sahara landscapes. They are rounded elevations, smooth as marble and sterile as naked rock, and of so uniform a colour that they never appear to blend or confuse with surrounding objects. During the day they wear the sombre hue of a landscape at sunset; and they seem to be at the mercy of the wind, travelling at its bidding to settle here and there, to rise and wander forth again.—*Chambers' Deserts of Africa.*

did not, however, resign his hopes without a final effort. On returning to the creek, he made an attempt to the north-north-east. He kept for two days upon this course, but it was in vain. The same salt formation appeared, and the same fiery red sand, which drifted upon them as they travelled, as if ready to bury and overwhelm them; and yet he was not without hope. From even where he returned, though the country was bad enough, they saw natives, and there were distant smokes to be seen beyond. There must certainly have been some improvement where natives could exist; but he was obliged to return. He reached the creek on the 14th. His furthest north was lat. 24° 30', long. 137° 58'.

Thus far their explorations extended, but not their labours. They did not get to the depôt without much suffering. Dr. Browne, endured very much from scurvy, and was scarcely able to keep his seat upon his horse; the others were equally exhausted. Well they might be. They had been living lately upon five pounds of flour each per week, and little else besides. The water failed upon their return, as they had expected. It is needless to go through the harrowing details of the journey back across the sand, with all the pains of fearful thirst upon them. How they got over the last stage was a mystery even to themselves, but they reached Strzelecki's Creek on the 29th, and were back at Fort Grey by the 2nd October. They had been absent eight weeks, and had travelled rather more than eight hundred miles. Had it not been that they took the precaution of deepening some of the waterholes as they passed, neither they nor their horses would ever have returned alive.

Poor Sturt was not yet baffled. He was determined not to give up hope until he had made one more effort. In order, however, that the safety of the whole party might not be compromised, he offered to leave Dr. Browne with all the men but three, while he continued his explorations. Dr. Browne did all he could to dissuade him from the hopeless effort. It seemed like tempting Providence to rush into the thirsty desert again. Finding Sturt inexorable, he nobly refused to leave the depôt until they could return together.

This course was not without risk to all. They had had
no rain since the showers when Mr. Poole died, and
the supply at the stockade was getting very low. It
might fail altogether before Sturt's return. The latter
was aware of this, and in leaving Dr. Browne in command he directed him, in case of scarcity, not to wait
for his companions, but to fall back upon Evelyn Creek.
These and a few other preliminary arrangements were
completed on the 9th, and then he started. His companion this time was J. M'Dougall Stuart (since so celebrated himself as an explorer), besides two men, and ten
weeks' rations for them all.

On the morning of the 11th they reached Strzelecki's Creek. It still contained abundance of water.
They then struck away from it to the north-west, over
flooded plains bounded by sand-hills. The end of the
day's journey was near a belt of trees, which was pretty
and picturesque, the country meanwhile improving.
Next morning the trees turned out more interesting
than they thought. They lined a splendid creek, containing abundance of fine reaches of water. The grass
was beautiful around it, and the reaches covered with
ducks. It was evidently at times a fine main channel
of drainage, more entitled to be called a river than a
creek; for though the country around seemed as if rain
had not fallen upon it for years, the reaches were
very deep, and well stocked with fish. Sturt named it
Cooper's Creek, after Sir Charles Cooper, the chief justice in Adelaide. It is necessary, however, to warn the
reader that this name is not preserved in the rest of this
work. The stream in question has been a most important point in connection with various explorations,
and has received very many names. Mitchell called it
the Victoria River, but we have one already in Australia. It was also proposed to call it the Cooper's River,
and the Gregory. Sturt's name, however, has been the
one most used, and that is open to the objection that we
have here to deal with a large river which is sometimes
two miles wide. The natives call it the Barcoo, and
this is the name by which it will be always alluded to
in this volume.

Such a splendid watercourse naturally would have kept Sturt along its banks, but it ran east and west, and he was determined to travel north. He left it with great regret, for it offered finer promise to the explorers than any stream he had seen on this journey. The river was succeeded by grassy plains of considerable extent, in which there were pools of water, left by a recent thunder-shower. This was their only supply, so they deepened every puddle they met to make them last the longer. The journey for two days was most promising, but again a terrible check awaited them. On the 15th the old and detestable red sand ridges commenced, but they did not continue long. Grassy plains again succeeded, and thus they thought they had escaped the sand. The plains were named the Plains of Hope. Hope deferred, they should have said, for the respite was a very short one. The 17th brought them again to sand-hills, through which they had to toil for two days. They fortunately found a little water, and this made Sturt continue, only keeping rather more to the west. The country was desolate beyond description, and Sturt considered that it must get better, for it could not possibly be worse. He reckoned without his host, for the summit of one of the sand-hills showed him a view which made his head reel with despair. Sudden changes, he had seen, was the rule in this country, but he had tried to forget it. The view now before him recalled the truth with cruel bitterness. No wonder he sat down and gazed stupefied upon the scene. The foot of the high sand-hill jutted out into the Stony Desert, which stretched on every side like a dark purple sea before him.

This was an awful blow to Sturt. He says, that coming upon it so suddenly again almost took his breath away. After gazing at it for a long time, courage enough at last returned to make him resolve to cross it again. Slowly they descended on to the barren plain, and tried to keep to the north-west, but it was all to no purpose. They certainly did again cross, but that was all. On the other side they met ridges from one to two hundred feet high, covered with stone fragments, and all

around the same sort of country seemed to continue.
This was in lat. 25° 58′, long. 139° 26′. The horses
were then so much reduced from scarcity of feed and
water that they were obliged to return. On his way
back, Sturt struck a little to the north-east. A day's
ride placed him out of sight of all high land, and the
desert was like an immense sea-beach, with large fragments of rock scattered over the surface or buried in the
ground, as if by the force of waters.

Such was Sturt's view of the Stony Desert, but probably he took an erroneous one of its nature and extent.
The desert was not the only place where such stony
plains are found. Readers can remember one already
mentioned in the description of Stokes Range. Recent
observations prove that the desert is not different. It
is most probably a series of plains instead of one vast
desert, and is not all equally thickly strewn with stones
or destitute of vegetation. Howitt found, in 1862, a part
where it was not more than seventeen miles wide, of
which only eight miles were bad travelling, and all
more or less grassed. The stones again are not in every
place of equal size. They are very small in some localities, and form almost boulders in others. Whether
small or large, the plains must not be kept on the maps
as a strip of land branching out for an unknown extent to
the north of Lake Torrens. The Stony Desert, if it must
still be marked, must appear as dotted patches amid the
plains for a considerable distance north, south, and west
of the Barcoo, with no special character peculiar to one
part more than another. But my readers will probably
be anxious to hear some explanation of the cause of
these stony plains. Many theories have been proposed,
the favourite of which is, that they are the remains left
by some long-continued current of water running
through the centre of the continent. My own opinion,
and it is but an opinion, is that they are the remains of
a decomposed highly ferruginous tertiary sandstone,
which abounds in other parts of the continent. Where
the strata contained a great deal of iron they formed
siliceous concretions which resisted decomposition, while
the rest of the rock fell away. Or it may have been

that the strata was itself composed in places of a sandstone breccia, like that found on the north coast, where
each ferruginous nodule is glazed round with quartz.
The red sand is certainly derived from a ferruginous
sandstone ; and if it be asked how the ridges should be
so high and uneven, and the plains so low and flat, I
answer, that when the strata decomposed, the lighter
portions drifted away into ridges, leaving the heavier
remains scattered below on the plains.

Be this as it may, Sturt now turned away from them
for the last time, cruelly disappointed, and enduring
much in mind and body. The horses suffered extremely
for want of water on their return, and so did the men,
for most of the wells they had dug were now dry. Had
it not been that one of them still retained a little fluid,
the party must have perished. One horse died in the
desert. This was their only loss, and they reached the
Barcoo on the 28th October. But their labours were
not finished. The men were all exhausted, and Sturt
perhaps worst of all, but still he was determined not to
leave the Barcoo until he had explored it for some distance to the eastward. This was the greatest risk of all.
The retreat might—nay, would—almost certainly be cut
off before he returned ; but proceed he would. It was
the only important discovery made on this unfortunate
expedition, and the men could hardly grudge him that.
He buried all his superfluous stores in order to lighten
the burdens of the horses, and then advanced. He found
the channel of the river to be dry, but there were many
reaches with abundance of water in them. Natives were
very numerous, and they formed a most remarkable
exception to the generality of savages, for they were
peaceable and communicative.*

On the 31st, as they proceeded, stony ranges appeared on the left, and seemed to fall back towards the
north. The river had now two channels, but only one
of them contained water. The banks were well grassed,
and wood was abundant. On the 3rd November, they

---

* This is a character borne out by every other explorer. It will be
related how they saved the life of King when Burke and Wills both died of
starvation.

reached several tributaries, which seemed to come from flats of large extent, in which Sturt believed that the river took its rise. From this point he turned back, for the boundless plains which met his gaze not only precluded all hope of penetrating further to the eastward, but he and one of his men were very ill, and the horses could scarcely drag themselves along. They returned to the buried stores, and they left the river for Strzelecki's Creek. Sturt first struck the Barcoo in lat. 27° 44′, long. 140° 22′, and his turning point was in lat. 27° 56′, long. 142° E. The furthest water-holes were covered with duck, cormorants, pelicans, and even sea-gulls, or birds which were very like them.

Their return from Strzelecki's Creek was the most terrible journey they had yet made. They were met in the plains by a terrific hot wind, which broke upon them with unrestrained violence. A thermometer, graduated up to 127°, burst from the heat, and the ground was so hot that if a match was dropped upon it it ignited immediately. The horses could not be got along. The last stage without water was eighty-six miles. When thirty-six had been got over, some of the animals gave in. One of them, named Bawley, was left in plains which still bear his name.* As the party were now reduced to great straits for want of food, Sturt rode on to send out assistance from the depôt. When he arrived there, it was deserted. He anticipated this, and yet it proved a great shock to him. "A sickening feeling came over me," he says, "when I found they were really gone. Not on my own account, for with the bitter feelings of disappointment with which I was returning home, I could have calmly laid my head upon the desert never to raise it again." He found a letter from Dr. Browne, explaining that he had left because the water had become putrid.

Sturt's companions soon arrived. The horses, with

* This horse survived, and was found many years after feeding near Lake Torrens ; at the end of fourteen years after his loss he was driven into the settled districts. He had, of course, become very wild, and was quite white instead of the roan colour he had when deserted ; his hoofs had grown to an enormous length.

one exception, were with difficulty brought up, and then
the party ate their ration of damper, which was the only
meal they had tasted. for the two previous days. In
searching about the camp they found some bacon fat and
some suet, which the dogs had buried. This was hailed
as a great godsend. It gave them new strength for the
rest of their journey. Then Sturt, though suffering
extremely from scurvy, thinking only of his companions,
rode on to the depôt for assistance. He kept on horseback for twenty hours, never stopping, except to relieve
for a moment the excruciating pains in his limbs. He
reached the tents on the 17th November. There, fortunately, was the relief he sought. Dr. Browne had
nearly recovered, and the men with one exception well,
so that assistance was easily sent to those coming on
behind. They all reached the camp in safety. There
was now no time for delay : the grass and water were
both scanty in the depôt, and the weather gave every
indication of a hot and arid season. Any attempt to
escape to the southward must be made at once, or they
might never expect to gaze again upon the dwellings of
civilized men.

Their position was soon found to be a fearful one.
A search for water was made along their route, and
then an alarming fact became known to them. From
the camp to Flood's Creek—a distance of a hundred and
eighteen miles—there was not a drop of surface water.
At Flood's Creek the messenger had found some, but it
was as black as ink, and so low that a few more days
would dry it up. Sturt was now so ill that he was
unable to move. He had never left his bed since his
arrival at the camp, but his mind was still vigorous.
Helpless as he was, he designed a plan for their escape.
Three bullocks were shot, and their hides filled with
water. These were sent on by the cart, and deposited
half-way to Flood's Creek. It was hoped that the
bullocks would, when disencumbered of every unnecessary article of baggage, be able to carry enough for the
intermediate portions of the journey. The plan succeeded admirably. It was a terrible journey, but
one which admitted of no delay. Flood's Creek was

reached at last, and the animals had not suffered very much.

But the end was not yet. Another stage succeeded, but not entirely destitute of water, and so they rapidly proceeded on their way homeward, across the Barrier Range, and, in all haste for Cawndilla, where they knew there was assistance, they hurried. Their last trial was the greatest. They were still seventy miles from the lagoon when all their supplies failed. It was a terrible suspicion to think that Mr. Piesse might not have reached the settled districts, and that there was still no help for them at Cawndilla. They travelled on day and night, almost afraid to hope. After thirty-six hours' incessant labour, they were relieved of their anxiety. They then met Mr. Piesse with the supplies, and thus all their troubles were at an end.

Poor Sturt suffered very much in the latter part of the journey. He had to be lifted in and out of the drays as they proceeded, so that it was sometime before he could leave the Darling, and pursue his way to Adelaide. Whatever disappointment his friends felt at his misfortunes, it was more than compensated by seeing that he nearly recovered the effects of his sufferings. But never completely. He shortly afterwards entirely lost his sight, and thus completed the greatest sacrifice to the cause of exploration ever made by one so unsuccessful.

This journey confirmed the idea that the centre of Australia was a desert; how unjustly has been since proved, as the reader will see further on. In other respects, the discovery of the Barcoo, and so much good country, amid sandy deserts, rather improved the impression as to the interior. Sturt's travels, published subsequently, form a fine record of what energy and perseverance can do against insurmountable difficulties. The story is told with a modesty, simplicity, and disinterestedness, which charm the reader into the warmest sympathy with all he relates. Though unfortunate, he stands in the foremost rank of Australian explorers.

CHAPTER VII.

WESTERN AUSTRALIA.

The Gregorys' expedition into the interior, in 1846—Discovery of immense salt swamp—Fruitless endeavours to cross it—Dense scrubs—Hills of volcanic rock — The Arrowsmith — Discovery of coal — Return to the Swan—Helpman's ocean expedition—The Coal River—Observations on the country around.

SINCE the time of its first foundation, Western Australia has never given up the subject of exploration. Unlike the other colonies, which have always gone into the matter by fits and starts, there have been almost continuous expeditions from Perth. But a reason exists for this which does not exist elsewhere in Australia. There is no colony which is cursed with so much unfruitful soil as Western Australia. Almost every excursion into the bush must lead to land almost unvisited. Away from the banks of the rivers nearly all the country is a thick scrub, as useless and almost as impenetrable as any scrub in Australia. But the colonists did not at first take all this for granted. With a zeal which deserved far better success, they kept sending parties to the westward, in the hope every time of finding some new and more promising features. Some of these undertakings were on so small a scale that they scarcely need any notice here. Others led to more important results, and among such is the journey we have now to record.

Three young surveyors, whose names have become celebrated since as most distinguished explorers, were sent on a small expedition to the westward. They were the brothers Gregory, of whom the famous traveller Augustus was the chief. Their equipment was of the slenderest possible kind, consisting only of four horses and seven weeks' provisions. It was not hoped that they could do much on so small a scale, but even a little patch of good ground would be an important discovery, and at any rate they could ascertain something of the nature of part of the unexplored interior. They started from Bolgart Spring, the most outlying of the settled districts, on the 7th August, 1846.

Their course was twenty degrees north of east. Of course the commencement of the journey was over worthless country. Had there been good land beyond Bolgart Spring, it would not have been the most outlying station. So their course took them over sandy downs, thickly timbered, and with small streams running down towards the coast. This was in lat. 31° 12′, long. 116° 50′ E. All at once, the land improved for a short space, giving them a grassy flat, with *Casuarina* trees, to travel over. The country was too level for the explorers to see anything beyond the nature of the land they were passing along, but towards evening a lake rose nearly north of them. This was out of their course, but water of any kind was worth examination in this arid tract, so they made for the basin. It was fresh, but so shallow that it was more entitled to be considered a swamp than a lake. In fact, the land around was very swampy, and the water was no more than the lowest part of a depression on the surface of the soil, which allowed rain-water to collect, and therefore gave rise to a better soil. The water was slightly oblong, and nearly a mile wide. It was a very exceptional case to find so large a sheet of fresh water in such a scrub, but absence of rain, and evaporation, no doubt soon render it as salt as any of its neighbours.

Messrs. Gregory resumed their old course when they had ascertained the nature of the lake. The country was scrubby, but not level now. Every few miles it swelled into sandy hills, leaving valleys between, rather more openly wooded. From one of these hills they observed shallow lakes, about five to ten miles to the north-east, so again they left their course, and steered towards them. Before they reached the water the tract became clear of timber, and an immense plain lay before them, studded with shallow salt lakes. The plain was not grassy; it was covered with that dank, noisome vegetation, half sea-weed, half rank swamp growth, which one finds on low, shallow sea-shores. It was evidently all one salt lake at times, but the dry weather had separated it into pools, glistening all round with a fringe of crystallizing salt. The explorers, however, easily found a native well, with some grass, where they made a good camp.

Again they resumed their course to the east. Leaving the large lagoons and the swampy country on their right, they were soon in the thicket once more. Not a scrub this time. It was an open gum forest, with tall trees rising high above their heads, and a thick undergrowth, which made travelling laborious and slow. It did not last long at first, and when the view opened, they could see the salt lagoons and the low marshes still keeping on their left. But when the forest closed upon them again, it was a succession of very dense thickets, till they reached an open grassy patch, surrounded by swamps. The gum forest continued until the 11th, when they saw before them the outlines of a mountainous horizon. They were approaching the granite hills described by so many explorers as forming a stony boundary between the scrubs and streams of the coast on one side, and the low sandy desert and salt marshes of the interior.

They steered towards the nearest of the hills. It was like most of the granite mountains which raise their heads from the scrubs of South Australia as well as the west coast. The summits are bare rocky peaks, or boulders, lying confusedly, as if piled by art, though broken by disintegration and weathering. In amongst these stones there are generally hollows or depressions where the rain-water collects. Sometimes even there are small springs of water at the base of the rock, but these are not permanent, and only due to the drainage of some heavy winter rains. The slopes of the base are always well grassed and lightly timbered; in fact, a granite hill, wherever it is met, is an oasis in the desert, where feed for horses and nearly always water can be found. Mr. Gregory now mounted the nearest of the hills he saw before him. The view was very extensive, as the prospect from any elevation, however small, must be in such level country. It extended over the usual vast, brown, rolling sea of scrub. The clear blue sky and transparent atmosphere of Australia is a painful addition to such a prospect. It makes even the most distant part of the dreary scene stand out, clearly and distinctly, as if to remove all doubt of the hopeless character of the interior. Gregory, however, could see breaks here and there. One was the Lake Brown (of Roe), lying like an irregular white spot on the open ground. Beyond this the horizon faded off into rugged summits, more and more faint, until they formed into the merest shadow in the filmy distance.

They descended the hill, and took a course bearing to the north, in order to avoid going over the ground discovered by Roe. The country was at first undulating and woody, with small watercourses trending to the southward. This lasted as long as they were among the granite rocks. They managed to camp near waterholes by the rocks on nearly every day during the first part of the journey, for there were a great number of granite hills in this latitude. The day's work on their course was simply going from one to another of their rocky summits. The intervening country varied but little. For the most part it was dense scrub, without water or grass, and difficult enough to travel through, but it opened into small patches of gum forest here and there, with a tangled growth of small wood underneath. The soil, however, was pretty uniform; it was nothing but sand.

On the 16th, in travelling through well-grassed country, they ascended a green hill, of a fragmentary or brecciated trap rock. From its summit they saw several others of similar character, while to the north were dry lakes. They struck to the shore of one of these lakes. Its banks were gypsum and red sand, rising into curious looking cliffs, often thirty feet in height. The water was salt, and altogether the view

was not encouraging. They skirted this desolate sheet
of water, and plunged into the dense Acacia thicket
which fringed the edge. The soil now was a red sand,
and supported nothing except the Acacia, Cypress, and
a few gum trees. There was no small vegetation
whatever. Next day brought them across a narrow
samphire flat, which they steered north to avoid. This
led them to a trap hill, with a few granite rocks at the
foot. The trap was a peculiar rock, striped red and
black, a sort of gneiss, in fact, about three hundred feet
high. The view was somewhat different from what
had been seen from the granite hills. There was a line
of trap hills extending to the eastward, while all else
appeared a sandy desert, as dry and as destitute of
vegetation as it was possible to be. They seemed on
the edge of a sandy desert, without a growth of even
scrub, for as they looked out upon its vast extent they
could see immense columns of red sand, or dust,
whirling over the plains in trembling pillars, some three
hundred or five hundred feet high.* There did not
seem much chance of water in such a desert, and yet
Gregory was determined to try to penetrate further.
One day's journey convinced him that it was in vain.
He could find no water, nor the prospect of any, so he
returned to his camp on the hill from which he had
seen the whirlwinds.

This conclusion of Gregory was only confirmatory
of what others had seen before, and what subsequent
explorers found. The experience of every exploring
expedition from Perth has been the same. Dense
scrubs, or gum flats, with granite rocks and salt lakes
in between, until a series of volcanic hills is reached.
Then the country changes. All beyond is a desert,
without grass or water. It is of unknown extent, and
it should ever be borne in mind by those colonists who
propose a journey across the continent, from east to
west, that this belt of country must be considered a

* In the vast expanse of desert we saw towards the north a number of
prodigious pillars of sand at various distances, sometimes moving with great
velocity, sometimes stalking on with majestic slowness. At intervals, we
thought they were coming in a very few minutes to overwhelm us, and small
quantities of sand did actually reach us.—*Bruce's Travels in Abyssinia.*

barrier, which, being insurmountable so near the settled districts, can scarcely be expected to be easily crossed from the eastern side.

Gregory, finding he could not travel any further to the east, turned back a little to the north of the way he had come. His object now was to get back among the granite rocks, and then to steer in a northerly direction until he found some more available country for making another attempt to the eastward. He was soon among the rock waters again, and also among the scrubs. For days subsequently the journey was what has been already described in connection with this granite rock country. Sometimes the scrubs were very dense, or again they were more open. But the country did not improve until they came again into the region of the salt lakes, considerably to the north of where they had formerly struck them. This was on the 25th. The first approach to the lakes was announced by the commencement of a vast samphire flat, which extended as far as the eye could reach. It seemed pretty safe, so Gregory resolved to cross it, though the half-withered vegetation of a salt marsh, with green slime, or white incrustations, told them that it might prove soft as they advanced. The horses got safely along for some distance, until they reached the dry bed of a lake. It was covered with a hard crust of gypsum and salt, which for half a mile bore the weight of the horses very well. At that distance it suddenly gave way, and three of the horses became bogged. This was very provoking to the explorers. The animals could not be extricated, and the men were obliged to wade their way back to the timber on foot, to make hurdles. With the assistance of these the horses were got out, and taken to a grassy granite hill, about three miles to the eastward.

From the summit of the hill they saw, next day, the nature of the obstacle before them. It extended ten miles to the eastward, and rather more than that distance on nearly every other bearing, except north-east. On that it stretched out beyond the range of vision, and formed the only visible horizon. It looked

an oozy, unwholesome place. There were large shallow
pools, about a mile in extent, occurring here and there,
while low wooded and high rocky islands were scattered
over the vast expanse of salt, gypsum, and white mud.
Such features remind us forcibly of Lake Torrens and
the area of the salt lakes in the red sand of South
Australia. No doubt they owe their origin to the
same cause. They are reservoirs of rain water in
sandy scrubs, where there is no drainage, and the
calcareous sand and marl of the soil is dissolved in the
liquid, and redeposited at each successive heavy rain.
Probably Lake Torrens is not so big as many lakes in
Western Australia, about which there has scarcely ever
been any mention made.

As the party were now enclosed on the north-east
side by this feature, they were obliged to turn south, in
order to skirt it. The granite rocks still kept along
the edge, and it was on these alone that they were
dependent for water. In travelling south, they found
that the lake edged more and more to the eastward,
until at last they thought they had got round the
southern boundary. They were very much mistaken.
In ascending a granite hill, on the evening of the 28th,
they found, to their disgust, that they were on a peninsula, formed by two branches of the lake, and that
further progress to the westward was impossible. The
south, too, was closed to them, for the marsh formed
the horizon in that direction. It was very hard to
have to retrace their steps, but there was no time for
deliberation. They turned east, and when they had
passed the south extreme of the eastern branch, struck
fairly into the scrub again. For a long time now they
kept to the east, amid the same succession of granite,
Acacia thickets and gum plains. It was not until the
30th that they turned north, where a more level tract
of open country enabled them to see that there was no
fear of the lake again. But they saw it before long.
In the middle of the day they found themselves at the
north-east extremity of it. It was of enormous dimensions. For five days it had prevented the explorers
from proceeding, and yet they had not seen the whole

of its extent. At this point it was about six miles wide,
and extended into the gloomy distance, to the south-
east, like a dusty white plain.

They now journeyed north-west. All hope of
getting to the eastward was abandoned, and the utmost
they expected to effect was to make towards the coast,
and try to explore the sources of some of the streams
of Grey. On the 1st September, they reached the
summit of a trap hill, which gave them an extensive
view. To the west were dry salt lakes, and ranges of
hills like the one they were upon. To the north, the
land was level for several miles, and then a low range
of granite hills occurred, covered with brushwood and
grass. All the land around on every side was clothed
with a dense Acacia scrub, and the only grass was
where granite hills started up, though that was in nearly
every direction. There was no variation whatever in the
country from what has been already so often described.
By the 2nd, they saw that they were approaching the
coast, because of the commencement of small streams
trending to the west. In the evening they crossed a dry
stream bed, about thirty yards wide; and near it were
a party of natives, who fled so precipitately, on seeing
the explorers, that they left their spears behind them.

On the 3rd, the land became more level, and the
stream beds more numerous. In the midst of them
there was another salt marsh, which from the summit
of a hill was seen to extend about fifteen miles to the
north-east, with a branch to the north-west. In that
direction the water appeared to trend in wet seasons;
though the dip of the country was so slight as to render
this very uncertain. The granite hills continued
almost like a range to the north, but on the course of
the explorers trap hills took their place. This was
a bad sign, because these rocks seldom or never contained water. Gregory, however, pushed forward.
In twenty-four hours he reached lat. 28° 24', long.
116° 42'; but there was no prospect of finding water.
With great regret he was obliged to turn back. All
he could hope to do was to reach the sources of the
Arrowsmith from the camp of the last water.

On the 5th, they commenced their journey to the
west. Need it be said again that it was through Acacia
scrubs and red sand? The country seemed rising as
they proceeded, and water became very scarce. They
sometimes had to journey as much as fifty miles without
a drink for themselves or the horses. On the 8th, the
land became much better; it was now a grassy gum
forest, and the soil an ironstone gravel. The streams
were rather numerous, and of considerable size; but
they all seemed to go too much to the south for the explorers' purposes. In travelling through the gum
forests on the 9th, a large watercourse of this kind was
passed. It seemed very promising, but Gregory
thought it better to continue his western journey,
especially as a grassy and lightly timbered valley was
before them. This led them to a small stream leading
north, and full of small pools. They followed it. It
was soon joined by a running stream of brackish water,
four yards wide. They left this when it turned south-
west, and again had to encounter a very thick scrub,
the soil of which was composed of fragments of granite
and trap. This suddenly terminated in a deep valley,
which the explorers entered by an extremely difficult
and abrupt descent. It could hardly be called picturesque, in the midst of so many rocks and such arid
soil, but it soon led to the river again, now changed
into a broad stream, running through a grassy flat, and
flanked by sandstone cliffs eighty to one hundred feet
high.

These banks of rock proved particularly interesting.
As the stream continued, they rose higher and higher,
making the dark valley look more sombre, and giving
it the appearance of a chasm rent in the rocks. There
were two formations. The lower were thin strata,
dipping to the east, with a high inclination, while the
superincumbent red sandstone was nearly horizontal.
As the explorers examined the lower beds, they were
surprised and delighted to find that they contained two
seams of coal, five and six feet thick, with several beds
of shale. They lost no time in collecting specimens,
and having cut out a quantity with an axe, had the

satisfaction of seeing a coal fire burning cheerfully before the tent. This was in lat. 28° 57' 10", long. 115° 30' 30".

On the 10th September, they commenced to follow the river, the general course of which was south of west. The valley widened as the stream went down, and the soil upon the banks was of much better quality. It seemed to be composed of decomposed bituminous shale and gypsum, producing luxuriant wild rye and oat grass. The green valley was altogether about two miles wide, but the grass flats were not more than a quarter of that, and were flanked by scrubby sand dunes. Beyond these, table-hills arose, the whole lying in an amphitheatre of sandstone cliffs. On the 11th, another large stream was found to join the one they were upon. It was so deep that the explorers had great difficulty in crossing. When they succeeded, the river kept a west-by-south course, through rich lime-stone valleys. This was near the mouth, when they had descended from the tableland. Like the most of the Australian streams, the *embouchure* was choked up with a bar. Gregory considered it to be the Irwin River of Grey; but in this he was mistaken. It was the Arrowsmith. Gregory's mistake was a very natural one, because the stream was only a mile and a half south of where Grey placed the Irwin; but he had no correct means of determining the latitude at the time, and his positions were often erroneous.

Gregory now retraced his steps, until he came to the sandstone tableland again; and when he had ascended this, he struck to the south of east. He knew that he might expect bad country from such a course, but his great object was to explore as much as possible upon the journey. All his anticipations about bad travelling were soon realized. He found himself en-tangled in the usual scrubs; and the horses could get nothing to eat, except white everlasting (*Helichrisum*) and scrub. The land was broken by valleys, and the soil, a red sand with ironstone gravel, producing scrub, *Banksia*, and grass trees, besides the usual patches of gum forest. Keeping more to the eastward, the country

I 2

became level, surrounded on all sides by hills. By this
time one of the horses was completely exhausted for
want of water. They were obliged to leave him, and
proceed to a small lake which they saw before them,
and on which their hopes were built. It turned out to
be salt. They dug in twelve places all around the sides,
in the hope of getting a little fit to drink. This plan
succeeded. A small quantity of fresh water was thus
obtained, and they then were able to rescue the abandoned horse.

They rested two days at the lake, and proceeded
next to a remarkable gorge in the range which lay
to the east and south of them. This was a branch
of the Moore River. From hence back to their starting-
place at Bolgart Spring the country was better than
any hitherto seen, except on the Arrowsmith. It was
grassy, and generally of a rich brown loam; but there
were mounds of scrub between, with the usual granite
hills, and many small watercourses. On the 22nd September, they arrived at Bolgart Spring, having thus completed their circuit through a very inhospitable country,
so badly watered that but for the surface pools in the
rocks, which are only formed in the winter season, they
could never have managed to penetrate so far. They
had been absent forty-seven days, and during that time
had travelled about nine hundred and fifty-three miles,
over three degrees of latitude, and nearly four and a
half of longitude. It was very significant of the nature
of this tract that they only once met with natives, and
these were near the coast.

Of course, the Government were very anxious to
follow up this discovery of coal, which was the only
important result of the expedition. With this view,
Lieutenant Helpman was despatched in the schooner
Champion to Champion Bay, and was directed to take
a party from thence to the alleged coal deposits on the
river. He sailed from Freemantle on the 4th December, 1846, and on the 6th anchored in Champion Bay.
He immediately commenced landing the horses, and
while doing so were met by seventeen natives. They
were very friendly, and showed where water was to be

found, at the back of a large patch of sand. This was a valuable piece of information, for the season was too far advanced to leave any on the surface, and their first efforts at digging wells were unsuccessful. In the afternoon nine more natives joined, all fine stout men. But their honesty was very questionable. While the crew were at dinner, they contrived to steal three tomahawks, and then suddenly disappeared.

On the 7th, everything had been got in readiness, and the party started towards the coal deposits. They did not at first travel up the Arrowsmith River. When Captain Grey discovered that stream, it will be remembered that it was only one of many which he found emptying themselves from the tableland on to the south-west coast. Besides the Murchison and the Arrowsmith, there were also the Irwin, the Chapman, the Greenough, the Hutt, and many other small streams. Captain Helpman commenced travelling up the bed of what he believed to be the Greenough. The natives followed him for some distance, and on this occasion were accompanied by the women, which is always with them a sign of peaceful intentions. They showed the explorers a well of bad water, but it was better than the river, for that was quite salt. They kept the left bank of the river for some distance. It was about fifty yards wide, and from the summit of a high sand-hill they saw it trending to the south-east. On the day following they found, as they traced it, that it became very much narrower, though still deep; and when it had passed through a fine open plain from a break in the hills, the bed became scarcely discernable. At noon, they had passed the head of the valley, and a dense scrub lay before them.

Shortly after entering the scrub, they came to a singular natural basin in limestone rock, about fifty yards wide, and twenty feet deep. Mr. F. Gregory, who accompanied Helpman, went from this to the top of the highest and nearest sand-hill to seek for some better route through the scrub. He saw at once that the timber and the nature of the country only left one route open to them, and that was to the north-east,

over ridges of very scrubby ground. The land, as far
as he could see, was similar to that which they were
on. The Arrowsmith was reached on the 9th. The
intermediate country was of a wretched character,
until they came to the high land dipping towards the
valley of the river; then it became of the fertile
character described in connection with the route of
A. Gregory. They found upon the lower banks a native
hut, which was very different from those about Perth.
It was well plastered, and about six feet high inside.
Altogether it was more commodious than the dwellings
of the natives are made, and was capable of housing ten
persons very easily.

It is not necessary to describe the journey up the
stream. It was the same track as the one Gregory had
followed, only this party had the disadvantage of having
a cart to take along with them. This was found to be
a great inconvenience, when they had reached the top
of the first tableland, not alone because of the scrub,
but also in consequence of the many gullies which ran
like gorges down into the bed of the river. The cart
had to be taken round all of them. The valley of the
Arrowsmith was more or less clothed with trees, but of
a poor and stunted growth, mostly gum trees and
wattle.

On the 12th, they reached the coal. The valley
was here about twenty-five yards wide, but the water
in the pools was salt. The coal fire left by Messrs.
Gregory was undisturbed. It had left nothing but
white ash, with no cinders. The men were not long in
digging out about 3 cwts. of coal, from a depth of four
feet. The seam was nearly six feet thick, and ran
entirely across the bed of the river, and under the bank
on both sides. They had soon a sufficient quantity of
coal in the cart, and then set out on their return. They
shortened their route over the tableland by avoiding
the gullies, and found a very easy road for the cart,
though the brushwood made walking rather uncom-
fortable.

In returning, Helpman was rather anxious to cross
a valley in which he supposed the Greenough to run,

and so he took that direction instead of going direct
back to the coast. On the 17th, after passing over a
generally scrubby country, they came to a large valley
extending to the north-west. This was very similar to
the one through which they had walked on their way
up the first day, though not so wide. It was not long
before the very thick brushwood compelled them to get
on to the high land. This was of limestone, and very
scrubby too. It soon brought them to the Greenough,
turning in a westerly direction, probably from Stokes'
Wizard Peak. It was now quite dry. The cart was
very much dilapidated from the journey, and could not
be taken round Moresby's Range, as Helpman wished.
He therefore sent Mr. G. F. Gregory to examine the
country south of the Hutt, while he moved down to the
ship.

Gregory started from Champion Bay on the 20th.
He followed the beach for a time, and then turned into
the scrub, crossing the Chapman, and reaching Mount
Fairfax early in the morning. Further on, the Chapman was found to have a large branch, with small
pools of water, and high steep banks. Beyond this the
country improved, until they reached a high flat-topped
hill resting upon granite, which was the western part
of Moresby's Flat-topped Range. Further east, the hills
were apparently grassy, and gradually rose from the
Chapman for eight or ten miles. Gregory's object was,
however, the north, and not the east. He journeyed
on, and soon met a large body of natives, who showed
him where water was to be obtained. The country did
not look so good when examined closely. The grass
was coarse, and very scanty; but still Gregory called it
fertile. This it might be in comparison with the rest of
that brown-looking sandy desert. It is difficult, however,
to imagine how any country could be considered good,
where the soil was a red sand, where every scattered
tuft of grass eked out a precarious existence at the foot
of tangled Acacia bushes, and where there was not an
inch of soil lining the banks of the streams, whose
extent was now disputed almost foot for foot by the
dense and tangled scrub. There were many streams,

and probably, if anything, this must be considered the best part of the western coast between the Hill River and Sharks Bay; but when the soil was sand, and the rocks red sandstone and granite, like the whole of the interior tableland, it must not be described as very different from the grassy patches found elsewhere near the granite hills. Gregory ascended the tableland, and found it clothed with the short scrub. From thence he could see no signs of improvement to the north-west, so he turned again down to the coast, down a deep gully. As he went back towards the ship, the country improved, though it was hard for it to do otherwise, because, from the range, Gregory had seen to the north nothing but a vast sea of scrub. On the 22nd, he found such an improvement that he said positively that it was a fine grassy country, extending ten or twelve miles, presenting to the view 60,000 acres of sheep pasture of fine description. Beyond it there was granite, with patches of grass tuft, but in no way equal to the rest. This was the last discovery made upon this expedition, which returned to the ship along the line traversed by Grey. On the 27th, the *Champion* returned to Perth.

The expedition resulted in nothing very important to the colony. With regard to the patch of land discovered, it was too small to be of any service. The coal, however, was all that Gregory reported it to be. Of course, the value of the mine would depend upon the fitness of the locality as a residence for miners. Unfortunately this deficiency rendered the discovery unavailing. The expedition of Helpman also served to clear up certain doubtful points as to the identity of the rivers of the west coast. The difficulties and privations which Grey had to overcome prevented his obtaining latitudes and longitudes at the various rivers which he crossed, and the map of his route to Water Peak was too long, and from thence to Perth too short by 14° 15'. All these errors were corrected by Helpman's voyage, and it was settled that the river which contained the coal was the Arrowsmith of Captain Grey.

CHAPTER VIII.

MITCHELL ON THE UPPER BAROOO.

Commissioner Mitchell discovers the Narran—The Bokhara—The Balonne—
The Culgoa—Sir T. Mitchell's party—The Maranoa—The Cogoon—
Fitzroy Downs—Mount Owen—The Warrego—The Salvator—The Nogoa
—The Claude—The Belyando—The Nive—The Nivelle—The Barcoo—
Return down the Maranoa—The Mooni River—Great floods—Return to
Sydney.

It has been related in the first volume how Sturt, in
1828, and Mitchell, a year or so afterwards, were employed in furthering Oxley's discoveries in the neighbourhood of the Upper Darling. Sturt had traced the
Macquarrie and Castlereagh to their junction with the
main stream, and Mitchell had seen something of the
other tributaries. Beyond the information thus obtained,
the knowledge of the country did not extend. That
there were other streams to the northward was more
than suspected, but the matter claimed no especial
attention from the colonists, and was allowed to rest for
more than ten years. During this time many settlers
on the edge of good country must have made explorations from time to time, even to some distance from their
stations. What they did is, however, unknown. Probably a resident among them might glean from an old
colonist how he went into the interior, and how much
of the country he knew before ever the Government
explored the surrounding land; but such information is
often very unsatisfactory, and if not untrue at least
untrustworthy.

In 1845, Mr. Commissioner Mitchell, a son of the
surveyor-general, Sir T. Mitchell, made an exploration
in the direction of the Macquarrie junction. The precise
time of his journey, or the character of the expedition,

I have not ascertained; but he could not have been absent very long, as far as one can gather from the dimensions and character of the country examined. He discovered two new tributaries of the Darling. The first is the Narran, which terminates in a marsh, not far to the north of Sturt's furthest point on the Macquarrie. Along the stream Mr. Mitchell proceeded. Its course was through open forest or barren polygonum plains, evidently liable to inundation. By diverging a little to the west, he found another tributary, named by the natives the Bokhara. It seemed to run the same course, through a similar country to the one he was upon. Both rivers ran to the south-west. When in lat. 28° 25', he came upon the junction of a very large river, called the Balonne in the native tongue; and when he had crossed this he found, in a few miles, another stream, quite as large, named the Culgoa. The country was good, and evidently liable to floods, and though seven degrees of latitude and nearly eight of longitude from the sea, the bed was only four hundred and ninety-four feet above its level. This showed nothing very hopeful of the interior, and explained why a little increase in the volume of water overflowed all the adjoining land.

These discoveries made little sensation at the time, but they were very useful to Sir Thomas Mitchell, who had been for a long time thinking of an expedition into the interior. In 1843, he had made an application to the Home Government for funds to conduct an expedition into the interior, by following the sources of the Darling until a dividing range or watershed was reached. The request was acceded to by the authorities, but owing to some unexplained causes, Mitchell did not get final authority to equip his party until the close of the year 1845. This was while Sturt was employed in the interior in making his escape from the central desert. With every possible celerity, Mitchell hastened to be in the field, and by the 17th November his party moved off from Paramatta. It consisted of Sir T. Mitchell; E. B. Kennedy, second in command; W. Stevenson, surgeon and naturalist, and twenty-six men. The equipment was eight drays, eighty bullocks, two boats, seventeen horses, three light carts, two hundred and fifty sheep, and provisions for a year.

In spite of all the haste made in starting the party, it was a very long time before they were upon the ground from whence their labours were to commence. As they made their way up the country, the water was found to be extremely scarce; and, finally, their progress became completely stopped on the banks of the Macquarrie. There was no water beyond them, and they were obliged to remain until the floods of the upper part of the river reached them. This took place on the 16th February. On the 4th March, Mitchell took his party to the Narran, and with some difficulty crossed the swamp which lies between that river and the Barwon, or Upper Darling. From thence it took him until the 1st April to reach the Balonne, along the open forests and sandy, barren flats of the Narran. On arriving at the point of junction, he crossed to the Culgoa, and found a very zigzag chain of ponds, (which the natives called the Cawan,) between the two streams.

The Culgoa was the starting-place. It was found to be a deep but narrow stream, lined with beautiful timber, and appearing more important than the Upper Darling. The banks were forty feet high, and very steep; and this made the passage for the drays extremely difficult. The water was abundant. This was fortunate, in more respects than one. Not only had the season the appearance of being very dry and hot, but the rain, if it had come, would have been a serious obstacle to them. The aspect of the country was such as to make them dread the effect of a few days' rain upon it. It seemed as if the least moisture would convert the loose and shifting soil into a vast quagmire.

Taking a northerly course from the river, the party traversed a fine grassy land, with *Acacia pendula* (the well-known plant of Oxley's dreary country), and a similar moist vegetation, though the soil was as arid as it was possible to be. The north course could not be continued long if they wished to follow the stream. It turned so much to the eastward that they had to travel

aside to reach it; and when they did so, they had
evidently reached the Balonne Major, or that part
above the Culgoa where the Lower Balonne joined it.
Their camp was in lat. 28° 27', and from this point
Sir T. Mitchell commenced marking his camps with
Roman numerals cut upon the trees. This was Camp I.

It was a memorable one to the party. The whole
of them were detained in it for a long time, in consequence of an attack of purulent ophthalmia with which
Mitchell and Kennedy were visited. On the 8th, they
continued northward, keeping the woody banks of the
river in sight. They crossed many grassy plains and
open country, the bed of the stream being only occasionally dry. This was their course until the 11th,
when the river opened out into an immense lagoon,
with islands upon it. A short distance in advance
there was another, and the next day they came to a
noble reach of the river, whose banks were one hundred
and twenty yards apart. The scenery of the spot was
magnificent. The gently sloping sides, so well wooded
and so thickly grassed, made the reach look like a
piece of ornamental water; and a natural bridge of rock
across it made the romantic wildness more picturesque
still. It was a good place for a depôt, and Mitchell
determined to make one of it, while he set out on horseback, with a small party, to explore the course of the
stream and examine the north-west country as far as
possible. Mr. Kennedy was sent on at once to make a
preliminary examination while the depôt at St. George's
Bridge was being arranged. He soon returned. He
found indications of the river for twelve miles, and
plains to the westward. From this account, Mitchell's
resolution was taken. He resolved to strike away from
the river, and advance to the north-west.

He started with six men, and for his first day's
journey provided himself with a cart-load of water.
This was a very necessary precaution. The route lay
through country which was occasionally scrubby and
abounding with game, but as arid as the desert. Next
day, polygonum flats, but no water. The grass and
gum flats still continued, but getting much poorer,

and the soil was only a red sand. The country soon
changed to heath, low and level, with no immediate
prospect of improvement. They camped again without
seeing water, and were determined to proceed; but in
the night a messenger arrived with news from Sydney.
The despatches contained the account of Leichhardt's
safe return, and a description of the rivers and mountains he had found in crossing to Carpentaria. This at
once altered Mitchell's plans. He would no longer
waste time in trying to reach the north-west country.
Leichhardt's journey made him almost certain that
there must be a watershed between the rivers of Carpentaria and the south coast. This he would try to
reach, and, with the help of the streams he there found,
be the first to cross the continent from south to north.

He accordingly returned to camp, and made preparations for a longer and more difficult journey. His
intention now was to trace the Balonne upwards, until
he found the mountains to the north-west, and from
these judge of the practicability of passing further
north. He started on the 23rd April, with a party of
eight men, two native boys, fourteen horses, the three
light carts, and eighteen weeks' provisions.

The first two days' journey was along the noble
reaches of the river, rendered very beautiful and picturesque by the rocky character of the banks. On the
second day they reached the junction of another, coming
direct from the north-west, through grassy plains. This
was just what they wanted, if it continued in the same
direction; but it did not. Its course was to the west,
and soon even to the south, and its bed completely dry.
Mitchell again turned to the banks of the Balonne,
crossing the new stream, which the natives afterwards
informed him was called the Maranoa. To prevent
Kennedy taking the same track, when he followed
with the heavy drays, a messenger was sent back to
him. This delayed the party until the 28th.

The Balonne, on the succeeding days, preserved its
important character. Its course was pretty straight.
A good many watercourses joined from the eastward
from time to time, and ferruginous dykes occurred in

many parts of the channel. The banks were fertile, as all the banks of these streams are, but in other respects the character of the scenery was like that near the Darling, and thoroughly Australian. There were belts of scrub jutting out here and there on to the edge of the river, though generally the eye wandered over an immense sandy plain, thickly timbered, and clothed with patches of coarse grass, which seemed as if it were flooded at times. The dry and flood-marks were very well marked now, for it was the warm season of the year, yet water was plentiful, and the distant smokes showed that the natives were numerous. Thus they found the stream up to lat. 27° 15', which they reached on the 1st May. Here they saw the junction of another river, while the Balonne took a north-eastern course, and went towards some distant hills, which were faintly visible in the sunshine. The new river was called the Cogoon, and Mitchell followed it. It was altogether a different stream from the one they had traced hitherto. It was a small tributary, and its waters, meandering through the plains in different channels, left the party at a loss which to follow. Latterly the Balonne had been cut by very numerous gullies, and its banks thickly timbered; but this was open, with large lakes on its course. The country was very fine. Here and there a Mulga scrub made it poor, and the travelling more difficult.*

The 3rd of May brought the party to the first hill they had met with among the rivers. It was called, in consequence, Mount First View. It showed them what they were all delighted to see, and that was the blue summits of very high ranges to the north-west. From another hill, reached two days after, the river was seen to pass along a fine valley to the northward, becoming more open and sandy, and the slopes less abrupt. All this was very encouraging, and proved that the watershed was a very important feature in this country. It threw off at times great bodies of

* Mulga is an Acacia. It grows in thick bushes with thin twigs and small leaves. Probably it is the most extensively distributed tree in all Australia. It extends right across the continent.

water to the southward, for there were large trees lying
in the channel, and this made them hope it would be
important enough to carry its northern waters completely to Carpentaria. Everything as they proceeded
confirmed this supposition. From a red rock, reached
on the 6th, the horizon was seen to be perfectly surrounded by hills. Better than all, the country was
found to be rapidly rising. Instead of the low, level
plains, scarcely elevated at all, and with a fall hardly
sufficient to make the water flow, they were now seven
hundred and forty-seven feet above the sea. The
country was beautiful; so well grassed indeed, and
provided with every mark of fertility, that Mitchell
called one of the hills Mount Abundance. It was very
cold, however. Notwithstanding their proximity to
the tropics, there was ice upon Frosty Creek, when they
went to get water from it in the morning. It is refreshing to read of such a thing in the interior of Australia.
Instead of an arid, sandy desert, a scorching heat, and
a copper-coloured sky, here were open, swelling downs
of emerald-green grass, which, in the bright-blue sky of
a shining frosty morning, seemed sowed with dewy
diamonds or silvered over with a hoar frost.

It was evident now that they were near the sources
of the stream along whose banks they had come thus far.
The channel had dwindled down to the merest creek,
and divided into the two branches. Frosty Creek was
followed as far as lat. 26° 42', and then Mitchell rode
to the summit of Mount Abundance with the most eager
anticipation, hoping that he at last had reached the
watershed between the northern and southern waters.
He was disappointed, however, for a time. All round
him lay beautiful grassy downs, which he called after
Governor Fitzroy; but instead of the watershed there
were ranges still in advance. One of these, lying like
a terrace amid the beautiful champaign country, he
called the Grafton Range. It was on this range that
Mitchell saw the bottle tree for the first time. It grew
like an enormous pear-shaped turnip, with only a small
portion of the root in the ground. In other respects
the vegetation was every day assuming a more tropical

character, which looked all the more luxuriant and rich amid such splendid downs.

On the 9th, they came again upon the Cogoon, but it had diminished very much, and soon dwindled down to a chain of ponds. When these failed, they still kept north, and came across another chain of ponds, where they camped. Next day, they crossed two more watercourses, travelling steadily north-west, over open downs, towards a high mountain. This they ascended on the 11th. Open downs were seen all round it, and beyond these there were two distant valleys, one of which fell to the south-east and another north-west, leaving rather an elevated tract between. This, then, was the watershed; at least, so Mitchell considered. It was not a mountain, but a series of downs, and differed from the usual character of the interior, because the underlying rock was basaltic trap. The highest part was fifteen hundred and sixty-three feet above the level of the sea.

Mitchell made all haste towards the north-west valley. The natives called it the Amby; but from one or two expressions which fell from them, he began to doubt whether after all the Fitzroy Downs were the watershed between the northern and southern waters, and whether the Amby were not a tributary of the Darling, through the Culgoa. In this case, the downs would be only the watershed between the latter river and the Balonne. At all events, he was on the right course for ascertaining the truth, and for carrying out the object of his journey, so he kept on. There was a flat range before him, which shut out all further view. It was a black ferruginous sandstone. It had a gap in it, which was a curious opening, to the westward, through which ran a watercourse fourteen hundred and fifty-eight feet above the sea level. Parallel to the range was another, of conical volcanic hills.

Proceeding along this watercourse, which ran almost due west, its channel was soon lost amid grassy plains, and the party were without water. But they had good hopes of finding some more at no great distance. There was a thick line of trees to the westward, which looked like another stream, and this they moved towards. They were agreeably surprised to find themselves soon upon the banks of a large river, whose course was nearly north and south, and as it was not running, it became difficult to say whether it were a northern or a southern water. It was as large as the Darling; the soil of its banks was sandy, but not barren, for there was plenty of good grass about, and the land was nicely timbered. It was not for water alone that it proved a useful discovery to the explorers. It was well stocked with fish; but what made them sure it was a northern water was, that they were of a different species from those of the Murray or Darling. But it was not a northern water. Little did they think that this was the Maranoa—the very stream which they had tried to follow at first, and were obliged to give up because it was dry.

Mitchell resolved to make a depôt there. It was hard to say whether he would find permanent water if he pursued his journey further on, and as he could not advance very much until Kennedy came up, he thought it best to wait for him there. He had, however, very strong hopes of still finding the watershed, if this should not prove to be beyond it. From an elevation near he could see distant ranges seventy or eighty miles to the north, and some tableland to the east; but in the south the land was very level, too much so, indeed, for them to imagine that this was a northern water. The rocks were a sandstone with plant impressions. The river seemed, at a little distance from the camp, to cut its way through rocky ranges, and to receive many tributaries. It had gravelly terraces for its beach in some places, and rocky escarpments of great height in others. The lat. was 26° 12'; but the weather was still very cold, and it was not at all an uncommon thing to find the pools in the river frozen over.

While waiting for Kennedy, Mitchell explored a little to the westward. At first the country was composed of rocky sandstone gullies, from a table range, which gave rise to many streams joining the river. He called this Riverhead Range, and it differed from all the others, in being a sort of diorite instead of sand-

VOL. II. K

stone. When the hills were passed, open downs succeeded, which were bounded on the south by other
elevations. From one of them (Mount Lonsdale), a
view of the westward was seen. There was a vast
level plain of good land, with a river in the midst. It
was unbounded except by the horizon, but whether all
was of fertility equal to that which lay at the foot of
the hills, Mitchell was then unable to ascertain.

On the 1st June, Kennedy arrived with the drays,
and Mitchell was again able to take fresh supplies, and
go on with an advance party. He did not tell Kennedy
to follow him, for he intended to move more rapidly,
and to take four months' supplies. He had by this
time become certain that the Maranoa was a southern
water, and he thought it was the best place to form a
permanent depôt upon. He now determined not only
to cross the watershed before he returned, but, if possible, to reach Carpentaria. He started on the 4th of
June. At first the channel proved rocky and difficult,
but subsequently it became more open and scrubby,
with numerous and important tributaries from the west.
Yet though there were very good patches of land here
and there, the stream was in no way equal to the
Cogoon in point of fertility. They left the channel for
the north-west on the 15th, along some chains of ponds.
The country was rising rapidly, and this stream was
1827 feet above the sea level. On the 17th, the country became nothing but heavy sand, with abundance of
pine, but the water completely failed. It was evident
that the course of the channel would soon do the same,
for its bed was now amid rocky gullies, which were too
steep to be lengthy, and too barren and sandy to be
very far from their sources. The change too in the
hills was most marked. Instead of sandstone tablehills,
now succeeded a long line of volcanic cones. One of
these, named Mount Owen, was ascended; but little of
the adjacent country could be seen from it; nothing
whatever of the sandstone gullies, by which the party
were shut in. The west was visible to a great distance,
bounded by low ranges, which seemed to have precipitous sides. Mount Owen was 2873 feet above the

sea, and 700 feet above the plains; but there were many other hills about, which were probably higher, and in consequence of the scientific tastes of the Major, were named after various members of the Geological Society.

It was not easy to find water amongst these sandstone gullies. It took Mitchell until the 26th of June to find a passage to the northward sufficiently supplied to advance along. Not that creeks were scarce; they were numerous; but were almost all dry, and formed the heads of watercourses to the south-west, and this was almost opposite to the way he wished to go. The country was all volcanic, and some fine hills were seen to the northward, evidently of considerable elevation. Generally speaking, the soil was good, though the land was frightfully rocky and precipitous. Their approach to a tropical climate was marked by the frequent occurrence of the *Zamia*, a plant which has been spoken of in connection with Leichhardt's expedition. It grew there abundantly.

The first of the more northerly hills which Mitchell was able to ascend gave him a view to the north, further on, but with no passage for a watercourse. Mountains were numerous on every side, and especially to the north-west; but the one he was on, Mount King, was higher than the most, being 2646 feet above the level of the sea. There was a creek proceeding from this hill, and Mitchell followed it, simply because he saw no other way of getting to the north, except by tracing every watercourse he saw. This one led to the south-west in a very short time, and though it seemed to become a very important feature, they were obliged to leave it. This stream was the Warrego, which was afterwards explored by Kennedy. It runs almost parallel with the Maranoa, through a very similar country, and is another of the numerous tributaries of the Darling.

They now turned to the northward, travelling through a very dense scrub, and apparently no immediate prospect of a passage to the gulf. At last, in turning down a sandstone gully, they came to water in

K 2

a valley which ran to the north-west. At first the
channel was scantily supplied with water, and was
hemmed in by bold precipices, terribly difficult to pass
along. But by-and-by these receded, forming beautiful
bold headlands on each side.   Then the country became
more open to the north, and at last, to their joy and
surprise, they met a small stream flowing to the northwards, with running water in it.   Thus the watershed
had been passed. It was too much to suppose that
there was no other between them and the gulf, especially as they were so near to the east coast; but it was
probable that some important streams would rise from
the north side, since so many were found flowing from
the south.

The scenery was magnificent—the river with its
limpid stream, the banks with their fine red stony
escarpments jutting out on to the grassy flats, like sea-
side promontories; the blue sky and the tropical
foliage made Mitchell forget he was exploring.   His
account is full of glowing descriptions of the views
which met their gaze upon every side. A mountain was
called Mount Salvator, and that was the name he gave
the river, for the whole prospect was more Italian than
tropical, and the scenery, says Sir Thomas, reminded
one of the gorgeous conceptions of Salvator Rosa.
The party commenced moving down the rivulet on the
6th July, starting from some picturesque rocky hills,
named the Pyramids. "We made sure," says Sir
Thomas, "of water for the rest of our journey. The
hills overhanging it surpassed anything I had ever yet
seen in picturesque outline; some resembled gothic
cathedrals in ruins; others forts; and contrasted with
the flowery outlines of evergreen woods; while a fine
stream in the foreground gave a charming appearance
to the whole country. It was a discovery worthy of
the toils of a pilgrimage. The better to mark them on
my map, I gave the name of Salvator Rosa to the
valley. The rocks stood out sharply from thick woods,
just as Martin's fertile imagination would dash them
out in his beautiful sepia landscapes. I never saw anything in nature come so near the creations of his

genius and imagination." Owing to this resemblance,
a range on the west, which was met soon after, was
called J. Martin's Range, and a lake in front of it,
Lake Salvator. Enormous eels, with spots upon them,
and a fresh-water mussel, different from those in the
Darling, were found in the stream. Altogether, it was
a place as rich and fertile as it was magically beautiful,
and many were the earnest wishes that it might continue across the continent. In this they were griev-
ously disappointed. The lake was very extensive, but
no river flowed out of it. There was only a dry watercourse turning to the north-east, and even this could
not be followed, because of its frightfully deep and
scrubby gullies. There was no alternative left for
them but to proceed to the north, and take their chance
of water.

Their progress was at first very slow. It was
through a dense scrub, intersected by dry watercourses,
falling into the Salvator, and joining a stream named
the Nogoa, as the natives informed them. They persevered through the scrub for a long time, but it turned
them back at last, so they retired to the Salvator,
with the intention of cutting a road down its banks.
In this they succeeded for a time, and the country
opened a little, but the stream was evidently making
direct for the eastward. Mitchell knew it was useless
to follow it further. It would only carry them into explored regions; so he left his party and rode to the
north, to make a reconnaisance with one or two companions. At first, a scrub impeded them, but they soon
emerged into more open country, with a luxuriant
growth of timber upon fine black soil. To the north-
west an opening in the hills seemed to promise another river. Proceeding to it, they came upon a stream
flowing from the westward, with water in it, and abundance of silicified wood upon its banks.

It was named the Claude. The rest of the party
were soon brought up, and they again moved northward, through fine scenery, admirable to any but those
who had to climb over the lofty and picturesque escarpments. The plains on the banks were the richest

Mitchell thought he had ever seen in Australia; but, unfortunately for their projects, both this river and another they met soon after were only tributaries of the Nogoa. Each watershed they passed seemed only to be divisions between the basins of the streams of the east coast. All the rich land was thickly strewn with fragments of fossil wood, agate, and chalcedony; and in one place, the remains of an entire branch lay together in a heap of ruins, the dilapidated fragments of a tree turned to stone. These downs were 1512 feet above the level of the sea. They were terminated northwards by impassable rocky gullies. This was a formidable obstacle to the party, who anticipated no such difficulties in travelling to the north. From the north-west to the south-west there was absolutely no passage to be obtained, so there was nothing left but to follow down a valley which was evidently the head of a watercourse falling to the east. Even on the sides of this the precipices were so abrupt that they had to travel in the sandy bed of the stream, and this was very slow work indeed.

On the 17th July they found an opening which soon led them among different scenes. By turning north, they came upon another watercourse, proceeding like the last from the Tower Almond and Mount Mudge Ranges, which lay to the westward. The gap through which they passed was called Stevenson's Pass, after the doctor of the party, because he discovered it. It was a perfect chasm or gorge, which led into a spacious glen, surrounded on all sides but the northward by mountains of matchless sublimity. At the gorge there stood a sort of watch-tower, so like a work of human skill that the explorers were startled at its first appearance, and imagined they had penetrated into the mysterious haunts of some natives, who still retained the arts of an earlier civilization. It was a turret, with a pointed roof, on the summit of a rounded hill. This was called Tower Almond. On the westward, the rocky range seemed to terminate in a point, and beyond the country to the north appeared open forest land. Their latitude was 24° 6', and their elevation 1234 feet

above the level of the sea. They were not long getting
to the point of the range, which they named Mount
Mudge. The view from it showed a watercourse to
the westward, and small ranges between them and the
coast to the eastward. But what was of most importance to them just then, they saw a watercourse,
evidently falling to the northward, or exactly in the
way they wished to proceed. Mount Mudge was
2247 feet above the sea. It was a calcareous grit, with
fine impressions of the Australian oolitic (?) coal plants.
At the base of the hill there was a basaltic gravel.
Natives were seen about, but they were not numerous,
and very shy.

Into the valley of this northern river they descended.
On the 21st July they met the stream. It was trending slightly east of north. The soil was a firm clay,
which was easy to travel over, but tributaries constantly impeded their progress. In a very short time,
however, they found that the bed was bounded on both
sides by an almost impassable scrub of Acacia and
other shrubs, and this continued with scarcely any
interruption as long as they traced it. One part was
exactly like another, and it would be useless to particularize the daily journeys along this monotonous
stream. The following facts form the result of all
Mitchell was able to ascertain about it. He learnt
from natives which were met in the upper part that
the river was called the Belyando. He traced it far
within the tropics, that is, to lat. 21° 30′ S., long.
147° 10′. During the whole of this distance, which it
took the party until the 12th of August to accomplish,
the stream varied scarcely at all. It consisted of a
number of channels winding amid the thick Brigalow
scrub, which was all the more difficult to travel as the
greater portion of it was dead. Amid so many beds it
was impossible to say which was the main one, or
whether there was more than an occasional stream in
any. But in latitude 22° this character was changed
to some extent. There the river was joined by another
stream from the south-west, and some fine reaches of
water commenced to show themselves. To the west-

ward, during a great part of their course, they saw
a low range of sandstone cliffs, about twenty miles
away. This was the only high land about. None
appeared to the northward, and it became evident to
Mitchell that their course, if continued, would take
them to the Suttor River of Leichhardt, and thence to
the east coast. This was not, then, the northern river
he sought. As yet, it was clear he had not crossed the
coast watershed, and until he did so, could have no
hope of reaching Carpentaria by an inland stream.
What was he to do now? The only stream he had
met with to the westward was the Warrego, and that
led to the south, and the country west of that seemed
deprived of water. But it was worth trying, and at
any rate he could not go back to the settled districts
without having made a final effort to reach the northern
watershed. In leaving the Belyando, he said of it,
"Like most of the Australian rivers, it maintained a
peculiar character throughout its course, with great
uniformity, even after it had received tributaries apparently larger than itself. All these lapsed into the
same concentrated line of ponds; at one time spreading
among Brigalow scrub, at another forming one well-
defined deep channel." He adds that rivers of this
kind are exactly suited to the dry climate of Australia,
as the spreading of the streams causes more ponds and
natural reservoirs to be formed upon their course. The
last camp on the Belyando was six hundred feet above
the sea.

After passing back through the beautiful country
already described, the party arrived, on the 5th September, at the head of the Salvator. They rested here
four days, and the maps were made up, and a despatch
sent back to Kennedy, reporting progress. It became
necessary to divide the party again, because of the
difficulty of taking on all the stores rapidly over such
rough country; and just now it was very necessary
that whatever was done should be done very quickly
indeed. After some little deliberation, Mitchell set out
with only two men, the native guide, two pack-horses,
and a month's provisions. With these small means, he

hoped to solve the question of the north-western river, if it were to be found.

The first journey was to Mount Pluto, one of the many volcanic cones in this high land. There were some watercourses near it, but all going into the Salvator. From a high pinnacle of trap rock, Mitchell could see the volcanic spur extending to the westward, and a range running right across the track he intended to pursue. This range they crossed on the lowest part, and yet that was over 2,000 feet above the sea. It was hard work enough to climb it, but it was succeeded by even worse travelling, through Brigalow scrub, matted vines, and a dense forest of young pines. It took a day to force a way through these; and though the scenery was romantic, and the stillness of the unbroken forest grand in its solitude, the obstacles were too wearying and incessant to create any emotions except impatience. They had not as yet left the southern waters, for their camp was on a stream called by the natives the Cunno: it ran into the Warrego. Still to the northward, Mitchell steered over low scrubby ridges and thickets, which brought him at last to the head of a stream. At length, he made sure he was successful. The stream soon led to some fine ponds of water, and, by-and-by, to a tributary which was called the Nivelle. Sir Thomas was confident he had found a river which would take him to the north-west, but he was again doomed to disappointment. The channel soon turned southward, and was followed twenty-two miles without discovering any water in its bed. This was a severe loss of time and provisions to the party. Mitchell felt this keenly, but he again struck to the north-west.

His journey was at first over an open Brigalow ridge, above 1800 feet high. He went towards a rocky gap, along the side of which a watercourse meandered. The party found water in this, and they camped on the east side of the gap, leaving its examination until the next morning. It well rewarded their perseverance. From the gap Mitchell beheld downs and plains extending westward as far as the eye could reach. It was

bounded on the south-west by woods and low ranges,
and on the north-east by higher ranges. This was
good, but there was something still better. The whole
country inclined to the north-west, in which direction a
line of trees marked the course of a river to the
furthest verge of the horizon. At this discovery, nothing could exceed Mitchell's transport. "Ulloa's delight at the sight of the Pacific," he says, "could not
have surpassed mine on the occasion. From that rock
the scene was so extensive as to leave us no room
for doubt as to the course of the river, which then
and there revealed to me alone seemed like a reward
direct from heaven for perseverance, and as a compensation for the many sacrifices I had made in order
to solve the question of the rivers of tropical Australia."

One can well understand this rhapsody by a man as
enthusiastic as Mitchell, but, unfortunately, in this case,
it was very premature. Who would think that it was
spoken of the Barcoo, of which we have seen Sturt
write so despondingly. Certainly, the upper part was
worthy of all that Mitchell said of it, and the lower
part equally deserving of Sturt's condemnation; and
although the Major could not foresee the nature of the
soil all down the banks, he pronounced on its north-
west course a little too soon. The Barcoo has occupied
a great deal of attention in connection with exploration,
and especially so in this part of the history. It is
worthy of remark that nearly every explorer had given
an account of it slightly different from his predecessor,
but that the general opinion is contrary to the first
impressions of Mitchell. However, the latter now commenced to trace it down, through richly grassed open
downs. At first, the bed consisted of firm clay, with
deep hollows and long reaches. It was dry, but contained so many mussel-shells that Mitchell thought
the dryness very unusual. Many small watercourses
came from the eastward, and the general course of the
stream was west-north-west. On the 17th September,
the bed was found to contain five long reaches of water,
with abundance of ducks and game upon it; but the

beauty of the downs was much interrupted by Brigalow
scrub.   The stream occasionally divided into four or
five separate channels, but was very monotonous.   It
varied so little that no more need be done than to
describe the main results of Mitchell's journey in a few
words.
    He followed its course for about ten days, to lat. 24° 14',
long. 144° 34'. The country did not improve as they went
down, though the reaches of water were splendid, and
the natives numerous.   The stream often divided into
arid branches, thus showing a very slight inclination of
the land and a sluggish current to the water. A large
stream with three channels joined from the north-east,
in the 145th parallel of longitude.   This was named
after the Princess Alice, as the stream itself was
named the Victoria, after the Queen.   The bed of the
rivers consisted generally of firm clay, and, where the
scrub was absent, boundless plains of fine grass lined
the sides.   The country was surprisingly level, and the
land seemed very liable to occasional floods.   The
natives, as already mentioned, were numerous. Among
them one was noticed who had an iron tomahawk, and
Mitchell was much puzzled to find out whence he could
have procured it.   Very probably it was one given by
Sturt to some of the aborigines met on a lower part of
the stream.
    Mitchell soon found that the means at his disposal
would not admit of the full exploration of the river.
He had, however, discovered, as he thought, all he
expected to find, and he had no objection to think now
of returning. He gave his men one day's rest, and
then returned on the 28th. They were highly elated
with this discovery, and no one doubted that the
general course of the river would be north-west, though
during the time they had been following it the direction was not much north of west.   On returning,
they were able to save a good deal of their time by
cutting off the windings of the stream, so that by the
4th October they had reached the junction of the Nive
and Nivelle. On leaving the Barcoo it was named the
Victoria, a name which has not been retained, as there

was already one upon the north coast, discovered, as previously mentioned, by Wickham and Stokes. The provisions were nearly exhausted before they reached the depôt camp, and as they returned through the scrubby volcanic ranges the water was found to have almost completely disappeared. By the 6th October they arrived in safety at the depot camp, at the Pyramids. Their companions were well. They had managed their provisions so economically, that now there was quite sufficient to support the party until they reached Mr. Kennedy's depôt.

They rested at the Pyramids until the 10th October, and then started, with the cattle and horses in such fine condition that they could easily make rapid stages. Water was abundant, for every crevice in the rocks contained some pools. As they went back they ascended Mount Faraday, a volcanic mountain, two thousand five hundred and twenty-three feet high. It gave them a fine view over the black summits of the neighbouring hills, but no new streams could be seen amid the waving scrubs which lined their sides. On the 14th they arrived upon the Maranoa. From thence they did not deviate from their outward track, except to cut off the bends of the channel, and on the 19th they reached Kennedy's depôt. They had been absent four months and fifteen days, during which time they had only lost one horse, which had fallen over the cliffs of the river two days before their journey terminated.

Mitchell now prepared for his return to Sydney. He determined, in going back, to keep down the Maranoa, and not turn off to the road by which he had come along the Cogoon and Balonne. He found, as he proceeded, that the Maranoa ran generally, in fine reaches, through a broad, deep valley. On each side were extensive level plains, well grassed, but occasionally scrubby. In the more southern parts the water was very scarce, until it joined the Balonne. This proved to be the place where Sir Thomas had tried to go up its banks, but finding no water, had turned to the Cogoon. St. George's Bridge was reached on the 5th November.

From the 5th to the 9th, Mitchell was employed in completing his maps and despatches. In the meantime, he sent Mr. Kennedy to the southward. He was to ascertain whether there was any stream watering the intervening country between the depôt camp and the furthest part of the Darling, reached by Mitchell's expedition in 1831. He did not return until the 15th. He had found the Mooni River, which ran nearly north and south as a chain of ponds, and that its banks were occupied by settlers and cattle stations, within a mile of the camp. This short exploration had cost the lives of two horses. Mr. Kennedy had mistaken magnetic bearings for true ones, and had thus ridden for sixty-three miles without finding water, while all the while his course was parallel with the Mooni. As the heat was very great, one of the horses had died, and all his men were very ill before they reached water. Upon the receipt of this news, Mitchell moved his whole party down the newly discovered stream. It could hardly be called a journey of exploration, for they journeyed past cattle stations and settlers' huts. On the 21st, their passage was arrested by a storm of rain, which lasted until the 7th December. It kept the rivers in flood, so much so, indeed, that the surrounding plains were uninhabitable, except at a sand-hill, to which the party were fortunately moved in time. When the rains had ceased, the boats which had been brought so far were at last found serviceable in crossing the Barwon, or Upper Darling, which was then running bank high. Their first use had been as tanks, to water their cattle on the Macquarrie. This was their last. How different was the Darling then from what it had been when first seen by Sturt, and the Macquarrie from what Oxley had found it! These facts give a better idea of the character of Australian rivers than pages of description.

Having brought Mitchell back to the country explored by him on his first journey, we leave him. This was his last expedition. He was certainly the most successful of Australian explorers. The care he took in equipping his parties, and the prudence and foresight

he displayed in applying his resources, have never since
been imitated. Had it been so with Leichhardt, he
would never have perished. It is true that one result
of this last expedition was not found to bear the test
of further examination; but every one must praise
Mitchell's care for the safety of his men, while, if it
left the work unfinished, it left us nothing to deplore.

CHAPTER IX.

WHILE Sir Thomas Mitchell had been making the
journey described in the last chapter, other expeditions
had been in progress, which will be alluded to directly.
It is necessary, in some measure, to disturb the chrono-
logy of this history for the sake of learning what was
the result of further investigations on the subject of the
River Barcoo. Sir Thomas had, in his report to the
Government, stated that it was his firm conviction that
the river would be found to flow to the north-west, and,
in his enthusiasm in favour of his discovery, he gave
the following glowing description of its course :—" I
pursued," he said, " the course of the river, through
open country, for ten successive days. It formed, in
part, splendid reaches, as broad and as important as
those of the Murray. I was convinced that its estuary
was in the Gulf of Carpentaria; at all events, the
country is open and well-watered for a direct route
thereto. That the river is the most important in Australia, increasing as it does by successive tributaries,
and not the mere product of distant ranges, admits of
no dispute, and the downs and plains of Central Australia seem sufficient to supply the whole world with
animal food. The natives appear few and inoffensive."

Now, with Sturt's account of Central Australia
before their eyes, every one thought that this glowing

description must be somewhat exaggerated. There
were some even who referred to Sturt's map, and
pointed out how, from the relative positions of Mitchell's
Victoria River and Sturt's Cooper's Creek, it was not
impossible that they might be found to be one and the
same stream. At all events, the question was one of
too great importance to be left undecided, and therefore Mr. Kennedy was given the command of a party
to explore the so-called Victoria River. He left Sydney
in March, 1847, with a party of eight men, all well
mounted, and leading spare horses. They had, besides,
two light carts, carrying eight months' provisions.

His route was across the Liverpool Plains to St.
George's Bridge, on the Balonne, and then to the
Maranoa. From thence he crossed the open flooded
plains to the Warrego, to a part much below Mitchell's
explorations. He thus cut off a large angle of the
former route. He then travelled up the Warrego to
Mount Playfair, and so on along the old track, until
the 13th August, by which time he had reached Mitchell's furthest point on the Barcoo. The very first
part of their discoveries destroyed all Sir Thomas's
pleasing anticipations. It was evident that there was
no chance of Carpentaria on such a stream. One mile
below the encampment it turned considerably south of
west, and then continued in that direction. Between
the latitudes of 24° 17′ and 24° 53′ it preserved generally a south-south-west course, with an unvaried
character, although the supply of water greatly diminished. It was divided into three channels, with
several minor watercourses, traversing a flat country,
lightly timbered, with flooded box. In the latitude last
named, and long. 144° 11′, the party had the greatest
difficulty in finding any water at all, and then the
supply was scanty and barely sufficient for their wants.
From this point, therefore, Kennedy rode in advance,
with two men. He found that the stream was by no
means exhausted, as he had supposed. Twelve miles
further down there was a very fine reach, below which
a large stream joined from the east. In lat. 25°, the
river turned south, and impinged on a low range on the

left bank. By this it was turned west, in one well-watered channel, for thirty miles. In this course the reaches were nearly continuous, and varied in width from one hundred to eighty yards. The soil was poor, white, and bare of pasture. In long. 143°, a considerable river joined from the north-east. This Kennedy named the Thompson, in honour of the colonial secretary of New South Wales. Like the stream to which it is a tributary, it has received a varied reputation from different explorers. Kennedy did not think much of it at this time; and Gregory reported subsequently that it flowed through an absolute desert, yet Landsborough was able, partly by its means, to cross the continent from north to south. In fact, this was the river which answered the description of what Sir Thomas Mitchell sought. It had its sources in the watershed which threw off northern waters into the Gulf of Carpentaria by means of the very long and serpentine course of the Flinders River.

Being satisfied that there was abundance of water to this point, the rest of the party were brought up, with the determination, it was now hoped, of following the river to the end. But the hope did not continue long. On the 25th August the journey was again renewed, and again there was a sudden disappointment. They had only proceeded one mile, when the river turned south-south-west, spreading over a barren waste, void of trees and vegetation of every kind, and broken only by shifting dunes of red sand. Here then commenced the red sandy desert described by Sturt. The sand-hills seemed to start up quite as unexpectedly as they did at Lake Torrens, and certainly they struck just as much dismay into the hearts of those who saw them. Yet they kept on, in the belief that they might yet reach more grassy soil. On the 1st September they camped upon a long though narrow reach, on the most western channel, at which point a low limestone ridge, strewed with boulders, closed upon the river. This was in lat. 24° 25', long. 142° 51', the only grassy spot for miles around. But the nature of the country hitherto warned Kennedy that any exploration they could make must

be done quickly. To enable them to advance quicker,
they buried all the stores; for though their instructions told them to advance from the most northerly portion of the stream towards Carpentaria, they saw that the
most they could effect was to explore the Barcoo to where
it joined Sturt's portion. This they were convinced was
now the obvious direction of the channel. The ground,
as they advanced, was most fearfully broken and fissured. The cracks were, at times, so wide that the
horses could scarcely stagger over them. It looked as
if the deluge had brought down all the alluvial soil,
and a drought ever since had split it into yawning
chasms. The water became scarcer and scarcer. The
river, in lat. 25° 55', was again turned aside by a range,
and then resumed its southerly course, spreading into
countless channels, and having marks of flood ten feet
above the level of the water. On the 17th September
they camped upon a small water-hole, in the midst of a
desert not producing a morsel of vegetation; but as the
water still continued, they pushed on. But next day,
even the water failed. This was virtually a stop to the
exploration. On the following morning, Kennedy took
one man with him, and made a rapid search in every
direction. All in vain. They were at the extreme
verge of what might be considered desolation—the
channel of a stream, long since dried up, in the midst
of a desert. They could not dare to trace it further, as
the horses were literally starving. This was the last
aspect of the vaunted Victoria River.

The furthest point was in lat. 26° 13', long. 142° 20'.
Kennedy said, in leaving it, that he thought there
could be little doubt that the Victoria was identical with
Sturt's Cooper's Creek. That was abandoned by its
discoverer, in lat. 27° 46', long. 141° 51', coming from
the north-east, and, as the natives informed him, in
many small channels, forming a large one. The lowest
camp of Kennedy was about a hundred miles from this.
On his way home he traced the Warrego down to the
southward as far as he could. It was a smaller stream
than the Maranoa, but much of the same character. Its
channel became destitute of water, and finally it was

lost in the desert. From this point, Kennedy struck across to the Culgoa, a journey for eighty miles through open plains, alternating with dense scrub. There was only one watercourse in the whole distance, and even that contained no water. Yet the open plains were liable to floods, if one might judge by the marks they bore. This is the contradictory character of all Australia. It is either a desert or a deluge. In spite of Kennedy's experience, there are times when the Warrego sends down such a flood that there are few places where it could be crossed between its sources and the Darling.

This was all that the public heard about the Barcoo at that time, and it was quite enough to destroy their further interest in it. Meanwhile, Leichhardt had not been idle since his return. Having been so successful in his journey to Port Essington, he contemplated another. This was nothing less than to traverse the country from east to west, and to place the nature of the interior beyond all doubt. He proposed to travel a good deal to the north before steering to the west, and as this would take a long time, his supplies were made sufficient for two years. His party consisted of eight persons besides himself, only one of whom had been with him before. The quantity of his live stock was tremendous. He took with him one hundred and eight sheep, two hundred and seventy goats, forty bullocks, fifteen horses, and thirteen mules.

On the 12th December the party reached their former station on Harley's Creek, which, it will be remembered, was at the edge of the scrub, above the Condamine River. Here their misfortunes commenced. First, a great many of the cattle and horses were lost, and they were not found again until the 4th January. It must, however, be stated that a part of this long delay was owing to their having been overtaken by a messenger with news of Sir Thomas Mitchell's return, and waiting for his despatches. They set out again, at last, and then pursued their journey very steadily along the former route. It will not be necessary to follow them over the old ground. On the 15th they

L 2

reached the head of the River Dawson. On the 24th
they were at Palm Tree Creek, exactly following their
old track. On the 9th February they commenced
ascending Expedition Range. By the time they reached
Comet Creek the country became rather marshy, in
consequence of the heavy rains which fell; and, at the
same time, as a natural consequence in such a climate,
fever and ague made its appearance among the party.
They were nearly all very bad, but they managed to
advance until they came to the Mackenzie River, and
there the whole were laid up in a deplorable state of
sickness. Without any covering, except their calico
tents, and with no medical stores, it may be easily
imagined what their sufferings were. Mr. Bunce, the
naturalist, has given the public a graphic account of all
they went through. If it was bad for the men, however, it must have been still worse for Leichhardt, who
thus saw all his resources wasted, and the time and
energies of his followers all melting before him. It
was not until the 6th April that they were able
again to move forward. They made an effort to reach
Peak Range, where it was hoped that the elevation
would benefit them. But they only made one day's
journey, and were again delayed until the 17th, partly
through fever and partly because they had lost the
whole of their cattle and sheep. Their situation was
as miserable as one can imagine. They kept moving on
when they could, but the weather became wet, and
fever kept its heavy hand upon them all. Then, when
further advance was impossible, they held their ground
as long as they could. Even in this, at last, they had
to give way, because all their cattle and sheep were
lost for want of proper looking after. Very reluctantly,
Leichhardt was obliged to own that he could not now
hope to prosecute his journey. He was the last to see
this, and certainly not until long after his followers had
tried to impress it upon him very earnestly. And so
the party made their way back, after an absence of
seven months, which had been almost one unmingled
course of suffering and privation for them all. This
expedition added nothing to the knowledge of the

interior. It, however, proved the permanence of the water found on the first journey, and the general richness of the country around.

When Leichhardt had given up all hope of prosecuting his journey further, he was put in possession of the results of Mitchell's expedition to the Barcoo. It will be remembered that when Sir Thomas reached the head of the Cogoon, in lat. 26° 53', he found splendid downs, bounded to the east by a distant range. These he named the Fitzroy Downs and the Grafton Range. These downs form part of the watershed between the Balonne and Maranoa. They were not very far from a part of Leichhardt's track to Port Essington, and the latter explorer was very anxious to connect the two lines, especially as some of the materials of his last expedition still remained to him.

And so, on the 9th August, 1847, he started from the Darling Downs, accompanied by Mr. F. N. Isaacs, Mr. Bunce, Mr. Perry, and a black fellow. They first continued along their old track until they reached Bottle Tree Creek, discovered on the former expedition in lat. 26° 20'. This was very nearly due east of Fitzroy Downs, so that their course was now to the west, and the intervening country was not more than one hundred miles wide in a direct line. This expedition will be more readily understood if the reader bears in mind one or two facts pertaining to the physical geography of the locality. Their course was along the foot of a range which runs almost east and west. This gives rise to a number of creeks, which run south into Dogwood Creek. Dogwood Creek runs south-west, until it joins the Condamine. So that, the reader will perceive, the journey of the explorers must have been at first over a succession of the spurs of the range which separate one creek from another. These dividing ridges were well timbered with box trees, and well grassed. Their sides were more often precipitous than sloping, and this turned the explorers to the south to seek better travelling; but when the steep sides of the hills disappeared, scrub commenced, and their progress was very slow.

In lat. 26° 32' they reached most beautiful open box ridges, well grassed, and perfectly sound, with a fine creek of reedy waterholes running by its side. All around the scenery was nice and open, except in one direction, and that one was unfortunately the very way they wanted to go. The scrub was too thick to the west for men to force, equipped as the explorers were, so they followed the creek. As they went down, the scrub came closer and closer to the banks, and it appeared as if it would hem them in soon if they proceeded, so they thought it best to face it at once. They did so, and nine miles' travelling brought them to beautiful box ridges. They were still running along the south side of some watershed, because the country trended to the south, and was full of creeks. First they found a well-watered one, which led five miles to the westward and then turned south. After passing a ridge they found another, and then another, and last of all a very large one with high flood-marks upon its banks. This was called Emu Creek, a name which is possessed by hundreds of others all over the country, as every one appears to know, except explorers, who go on pertinaciously naming them as if they were the first inventors of such an appropriate appellation.

To the creek succeeded scrub, which turned them again to the south along a watercourse. This they followed to below lat. 26° 55', when it became rocky, and joined a large creek with more of the flood-marks upon the banks. These were formed by perpendicular rocks, amid a very barren country. This was Dogwood Creek again, but its character was much altered by receiving so many tributaries, and it now assumed the proportions of a river. It went too much to the southward to suit the explorers, so they again turned to the west, through a very scrubby country. At twelve miles they came to a river from the northward with high but irregular banks, lined with large water gum trees. Its bed was sandy, containing pebbles of fossil wood, broken pieces of agate, and variously coloured flint and quartz. Tracks of horses were noticed upon the banks. This showed that either settlers were near, or that explorers had been there before. In either case it was an unfortunate circumstance, for the stream received in consequence the awkward and ugly name of Horsetrack River. Yet Leichhardt considered that it should be called Robinson's Creek, because its features were very similar to a stream of that name which had been crossed about ninety miles to the north, on the first expedition. Fourteen miles beyond the Horsetrack, they met another large channel. The explorers were evidently in the humour for harsh names, so this river fared no better than the others. It was called Yahoo River. The intervening country was generally scrubby, and, as far as appearances went, no one could guess that they were approaching such a fertile tract as Fitzroy Downs. Another creek, ten miles to the westward, was called Bunce's Creek. This, Leichhardt thought, was the stream which Mitchell had seen from the summit of Mount Abundance, and had mistaken for the continuation of the Balonne. They had now passed a great number of watercourses, all of which drained into the Darling. Let the reader bear in mind what Mitchell and Sturt had found that river to be—an almost dry channel, with long reaches of still water. Now, does it not seem extraordinary that such a stream should form the main bed for all those creeks and rivers now mentioned, as well as the Condamine, the Maranoa, the Macquarrie, Castlereagh, and a host of others? Surely this should serve better than any description to give a true idea of the nature of the country and the character of the climate of Australia.

After Bunce's Creek, an almost endless succession of sandstone Acacia ridges succeeded. They were so great an obstacle to the party that at last they were obliged to diverge to the south-west. This brought them to a water-hole, and some natives near it, who could or would give them no tidings of the Cogoon River, though they had evidently seen whites before. It was singular that this reluctance to give information was only displayed by these savages, which must have belonged to the tribe that had furnished Mitchell with so much. Six miles beyond where they were seen, Leichhardt came upon the

Cogoon, exactly fifty-four miles west of the Horsetrack River. Mitchell's tracks could not be seen upon its banks, so Leichhardt struck to the west to intercept them. To his great surprise, he came upon a creek flowing from the westward, in lat. 27°. He followed this for about four miles, but it turned north, so he left it, and continued the west course with his companions. Their journey was over very mountainous country, with numerous interesting creeks. One, which ran to the south-south-west, was followed for about ten miles; and while the party were camping near a water-hole, they heard the neighing of a horse near them. They had long noticed the tracks of settlers on the banks of a creek, and expected every mile to come upon a station, so that they were not much surprised when, in answer to a gun-shot, they heard the cracking of a stock-whip. In a few minutes afterwards they were comfortably ensconced in the station hut, and their exploring terminated.

Leichhardt could not pursue his investigations beyond this point. He did not reach the Fitzroy Downs, because his southerly course had brought him about fifteen miles below where they commenced. He was of opinion that there was good country at the heads of the creeks he had crossed, but not good enough to be called downs, and this was the only important result of the journey. It is worthy of remark that Leichhardt found on the Horsetrack and Cogoon Rivers several trees marked with the letter L. This should be borne in mind, when much stress is laid upon the L marked trees found by Hely and Gregory on the Barcoo. They might all have been made by the same person, and if so, not by Leichhardt, for here he draws attention to them; not by Kennedy's party, for it had not been there at the time; not by Mitchell's, at least for any reason one can see, for there was not a single man in his party whose surname or first christian name began with the letter L.

As soon as ever Leichhardt got home, he was busy again trying to equip another expedition. Funds, of course, were his greatest difficulty, because the loss entailed by the last journey was very serious; but his zeal and energy were great, and the public had every confidence in him, so that it was not very long before he was ready again. But he was not so well equipped this time. His party was smaller than ever, and miserably provided. Very likely he feared that his plans might be for ever laid aside if he did not try to accomplish them then. He little thought he was bartering away his life for his project. He started in 1848. The plan was the old one—that is, to traverse the continent from east to west, and to take about two years in its accomplishment. He intended to vary the commencement of his route to some extent by travelling along Mitchell's track, at least as far as the basaltic tableland at the head of the Maranoa. His route beyond that was uncertain, and has been much disputed by his friends when a search for his missing party was projected. However it may be, the last that was heard from him was from the Cogoon, and is contained in the following letter :—

" McPherson's Station, Cogoon, April 3, 1848.

"I TAKE the last opportunity of giving you an account of my progress. In eleven days we travelled from Mr. Burell's station on the Condamine, to Mr. M'Pherson's on the Fitzroy Downs. Though the country was occasionally very difficult, yet everything went on well. My mules are in excellent order; my companions in excellent spirits. Three of my cattle are footsore, but I shall kill one of them to-night, to lay in our necessary stock of dried beef. The Fitzroy Downs, over which we travelled for about twenty-two miles from east to west, is indeed a splendid region, and Sir Thomas has not exaggerated their beauty in his account. The soil is pebbly and sound, richly grassed, and, to judge from the Myalls, of the most flattering quality. I came right on Mount Abundance, and passed over a gap in it with my whole train. My latitude agreed well with Mitchell's. I fear that the absence of water on Fitzroy Downs will render this fine country, to a great degree, unavailable. I observe the thermometer daily at 6 A.M.

and 8 P.M., which are the only convenient hours. I have tried the wet thermometer, but am afraid my observations will be very deficient. I shall, however, improve on them as I proceed. The only serious accident that has happened was the loss of a spade, but we are fortunate enough to make it up on this station. Though the days are still very hot, the beautiful clear nights are cool, and benumb the mosquitoes, which have ceased to trouble us. Myriads of flies are the only annoyance we have.

"Seeing how much I have been favoured in my present progress, I am full of hopes that our Almighty Protector will allow me to bring my darling scheme to a successful termination.

"Your most sincere friend,
"LUDWIG LEICHHARDT."

It is strange that no allusion is made in this letter to what his immediate plans were. One would think that he should have said which way he meant to travel from the Cogoon, but here, unfortunately, the mystery connected with his fate commences. This was the last that was heard of him. Other tidings there were which we shall have to comment upon, but the secret of his fate has not yet been cleared up—probably it never will be. Yet it seems hard to suppose that the journals, even in the worst privations, were not carefully guarded. They are hidden perhaps in some untrodden portion of the continent, and may yet see the light; but they will not tell us all. Gregory, in 1858, found what was thought to be one of the camps upon the Barcoo. The party may have perished in trying to cross the desert which baffled Sturt; but this is only conjecture, and we have no other clue. The name of this brave and enterprising man must be added to the list of victims to Australian exploration. His fate, and the fate of those who followed him, will be mourned as long as Australia affords a home to those who have benefited by his discoveries.*

* See Appendix, on the loss of Leichhardt.

CHAPTER X.

ANOTHER DISASTROUS EXPEDITION.

Kennedy's expedition to Cape York—Lands at Rockingham Bay—Difficulties
—Encounter with the natives—Fearful scrubs and swamps—High ranges
—The toilsome climbing over the watershed—The Mitchell River—
Attacked by natives—Great exhaustion of the party and failure of sup-
plies—Advance of a portion of the expedition, while the remainder stay at
Weymouth Bay—Jackey's narrative—Awful accident—Three more men
left behind—Cruel attack of the natives—Death of Kennedy—Jackey
arrives at the ship—Relief sent to Weymouth Bay—Frightful sufferings
of the party there—Death of all but two—Their rescue—Recovery of
Kennedy's papers.

IN New South Wales, zeal for exploration had taken
a very strong hold on the colonial public, nor were one
or two failures sufficient to shake what was left of it in
1848. Yet such matters had not been very prosperous
during the previous years. It is true Leichhardt had
successfully accomplished his first undertaking, but the
effect of this was more than counterbalanced by his subsequent failure, and the knowledge that the main object
of the journey to Port Essington had not been accomplished as yet. Mitchell's good news had given a tem-
porarily bright aspect to the character of the interior, but
Kennedy's journey had dispelled the vision most effectually. Yet, in spite of every drawback, a large portion of the public were as keen as ever for the accomplishment of the original design which had sent Leichhardt and his followers to Port Essington : that was, to
discover a short and available route from New South
Wales to the north coast, and thus open up trade to the
East Indies. Until that was done, or at least tried,
funds were always easily collected in Sydney for exploration purposes. There was a good reason for this.

Sydney had long been the capital of the only colony in Australia. Only a few years before, separate colonies with separate capitals had been created. Just now their competition had begun to be seriously felt by the old city, and to heighten the gloom of the prospect, the Port Phillip settlement was loudly clamouring to be declared a separate colony. The only chance for Sydney to maintain its superiority would be by making the utmost use of its geographical situation. The overland route to an Indian trading port was just the idea which suited the position.

As Leichhardt's route to Port Essington was much too long to be seriously thought of, it was intended first to send a party to explore on the east side of Carpentaria, and to see what could be done with the country about Cape York. They could reach this ground by sea, and, landing at Rockingham Bay, would soon, it was considered, obtain an accurate knowledge of the country up to the cape. A party was soon equipped upon these conditions. It was placed under the command of Mr. E. B. Kennedy, whose experience on the Barcoo had not tired him of exploration. His companions were Mr. W. Carron, as botanist; Mr. T. Wall, naturalist; and nine men, without counting a native, named Jackey Jackey, who was destined to bear a very prominent place in the records of this sad journey. The provisions were a very scanty supply, being no more than one ton of flour, 90 lbs. tea, and 600 lbs. sugar. This, had the nature of the country been known, would have been quite enough for the distance they had to traverse; but as it was not, and as the only thing certainly known was that the mountains were very high, and the party might meet with scrubs of a frightfully difficult nature, it was a crying shame to let thirteen men set out with so meagre a supply. They had, however, 100 sheep (almost certain to be lost), and 28 horses; and the carts, tents, ammunition, &c., were quite equal to the requirements. Thus they were equipped—for death, as it proved to all but three.

They sailed on the 29th April, 1848, on board the barque *Tam O'Shanter*, and H.M.S. *Rattlesnake* bore

them company. She was to see them safely landed in
Rockingham Bay, and then afterwards, it was hoped,
would be able to meet them again at Port Albany, when
they had traversed the peninsula. Port Albany is a
bay on its extreme north-east side.

The first part of the journey was not very encouraging. It took twenty-one days to reach the port, and
three more to select a proper place for landing. This
was in a very nice part of the bay, where not only were
the grass and water abundant, but the few natives that
were seen were of a peaceful and harmless disposition.
But in spite of its advantages, everything was not got
ashore until the 30th May, and then the list of their
effects included the carcase of one dead horse, who was
drowned before he could be got to the land. Their
camp was in lat. 17° 58', long. 148°. The land was
wet from a small stream running near them. It was
poor and sandy, besides being strewn with tropical
shells.

Before moving his party, Kennedy made a preliminary examination of the country, to see the nature
of the difficulties he would have to deal with. One thing
soon became very evident ; there would be plenty of
marshy ground. After passing along a mile of open
land, which was covered with long rushy grass, and
a hill of bushy timber near the beach, he reached a
large mangrove swamp. This was only the edge of a
larger one of fresh water, not, of course, covered with
mangroves, but by a scrub far more formidable to the
explorers. It was a tea tree, lashed together by the
Calamus Australis, a plant which Kennedy now saw for
the first time, but which he had good reason to remember. It was almost the greatest obstacle the explorers
met with ; and as it led to some of the disasters of this
journey, it is worth describing. It is a strong climbing
palm. From the roots as many as ninety shoots will
spring, and they lengthen out as they climb for hundreds of feet, never thicker than a man's finger. The
long leaves are covered with sharp spines ; but what
makes the plant the terror of the explorers, is the
tendrils, which grow out alternately with the leaves.

Many of these are twenty feet long, and they are
covered with strong spines, curved slightly downwards,
so as to support the branches in their rambling growth.
The tendrils lay hold of the surrounding bushes and the
branches of the trees, covering the tops of even the
tallest, and turning in all directions. It thus forms a
thicket like a wall, which is difficult even to cut
through. Kennedy's party found it especially so.
Each stem as it was released by the axe caught upon
the clothes of the assailant by its recurved spines, and
it was often hours ere he could rid himself completely
from its tenacious embraces.

Having seen this much, Mr. Kennedy returned on the
3rd June, convinced that it would be impossible to proceed in a north-west direction. The swamps he had
found were impassable, and the party would, therefore,
have to cross a river on the south instead. They did
not start until the 5th June, and in two miles came to
the Mackay River. It was salt, about 150 yards wide,
and skirted by mangrove swamps. A boat had been
sent up the river by Captain Stanley, of the *Rattlesnake*,
and with its aid they crossed easily, but had to journey
a long way up the stream to get fresh water for the
evening. They then proceeded inland, but were stopped
at three miles by the swamps, which continued to run
parallel with the coast. So they had to return to the
beach, and soon came upon another river, much wider
than the first. It was salt in the middle, but the large
swamps draining into it made it fresh at the sides. It
took them three days to cross it, and this was only
effected by floating the dray by the means of empty kegs,
and using it as a raft. Meanwhile, Mr. Kennedy was
employed in looking for a passage inland, but still the
unbroken line of swamps continued. The 11th brought
them to another river, which they crossed as before, assisted by the natives, who were numerous, and at this
time inoffensive. Everything seemed, however, to combine to delay them, for two days were lost here in looking for one of the men who was missing. The poor
fellow was nearly an idiot—a character one would think
which should never have been employed on such a

service. He had absconded with a little food which he was sharing with the natives when he was found. This day also a large alligator was seen in the stream.

Mr. Kennedy now made every exertion to find some place by which he could cross the swamps which kept him upon the coast. Thus the time was spent until the 23rd June, and then he was obliged to give up the search, and keep to the southward. But this travelling was almost as bad as crossing the swamps. Little salt-water streams, boggy, and lined with mangroves, continually impeded their course, so that by the 26th they had only advanced a very few miles, if it can be called advancing to have to go southward when they wanted to move north. The natives followed them all the time. They were painted all over with red earth, and armed with spears. Some of them had already learned to address the men by name, and they seemed pleased when they got an answer. They were peaceable, but much inclined to steal, even though Kennedy frequently made them small presents.

On the 26th, they were at last able to move westward. The country seemed rising, and became more dry; but almost as great an impediment as the swamps was found in the small creeks running eastward, to say nothing of the thick forest entangled with the dreaded *Calamus.* Yet this was only the commencement of the difficulties. Two of the men soon were prostrated by the ague—a disease to be expected in such damp and thick forest. While they were recovering, Kennedy went out exploring until the 1st July, and on his return reported that the party could advance forty miles without much difficulty. But the two men were still too ill to move. Kennedy again set out on foot with three companions. He only went a short distance, and as he was returning the natives followed, making very threatening demonstrations with their spears. After some hesitation one spear was thrown, and Kennedy ordered his men to fire. They did so, and four of the natives fell. One was killed on the spot, and the three others were immediately carried off into the scrub. Such wholesale slaughter seems to have been rather un-

necessary. One shot would have done all that was
required ; and even this need not have been resorted to
until the effect of firing over their heads had been tried.
The subsequent hostility of these savages was retribu-
tive proof of the effect of this harshness.

On the 6th July, the sick men were able to travel,
and the party started again. They crossed two creeks,
the second of which had banks twenty feet high. It
caused much delay, because the drays had to be lowered
by pulleys. On the further side the travelling was
very slow, as the rank grass was high, and the scrub
thick. And it soon became thicker, for they were
occupied until the 13th in cutting a road through a
brushwood of appalling density, where, as usual, the
Calamus was the greatest obstacle. There were, however, some patches of open ground, but even with the
aid of these they barely advanced five miles daily. The
soil became very uneven when the scrub was passed,
and very difficult to travel over. First one and then
the other cart gave way, and it was evident that they
could not be taken much further. Mr. Kennedy at
last determined to abandon them altogether, and to take
on what he could upon the pack-saddles. Many valuable articles were thus left behind, as being too heavy
for the horses. This was the commencement of the
abandonment. Already their route began to bear the
traces of their difficulties, and gloomy anticipations were
felt as to the endurance of the horses with such increased
weight upon their backs. Nearly every day some effort
had to be made to lighten their labours, and the track
began to look more like the route of a retreating regiment than that of an exploring party.

In the following nine days they travelled over an
irregular mountainous country, intersected by numerous
creeks, with a thick belt of scrub on each side, which it
was always necessary to cut through. Often the winding course of a creek would oblige them to cross it
several times, and they had, moreover, to turn in every
direction to avoid the deep gullies and scrub which they
constantly met. On the 25th, they met the channel of a
river which divided into two branches ; one going to the

south, and the other east. It was about two hundred yards above the junction, and as it went to the north-west they followed it in that direction. But they could not do so long. The ground soon became so rocky that the horses were continually falling, so they crossed the stream and again plunged into the scrub. The change was from bad to worse. They had to cut their way through for the whole of the first day, until they reached a high hill, where they encamped. The rocks then became an impediment to them, and though they were very high and perpendicular, there was a range still higher and more precipitous straight in their path. One can judge of their position from the fact, that at one encampment a horse, even when tied to a tree by a tether rope, fell in feeding, and was dashed to pieces.

Mr. Kennedy saw that the rocks would soon stop them, so he went on in advance of the party to find a passage over the range. He returned on the 31st, and then five men were sent to clear a passage through the scrub. On the 3rd August, the whole party again moved on. They proceeded up a spur of the range in a north-west direction; but it was only with the most tremendous exertion that the horses were got up to the camp. Fortunately, only one was lost. There were many creeks in this locality, running rapidly, and tumbling over rocky falls. Kennedy supposed that they all ran into the swamps they had passed, and thence into the rivers of Rockingham Bay.

The difficulties of the journey had now increased so thickly upon them, that it became necessary to divide the party. Six went to clear a path through the mountains, while four remained to guard the stores, and three to follow the sheep and horses. The animals were suffering extremely, as may be imagined. The sheep were dying rapidly, and on the 7th one horse had to be abandoned. That night the camp was most miserable. It was raining heavily, and as the horses could scarcely be got along, they had to be tied to a tree, and the men lay down beside them without a fire or any comfort whatever. Next day they travelled up the hills, but they made very little progress owing to the numerous steep

ascents.   Fortunately, they were able to make a fire that
evening ; but this was scarcely compensation for another
inconvenience they suffered.   On rising in the morning
they found themselves covered with blood, for the grass
was full of leeches, and they had made the greatest use
of the rare opportunity of white blood to feed upon. *

Next day they reached a river, which they crossed,
and then they were travelling for some time through
uneven forest land, with the terrible scrub here and
there.   The country had a broken appearance.   Huge
blocks of rock were lying upon the open ground, of
various shapes, and often irregularly piled.   The stone
was either granite or trap.   On the 16th, another horse
fell.   His death revealed a significant fact with regard
to the state of the provisions, for poor as the animal
was, the men were glad to cut him up for food.   Another
died on the 19th ; and for the first time since their
starting, the party were able to increase their provisions by shooting a wallaby.   Their position was
now in lat. 17° 30', long. 145° 12'.

They had crossed the Dividing Range it was evident,
for the country fell to the westward, and all the creeks
and watercourses took the same direction.   The travelling was much better, for they journeyed for eight days
through open undulating downs, with occasional thick
scrubs.   Their only delay was in looking for one of the
men who had strayed, and in the meantime two more of
the horses died.   On the 29th they camped by the side of
a very broad river.   It was not running, for there was
water only in the holes and reaches, but evidently a great
deal of water ran at times, as the bed was six hundred or
seven hundred yards wide, with two or three channels.
They tried to keep along the stream, thinking it might
lead to Princess Charlotte's Bay ; but the country
became very mountainous, and so full of scrubby gullies,
that the banks could only be seen occasionally.   Their

* There are many places in Australia where leeches exist in abundance
in the long damp grass. Horses and cattle suffer fearfully from them. It
may almost risk a person's life to sleep on the ground in such localities, and
an early walk in the morning costs an ounce or two of blood from the legs.
According to the Abbé Huc, some places in Tartary have the same unpleasant
peculiarity.

course was nearly west, but the river wound in all
directions in the rocky ground, and sometimes the bed
was the only available road.

On the 9th September, they had a fine view over
the surrounding tract from the top of a high hill.
To the west, and round to the south, it appeared to be
a fine undulating forest land, intersected by numerous
creeks and rivers. They could see also that the river
they were upon kept too much to the west to suit them,
so they left it and kept to the north. It was a pity they
did so, for they might have easily followed the coast to
their destination. As it was, their course was through
a lightly timbered, stiff clay soil, with occasional sand-
hills—all very difficult for the horses. Water was
abundant. They could get no game of any kind. On
the 15th they met another river, with a fine
broad bed, and steep banks on both sides. Mr. Kennedy
considered that this stream rose somewhere near Cape
Tribulation, and, after running northward for thirty
miles, to turn south-west, which was its course when met
with. It was crossed easily, and as the party camped
upon its banks, they found an important addition to
their provisions in the fish which were caught in the
pools. This was the only thing in the way of "game"
which they could procure; and though the expedition
was far from its termination, the effect of suffering and
fatigue was beginning to tell very much upon the
organization of the party. In truth, they were very
miserable, with all the inconvenience of hunger and
exhaustion to bear, in the midst of a terrible country.
Their camp upon this river was rendered more distressing from the hostility of the natives. At first, they
seemed cautious in their attacks, and were easily driven
off by the sound of fire-arms; but subsequently they
gave battle in a most determined manner, and several
spears were thrown into the camp, after the grass all
around the explorers had been set on fire. The latter
now retaliated in earnest, and though they were unable
to see the effect of their shots, they had every reason to
believe that it was not the sound of the guns alone
which made the savages decamp.

M 2

Such victories did not elate the party nor brighten their prospects; on the contrary, they increased the gloomy anticipations of the country yet to be travelled over; the days' stages were getting shorter, and the men getting weaker. How long they might be able to resist such attacks was painful to speculate upon. They left the river because the country around was well watered by creeks, and very fair travelling. Soon they came upon what they considered the Mitchell of Leich- hardt, with its fine open reaches and sandy bed. But such improvement in the travelling did but little to better their position. The heat was so oppressive, and the scorching glare from the red sand, or the red sky, so overpowering, that only very short stages could be made. The men were willing to do their best, though each delay made the probability of starvation greater; but the heat was more than they could endure. Thus they went on crossing small streams, and tra- versing sandy plains, until they reached the sea. The incidents of the journey were varied only by the hos- tility of the natives, who once nearly burnt the camp; or by the death of some of their exhausted animals from the heat. As they approached the shore, the soil became incrusted with salt—the only production which could be made of use to the explorers. By its means they were able to preserve their supplies of horse-flesh, now their main subsistence. Even this was a very slender supply, for the last horse that was killed weighed only sixty- five pounds.

The part of the coast they reached was Princess Charlotte's Bay, in lat. 14° 30', long. 143° 56'. The object of coming to this point was in consequence of an arrangement that H.M.S. *Rambler* should wait for the explorers during the month of August. It was now October, so the chances of the ship being still there were very slight; and yet the party had clung to the hope of finding her. With a feeling of disappointment they turned away to make for Port Albany, which was the next rendezvous; and it was with the gloomiest an- ticipations they again turned their faces towards the rocks, scrubs, and precipices of the Dividing Range.

In coming to the bay they had found a pretty large salt-water river, and here they were again attacked by the natives, though a tribe met the day following manifested the most friendly dispositions.

A horse was killed by accident on the 16th, and, of course, cut up for eating. The whole of the animals left were too weak to carry much more than the saddles. They were repeatedly falling, especially during the next four days, as the country became very uneven. The baggage was not much to carry, for the whole stock of flour was reduced to two hundred pounds, and thus many of the men became weak from the smallness of the rations. Judge then their sufferings, when, after four days' travelling from the coast, a terrible rocky route was before them, every step leading into more mountainous country. Through these ridges and deep gullies they journeyed until November 2nd, when one of the men became too weak to walk, and another horse had to be killed. Yet they struggled on through the ravines, which became steeper at every step, and daily worse supplied with water. At last, on the 10th November, Mr. Kennedy found that the majority of his men would perish if he tried to advance them much further. It was clearly impossible for them all to reach Cape York before the provisions were exhausted; and their only chance of life was to form an advance party, and try to obtain assistance for those who remained behind. Mr. Kennedy resolved to go himself. He selected three men, and Jackey Jackey, the native, and then advanced down a valley, and formed a depôt as near Weymouth Bay as possible. There were nine horses left, of which number it was proposed to take seven, and proceed to Cape York, and obtain assistance from the vessel waiting there. When they had chosen the depôt, the whole party rested for two days before separating. The last sheep was killed, and every precaution taken to provide for the safety of the camp. Mr. Kennedy then gave Mr. Carron written instructions how to act during their stay at Weymouth Bay. He expected to meet the relief ship at Port Albany, and then could send round by sea for his companions. He calculated that it would

take him ten or fifteen days to reách that place; and Mr.
Carron was directed to keep a sharp look-out for a
vessel; and if he should see one, to hoist a flag upon the
hill. Rockets were also left to fire as signals. The party
left were eight in number, and the provisions were two
weak horses, and twenty-eight pounds of flour. It was
a pitiable thing to be reduced to this, yet their lives depended upon nothing else. The provisions were to be
served so as to last six weeks, in case of accident.
Heaven only knows how it was to be done so as to
keep eight men from starvation! Yet Kennedy did not
spare himself. He took with him only eighteen pounds
of flour, and seventy-five pounds of horse-flesh.

He started on the 13th November. The devoted
little band went forward full of hope, though only one
of them was destined to see the faces of white men any
more. What they did and what they suffered is nearly
unknown to us. Unfortunately, they disappear from
our sight as they disappeared from that of their companions. The only record left is a very imperfect narrative given by Jackey Jackey, the sole survivor, whose
statement, so full of interest, is all that remains to us of
the closing scene of this disastrous journey. I make no
apology for giving the mournful tale in the original
words of the survivor. The confusion of dates occurring
would prevent an abridgement in any case, and certainly
the tragedy can be far better seen in the pathetic simplicity of Jackey's language. When he arrived at Port
Albany alone, and in the last stage of exhaustion and
emaciation, and when, as he imagined, his life was fast
ebbing away, he told in feeble accents the following
sad tale of suffering and death :

" I started with Mr. Kennedy for Cape York. We
went until we came to a river which empties itself into
Weymouth Bay.* A little further north we crossed
the river. Mr. Kennedy and the rest of us went on a
very high hill and came to a flat on the other side, and
camped there. I went on a good way the next day.

---

* The broken and disjointed style of this narrative is a good specimen of
the manner in which the natives express themselves in English. For the
manner in which the story is told, and the confusion of dates and places, of
course, Jackey is alone responsible.

A horse fell down a creek. The flour we took with us lasted three days. We had much trouble in getting the horse out of the creek. We went on, and came out, and camped on the side of the ridges. We had no water. Next morning went on, and Luff was taken ill with a very bad knee, and we left him behind; and Dunn went back again and brought him on. Luff was riding a horse, named Fiddler. Then we went on, and camped at a little creek. The flour being out this day, we commenced eating the horseflesh which Carron gave us when we left Weymouth Bay. As we went on we came to a small river. We gathered noondas, and lived upon them and the meat. We stopped at a little creek, and it came on raining, and Costigan shot himself. In putting his saddle under the tarpaulin, a string caught the trigger, and it went off, and the ball went under the right arm and came out at his back under the shoulder. We went on this morning all of us, and stopped at another creek in the evening.

"The next morning we killed a horse, named Browney, smoked him that night, and went on next day, taking as much as we could with us, and went on about a mile, and then turned back because Costigan was very bad and in much pain. We went back again because there was no water. Then Mr. Kennedy and I had dinner there, and went on in the afternoon, leaving Dunn, Costigan, and Luff, at the creeks. This was at Pudding Pan Hill, near Shelburne Bay. We left some horse-meat with the three men at Pudding Pan Hill, and carried some with us upon a pack-horse. Mr. Kennedy wanted to make great haste when he left the place, because he wanted the doctor to go down to the men that were ill. This was about three weeks after leaving Weymouth Bay.* One horse was left with the three men at Pudding Pan Hill, and we (Mr. Kennedy and myself), took with us three horses. The three men were to remain there until Mr. Kennedy and myself had gone to Cape York and returned for them. Mr. Kennedy told Luff and Dunn, when he left them, if

* This is either an error in Jackey's calculations, or shows that a great deal of what preceded is omitted.

Costigan died, they were to come along the beach till
they saw the ship, and then to fire a gun. They
stopped to take care of the man that was shot. We
killed a horse for them before we went away.[*]

"Having left these three men, we camped that night
where there was no water. Next morning, Mr.
Kennedy and me went on with the four horses—two
pack-horses, and two saddle-horses. One horse got
bogged in a swamp. We tried to get him out all day,
but could not. We left him there, and camped at
another creek. The next day Mr. Kennedy and I
went on again and passed up a ridge, very scrubby, and
had to turn back again, and went along gullies to get
clear of the creek and scrub. Now it rained, and we
camped. There were plenty of blacks here, but we
did not see them, but plenty of fresh tracks, and camps,
and smoke. Next morning we went on and camped at
another creek, and on the following morning we continued going on, and camped in the evening close to a
scrub. It rained in the night. Next day we went on
in the scrub, but could not get through. Then I
changed horses, and rode a black colt to spell the others,
and rode all day; and in the afternoon we got on clear
ground, and the horse fell down—me and the colt.
The horse lay on my right hip. Mr. Kennedy got off
his horse, and moved my horse from my thigh. We
stopped there that night, and could not get the horse
up. We left him there. We had some horse-meat
left to eat, and went on that day, and crossed a little
river and camped.

"The next day we went a good way. Mr. Kennedy
told me to go up a tree and see a sandy hill somewhere.
I went up a tree, and saw a sandy hill a little way down
from Port Albany. The next morning we went on,
and Mr. Kennedy told me we should get round to Port
Albany in a day. We travelled on all day till twelve

[*] Jackey, in the following statement, makes many mistakes about the
number of the horses; but the aborigines, however civilized, cannot count,
and therefore the errors may be excused. Let it be borne in mind, that
Kennedy left Weymouth Bay with seven horses. Two are already accounted
for as killed; one was left with the wounded man; and therefore Kennedy took
four on with him; but Jackey speaks alternately of three and four.

o'clock (noon), and then we saw Port Albany. Then,
he said, 'There is Port Albany, Jackey; a ship is there.
You see that island there,' pointing to Albany
Island. This was at the mouth of Escape River. We
stopped there a little time. All the meat was gone.
I tried to get some fish, but could not. We went on in
the afternoon about half a mile along the west side, and
met a good lot of blacks, and we camped. The blacks
all cried 'Powad! Powad!' and rubbed their bellies,
and we thought they were friendly, and Mr. Kennedy
gave them fish-hooks all round. Every one asked me if
I had anything to give away, and I said 'No;' and
Mr. Kennedy said, 'Give them your knife, Jackey.'
This fellow on board [a prisoner to be spoken of here-
after] was the man I gave the knife to. I am sure of
it. I know him well. The black that was shot in the
canoe [to be mentioned just now] was the most active
in urging all the others to spear Mr. Kennedy.

"I gave the man on board my knife. We went on
this day, and I looked behind, and they were getting up
their spears and ran all round the camp which we had
left. I told Mr. Kennedy that very likely those blacks
would follow us, and he said, 'No, Jackey; those blacks
are very friendly.' I said to him, 'I know those black
fellows well; they too much speak,' and we went on for
some two or three miles, and camped. I and Mr.
Kennedy watched them that night, taking it in turns
every hour all night. By-and-by, I saw the black
fellows. It was a moonlight night, and I walked up to
Mr. Kennedy and said, 'There is plenty of black
fellows now.' This was in the middle of the night.
Mr. Kennedy told me to get my gun ready. The
blacks did not know where we slept, as we did not
make a fire. We both sat up all night. After this,
daylight came, and I fetched the horses and saddled
them. Then we went on a good way up the river, and
then we sat down a little while, and then we saw three
blacks coming along our track, and then they saw us,
and one ran back as hard as he could run, and fetched
up plenty more, like a flock of sheep almost. I told
Mr. Kennedy to put the saddles on the horses, and go

on; and the blacks came up and they followed us all
day. All along it was raining, and I now told him to
leave the horses and come on without them, that the
horses made too much track. Mr. Kennedy was too
weak, and would not leave the horses. We went on
this day until towards the evening; raining hard, and
the blacks followed us all day, some behind, some before.
In fact, black fellows all around following us. Now we
went into a little bit of scrub, and I told Mr. Kennedy
to look behind always. Sometimes he would do so, and
sometimes not.* Then a good many black fellows came
behind in the scrub, and threw plenty of spears, and hit
Mr. Kennedy in the back first. Mr. Kennedy said to
me, 'Oh, Jackey, Jackey! shoot 'em! Shoot 'em!'
Then I pulled out my gun and fired, and hit one fellow
all over the face with buck-shot. He tumbled down,
and got up again and again, and wheeled right round,
and two black fellows picked him up and carried him
away. They went a little way and came back again,
throwing spears all round more than they did before—
very large spears.

"I pulled out the spear at once from Mr. Kennedy's
back, and cut out the jag with Mr. Kennedy's knife.
Then Mr. Kennedy got his gun and snapped, but the
gun would not go off. The blacks sneaked all along by
the trees, and speared Mr. Kennedy again in the leg
above the knee a little, and I got speared over the eye,
and the blacks were now throwing their spears all ways,
never giving over, and shortly again speared Mr.
Kennedy in the right side. At the same time we got
speared the horses got speared too, and jumped and
kicked all about and got into the swamp. I now told
Mr. Kennedy to sit down while I looked after the
saddle-bags; and when I came back again I saw blacks
along with Mr. Kennedy. Then I asked him if he saw
blacks with him. He was stupid with the spear wounds,
and said, 'No.' I then asked him where was his

* I learn from Mr. David Edgar, who was very intimate with Kennedy,
that he was so near-sighted that he could scarcely distinguish anything at
ten yards' distance. This is probably the reason why he neglected to look
behind him, as Jackey directed, and why he was so easily speared by the
natives.

watch.   I saw the blacks taking away his watch and
hat as I was returning to Mr. Kennedy.   Then I
carried Mr. Kennedy into the scrub.   He said, 'Don't
carry me a good way.'   Then Mr. Kennedy looked
this way, very bad [Jackey rolling his eyes].   I said to
him, 'Don't look far away,' as I thought he would be
frightened.   I asked him after, 'Are you well, now?'
and he said, 'No.   I don't care for the spear wound in
my leg, Jackey; but for the other two spear wounds in
my side and back,' and said, 'I am bad inside, Jackey.'
I told him black fellow always die when he got spear
wound in there.   He said, 'I am out of wind, Jackey.'
I asked him, 'Mr. Kennedy, are you going to leave me?'
and he said, 'Yes, my boy; I am going to leave you.
I am very bad, Jackey.   You take the books, Jackey,
to the captain, but not the big ones; the governor will
give anything for them.'   I then tied up the papers.
He then said, 'Jackey, give me the paper and I will
write.'   I gave him pencil and paper, and he tried to
write, and then fell back and died.

"I caught him as he fell back and held him.   I then
turned round and cried.   I was crying a good while until
I got well.   That was about an hour, and then I buried
him.   I digged up the ground with a tomahawk, and
covered him over with grass, thin logs, and my shirt
and trousers.   That night I left him near dark.   I
would go through the scrub and the blacks threw spears
at me a good many, and I went back again into the
scrub.   Then I went down the creek which runs into
Escape River, and I walked along the water in the
creek very easy, with my head only above, to avoid
the blacks, and get out of their way.   In this way I
went half a mile.   Then I got out of the creek, and got
clear of them, and walked on all night nearly, and slept
in the bush without a fire.   I went on next morning,
and felt very bad, and I spelled here for two days.   I
lived upon nothing but salt water.   Next morning I went
on, and camped one mile away from where I slept, and ate
one of the pandanus fruits.   Next morning I went on
and sat down; there I wanted to spell a little and then
go on; but when I tried to get up again I could not,

but fell down again very tired and cramped, and I spelled two days.

"Then I went on again one mile, and got nothing to eat but one nonda, and I went on again that day and camped, and on again next morning about half a mile, and sat down where there was a little water, and remained all day. On the following morning I went a good way; round a great swamp and mangroves, and got a good way by sundown. The next morning I went and saw a very large track of black fellows. I went clear of the track and of swamp on sandy ground. I came to a very large river and a large lagoon, about ten miles from Port Albany. I now got into the ridges by sundown, and went up a tree and saw Albany Island. Then next morning, at four o'clock, I went on as hard as I could go all the way down over fine clear ground, fine ironbark timber, and plenty of good grass. I went on round the point [this was towards Cape York, north of Albany Island], and went on and followed a creek down, and went on the top of the hill and saw Cape York. I knew it was Cape York, because the sand did not go on further. I sat down then a good while. I said to myself, 'Then,' I said, 'this is Port Albany.' I believe indeed, somewhere, Mr. Kennedy also told me that the ship was; inside, close up to the mainland. I went on a little way, and saw the ship and boat. I met, close up here, two black gins and a good many piccaninies. One said, 'Powad! Powad!' then I asked her for eggs, and she gave me turtles' eggs, and I gave her a burning-glass. She pointed to the ship which I had seen before. I was very frightened of seeing the black men all along here, and I was on the rock " coo-ing," and *murry murry* glad when the boat came for me."

This was the end of Jackey's narrative; and contains all that is known about the end of poor Kennedy. A braver or better man never had command of an exploring party, and it is with greatest sorrow one reads his hard fate. Jackey tells the tale with so much simplicity and truth of detail, that one can picture the whole scene—the dense scrub through which the dusky

forms of the savages could be seen stealthily creeping;
the small vacant space amid the trees, with Jackey
supporting his poor master's dying head while the life
blood was rapidly staining the soil around. All is
described most minutely, even to the wandering gaze
of the eyes glazed in death, while the poor victim makes
a last effort to write something of his fate and sufferings for his fellow men to read. A death more lonely
and pitiable, more utterly destitute of every consoling
feature, has not been met with in the annals of
exploration.

Jackey arrived at Port Albany about eight o'clock
in the morning of December 23, 1848. The vessel
he reached was the *Ariel*, which was under the command of Captain Dobson, and waiting for the arrival of
Kennedy's party. He had waited so long already that
he had begun to think that the whole expedition had
perished. Just as they were debating how much
longer it would be considered expedient to wait, some
of the crew saw a black on the shore with a shirt and
trousers on. He was making signals and shouting as
loud as he could; but when the boat reached him, joy
and weakness made him scarcely able to speak. He
was haggard, awfully emaciated, and very lame; and
when the men put him into the boat he could only lie
down in the last state of exhaustion. He was barely
able to whisper as he was being rowed to the ship, that his
name was Jackey; that Mr. Kennedy had perished; and
that the rest of the party, if they still survived, would
be found at Pudding Pan Hill, and Weymouth Bay.
When placed on board, and restoratives and cordials
had been given, it seemed very doubtful whether
Jackey would ever recover. His statement was taken
down in writing, and then a council was held on board
as to what was best to be done after, under the circumstances. It was decided at once to proceed to Pudding
Pan Hill without delay, and to search for the three men
left there. If the search was unsuccessful, they would
lose no time, but go on to Weymouth Bay for the main
body of the party.

The crew of the *Ariel* made instant preparations,

and she sailed next day through Torres Straits. On the
day following, as she steered cautiously along the coast,
looking out for every sign of Costigan, Dunn, and Luff,
they came suddenly upon a canoe, with seven or eight
natives in it. Jackey was brought on deck, and he
readily recognised all of them as having being concerned
in throwing spears at Mr. Kennedy. One of them came
fearlessly on board, and Jackey identified him as the
man to whom he had given his knife. He was accordingly seized, and after a stout resistance, made a
prisoner. His companions jumped overboard on the
first alarm, and were paddling away without molesta-
tion, when it was found that the prisoner had some of
Mr. Kennedy's property about him. A chase after the
canoe was now made, and very few strokes of the oars
placed the boat's crew alongside. A shower of spears
was the first salute, and one sailor was wounded in the
arm. Of course, a volley of musketry was the answer.
One savage fell dead to the bottom of the canoe, and
all the rest jumped overboard and swam ashore. The
canoe was now searched and a great deal of Kennedy's
property found in it—all showing that Jackey's identi-
fication was correct, and that the punishment had really
fallen on the murderers. The prisoner, however,
escaped easiest of all. During the night he managed
to get free from his bonds, and, plunging overboard,
swam ashore.

On the 26th, the *Ariel* anchored in Shelburne Bay,
close to where Pudding Pan Hill was supposed to be.
Unfortunately, the water was so shallow that they
were not able to bring the ship closer than three or
four miles from the shore. As soon as she was
anchored, four men started under Jackey's guidance, in
search of Costigan and his companions—for Jackey was
now recruited in an astonishing degree, and on a fair
way to recovery. They marched inland for about an
hour through dense scrub, and then Jackey found that
they were too far to the north, and so they returned
disappointed to the boats. Another search ensued on
the same day, but by some bad management, they
could not reach within eight miles of where Jackey

said the party had been divided. The weather now changed, and as the schooner had been left with only two hands in her, Captain Dobson was reluctantly obliged to give up the search, and think only of saving the men at Weymouth Bay.

They arrived at the latter place on the 30th December. No time was lost in anchoring and making the vessel fast, and a party at once set off, under Jackey's directions, to search for the camp. They were not long before they came upon natives who shouted "White men!" very often, and pointed to a mountain near. A few lines were written to the party in the depôt, stating that a vessel was in the bay, and the bearer, one of the natives, would take them to the beach where the vessel lay. This was given to one of the blacks, who started off rapidly with it, while the relief party moved slowly forward. In about two miles Jackey was in country that he had seen before. He redoubled his pace, and soon shouted out, " I see camp!" The others pressed forward and there, in truth, was the camp; but alas! tenanted by two men instead of eight, and these so sadly wasted by famine and disease as to shock their deliverers as much as if they had found their corpses.

The survivors were Mr. F. Carron, the naturalist, and Mr. Goddard. It was with the greatest difficulty that they were got down to the beach, and it seemed for a long time doubtful whether they had been reserved for anything except to die in the arms of their pre- servers. The savages surrounded the party as they returned, so that every article in the camp except the instruments, charts, and botanical specimens, had to be abandoned. It required the greatest caution to avoid a collision, but, fortunately, the poor sufferers were brought on board in safety.

When Mr. Carron was sufficiently recovered, he told a harrowing tale. What they had suffered would have been incredible, unless it had been corroborated by the awful visages of the actors in that tragedy. Two days after Mr. Kennedy's party had left, one of the men died; and, subsequently, fifty or sixty natives made an

attempt to attack the camp. They did not however
throw any spears, but went away as suddenly as they
had come. When they had gone another of the party
died. On the 21st November, about sixty natives came
with a supply of fish, and tried to entice the whites to
come for them. The whole band were so fully armed
with spears, boomerangs, and clubs, that none of the
men dared venture among them, hungry as they were.
Finding that stratagem would not do, the savages began
closing round in all directions; preparing their spears
and pointing to their own necks and sides, and showing
by their postures how the explorers would writhe when
they were speared in those parts. Then they would
change their tactics, and pretend to mean no harm, lay-
ing down their spears, and making every demonstration
of peace. All the explorers could do was to sit huddled
together and anxiously watch their movements. Few
were strong enough to place their guns to their
shoulders, but they placed them across their knees,
resolving, as long as strength remained, to sell their
lives as dearly as they could. At length the fight
commenced in earnest. Spears were thrown on one side,
and were answered by the muskets. The spears did no
harm; but several natives were wounded, and when this
was ascertained, they withdrew in haste, leaving the
field clear, and the victory very decidedly on the side
of the explorers.

These incidents were almost daily repeated, until
the party were relieved. Skirmishes took place constantly; the victory was always their own; yet the
numerical strength of the party diminished daily. The
spears of the natives did no harm, but death threw his
shaft of famine with an unerring hand. The men
withered away rapidly. But they died very easily.
Some of them expired in the camp, and others on their
way to the creeks to which they tottered for water.
They seemed to hope to the last, and when their trembling feet would bear them no longer, they would calmly
lay their heads upon the earth and breathe their lives
away without a struggle. At last, the number of the
survivors was reduced to two. The natives came down

every day, and watched with pleasure the rapid dimu-
nition of the numbers. At first, the survivors were
able to hide the corpses; but the last two or three were
left where they died. Their companions were even too
weak to cover them over, so they remained, a ghastly
sight for their comrades—enough, indeed, to stifle all
hope. Even the natives were a sort of company to
them, had they been strong enough to resist them;
and, probably, they would have made a last effort for
life by going among them; but the fear of such a death
as these savages would inflict kept them back.

On the 1st of December, a schooner was seen crossing the bay. It was thought to be the *Bramble*, and
joy and hope with the most intense anxiety were felt,
whilst they watched her course. Every effort was
made to attract her attention. They fired their rockets,
discharged their pistols, and lighted fires; but all in
vain. The vessel passed on, and as she disappeared
from view, the chill feeling of despair and disappointment was worse than death to the explorers. It seems
cruel almost to tell the story of such a disappointment.

A short time before they were rescued, the natives
made a very daring attack upon the two unhappy men.
Goddard, who was the strongest, stood with his gun,
presented; but Mr. Carron had fallen down in his
attempt to present his gun, and could only feebly keep
it resting on his knees as he sat upon the ground. This
demonstration served to keep off the savages. Their
conduct was very strange. Sometimes they would
wind up their warlike proceedings by giving fish to the
poor men; and such seasonable supplies assisted much
in keeping them alive. These, a few pigeons and their
dogs, were their only sustenance.

One day, while Goddard was away, searching for
food, the natives suddenly arrived, and brought the
paper given by Captain Dobson. "For a moment,"
says Carron, "I was almost out of my senses with joy."
He gave the natives some presents, and a note for Captain Dobson; but instead of hurrying off with it, they
assembled round the two survivors, and made preparations for an immediate attack with their spears. The

gleam of hope was rapidly dying out in the minds of
the unfortunate men, for they now expected death every
moment. But who can describe their feelings, when,
just as the conflict was commencing, the relief party
came in sight, and they were saved? On their arrival
on board the *Ariel*, they were taken charge of by
Dr. Vallack, and after a protracted voyage they reached
Sydney in safety.

Directly the result of this disastrous expedition
was made known, a brig, named the *Freak*, was chartered by the Colonial Government, to call at Shelburne
Bay and Escape River, on her way to Port Essington.
It was to ascertain, if possible, the fate of the three
men still unaccounted for, and to recover the papers
secreted by Kennedy. Jackey Jackey went in the *Freak*,
to point out the localities. They arrived, first, at Weymouth Bay, and immediately visited the camp. They
found the remains of six men, and had them decently
interred; and then such portions of the equipage
and charts as were worth removal were taken to the
ship. The camp at Shelburne Bay was not visited.
The coast was very diligently searched, but no traces of
the missing men found. Escape River was then examined. Jackey was able to indicate the precise spot
where the papers were secreted, and they were found,
but much damaged and almost illegible. Jackey also
pointed out every spot connected with the tragic end of
Mr. Kennedy, and the truth of his identifications was
borne out in every case. He brought them to the spot
where Kennedy died, but the grave had been disturbed,
and the body was not found. Poor Jackey shed many
tears as he recognised the place, and his feelings
against the natives were so bitter, that he was anxiously
looking out for some to be revenged upon. His recollection of every place was so acute, that he would point
out places in the scrub where he had thrown things
away, and they were always found. These were the
only results of the visit of the *Freak*. The fate of the
three men left at Shelburne Bay is a mystery to this
day.

Thus ended this disastrous expedition. Kennedy

was an able and courageous explorer ; but, probably, he was not strict enough as a disciplinarian. All accounts agree in stating that the provisions were wasted on the first part of the journey, and to this is owing all the misfortunes. If the catastrophe was then, in any measure, due to Kennedy, it is a consolation to think that the fault proceeded from his generosity and kindness of heart. All his men loved him, and he earned their affection by his disinterestedness. They, one and all, believed that he would have freely given his life to save theirs; and having fully examined all that has been said by those who knew him well, I can well believe that they were right.

180

CHAPTER XI.

ROE, GREGORY, AND FITZGERALD IN WESTERN AUSTRALIA.

THE experience of so many different explorers in Western Australia had not, as yet, discouraged the inhabitants. As soon as failure was reported in one direction, they lost no time in trying another; and as long as any promising part of the country remained unvisited, they were always sanguine in their hopes of discovering good tracts of country. Unfortunately, however, there remained now few directions in which an expedition could proceed. The west coast, north of Perth, had been pretty minutely examined; and the reader has already been told that the results were not very encouraging. To the south, the country was known—too well known, indeed, to leave much room for hope. But there was still, it must be admitted, a great deal of exploration to be done. To the east of King George's Sound, the country was quite unknown, unless from the scanty details brought in by Mr. Eyre. There was a very good reason also for exploring in this direction. Mr. Eyre had crossed a good many small streams, and had found some very fair country; but, more important than all, he had seen a fine range of mountains, named by him the Russell Range; and it was considered certain that such a range must have a good deal of available land in its vicinity. It was in this direction, therefore, that the Government determined to send an exploring party.

The command of it was given to Mr. Roe, then surveyor-general of the colony. He had been with King on the north coast, and, as already stated, was concerned in nearly every exploration that was made at the first settlement of the colony of Swan River. Though little known to the public, he is the oldest living explorer, and certainly takes rank as one of the most eminent. His party, on this journey, consisted of six persons and eleven horses, carrying provisions for about four months.

The expedition started from York, in West Australia, on the 14th September, 1848; and took its final departure on the 17th, from Nalyaring, the furthest settlement in the district. The course was east and south, as intermediate between tracts of country previously explored; and it was intended to proceed to Cape Riche, and from there along the most favourable line to the Russell Range. They soon found, after leaving the settlement, that the limit of the grass country had been passed, and had to pass over the usual sand plains of *Eucalyptus* thickets, so often described in connection with this part of Australia. At thirty-four miles inland, they met with a tribe of natives, who, though at first alarmed and suspicious, soon became friendly and useful. They showed several springs of water, extending fifty miles to the boundary of their own country. At this time, the party had descended from an elevated tract of sandy plains covered with low scrubby vegetation, and were threading a vast chain of small shallow salt lagoons in a wide scrubby valley evidently connected with the river Avon. It came from the south-east, in which direction the natives

said the ground was poor and worthless; so Roe left it,
and proceeded eastward. But a worse country met him
in that direction. He could see a desert for, at least,
twenty miles in advance; evidently, a part of that
hideous scrub which lined the east side of the colony.
There was nothing to be gained by trying to push
through such a region, so he turned to the south-west,
towards the Stirling Range.

At the end of twenty-five miles, the party recrossed
the salt lakes of the Avon valley, and gradually
ascended an elevated tract of sand plains, which supply
the tributaries of the rivers flowing down on to the west
coast. On this tract, the air was sharp and keen, due to
an elevation of about two thousand feet above the sea
level. The party found the temperature particularly
disagreeable; especially as they were exposed to a
biting south-west wind, often driving up heavy storms
of hail. From the tableland they descended to the
southward, through very thick country, or scrubby
sand plains. They forced their way through these, and
in lat. 33° 16′, met an intricate and wide valley,
evidently a watercourse, though it now contained only
scattered salt-pools. This was considered to be part of
the Buchanan River, which was only known to about
eighty miles from here. Further south, the country
continued poor and unpromising for fifty-five miles, and
very difficult for the men to force a way through. At
last, they emerged upon the waters of the south coast,
with abundance of both water and grass. From this,
they were not long in reaching a settlement, where
they rested the famished horses for a time; and, in the
meantime, made preparations for the second part of
their journey.

On the 18th of October, they commenced ascending
the Pallinup River. This, it will be remembered, was
the last stream crossed by Eyre in his journey to
Albany. It was a fine river where the party commenced ascending, coming in long reaches from the
north-east, amid fine grassy banks. At seven miles,
they quitted the main river, and ascended a north-
easterly branch. This flowed between red and white

sandstone cliffs; but with no signs of coal, though
search was made for it at every section. The river
suited the explorers in every respect but one, and that
was, that its direction was from the west of north. The
valley was so wide and so well grassed, that the explorers left it with regret; especially as the rocks had
changed to trap, and gave every indication of further
improvement. They now, however, steered north-east,
and crossed several good streams running to the south
through grassy valleys. All indicated that the coal
formation had now ceased, and in its place there were
sheets of granite and quartz spreading out in bare
masses on the surface. They passed over a ridge of
this on the 22nd, and then were gladdened by a view of
a large tract of good grassy country to the north-east,
lightly timbered, and at this time well watered by
a river with numerous branches. They descended for
two and a half miles, by a well grassed valley, with
beautiful lightly wooded hills and slopes on both sides.
But the water of the river gave a sad commentary on
the appearance of a fertile season. It was a little
brackish, but showed a rank salt vegetation in the
pools of granite rock. Yet, grasses of the best description filled the valley and covered the gently swelling
hills on each side, and, altogether, the soil was promising
and fertile.

On the 23rd, Roe followed a branch which led to
the north-east; but at four miles the grass and water
diminished so much as to render its further exploration
unimportant. He left it, and proceeded on his course.
The land soon became poor and scrubby, and they
encamped late on a chain of salt and brackish pools,
dipping east in an almost level country. One cannot
help sighing over the prospects of a colony, where the
smallest amount of fertility is thus in a moment
succeeded by so much that is arid and worthless. It
seems as if the scrub waited like a beast of prey upon
explorers directly they emerged from the poor comforts
of a valley of brackish and salt pools.

Following down these pools, on the 24th, they soon
reached a continuous river of brackish water, between

banks of granite or sand, twenty to thirty yards apart.
It flowed to the south-east, over open scrubby plains.
The explorers would have gone further this day, but
heavy rain came up from the south-east, and continued
the whole of the day following. When they resumed
their north-east course, they passed over worthless
sandy downs, divided here and there by belts of scrub,
which only an axe could find a passage through. The
country was high and level; the watercourses had disappeared, and in their place were many small salt or
samphire lakes. This was the only place Roe could
find to camp upon, with nothing but brackish water for
the horses, and coarse rushes for them to eat. But they
soon had better water and rather more abundantly than
they wished. They were visited by a very severe
thunderstorm; which seemed, says Roe, to vent the
whole of its force in the midst of the little party. The
lightning darted through and amid the tents in fearful
flashes, and the thunder was deafening.

On the 27th, the salt lakes and swamps increased in
number and size as they proceeded north-east; but after
four miles, they ceased, and the route lay up a long
ascent to a more elevated country, poor, and covered
with dense scrubs. Thick showers greatly confined the
view of the party; but the surrounding land seemed of
the same description. Whilst despairing of being able
to feed the horses, they suddenly came upon a small
fresh lake, in a clump of trees, surrounded by good
grass. They gladly encamped there, having come upwards of sixteen miles without seeing grass, or any
water, except the rain. Fourteen miles beyond this
oasis, another was discovered; but it was like its predecessor, of very small extent. Mr. Roe would have
staid a day or two at the second, for the purpose of
drying his provisions, which were thoroughly soaked by
the rain : but, after the first night, every bit of available
grass had been eaten off by the horses. So they moved
forward again. In a short distance, the highest part of
the sandy plain was attained; and this gave them, for
the first time, a view over the country in advance. It
was not encouraging. The same sandy desert seemed

to continue as far as they could see. The plains were undulating, and only diversified by dark lines marking the thick belts of scrub. There were, however, two exceptions to the general monotony. There was a granite hill, named Mount Madden, to the east; and some white sandy lakes, evidently salt, to the north-west. It was determined to proceed to the Mount, and from its summit ascertain the nature of the ground further east.

The way to the hill was no exception to the general sterility of this wretched country. Here and there, the sand was broken through by large sheets of granite, which seemed like patches of the under-lying rock which had resisted decomposition better than the rest. They often contained small pools of rain-water, and were surrounded by a bright green fringe of velvet moss; but this was the only mark of verdure they bore; in other respects they were as barren as the desert. A long and fatiguing march through close thickets, or soft boggy land, brought the party to the base of the mountain mass of red granite. Again, a view to the east gave the usual cheerless result. There seemed to be not the slightest improvement; on the contrary, the country became worse.

To describe one day of the journey, for some time after, is to describe it all. The party kept on through sand, thickets, dry watercourses, and dry salt lakes. At first, they found small quantities of grass and water; but these soon failed, and they reached a depression or salt basin, where only salt water was to be had. This was on the 2nd of November, and they had been steering towards a range of hills which appeared to promise springs. Of course, they had to press forward to them in all haste. They reached them after sunset, and were greatly disappointed to find them only a collection of loose stones and trap rocks. They found their way, at once, to a deep valley beyond. The darkness and almost impracticable thicket soon obliged them to halt, and they tied their horses up to trees, without water or grass for them. The range was a succession of steep, narrow ridges, densely covered with scrub and small

timber, but no grass. The soil was coloured a deep red
by the ironstone at the surface; but the rock was principally trap and quartz. This description seemed to be
applicable to the whole range, which extended six miles
north-west. The view, says Mr. Roe, was very much
confined by the thickness of the wood, and the setting
sun was glaring like burnished gold on some water to
the west, which was evidently a continuation of the salt
lakes already passed. The range was named the
Bremer Range.

With difficulty, sufficient water was found for the
animals on the 3rd. It was obtained partly by digging
and partly from a small pool upon the road. But still
there was no grass of any kind, and the horses could
not subsist much longer without something to eat : food
for them was, therefore, the first consideration now.
There appeared but little prospect of obtaining it upon
a more northerly route ; and as there was a great salt
valley on the south, Roe steered south-east towards a
peak of granite, which was about twenty-eight miles
distant. Anxiously they watched their progress towards
it, as they felt sure it would afford them pasture enough
to rest their exhausted limbs for a day or two. But
every effort to make the stage in one day failed. They
had travelled twenty-four miles by sunset, but then the
horses gave up. The poor, famished animals were
unable to proceed further up a continued ascent, and
Roe was obliged again to halt them amid coarse rushes
and scrub. Their existence seemed to depend upon
finding water on the morrow.

Next morning they commenced their ascent. The
summit was reached at last, but with it a cruel disappointment : there was no grass. Despair gave new
vigour to the search, and they at last found both water
and feed on the northern side of the mountains. They
were named Fitzgerald Peaks, and the party encamped
upon them for several days : the highest was elevated
about a thousand feet above the level of the plains, and
gave an extensive view : it was a very sad one indeed.
In every direction lay spread out one vast sea of dark
scrub and thicket, intersected by broad belts of salt lakes

and samphire marshes, the only exception being the
Bremer Range, and another somewhat further off in the
north-east. Roe says that he felt anxious to proceed to
the latter; but that when he examined its character
through a telescope, and glanced over the intermediate
character, remembering that the horses had been five
days without grass before they reached their camp, he
dared not risk such a journey. On the 9th of November they again launched out into the frowning sea of
scrub, and soon came upon a country whose barrenness
fully came up to what it appeared at a distance. They
struggled with this formidable country for three days,
and by forced marches accomplished a distance of fifty
miles from the peaks, but their position became every
day more perilous. The party became entangled in a
very extensive series of salt lakes and marshes, one
false move amongst which would have proved its entire
destruction. They fortunately came upon a patch of good
grass, but the horses were sadly distressed for want of
water, which had only been met with once since leaving
Fitzgerald Peaks. It was now found to be quite impossible to continue the exploration further eastward
until the animals could be recruited. For this purpose,
therefore, Roe steered to the south. No improvement
took place at first; but soon the land seemed to get
lower, and there was a mountain to the south-east. But
it was at least thirty miles away, and the intervening
scrub seemed as bad as any they had passed.

The journey to Mount Ridley was a terrible one.
The horses were got along with the utmost difficulty,
and all efforts to get water for them had to be resorted
to. During the night, dew and rain were collected on
plates and pannikins, but this scanty supply could not
save two from giving up long before the hill was
passed. As they went along they passed many salt
lakes, and into these the horses would dash and drink
before they could be prevented. After four days
and three nights without water, they encamped once
more upon a verdant spot. One of the horses
was brought on next day, but in so exhausted a condition that they were obliged to rest another day to

restore him.   This was an unfortunate circumstance, as
the grass round Mount Ridley was scanty and poor,
and there was a probability of getting better at some
hills which appeared twenty-five or thirty miles further
eastward.   Mount Ridley was a huge mass of granite,
about seven hundred feet above the plains, and the view
was but little different from what had been seen before.
Several hills, like the mount, were visible to the south
and east, and the dark scrub spread all round, only
broken by chains of salt lakes and samphire flats.   The
horizon was as level as the ocean, only more dark and
gloomy looking.

On the 15th they started again; but at fifteen miles
one horse gave in and would move no further.   They
gave him a portion of the water they carried, and two
men (Messrs. Ridley and Gregory) remained with him,
while Roe pushed on for a granite hill, rising like an
island out of the salt lake, and thickets, about nine
miles away.   With a star for their guide, they groped
their way after dark through the thick brushwood.   They
reached the hill about nine o'clock, and turned the tired
horses loose, to find the best feed they could.   Water
they had already passed through in thick tea-tree
swamps, and next morning an excellent spring was
found at the eastern foot of the hill, amid splendid and
luxuriant grass.   Soon after they had camped, the
absentees arrived, but the horse they had been obliged
to leave behind, about four miles away.   The attempt
to bring him on was renewed, but at night he was still
a quarter of a mile from the grass, and could not be
advanced until next morning.   Such a specimen as this
of the state of the animals gives one a good idea of the
nature of the country.

The Russell Range was still fifty miles distant,
and from this hill its lofty and rugged outline was dis-
cernible.   Although so near, there was no mistaking
the country which intervened.   Need the features be
again repeated of a desert land, as inhospitable as any
the sun ever shone upon. But this was worse than what
had preceded, for there were no more granite hills
between, and even the misty range caused a doubt as

to the nature of that huge mass of rock which rose so abruptly out of the sea of scrub. The whole horizon between this range and Mount Ridley was unbroken by a single hill, though it seemed to ascend gradually to the north, covered with salt lakes and scrub. Here, on the evening of the 17th, they could see the fiery flashes of the Aurora Australis, extending over the silent desert, and its peculiar mystic character looked doubly curious amid a haze which hid the scintillations, and made the scene around glare as if illumined by a conflagration.

Into the scrub they again launched on the 18th, leaving the tired horse to be taken up as they returned. They had not overrated the obstacles before them. The track was at first more open, and they hoped for better travelling. But as they persevered in their way to a small granite hill, numerous salt lakes again obtruded their unwelcome presence, fringed by thickets, so closely and densely matted together, as to require the use of the axes to make a road for the horses. When they reached the granite hill there was neither feed nor water upon it. The latter was got by digging; but in place of feed they were obliged to tether the animals among the rushes, and let them do their best. In working onwards through the scrub next day, they came suddenly upon a native camp. It had been abandoned on the approach of the party, so hastily, indeed, that the natives had left behind their weapons and their food. This was not the only time that the party had seen traces of natives; and one cannot help thinking that there must be some better land near, or they never would have been found at all in such a place.

Although the country continued as thickly clothed with scrubs as ever, it lost its generally flat character. Fresh water had lodged in no less than three places met with this day, and the salt lakes seem to have been left behind. But the scrubs became thicker than ever. They encamped on the 19th without grass or water, and the hungry horses consumed the bark off every tree and the top off every bush within their reach; some of them even ate the dry sticks under their feet. Six

miles further next day brought them to a nice patch of
grass; but it was only a temporary respite. Next day
again they could find neither water nor feed, while they
had still twenty miles of scrub between themselves and
the Russell Range. Mr. Roe gives a fearful description
of the hardships which followed. He says that he,
with much anxiety, climbed a hill, which showed the
route before them; and as he looked towards it he turned
over in his mind the long list of the horses which he
feared would never have strength to reach the range.
Granite hills were abundant to the southward within
the same distance, but he cared nothing for them; and
to the north the interminable scrub frowned upon him.
The only relief in their route was a granite hill, about
sixteen miles away. To this he went in all haste. The
poor horses staggered up to their saddles with de-
spondency in their aspect, and seemed to upbraid the
men with their treatment. Roe would gladly have
examined the difficulties before he put the animals to
face the scrub; but he tells us that in so fearful a
country delays were utterly inadmissible; and to have
halted the party would have doomed it to destruction.

Travelling now became difficult in the extreme.
To avoid sapling thickets twelve to fifteen feet high, so
closely packed that axes only could have opened a
passage, they were compelled to deviate a good deal,
and force through easier scrubs. Yet even these were
so thick that at three or four feet away no part of a
horse could be seen, and the greatest care was necessary
to keep them close together, and in line. But this could
not last long. Half way to the hill four of the horses
gave up. Roe determined, in consequence, to abandon
the provisions for a time, and to push on, to save the
animals. While unloading them they seemed to revive,
so he made another effort, and reached the hill that
night; but only to increase the embarrassment of his
position. There was no grass and no water on the
spot; and now that the animals had been exhausted in
pushing on to reach thus far, it was difficult to say
what to do. The Russell Range was only four miles away;
it rose as a naked mass of rock, six hundred feet above

the level of the surrounding plains, and not a sign of
verdure was to be seen upon it. As there was no time
to deliberate, they made for the nearest part of the
range.   The bush was more open, and the horses
staggered through it with less difficulty, but the utmost
exertion was necessary to prevent them lying down.
As they proceeded, the range appeared more fertile,
and it was the greatest possible relief to all to find
themselves soon upon a patch where both grass and
water were abundant.

The party remained four days upon the Russell
Range. It was found to be in lat. 33° 27'. It consisted of narrow ridges of sharp rocks of gneiss, intersected by quartz veins and deep fissures, as if the
mountain chain were breaking up.   The view all
around gave no new hopes of a better country less
irreclaimably sterile than it had proved hitherto to be.
All around the dark brown foliage of the scrub lay
like a gloomy drapery, keeping the earth from the
sunlight.   In the south alone the prospect was broken.
In that direction the distant ocean could be seen,
extending in a heaving outline, fringed by the arid
sand dunes, and relieved here and there by the thin
columns of smoke from native fires, which curled into
the air, like a protest against the lifeless stillness on
every side. It was useless thinking to advance further
into such a region. Whatever hopes had been formed
of the Russell Range they were now destroyed, and
Roe prepared to return to Cape Riche by a more
southerly route, for the purpose of intercepting or
examining any stream that might fall upon the south
coast.

The course was, therefore, south-west. As they
proceeded, the soil and vegetation improved, and there
was game to be found at times. There were fresh-water
lakes, and always sufficient grass for a camp. Fragments of oolitic and variegated limestone strewed the
surface, and the same rock formed the basis of the low
rocky ridges which traversed the level country between
the granite hills. The latter were usually bare masses of
granite or gneiss, three to five hundred feet above the sur-

rounding plains, from which a sloping platform ascended
for half a mile to the base of the bare rock. These
hills were frequently rent for their whole length by
fissures some three feet wide, either open or filled with
the *débris* of decomposed rock.

In returning, Mr. Roe was able to send for the
abandoned horse, and when it was brought to camp he
went with the whole party to Esperance Bay. From
thence he journeyed along the coast, and his route was
not of much interest, neither did it differ very much
from that of Mr. Eyre. To the west of the bay the party
crossed several streams of brackish water running into
salt swamps. These were the first watercourses met
with for four hundred miles, the surface water of the
country, when running at all, being found in small
melon-holes or circular spaces five or ten yards in
diameter. From Esperance Bay to Recherché Archi-
pelago, salt lakes were of frequent occurrence immediately behind the sand-hills of the coast.

On the 13th they met the first of a series of rivers
which they crossed in their passage towards Cape
Riche. They were none of them important streams;
and though some had grassy banks and fine fresh
water-holes, yet they extended no distance into the interior. Near their mouths the red sandstone or coal
formation made its appearance; but though every
search was made for the coal shales, none could be seen.
Thus it was with the rivers Gore and Lort, Young and
Stokes' Inlet, in all of which promising indications of
coal were found. After this, the coast turned to the
south-west; and to avoid the windings, Roe struck
west for Cape Barren, where the native guide told him
a large river would be crossed. The river was found
as predicted on the 20th. It was a very important
though grassy stream of good width. Descending its
steep and rugged slope, the party encamped in the
midst of a valley half a mile wide, with very luxuriant
grass all round. The scenery was rich and beautiful;
and after their long experience of scrubs and sand they
were never tired of gazing upon it. It was, however,
limited; and the effect was chiefly produced by the

abutment into the rich, grassy valley, of several small
projections from the higher land, composed entirely of
fragments of red sandstone, quartz, and thin scales of
micaceous sandstone, of every hue and colour. These
projections, and the grassy ravines between, were beautifully dotted with Acacia and small ornamental trees;
and above all rose a dense mass of dark-green foliage,
painfully reminding the explorers of the terrible thickets
they had passed through.

This river, which was named the Phillips, was
found to contain a good deal of coal shale; but time
did not admit the search for the coal itself, because the
native guide stated that the real beds would be found
on a river further westward. Before proceeding to it,
the course of the Phillips was explored as far as the
means of the party would admit. It was found to come
from the west of north, with many tributaries, some of
which cut their channel through high and perpendicular
sandstone cliffs. The other river, the Fitzgerald, was
reached on the 26th. It wound to the southward, in a
very tortuous course, at the bottom of a steep valley,
three-quarters of a mile wide. Here occurred the
white-streaked and coloured sandstones similar to those
on the Phillips. Climbing to the edge of one of the
cliffs, a complete section of the formation was to be seen.
The cliff was a hundred and fifty feet in height, and
in the soft, underlying, white sandstone, caverns were
excavated by the atmosphere, which gave a peculiar
appearance to the view. The surface of this country
was very rugged, and Roe was glad to travel southward to more even soil, by following the edge of the
valley. The sandstone cliffs made the scenery very
fine, but the scrub was far too thick for it to be agreeable to the travellers. When they got down into the
vale it was found to be composed of granite on one
side, and the high sandstone cliffs on the other. There
were horsetracks in it, and these were supposed to
belong to a Mr. Drummond, who was out botanizing
and exploring on behalf of the Government. Very
near these tracks extensive beds of coal were found in
the lowest levels of the channel. The portion exposed to

view was twelve to fifteen yards wide, and sixty-one in length, the further parts being concealed by loose drift-sand, covered with the thick scrub, which occupied the whole of the valley.   Mr. Ridley afterwards found among this scrub another flat bed of even better-looking coal, eighty yards long and six feet wide.   It seemed to lie horizontally, but the dip was found to be the same as that of the shales in the Phillips River.   From the description of Mr. Roe, however, it would seem to be doubtful whether these beds were anything more than brown or tertiary coal.   He says its appearance was that of carbonized wood, some pieces of which were scarcely converted to coal, and the bitumen was found in elongated pieces of various sizes.   But the coal burnt with a good flame, was easily converted to gas, and left only a white ash.   The river was here two or three hundred yards wide, between very steep banks, filled either with rank grass or very thick scrub.   Many marks of flood were visible to the height of at least twenty feet.

This discovery of coal seemed so important to Mr. Roe that he at once explored down the river.   He found that the stream terminated in an estuary, and this contracted to the width of about a quarter of a mile.   It was choked up by a dry bar of fine white sand, at least three hundred yards across to the sea rollers. From appearances within this bar, and from the general absence of marine shells on the shores of the estuary, it seemed that the sea seldom or never broke into it. The coast was composed of sand dunes and sandstone cliffs, and the land in front was swampy and thickly covered with tea trees.   The river was not navigable, even for boats, six miles above the bar, and there was about eight miles of rugged country between that point and the coal.   A small tributary of the stream was discovered in these examinations, and it was named the Elwes, after the lady of Governor Fitzgerald.

Leaving the river on the 30th December, the party entered on an extensive level flat of kangaroo grass. Beyond this they emerged from the valley of the river by ascending one of its western tributaries.   The country was then extremely rugged, rocky, and scrubby.

At the end of five miles they crossed over a poor, sandy ridge at the source of this branch, and then crossed two others belonging to a different stream, which seemed to have its exit to the sea by a break in the coast hills three or four miles to the southward. In the most westerly of these branches they crossed a briny salt stream in pools at the foot of some sandstone cliffs, commencing ninety feet below the general surface of the country. In three miles further they reached open gravelly sand-plains, covered with heathy vegetation.

The rest of the journey over this tableland need not be entered into. What has already been said describes the whole. They were keeping along the coast, and therefore frequently met with river valleys and craggy inlets; but with these exceptions the course was over a scrubby or heathy tableland. Mr. Roe made one excursion on to the beach again, to look for any further signs of the coal shales. But he found nothing but granite rock. As he came back his route lay across one of those barren wastes of drift sand so common on all the Australian coast, where the surface is kept continually moving onward by the prevailing wind. On this occasion the entire sand-patch was in motion, enveloped in a cloud of dust, drifting along like smoke. While crossing such a dismal scene, Roe and his guide came suddenly upon the skeleton of a human being, reposing upon a limestone slab, about two hundred yards behind the beach. The native immediately explained that he was one of three seamen who had quitted a whaler some eighteen months previously. The vessel was anchored near Middle Island, at least three hundred and fifty miles from Albany. This was one of two who died of thirst on the journey, while the third reached a settlement near Cape Riche. The body had evidently been much disturbed by native dogs; and, as it lay there withering on the sand, it formed a practical commentary on the nature of the surrounding country, and seemed quite in keeping with its desolation.

This was the last "adventure," properly speaking, of the expedition. From the camp where Roe had left

o 2

his companions, to the Pallinup River, and from thence
to the settled districts, easy stages were made.   Before
returning to the Swan, Mr. Roe made some further
explorations amid the sources of the rivers which flow
from the tableland down upon the west coast; but
they resulted in no important discovery, and did no
more than increase the knowledge of the interior tableland.   For the sake of the colony of Western Australia
it is also to be regretted that the more the land became
known the worse its reputation became.   On the
2nd February the party arrived at Perth.   The result
of the expedition is best summed up in Mr. Roe's words.
The explorers had traversed nearly eighteen hundred
miles of country ; and although, from the nature of the
interior, no great addition had been made to the land
available to the colony, much useful geographical knowledge had been obtained of a country almost unknown
previously.   Independent of this, the coal seams, and
the timber forest found on the tableland, were thought
to be a valuable addition to the resources of the
country, provided that the nature of the surrounding
country would not prevent settlement.

This, then, was the result of the expedition to the
Russell Range ; but it was far from being the only
effort made about that time by the colonists.   When
Mr. Roe was starting to the westward, another expedition was fitted out to explore to the northward—that is
to say, the favourable country about the Gascoyne
River, which had been so highly spoken of by Grey
in 1839.   Such unremitting efforts on the part of the
colony is a very good commentary on the state to which
it was reduced in struggling against its physical disadvantages.   This is alluded to forcibly in the instructions
issued to Mr. A. C. Gregory, to whom the command of
the expedition was given.   He was directed to proceed
to the Gascoyne, and then, in a southerly direction, to
search for an unnamed river in Sharks Bay, described
by Grey ; but he (Gregory) was to bear in mind that
the primary object of the expedition was the examination of the country for practical purposes by practical
men, and that the discovery of pasture land was of

paramount importance, on which the interests, and perhaps the fate, of the colony depended. The expedition consisted of six men in all, with twelve horses, and three months' provisions.

On the 9th September, the party started from the furthest settlement, about eighty miles from Perth. They steered north-west for the first twenty miles, and then entered the extensive grassy plains which occupy the whole country between the Moore and Arrowsmith Rivers. The rainy season had scarcely ended, so that they found both water and grass for the horses almost every night; and by the 15th they had reached that part of the river where coal had formerly been discovered. From this they went up the bed, through a steep and rocky valley, with sandstone cliffs often abutting upon the stream. These cliffs were level on the summits, and it seemed as if the stream had been cut down into the tableland, like, in fact, all the streams which flow down from it. The upper stratum is a hard red sandstone, resting on a softer rock of clayey character, beneath which the coal shales lie unconformably, dipping at a very high angle. When the sandstone ceased, the river divided, and granite rocks made their appearance; and this alteration of the tableland was the junction along which Gregory intended to make his journey to the northward, because that line was the most probable one for surface water and rock pools.

For nearly four days the north course was kept without much difficulty; but on the 21st, the level appearance of the country, the denseness of the Acacia thickets, and the scarcity of water, obliged the explorers to turn north-west. They had not gone far in this direction, when they got an extensive view from a scrubby sand ridge. No hill nor valley could be seen in advance; nothing but an immense thicket of Acacia and Cypress, lying unbroken on the ground, as if it were a coat of paint. This disheartening view made them turn to the west, because it became very necessary to reach the heads of some of the coast streams ere the party suffered much for want of water. Fortunately, they met in this direction a small native well, and this enabled them to reach the Murchison River. But not without difficulty. The scrubs were thicker than usual, and cost tremendous labour to force a passage through. The Murchison had ceased to run. Its channel was fifty yards wide, and the bed steep and rocky. Where crossed it ran over a dyke of trap rock. What water there was lay in long shallow pools, with samphire upon the banks. The valley was wide, and very poor, while sandy plains and scrub surrounded it on both sides.

The discovery of this river enabled Gregory to try a north course again, because the country was certainly more open. After passing sandy plains, and between sandy ridges, only lightly covered with scrub, the scenery reassumed its old repulsive character. By the aid of some burnt patches, Gregory was enabled to penetrate the scrub to some distance; but he had to camp without water. He then went west. The trees opened out a little, and he went north again. But the same result ensued. The thicket became impassable; and when a view could be obtained, there was the same cheerless prospect in advance for miles and miles, with a surface as level as the sea. It is needless to give more than the result of the exertions that were made for the next few days. All that could have been done to get further north was done; but the country was utterly impracticable. Not in one place alone, but in every direction, a thicket like a wall obstructed further progress; and this could be seen extending as far beyond as the southern limit of Sharks Bay. By a great effort, and at much loss to the horses, they reached lat. 27°, or about three hundred and fifty miles north of Perth; but this was the limit of the expedition, and they returned, very much dispirited, to the Murchison River.

The next plan was to explore the stream to its mouth; and when the men had returned to a favourable spot, Gregory formed a depôt, and went with one companion to examine the sources. As they went up it, they found the channel averaging one hundred yards

in width, full of rocks, small trees, and sandbanks, with
many shallow, brackish pools of water, few of which
seemed likely to withstand the heat of summer.   On
the first day they came upon a party of natives, five of
whom came up, and followed the explorers.   No
information could be got from them.   When spoken to
in the York dialect, they only mimicked the words, and
evidently could not understand a syllable.

When the red sandstone rock disappeared, granite
took its place, and the country became quite level.   It
was covered with one universal thicket of Acacia and
Cypress, except in the valley of the Murchison.   This
was only a very slight depression, about three miles
wide, with the bed of the stream about one hundred
yards, though evidently being three times that width,
and thirty feet deep in some seasons.   The valley was
not more than one hundred feet deep; and even that
had an Acacia scrub on it, except near the stream, where
there were grassy flats, well lined with gum trees.
The only rising ground seen was about sixty miles from
the camp.   From its summit the explorers had a very
cheerless view, and as no alteration seemed to take place
in the river as far as the eye could reach, Gregory
returned to his companions.   He was of opinion that
the river took its rise in distant salt lakes to the eastward; and this surmise was borne out by Austin's
discoveries in 1854, to be mentioned very shortly.
The only discovery of importance on this river was the
existence of a lode of Galena, found not very far from
the depôt while Gregory was away to the eastward.
This seemed a valuable fact; and with no other result
from their journey to the northward, the party now
prepared to examine the coast country on their way
home.

The land round the Moresby Range and Mount
Fairfax first claimed their attention.   It will be remembered how much the character of this tract had been
disputed.   It had been very much praised by Grey,
who first discovered it; but this report was quite contradicted by Captain Stokes, who spoke in the most
desponding terms of the quality of the soil.   Gregory

now contradicted him again. Like Grey, he had just come from a desert, and could appreciate the slightest improvement. He thought he had found grassy land enough to relieve all the wants of the colony. There were, he considered, 225,000 acres of pastoral land, near Champion Bay, to say nothing of 100,000 acres of agricultural land upon the Arrowsmith. This certainly was a very encouraging result for the expedition; but the practical commentary on it all is, that the country remains unoccupied.

There were many other explorations in this neighbourhood before, and therefore we need not follow Gregory's expedition further. The party returned to Perth on the 17th November, having travelled over fifteen hundred miles in ten weeks. Altogether, the results were considered satisfactory, and the exploration a successful one, though it had failed in reaching as far as it was intended to do. What caught the public attention most of all was the mineral discovery on the Murchison River, and this, it was at once deemed desirable, to investigate further. Governor Fitzgerald determined to proceed to Champion Bay by sea, and, by means of horses taken with him, to cross over to the mineral deposit. With this view, he sailed from Freemantle on the 3rd December, accompanied by Mr. Gregory, Mr. Bland, and three soldiers of the 96th Regiment. By the 7th, the lead vein was reached. It was found to be far more important than it was at first believed. It was traced for three hundred and twenty yards along the bed of the river, which was nearly dry. On clearing the sand and loose stones from the surface, the width appeared to vary from eight to twenty-four inches in width, with an average of twelve, dipping from the horizon at an angle of 80°. Throughout the whole length it appeared to be one solid mass of Galena, the northern end being lost at a vein of schistose rock, which intersected the adjacent strata. To the south the lode was covered by several feet of sand, and the whole included by the banks of the river, and mostly covered by shallow water. Some traces of copper were seen. The rock on each side of the vein was a hard compact gneiss, abounding with garnets of good colour, but full of flaws. The dip of the beds was nearly perpendicular, and to the westward.

On the 9th, they set out to return to Champion Bay. When they were crossing the Bowes River, on the 11th, they saw several natives, who hid themselves at first, but afterwards joined the party. At first they did not exceed ten in number, but they were soon joined by others, and gradually increased to about fifty. They then changed their manner, and began to bring up their spears; but the party kept on resolutely, without heeding them. About six in the morning, the explorers passed to the west of King's Tablehill, and as the country was covered with dense Acacia thickets, the natives took advantage of the ground, and completely surrounded them. They first began to threaten to throw their spears, then to throw stones, and finally one man caught hold of Mr. Bland by the arm, and threatened to strike him with a club; another threw a spear at Gregory. Immediately the governor fired, and killed the foremost of the assailants. A shower of spears was the consequence, one of which went right through Governor Fitzgerald's leg, just above the knee. Notwithstanding this, he continued to direct the party; and although the natives made many attempts to approach again, so as to use their spears with effect, the explorers were enabled, by keeping the open ground, and checking them by an occasional shot, to avoid their attacks. They followed closely for seven miles, after which they were only seen occasionally. The party now reached the beach, and were able to travel more rapidly. One of their ponies knocked up; but in spite of this, they got to Champion Bay that afternoon, and by sunset the whole expedition were on board their vessel again. Just before dark, the natives came down upon the beach, concealing themselves behind the bushes, whilst one man stood unarmed at the water's edge, and called to the sailors to come on shore, no doubt hoping thus to be able to make a sudden attack upon the boat. As this kind invitation was unheeded, no more of the savages was seen, and after dark they slunk quietly away. Next morning the *Champion* sailed for Perth. Fortunately, the governor's wound did not prove very serious, and the result of the expedition was that the colonists had the satisfaction of seeing a flourishing mine shortly afterwards established in working order upon the Murchison River.

CHAPTER XII.

LAKE TORRENS AGAIN, AND A SEARCH FOR LEICHHARDT.

Messrs. Oakden and Hulkes on Lake Torrens—Misgivings about the fate of
Leichhardt—His probable route—Mr. Hely sent—First tidings—Pro-
ceeds to the Maranoa—Dry state of that river—News from the natives—
Story of the murder of Leichhardt's party—Two of his camps discovered.

AFTER the experience of Gregory and Roe, exploration
languished for a little while in Western Australia. It
had died out altogether in New South Wales. Leichhardt was away, and the colonists were anxious to hear
of his return before they did anything more; and in
any case the melancholy fate of poor Kennedy had
quite dispirited them for a time. In South Australia
nothing had been done for some years. Since the
failure of Sturt, the central desert was looked upon as a
complete barrier to further efforts. The colony was
believed to be surrounded on the north by the horseshoe
of Lake Torrens, and that beyond this all was an inhospitable desert. Yet there were some few who did not
accept these conclusions. They believed that if Sturt
had tried the west side of Lake Torrens, his course
would not have been impeded, and he would have found
better country. To try the truth of this problem
seemed the only way to re-open the question of exploration in South Australia.

In 1851, Messrs. Oakden and Hulkes undertook its
elucidation. They started from the head of Spencer's
Gulf, and having got to the west side of Lake Torrens,
explored a great deal of the country. The precise
course they took, or the nature of their discoveries, is
not known. It was a private expedition, and they were
only in search of a sheep-run. It appears, however,

that they found one; and all that we know further is
from the information supplied to the Commissioner of
Crown Lands when they applied for a pastoral licence.
In this application they stated that they had penetrated a good distance to the north-west. They had
discovered a lake of fresh water, not less than five or
six miles in circumference, and of depth sufficient to
confer the deep blue of the ocean. The natives also
gave them an account of other lakes, extending to the
north-west, some of which in size exceeded the one they
had already found. They gave the names of ten such
lakes, which were surrounded by grass, and abounding
with game. They also told of creatures which the
excited imagination of Mr. Hulkes concluded to be
alligators, and another which he suspected to be a
buffalo. Kōkătta was the name applied by the aborigines to the district, and Karndan Yūmbo the lake they
visited. During the journey, two specimens of the
Moloch horridus were found—a lizard of fearful ugli-
ness, which was previously supposed to be confined to
North-West Australia; and Mr. Hulkes concluded from
this, and many other circumstances, that he was on the
verge of a north-west watershed. But fortunately for
his hopes and fears, he was obliged to return at this
point. The water on their run was evaporating, and
the men were very anxious to go back. Besides this,
the horses were knocked up, and could not with safety
be taken any further. Accordingly, Messrs. Oakden
and Hulkes returned, resolving to revisit the locality at
no distant time. This, however, they were unable to
do. The gold diggings were discovered very shortly
afterwards; and for some years subsequently the sand,
and lakes, and plains of Kōkătta were left again to their
solitude.

But what opinion are we to form of these discoveries? I fear we must consider them as of very
trifling importance. The stories of the blacks cannot
be much relied upon at any time; but even if true, we
must suppose them to have referred to the immense salt
lakes which are found to abound in this district. It has
been examined very carefully by many explorers since

then, as the reader will see, and no very favourable opinion arrived at.   There is fresh water on the ground at certain times, just as there is upon the tablelands of Western Australia ; but it only remains for a month or so after the rainy season, and becomes salt as it evaporates.   There are, however, some watercourses, with fine fresh pools in them ; but they are, like the grassy plains, few and far between.   Here and there patches of good grass and better soil may be found, but the general character of the district is sandy, and unable to support any vegetation which would entitle it to be considered a fertile tract.

During this year also occurred the search for Leichhardt, which led to the opinion that he had been murdered by the natives, and his party destroyed. Readers will remember that he was last heard of in April, 1848, and he was then at Mount Abundance, on the Cogoon.   He intended to cross the continent from east to west, but the mode in which he proposed getting over the first portion of his journey was uncertain. Some said that he intended to go first to Peak Downs, to recover some stores left on his return from the second unfortunate expedition.   Others thought that he would follow his outward route as far as Carpentaria, without any deviation.   Those who knew him well gave a very different account.   They said that his firm intention on leaving was to go to the Barcoo of Sir Thomas Mitchell, and running it up to its junction with the Alice, travel up that river in its supposed north-west direction.   He would thus find the watershed of the gulf rivers, and any running to the westward.   There was no occasion for him to go to Peak Downs for stores, as he was amply provided with everything ; so that this explanation of his movements appears to be almost certain.   It was confirmed by the shepherds who had seen him leave the most outlying portion of the settled country, and who stated that he was then going west, and not north.

Three years went by before any great anxiety was felt for his safety.   He had said that he would be two years away ; but by managing his provisions, as he was

known to do, the period might be extended to three.
But about the middle of the year 1851 the colonists
began to be very uneasy about him. Rumours of
various kinds reached Sydney, all of which seemed to
indicate that he had been murdered not very far from
the settled districts; and as time wore on, the absence of
any tidings gave a certain colour to them. At length
the Government equipped a party for the purpose of
following up his tracks. It was placed under the command of an experienced bushman, Mr. Hovenden Hely:
and he was furnished with a party of six, with provisions for twelve months, and the requisite beasts of
burden. The Government did not exactly know what
instruction to give, but thought it better that he should
allow himself to be guided by circumstances. In a
general way, they said that he should proceed from the
Condamine to Peak Range, and search for any record
left there by Leichhardt; but it was not intended that
this course should be followed, if there was a greater
probability of his having adopted another route.

Mr. Hely left Sydney early in 1852. By the
19th February he was at Brisbane, and he then informed
the Government that, from what he had heard, he
thought it best to follow Sir Thomas Mitchell's track
along the Alice, and if he found no traces of the missing party, he should return up the Victoria, and then
run down the Nogoa to the Peak Range. But by the
time he got near the Condamine, he changed his plans
again, in consequence of some very important news
which he received. He was met at Surat (about forty
miles from Mount Abundance) by a stockkeeper, who
had been out collecting cattle. The wild blacks had
informed him that the white men and their horses had
all been killed on a creek, about two hundred miles
west of the mount. They stated that the blacks had
followed on the tracks of the party until they mustered
a sufficient force, then attacked them in the night, killed
all the white men and the horses (as they were hobbled),
also some of the cattle, and plundered the camp. Two
blacks offered to take the stockkeeper and show him
the bones of the men and horses, and also the iron-work

of the saddles, bridles, &c. Hely became so convinced of the truth of this statement that he determined at once to proceed in the direction indicated.

He started with a very light party, and ten weeks' provisions; and to assist his search, he fortunately secured the services of two natives, who professed to know all about the murder. Whether they did or not, they certainly knew all about Leichhardt's movements, for they described with the greatest accuracy the route by which he reached the Maranoa. But their zeal was not at all proportionate to the importance of their information. By the time they had reached Mount Abundance, they said they had gone far enough, that the country was too dry to travel further, and that if they succeeded in doing so the blacks would kill them. Hely, however, thought differently. He determined to push at once to Mitchell's old depôt on the Maranoa. The distance was forty miles, and so dry was the season at that time that not one drop of water could be found between the two places. Nor was the aridity confined to that. The depôt, which Mitchell had described as a fine reach of water and full of fish, was nothing but a dry sandy bed, covered with reeds, and only a shallow pool of brackish water in the middle.

To Hely's surprise, the natives now said that this was the spot, and they pointed out old sheep-bones and tin canisters, left by Mitchell's party, in confirmation of their story. This was a very disappointing result, after having come so far with only a portion of the equipment, and it made the whole story seem like a pure invention. But still the guides persisted in their statement, and now added some circumstances which gave a greater probability to it. They mentioned that only one black fellow had been shot in the encounter, but that not one white had escaped. They accurately described the appearance of the natives in Leichhardt's party, and added further, that the bullocks were still to be found along the course of the river. They said that the murder had taken place a very long time before; so much longer, indeed, that the younger of the two was a mere boy at the time. Yet with all these circumstantial facts, there were doubtful points in the story, and these were confirmed when one of the guides escaped during the same night.

Hely determined to test the accuracy of the statement in every possible way before leaving the locality. He searched every bend and reach for four or five miles up and down the river, but without finding any trace, not even a mark upon a tree. It is true that the blacks thought they could see tracks of a number of cattle or horses, but these were very indistinct, and could not be followed for any distance. When five days had been spent in the search, the remaining guide suddenly altered his story. He said that the other had deceived them, and that the scene of the murder was still many miles distant. He explained the previous deceit by saying his companion did not like to show the bones of the murdered men, because if he did the natives would kill him, but if they proceeded at once, the locality could be easily pointed out.

Upon this new turn in their affairs, Mr. Hely followed his guide again. On the second day, they met fresh cattle tracks; and on the third day, a black fellow and an old woman, who repeated the story of the massacre, and volunteered to go with the party. Hely now struck to the north-west. The lubra said that it was seven days' journey to the place where the saddles and guns were, and that they would find plenty of water. In this respect her story was certainly not true. The country was as dry as it could possibly be, and when the party got to the Warrego, its bed seemed as if it had not had water in it for a very long time. On the 25th June, two more native women were met, who repeated the story as usual. They said that the place was four days' journey away, and that if Hely would meet them next morning, a little distance from the camp, they would take them to some blacks who would show them the place. But on going to the rendezvous, they were not to be found, and Hely was obliged reluctantly to track them and bring them along by force. They seemed much distressed; and then one offered to shorten the journey very much, and to take

them to the place that evening. She brought them
through a Brigalow scrub to a small water-hole, and
told them that was the spot. When asked what had
become of the saddles and guns spoken of, she said that
a big flood had carried them away. Her account of
the murder was very minute. She said she had been
there; that the black fellows had followed the whites
for several days, and that the natives, who were as
numerous as ants, formed a large circle, and gradually
closed up upon the white camp. That just at dawn, all
the whites being asleep, the blacks rushed on them and
speared them as they lay. Only one white man awoke,
and he fired his gun once, shooting a black fellow, but
that he was immediately killed; and that the black
fellow who was wounded went away and died in the
bush. That previous to this, the blacks had, in the
early part of the night, driven away the stock, but that
some of the cattle got away. That for a long time
afterwards there were quart pots, pint pots, red shirts,
axes, and other things in the blacks' camp, but that
now they were all gone. She persisted, however, in
saying that the whole scene happened on the spot she
indicated.

This Hely was able to contradict from personal
observation. About ten miles lower down he found an
old camp of Leichhardt, marked L, with the letters
X V A cut inside it. That it was a camp there could
be no doubt, for there were also the tent-poles and forks,
and the heavy saplings upon which he had placed his
packs, and even the forked sticks and cross pieces in
front of the fire. There was evidence also that the
weather was very wet at the time.

Near the camp, other native women were found,
who repeated the old story. Hely was in the habit of
detaining every black, and he had now in camp nine
native women. His object in keeping them was to
prevent the men leaving the neighbourhood; and
accordingly, finding that they could not get away, an
old lubra took them to the native camp upon the 29th.
On going up to it, the inmates repeated the same story,
but said that the place was three days' journey away.

Two of them very readily agreed to accompany Hely, so all the women were allowed to go.

Travelling with them for about fifteen miles, on a west-north-west course, they reached a large, deep creek, half-bank high, in lat. 25° 30', long. 146° 45'. The country was magnificent open forest, or rather plains with clumps of trees, and well grassed. From this creek they turned off in an entirely different direction, and now said that the scene of the massacre was eight days' journey distant. Their insincerity was apparent, and they admitted to the interpreter that they really were afraid to show the place. Next day they suddenly disappeared from the camp, and were soon followed by the interpreter, so that Hely was obliged to give up all further hope of finding the missing party.

He was upon the Nivelle of Mitchell when he turned back, and on his return, found another of Leichhardt's camps, marked with the same letters as the former. It was not easy to explain the X V A, but as the letters were repeated in the two camps, they could hardly refer to any date. This could not either have been the scene of the massacre, if such an event ever took place, but Hely had been forty-five miles beyond it, and had searched in every direction, and yet could find no traces of the missing men. Accordingly, he retraced his steps, and reached the Balonne River on the 22nd July, 1852.

Now what are we to believe about this mysterious story of the natives? There certainly does seem a kind of probability about it which makes one inclined to give it some weight; yet there are grave doubts which beset it. Any one familiar with the natives knows their ingenuity in framing a story to meet what they believe you want to hear. Many instances of this might be given, but one occurred very recently, which is very much to the point. Mr. M'Kinlay was sent out to search for traces of Burke and Wills. He met with the grave of one of the party, and the natives assured him that the whole had been murdered. Not one black, but every one, told him the same story, and described the fight in the most circumstantial manner.

yet not one syllable of their narrative was true.   The only fact it was founded upon was the death of one of the party from natural causes, and his burial there. Now certainly there was something very striking in the uniformity of the recital given by the natives to Hely, which was partly borne out by his meeting among them three tomahawks, apparently rudely formed from the plates of saddle-trees.   They appeared to have been made by doubling and hammering together the gullet plates, which were sharpened at one end and fastened into cleft sticks.   But such confirmatory evidence is very questionable.   On the whole, the loss of Leichhardt is so much mixed up with subsequent explorations that I have preferred to treat the question separately as an Appendix, to which the reader is referred for a full statement.

CHAPTER XIII.

AUSTIN IN WESTERN AUSTRALIA.

Gold search in Western Australia—Cowcowing—Salt Lake—Mount Kenneth
—Horses poisoned—Recruit Flats—Mount Margaret—Attempt to reach
Sharks Bay—Dreadful scrub—Fearful sufferings for want of water—
Mount Welcome—The Murchison River—The Geraldine Mine.

WE have already said that exploration languished very
much in Australia for some time after the discovery of
gold. It was natural that it should do so, for apart
from the fact that such a discovery was like a revolu-
tion in the colonies, no men could be found for any such
hazardous employment as exploring while there was a
chance of a fortune on the gold-fields. The first of the
colonies to wake up again to the importance of again
examining the interior was, as usual, the indefatigable
colony of Western Australia. It had not participated
in the auriferous deposits which seemed to spread everywhere else. It was almost far removed enough from
the diggings to be out of reach of its immediate influence. Besides, there was another reason for sending out an exploring party. Gold might yet be found
in the unknown interior. It was known that there
was abundance of quartz, and other favourable indications, and it was considered desirable to know their
nature as soon as possible.

In 1854, an exploring party was sent out by the
Government. It was placed under the command of
Mr. R. Austin, the assistant surveyor-general, and
included, in addition to the leader, nine men, one of
whom was a native. They were provided with twenty-
seven horses, besides provisions and stores for one
hundred and twenty days. It was thought advisable

that the course of the party should be to the north and
east of the settled districts, and then if gold could not be
discovered, there would be at least some chance of
reaching the Gascoyne, and finding good country.
Besides this, they could look for the large inland sheet
of water, named Cowcowing by the natives, which was
supposed to be upon the Gascoyne River. At the
latter place, a vessel was to meet the party, and with
the exception of his being at the rendezvous at the
appointed time, no very definite course was prescribed
to the leader. Two men, with forty days' rations, were
to proceed with the party as far as Cowcowing, and on
their return to report to head-quarters.

On the 10th July, the party left the rendezvous,
which was at Mombekine, fourteen miles north-west of
the town of Northam. They crossed the salt river, or
Short Lake, and travelled thence across a belt of elevated
sandstone conglomerate to extensive *Casuarina* plains.
These were dry, but they retained marks which showed
them to be liable to very considerable inundations, like
all the better class of country in these regions. A low
range separated these plains from others, where the
party made their first camp, in lat. 31° 11', long. 117°.
Having learned from two of the men, who were sent to
the northward, that the country was unfavourable in
that direction, Mr. Austin resumed his course to the
east. They travelled six miles, over undulating sand
plains, to a spring on the north side of a large salt lake.
This was ten hundred and twenty-five feet above the
level of the sea, and so very densely wooded that it
was necessary to leave the cart with the natives, who
followed, and make a *détour* to the northward. They
pushed thus over scrubby sand and through dense
thickets until they found a spring, where they encamped.

On the 16th, they struck the north-west shore of
the great salt lake, called Cowcowing. It was dry.
The edge was skirted by a gum and Acacia scrub, and
the bed was yellow and saline, with large patches of
samphire and immense numbers of small shells. There
was considerable difficulty in finding either feed or
water in such a spot ; and though wells were sunk, the

men were for a long time unsuccessful in their search.
At last, about seven miles to the north-east, a spring
and some grass were discovered, and an encampment
was made there on the 18th. There the lake presented
three large arms, stretching north-east, north-west, and
south-west, but the flow of water was to the southward,
and the height about one thousand feet above the sea.

Mr. Austin, with two companions, left the party on
the 20th, to examine the country round the lake. He
crossed one of the arms with much difficulty, for it was
very soft, and then entered a dense scrub. It was like
all the other thickets, gum or Acacia bushes, growing
on red sandy loam, without grass or weeds of any kind.
This continued for ten miles, and then Austin changed
his course to north-north-west. At first he passed over
scrubby sand-hills and granite rocks, and then another
scrub succeeded, so he resolved to go to the eastward
next day. This brought them through seven miles
more scrub, and then to another arm of the lake. It
was a cruel country to travel through. The scrub
would have reigned supreme but for useless sand-hills
and dismal salt lakes. If one compares the journals of
Austin, Gregory, and Roe, there will be considerable
difficulty in discovering any difference between the
country they severally passed through.

Austin floundered his horses across this second arm
of the lake. Five miles of the usual scrub on the other
side brought him to a spur of high land. Near this
was another salt lake, with samphire flats and pools of
shallow water, evidently communicating at rainy seasons
with Cowcowing. Austin continued along the edge of
this lake for five miles. When he arrived at the eastern
extremity, a gum forest with small lakes succeeded, and
then a stony quartz plain, with patches of scrub. This
was nine miles wide. It terminated at the foot of some
high, wooded, granite hills, and on the other side of
these there was a small area of grassy land, with a
brook running through it. This was the extensive
patch of agricultural land near Cowcowing, of which
the natives had said so much. It was composed solely
of the *débris* of the granite hills, but having very little

moisture, supported only an open forest of stunted gum and Acacia trees, and was bounded all round by a waving sea of dense, sombre scrub. There were no granite hills, except some a little higher in the north-east.

The whole party were brought up to the plains on the 25th, and when they had arrived, Austin determined to move forward to the higher ranges. This would take him between Roe's track and that of Gregory, in 1846, and therefore afforded the only chance of finding fertile country. It would be wearisome and tedious to the reader to have to follow the daily journeys. These expeditions are not like those in other parts of Australia, where large rivers, bold mountain ranges, and fertile plains continually encourage the explorer and give an interest to his journey. Here not one remarkable feature met the party. Day after day the same tiresome record of quartz hills, granite mountains, *Casuarina* plains, and scrub occurs. Only now and then grassy patches and water were reached, and altogether the principal interest was derived from the labours and fatigues of the party. For this journey it must however be said, that Austin was far more fortunate in finding grass and native wells than either Roe or Gregory had been before him.

On the 4th August, the expedition had reached lat. 29° 53′ long. 118°, and were encamped at a grassy spring, where Gregory and his two brothers had rested on their expedition in 1846. Here Austin sent back the two men who were intended to come as far as Cowcowing. The report they took with them was not, of course, very encouraging thus far. The expedition had passed to the eastward of those plains were Gregory had seen the whirling columns of sand in 1846. They had found no large salt lakes there, but much scrub, and the country was utterly valueless. On the 6th, they moved on again, in a north course, towards a singular looking hill. It took two days to reach it. A little red sandstone at first varied the character of the ground, and there was rather more grass, but salt lakes were more numerous than ever. The hill was a rocky tableland of sandstone, covered with scrub, sloping to the westward, but terminating to the east in an escarpment one hundred and forty feet high. They could not stop on the hill when they reached it, for though there was plenty of grass upon it, there was no water. They plunged into the scrub again, towards another and more promising tablehill, which was named Mount Kenneth. It was a good distance away, though not very high, but the country was so very level that the smallest elevation could be seen a very long way off. The intervening scrub took them four days to get through, and it was one of the worst journeys they had hitherto made. Many small watercourses were passed in approaching the mount, and they all flowed either west or south. There was a good deal of trap rock and greenstone lying about in fragments all over the plains, but still scarcely a scrap of grass for the horses, who now subsisted entirely on the young shoots of the Acacia trees.

Mount Kenneth was only a hundred and eighty feet above the plain, but it was fourteen hundred feet above the sea level. The country was evidently rising, and the tableland increasing in elevation and barrenness at the same time. From the summit of the mount a most commanding view was obtained. As far as the eye could reach to the north and east, flat-topped sandstone ridges extended with a singular appearance, for their tops were red, and their sides white. Here and there jutted out peaked hills of stratified quartz rock, resting on greenstone. From north-west to west rounded hills of greenstone, covered with scrub, gave the country a more undulating appearance, while to the south a vast rolling sea of scrub extended to the verge of the horizon. The geology of this remarkable country was not different from the rest of the tableland, and yet it possessed features which were rather exceptional. There was no coal, but a soft, black, bituminous substance exuded from between the sandstone strata. Three miles to the east of Mount Kenneth the section of the watercourses showed them to flow over bare granite and gneiss, composed of green and white ribbons of hornblende and quartz, twisted, curved, and seamed by small quartz veins.

From the mount, after a short rest, the party moved north again. Open stony plains and scrub succeeded, until they came upon a salt marsh, which stopped their progress for a time. It was similar to the marsh met with by Messrs. Gregory in 1846, but much larger, and it seemed as if it was the principal source of the Murchison, in times of flood. Probably, this one is among the largest in Australia, the surface of which is to an almost incredible space occupied by these terrible features. This one was disagreeable enough to the explorers, for it impeded them for a long time, and in crossing it they had to thank the dryness of the season that it was passable at all. The usual scrub succeeded until lat. 28° 43′ long. 118° 38′.

It was remarked here, that the grass had a strong ammoniacal odour, but they did not pay much attention to it then, for the horses were glad to eat anything in such wretched country. Unfortunately, the nature of the feed was not known until it began to have the most disastrous effects. The next day, nearly the whole of the animals were suffering from the effects of poison. They were attacked quite suddenly, falling down and kicking violently; and in a short time their heads and bellies would swell to an enormous size. The plant which seemed to have caused the mischief was a small species of *Gompholobium*, which was known to be very deleterious to animals, but had never produced such sad effects as those witnessed on this occasion. In the course of a few hours, nearly every horse was more or less affected. Such a crisis, of course, demanded the most active and urgent proceedings on the part of the party. Their lives depended on those of the horses, and it was of the utmost importance that they should be moved to some other camp as soon as possible. On the 22nd, three of the horses, which were very weak, were taken to another place, and while the more sickly animals were left in charge of five of the party, Mr. Austin pushed on, with sixteen more, and ten days' provisions, in a north-east direction.

Travelling nine miles on this course, through stony, undulating country, wooded with Acacia, he entered a sandy plain, covered with tufts of dry, soft grass, under Acacia bushes. Here he halted, and turned out the horses. Four more of them immediately became affected with symptoms of poisoning, and there remained now only eleven fit to move; these, unfortunately, the weakest. That night heavy rain fell, and relieved any apprehensions about finding water. It was determined next day to keep the animals moving as fast as possible, as that seemed to revive them. Accordingly they journeyed twenty-one miles the first day, over small hills of ironstone, with thinly grassed flats between. The soil was light red on the surface, but quite white, like lime, underneath, evidently from decomposed felspar. There was a high range in advance of them, which Austin was very anxious to reach. At first the country was broken and scrubby, but it soon opened into level open plains, with salt bush, coarse grass, and surface water, which extended right up to the foot of the range. It was just the place for the horses, in their famished and weak condition, and was called in consequence, Recruit Flats. While the animals were resting, Austin went to the highest part of the range, named Mount Magnet. It was a gneiss rock, fifteen hundred and sixty-nine feet above the sea, but only four hundred above the plains. The view from it showed wooded hills and extensive plains to the north and west, while the eastward was scrubby and unpromising. As yet there was evidently no change in the dismal character of the country.

Mr. Austin now determined to bring up all his party to Recruit Flats. He found to his dismay, when he reached the depôt, that during his absence seven of the horses had died, and five others were in a most precarious state. It was at once resolved to abandon everything which was not absolutely indispensable to carry the party to Sharks Bay, and move on rapidly to some better feed, which had been found about ten miles to the eastward. In all haste they made up the loads, but with every reduction some of the horses were scarcely able to move. Yet there was no time to be lost, and though they had to abandon three dying horses on the road, they moved on quickly to the new camp. When they were fairly settled in it, Mr. Austin went to examine the country around. Desolation still met his gaze on every side. On his return, he met a native, who made such a determined attack upon the explorers, single-handed as he was, that, reluctantly, they were obliged to drive him away with small shot. Near where he was encountered there was a fine spring, and the signs of an extensive native camp.

On the 4th September, the whole party were moved forward. The horses were now reduced to thirteen, but the baggage was confined to such provisions as were considered necessary to carry the party to Sharks Bay, with twenty-four days' flour added, to enable them to fall back on the mining settlement, at the Murchison River, in case of any unforeseen accident. On the evening of the 5th, they reached Recruit Flats. Here the horses were rested, while Austin pushed on to examine the country to the north-west. He hoped to find a passage to Sharks Bay in this direction. Again occurred the same wearisome repetition of rocky hills, scrubby plains, and dense scrubs. The chief interest of the expedition now was the heroic exertions of the party which composed it. Their position was most critical, as they were soon fairly entangled in a scrub, poorly watered, and almost totally devoid of grass. To heighten their inconveniences, they would every now and then come upon a patch of the poisonous herb. The men began to be so weakened that they begged their leader to abandon the horses, as the care of them very much increased their labours. This, of course, Mr. Austin would not do, and the lives of the men, no doubt, depended on this wise decision.

Close to Mount Magnet, and stretching north-west away from it, an immense salt lake was found. Its extent was not ascertained, but it reached beyond the range of vision, and was, at the edge, fifteen hundred feet above the sea level. Large quantities of the euro, or red kangaroo (*Osphanter rufus*), abounded in this country, and they formed at times a valuable addition to the scanty provisions of the explorers. After leaving

the salt marsh, the whole party advanced through a
very arid country, where they suffered fearfully for
want of water. On the 21st, they lost two horses from
exhaustion and thirst, but on the same day, in
lat. 27° 43′, long. 118°, found a spring, near a cave in a
quartzite cliff. This cave had some singular carvings
in it. There were representations of seven left hands,
of the ordinary size, with one large right hand above.
On the left of this were five pairs of kangaroos' feet,
and the feet of three emu. They were very well
executed, and had just the appearance of impressions
made by the objects they were intended to represent.
The surface of the rock seemed to have been stained by
some fluid. They were evidently ancient, and quite
beyond the capacity of the present race of natives.
This was shown by several rude imitations which had
been more recently made beneath them, and Mr. Austin
found underneath a stone instrument, which had been
used in the modern attempts. They evidently belonged
to the description of carvings found by Grey, near
Hanover Bay.

The cave was memorable to the party in more
respects than one. Near it, a lad named Farmer
accidentally shot himself in the arm, and died of lock-
jaw a few days afterwards. When they had buried
him, the party moved on again, struggling through the
scrub, and subsisting on the rock waters they met from
time to time. On the last day of September they were
obliged to abandon another of their poor horses. The
number was now reduced to eleven, but that was enough
to carry all that was wanted. There was still a good
supply of rations, and provided they could only find
water, they had good hopes of getting through to
Sharks Bay.

On the 5th October, they crossed a river flowing
south of west, named the Sandford. The intervening
country was still the usual scrub, with granite and trap
rocks, and a little surface water. After passing a
granite hill, named Mount Luke, upon the 6th, it became
more rocky, but open, and of so good a quality that they
found grass and water every night. A high range was

reached on the 8th, in lat. 26° 24′, long. 116° 28′. They
halted upon it one day, and called the highest summit
Mount Murchison. It was composed of trap and greenstone, about four hundred feet above the plains, and
probably fifteen hundred above the sea. Resuming
their march, they struck a part of the Murchison River,
flowing to the south-west. This was a long long way
above the point to which Gregory had traced it, and
still the bed was wide and deep, cutting down through
about thirty feet of red sandstone rock. It was lined
with fine gum trees, but quite dry, and there was
nothing whatever to indicate that it ever retained water
for any length of time. Five miles beyond the river
they entered a patch of rocky country, with red sandstone cliffs and conical hills of trap rock. This terminated in a plain, which was perfectly white, from the
thickness with which it was covered with quartz fragments, very like Sturt's Stony Desert, and probably owing
its origin to the same cause. After this, scrub again
succeeded. The party pushed through this as well as
they could, for a time, without the slightest sign of any
improvement or change in the dead level before them.
They reached within about a hundred and ten miles of
Sharks Bay, but were obliged to give up the idea of
going further, for they had been then three days without
water. On retracing their steps they found a native
well, about twelve miles from their furthest point. It
afforded a scanty supply for the horses, and they gladly
rested by it for a single night. Then, for the next two
days, they returned, keeping more to the west. Water
was not to be found anywhere, except at another well,
discovered on the second day; and even before that was
reached another horse died of exhaustion. The well
was discovered by the merest accident; it was in a bare
ironstone plain, where none would have thought of
looking for water, and yet, had they missed this supply,
all the horses must have perished. How it subsisted
under a scorching sun, which the red sand and ironstone
made more fiery and unbearable, was a mystery to those
who saw it. It was a fortunate discovery in every
respect, as well as a grassy patch of land about eight

miles beyond, for it enabled Mr. Austin to make a depôt while he examined the country in advance.

With two companions he went away from the camp, and on the 18th October reached the Murchison again, about twenty-five miles south-west of where he had seen it at first. It was the same width as before, and still cut down into the red sandstone of the tableland. At any part of its course this channel seemed recognisable by its hideous character of sterility and desolation. There was water in it now, in pools, but giving no comfort to the explorers, for it was as salt as brine. Up and down, and in every direction, Mr. Austin searched, but in vain. He scooped under the rocks, and dug into the bed of the river, but there was nothing but salt water to be had; yet there were high flood-marks upon the banks, and the river seemed liable to extraordinary inundations. Mr. Austin was now seriously alarmed, not only for his horses, but for his whole party. It was useless to rely on the grass or water at the camp, because they were probably exhausted by this time, and therefore some relief he must find before going back to his companions. In the midst of his anxiety he noticed a small native track, going off to the south, and he followed it in the hope that it might lead to water. It was traced till night over the red soil, amid a heat that seemed to burn up everything, and when the sun set, like a ball of fire, amid the brown foliage, there still seemed no chance of relief. Another fearfully hot day succeeded, and still the little band kept on their search amid the desert, which was quite in keeping with the coppery appearance of the sun and sky. In the afternoon they were almost in despair, and they turned, as a last resource, to some hills, about ten miles to the eastward. When they reached them their anxieties were ended for a while. The place contained both grass and water in abundance, and Austin, in gratitude, called it Mount Welcome. This was in lat. 26° 24', long. 116° 24'.

While the party were moved up to this camp, an examination of the country was again made. On the 24th, more water was found, fourteen miles to the west

of north, and this made an alteration in the plans of
Mr. Austin. He had found water a good deal to the
west of his former line, and so he thought it might be
still possible to get across to the ship, at Sharks Bay.
On the 25th, therefore, the party were again upon their
old course, to Gascoyne River. In ten miles they
entered a rugged, densely wooded country, of sandstone,
quartz, and gneiss, destitute of water and feed. Two of
the party, who were sent ten miles further, brought the
same account, and stated, that when they passed the
Murchison River, its bed contained only pools of salt
water. Soon afterwards they captured an old native,
and made him show them a well. He did so without
difficulty, in a hole which they would otherwise have
certainly passed over. This useful piece of information
cost the poor native his liberty, for it was deemed
necessary now to keep him until the worst part of the
scrub had been passed, in order that he might show the
place where the natives obtained water. They resumed
their journey to the westward, taking the old man with
them. They crossed eight miles of scrubby plains, and
then again reached the Murchison River, where its
channel divided. Beyond this the bed had become
very stony, with large angular fragments of quartz
and gneiss, and densely scrubby. For nine miles more
of this wretched country the native brought them to a
water-hole, with very little grass, and surrounded by a
dense thicket. The poor savage was undoubtedly very
useful here, for the explorers would never have thought
of entering this scrub but for their guide. From this
point the scrub became a little more open, but terribly
difficult for the men to get through. The native made
urgent entreaties to be taken to the south, plainly indicating that there was no water to the westward, and
that the blacks never penetrated into that tract; but
Mr. Austin kept his course. The country soon became
worse in every respect, and at last led to a deep rocky
ravine, which they could scarcely cross. The old
native depended on finding a supply there, but when
he gazed into its depths, and found it dry, he seemed
quite disheartened.

As the red dawn beamed over the desert, on the 29th, the party separated to search for water. In an hour or so they met together again, perfectly unsuccessful. The native then pointed nervously to a hill, some ten miles to the westward, but seemed doubtful. Thither Mr. Austin proceeded, while the old man, overpowered by heat and thirst, scraped a hole for himself under a bush, and lay down. Austin crossed to the hills over some salt bush flats. He found plenty of water-holes, but they were sandy and dry. He returned in all haste to the party, and found that the heat had nearly exhausted them, and they lay in holes under the bushes, almost dying of thirst. When the native heard that there was no water on the hill he burst into tears, and the news seemed equally to appall the rest of the party. Mr. Austin tried to encourage them as well as he could, and told them that if they would be firm, and obey his orders, he was sure that he could bring them back safe. This revived the men to some extent, and preparations were made that evening to return to the Geraldine Mine. This was Austin's furthest point, in lat 26° 15', long. 115° 16'.

That night they started. They marched through the whole night, and, in order to get the benefit of the dew, stripped off all their clothes except their boots and trousers. Two of the party went on in advance to reach the last well, and bring back water to the party. It was a terrible journey, but they soon reached their camp of the 28th, and had now only another day's stage to reach the well. They made a slight *détour* to the northward to avoid the ravine and rocky ground, but this brought them to a still more difficult cliff, where the tableland terminated abruptly. The fatigue of descending this was as much as some of the men could stand, and they began to give in. They dropped behind, one by one, and laid themselves down to die under the bushes. Mr. Austin tried to rouse them, but it was useless, and so the rest pushed on, making a well-marked track in a single file for the others to follow when rest should have restored them. After a fearful ride through the whole of a burning day, Mr. Austin and one companion

reached the waterhole in the evening. He instantly
filled the keg, and went back to his companions. They
were all, as it were, on the point of death and were
found one by one upon the road. The water soon restored
them. Leaving them to walk slowly to the camp,
Mr. Austin hurried to the cliff, where three horses had
been left with their loads. The poor animals were dead,
but the loads were still undamaged. He took with him
such provisions as were necessary for the immediate
wants of the party, and then went back to the water-
hole. One can imagine how fatigued and exhausted he
must have been, but his trials were only at their beginning. When he reached his companions he found to
his horror that the water was exhausted, and it seemed
as if with this little pool all their chances had melted
away. How to save provisions, horses, and men amid
such terrible obstacles was a problem that might have
made any man despair. Austin, however, was equal to
the occasion. There was not a moment to be lost. One-
half of the party were sent back for the stores, and the
rest moved hurriedly on towards Mount Welcome. On
the second day's journey they reached a fine pool, which
terminated all their anxieties for a time, but one more
horse died in going back for the stores.

When all the baggage had been brought up, and the
party were steering for Mount Welcome, Mr. Austin
and the native started to make another search down the
Murchison for water. He was unsuccessful, and the
native became so much exhausted on the journey that,
unless he had been washed with brine from the stream,
he would hardly have come back alive. On the 6th
November the whole party reached Mount Welcome. But
there was no rest for them even here. As soon as they had
watered the horses and filled the kegs the springs failed,
so they had to move down the Murchison at once, whether
they would or no. They had a fearful part of the journey
still before them. It was one hundred and sixty miles,
in a straight line, to the Geraldine Mine, and they were
ninety miles from Mr. Gregory's last watering-place on
the river. To accomplish this long march, they had only
eighty-one pounds of flour and two and a half pounds of

tea, and this was the whole extent of their provision. To make them last, the rations were reduced to ten ounces of flour per man daily, and by this means they could be eked out for twelve days longer.   They then buried everything which was not absolutely necessary, and left Mount Welcome at midnight, steering south-west, and carrying water for three days. With great difficulty, and by long night and day marches, they arrived at Gregory's furthest camp on the 12th. Water was obtained here for the first time by digging, and they camped on a beautiful patch of grass in the bed of the stream.   Their course between Mount Welcome and this place led over extensive plains, across which, in wet seasons, some streams flowed into the Murchison.   In many places their progress was almost stopped by the dense scrub, and only one water-hole was found in the whole distance.

On the 14th, they resumed their march down the river.   Below a great bend, the waters from the east-ward are concentrated and fall into it, and after this plenty of fresh water was found in springs along the bed, or under the sandstone cliffs which lined the stream. For thirty miles lower down water and grass were more scarce, and the hills, which hitherto lay back from the river, now closed upon it, and made the passage difficult. Dense scrubs also appeared, which prevented the party from cutting off the bends. The prevailing rock changed, and the hills were formed of trap or gneiss, with dykes projecting into the bed. On the 20th the expedition reached the mines, and thus their labours terminated. The men were most kindly received, but owing to their long abstinence from food, and their emaciated condi-tion, they were all soon laid up. On the 24th, however, they were able to proceed to the coast, and arrange-ments were made to relieve the vessel waiting for them in Sharks Bay. After this the party was broken up, and Mr. Austin proceeded to Perth.

After giving a tribute to the energy, perseverance, courage, and indefatigable zeal of Mr. Austin, which undoubtedly saved the lives of the party, it must be ad-mitted that the results of the expedition were of very little importance to the colony of Western Australia. Austin imagined that he had found indications of gold, but the metal has not been found yet. The only discoveries were that the salt marshes and trap rocks extended in a line for a good distance to the north, but probably not beyond the Murchison. It was also seen that the tableland of the west coast rose to an altitude of about 1890 feet above the level of the sea, and that the drainage was from one salt lake to another, until it flowed into the river near Perth. Of the nature of the rocks in this direction sufficient has been said in connection with this and other expeditions; but attention may perhaps be drawn to the singular belt of trap mountains which breaks through the tableland in place of the granite. Altogether, the useless and arid nature of the ground in this direction gives a sinister aspect to the future of a very large portion of Western Australia, and now that exploration has proved beyond a doubt the universal aridity of the desert which almost surrounds that colony, one can hardly be astonished that it has made comparatively so little progress during the last thirty years. In reading such expeditions as the foregoing, one cannot, however, help being struck with the fact, that it was only such a desert that could overcome the indomitable exertions and energy of the colonists that chose it for a home.

CHAPTER XIV.

In 1855, the colonial public began to think of something besides gold digging. Leichhardt had been more than four years overdue, and it became a matter of certainty that he would never bring in any fresh news about the interior. As long as gold was plentiful, and there was a chance of the party being still in existence, no one gave themselves much trouble on the subject; but when all chance of saving his life was gone, men became suddenly very zealous, and expressed their wish that a search should be made for his remains. The humanity of the project was plain. Apart from the curiosity of the public to know what had become of him, and how he had perished, there was a desire to know what he had done, and how far he had gone. Very few believed in the native account of his loss brought in by Hely, and it seemed very desirable that some better information should be obtained.

All these discussions led to no result, as far as Leichhardt was concerned, but the attention of the public was directed to the subject of exploration, and something came of that. An expedition was set on foot to remove a little of the mystery which still hung over so large a portion of Australia. There was great discussion as to the locality from whence the expedition should start. It was required to reach the interior in the shortest possible space of time, and yet to travel along some path which would secure water to the party. These requirements were rather difficult to fulfil, but at length a course was decided upon. The Victoria River had not been explored since the time of Stokes. It was the largest river known in Australia, except the Murray, and there was not perhaps a problem of greater interest in all the wide subject of Australian geography than to ascertain its course. It might conduct to the centre of the continent, but even if it did not, it was certain to be a well watered track to follow. This then was the object for which the party were equipped.

The command of the expedition was given to Mr. A. C. Gregory, the explorer who has already so often figured in these pages. He was accompanied by a party of eleven men, among whom was Dr. Mueller, the celebrated botanist, and Mr. Wilson, the geologist. They sailed with two vessels—one the *Monarch*, with the horses and supplies, and another the *Tom Tough*, which was to remain and co-operate with the party along the Victoria. It will not be necessary to detain the reader with the details of the early part of the journey. The first news which was received of the expedition was on the return of the *Monarch*, after landing the horses and supplies. It reported that the horses were reduced to forty-one in number, through sickness during the voyage, but up to the 24th September, 1855, everything else had succeeded perfectly well.

Immediately after the sailing of the *Monarch*, Mr. Gregory organized a land expedition to proceed with the horses to the upper part of the river. This party consisted of the leader, Dr. Mueller, and seven men. While they were absent, Mr. Wilson was directed to ascend the Victoria to some place available for landing the sheep where they were to camp. Gregory started on the 28th, but the horses were so weakened by the voyage that they were scarcely able to travel. They proceeded on an easterly course, through level forest country, poor in quality. In six days they reached Macadam Range, which had been so named by Stokes, because of its stony character. Gregory found it to be the deeply serrated edge of the sandstone tableland which occupies so much of the interior, so that the river is little more than a large chasm in it. The party took eight days more to reach the Fitzmaurice, and in the interim lost two of their horses, for the country was very stony, and the travelling bad. They camped on a small dry tributary of the river. During the night this was filled by the tide, and with the water a large number of alligators came to the camp. Unaware of their presence, the men slept soundly; and though they escaped, the horses did not. Three were wounded by them, one so severely that it was abandoned.

On the 13th October they crossed the river at a ford, where the stream was scarcely twenty yards wide. They then steered through grassy valleys, and reached some more stony land, where two more horses had to be abandoned. It was not until the 18th that they reached the upper part of the Victoria, after a difficult ascent of the sea range; and on the 20th they reached the point where the vessel was to commence landing the stores; but here everything was in confusion. Gregory learned, to his great mortification, that the schooner was grounded about eight miles lower down, and very much damaged. There was three feet of water in the hold, and more than half the ship's stores were destroyed, besides a ton of flour, a ton of rice, three hundredweight of salt, and eight hundredweight of sugar, belonging to the expedition. Of course, Gregory immediately repaired to the spot, but it was only after nine days' untiring exertions that the vessel was got off the bank. The greatest loss to the expedition was in the sheep. Owing to their long detention on board, only forty-four were saved out of one hundred and sixty-one, and these not in a condition which would enable them to stand travelling.

The early part of November was devoted to the erection of a store and emptying the vessel, so as to repair her injuries. On the 15th of that month Mr. Gregory tried to ascend the stream in a gutta-percha boat, but he was obliged to return without having accomplished anything, except destroying the boat by the heat to which it was exposed. Finding this method of exploring the stream quite out of the question, he made up another land party of five, with seven of the best of his horses. He left the stream at first to cut off the bends, and passing through a grassy valley reached it a short distance above Stokes' furthest point. From this they followed the river to the east of Fitzroy Range, and entered a deep gorge, bounded by cliffs of sandstone from fifty to three hundred feet high. Through this ravine the river wound, forming deep reaches, sometimes several miles in length, and only separated by narrow banks of shingle or rock. The average course was nearly south, so that their latitude rapidly increased, and when they had attained lat. 16° the valley suddenly expanded into a vast plain, covered with excellent grass. In this plain were several isolated hills of trap rock. They did not go beyond it in this preliminary expedition, but having ascertained the nature of the country so far, Mr. Gregory returned to the camp. He reached it on the 13th December, after a good deal of very difficult travelling, for the rainy season had now set in, and where the ground was not rough and stony it was soft and boggy.

On the 3rd January, 1856, Mr. Gregory again started. On this occasion he had eight men with him, besides thirty pack and six saddle horses. Their progress was at first very slow, owing to the soft and rugged nature of the country, and this entailed so much fatigue that by the time they had reached lat. 17° two of the horses had died. To diminish the baggage as much as possible, Mr. Gregory made a depôt at this point, and proceeded with only four men and eleven horses, and leaving the greater part of the stores behind. With their load lightened, both men and horses travelled more rapidly, and they soon—much sooner, indeed, than they had expected—reached the head of the Victoria River. This was in lat. 18° 12', long. 130° 39' E. I should like very much to give my readers a more detailed account of the journey through this most interesting part of Australia, but, unfortunately, it is not in my power. The only published narrative of the expedition is Mr.

Gregory's concise report to the colonial government, and
as this is as brief as possible, and containing no more
than the main results, it is impossible to gather anything from them beyond what is given here, almost in
the words of the author.

The dividing range between the northern and
southern waters was only thirteen hundred feet above
the level of the sea, and beyond it the party found that
whatever little surface water there was fell towards the
interior.   From the watershed they descended into a
level and depressed country, with a small watercourse
trending to the south-east.   At first this was easily followed, for the banks were nicely grassed, and there was
a little water in the deeper portions ; but in lat. 18° 22'
it was lost on a wide grassy plain, surrounded by a level
sandy country.   They penetrated a few miles beyond
this, but were soon obliged to retrace their steps.   The
country for a long way to the south was apparently a
desert without grass, and as for water, very little of any
kind seemed to have fallen south of the dividing range,
even during the rainy season.   They were evidently
fairly upon the sandy tableland, for the height was one
thousand feet above the sea level.

Gregory now determined to follow the northern
limits of this desert, in the hope of finding some creek
or river descending from the ranges to the north, which
would enable him to penetrate the desert, or even cross
it.   He therefore kept to the west, along the foot of the
sandstone range ; and on the 15th, in lat. 18°, long. 130°,
came upon the head of a stream. It first took a northerly
course, and then ran continuously to the south-west.
For the first hundred miles the country on the right
bank consisted of level plains of rich soil, covered with
beautiful grass.   The left bank presented a strong contrast to this.   It consisted of low sandstone ranges and
stunted trees. Gradually, however, both sides became
alike in their barrenness, and the country changed to a
desert.   It was very like the one described by Sturt,
consisting of low barren sandstone hills and long parallel ridges of drifting red sand, straight, equal in height,
and with a direction exactly east and west.   Yet it was

not altogether destitute of vegetation, though whatever there was was scattered and stunted.

The party followed the stream-bed for nearly three hundred miles, and at last its channels terminated in a series of dry salt lakes. These occupied the lower portion of a large depression in the sandy desert, only three hundred feet above the sea, in lat. 20° 16', long. 127° 35'. An outlet for the waters was carefully sought for on the southern, and on every shore of the lake, but none could be found ; in truth, the lakes themselves seemed capable of receiving all the drainage from the creek, because there were many marks of inundations high above the water level. From the height of these it was evident that such floods left permanent water for a long time, because there was an abundance of mussel shells buried in the soil, twenty feet above the surface of the lake, and more than a mile beyond its ordinary limits.

The stream which had led the party so far was named Sturt's Creek. Beyond the lakes, Gregory thought it useless to penetrate. The water had failed them, and for the last three days they had been subsisting upon some puddles left by a thunder-shower. The desert beyond seemed utterly impracticable, as no rain seemed to have fallen on it for the last twelvemonth; so Gregory returned. No doubt he was right in doing so, but I cannot say that I agree with his conclusions. One may reasonably doubt the inferences about the drainage of the lake, aided by the further knowledge of the interior which we have since obtained. Mr. Eyre, in 1839, traced down the Wimmera to Lake Hindmarsh, and could find no outlet beyond ; yet that lake is known now to drain into Lake Albacutya, and probably, in very rainy seasons, across the mallee scrub, from swamp to swamp, until it reaches the Murray River. The case of Sturt's Creek is very similar. Again, we need not believe that the desert of red sand is very wide. The experiences of Gregory himself, Burke, Howitt, Stuart, and M'Kinlay, all tell us that such sand deserts are only in patches, and that they are always bounded or interrupted by grassy flats, with small watercourses in scrubby plains. The lower the tableland the more fre-

quently are these patches and creeks found. Had then
the water allowed Mr. Gregory to travel far to the east
or west, he would have found more grass and water, and
might have advanced much further into the interior;
but when I say this, I must also say that the indefatigable zeal of Mr. Gregory had done more than could
have been expected of him—more, indeed, than any
previous explorer could have done, which is saying a
great deal.

As they returned, most of the puddles were found
to be dry, and they were obliged in consequence to
travel by night. On the 24th March they reached the
head of the creek, and then struck eastward to avoid the
waterless country traversed on the outward route. Consequently they crossed the dividing range further east,
where it was sixteen hundred and sixty feet above the
sea level.

Now, bearing in mind what a large stream the Victoria River is, the moderate elevation of the watershed
must prove the depth and violence of the rainfall in
this locality. The height of the tableland near Sharks
Bay is much greater, as we have seen from Austin's
journal, and yet there are no large rivers there at all.
At any rate, it would seem as if the supply on the Victoria is greatly in excess of any other part of the coast.

After crossing the watershed, the party reached a
valley, with a creek running to the north-west. This
they followed for thirty miles, and then steered east for
fifty miles, over to a level grassy country, destitute
of water. They reached the depôt camp on the 28th,
where everything had gone on well meanwhile, and the
horses were in good condition. While those employed
on the last journey were resting, Mr. Gregory took six
fresh ones and three men to examine the country to the
eastward. He traversed sixty miles of splendid grassy
country, of volcanic formation, well watered by numerous creeks, and then reached the eastern boundary of
the valley of the Victoria. He then turned northwards,
and traced the river down to lat. 16° 26', thus connecting this route with that of December of the preceding
year. After returning to the depôt camp, he examined

the lower part of the Victoria for any tributaries which might occur, and on the 9th April the whole party were together again at the main camp.

The *Tom Tough* was evidently an unfortunate vessel, for she was in trouble again when Gregory arrived. One man had died of scurvy; there were several more sick on board; but a supply of fresh provisions put all that to rights; and in other respects the repairs which the schooner required had been effected, and all went well. To secure some necessary supplies, Gregory determined to send her to Coepang, while he explored towards the Gulf of Carpentaria, with seven of his party. The others were to proceed in the schooner, and were to meet him again at Albert River, from which point all the party would go overland to Moreton Bay. The provisions, however, had been so divided, that even if the *Tom Tough* did not meet them at Albert River, the party would have enough to carry them on to the settled districts. Thus the second portion of this expedition was an undertaking greater than Leichhardt had first projected in his celebrated journey to Port Essington.

Gregory left his camp on the Victoria on the 21st June, 1856. The party consisted of himself, his brother (Mr. H. Gregory), Dr. Mueller, Mr. Elsey, the surgeon, with three men, and thirty-four horses. Their baggage, including the ammunition, was about two tons, so that the animals were not impeded by weight from advancing rapidly. The first course was to proceed to the eastern bend of the river, in lat. 15° 38', and then they left it to follow up a creek which came from the eastward. The travelling, at first, was rocky and bad, except on the immediate banks of the creek, but at its source the rocks became basaltic, and the country good, though thinly timbered. Beyond the creek, in lat. 15° 33', long. 131° 40', a low sandstone tableland commenced, about seven hundred feet above the sea level. It was thinly grassed, and covered with a forest of stringy bark, but, with the exception of one creek, quite destitute of water. The creek was followed to lat. 14° 54', where it turned to the north-west, leaving the table-

land, which here seemed like the northern extension of
the interior desert.   It took them five days to search for
another creek.   At last, they found one to the eastward,
and the party were moved up to it on the 12th July.
A south-east course was then attempted, but they were
soon driven back for want of water, and they had to
keep down the creek to its junction with the Roper
River, which was first discovered by Leichhardt.   The
country was volcanic and good, and continued so as long
as they followed the river.   But this was only for
twenty miles, when they again turned south-east, over
a poor sandstone country.   On the 19th July they encamped upon a small creek, with a few water-holes, and
while they were resting, some blacks made a very cun-
ning attempt to surprise them.   They were discovered
in time, and were evidently quite sufficiently punished
by a discharge of small shot among them.

On the 20th they continued their south-east course,
encamping at a spring in a sandstone ravine.   No
poisonous plants were noticed about, so before precautions could be adopted, two horses died from eating
some.   Leichhardt had mysteriously lost a horse in this
neighbourhood, but was unable to say whether it was
from poison or the bite of a snake.   The mystery was
now solved by Gregory's horses, and, fortunately, the
disaster was not as serious as that of Austin under
similar circumstances.   The explorers continued to traverse the sandstone tableland, which was now frequently
interrupted by very scrubby valleys.   In these, small
creeks took their rise, and evidently formed part of the
heads of the Limmen Bight and Wickham Rivers.
The water was very scarce, and they were compelled to
return to the northward, travelling along the broken
ridges at the edge of the sandstone tableland.   On the
4th August they reached the head of Leichhardt's
M‘Arthur River, in lat. 16° 25'.   The channel did not
exceed twenty yards in width, and so little water
remained even at that season, that it had to be followed
down for some miles before a sufficient supply could be
obtained.   From this they again struck south-east,
crossing the spurs of the tableland.   In the valleys

)etween, many small creeks take their rise, forming the
1eads of the rivers which flow into the Gulf of Carpen-
aria.   The principal feature of the country was sand-
itone, though basalt and limestone cropped out in small
)atches of grassy land.   This seemed to expand into
)lains to the northward ; but to the south, the level of
;he sandstone tableland was of an unvaried sterile character.   Its elevation reached nine hundred feet, but in
lat. 17° 40', long. 137° 40', a detached mass projected,
which was thirteen hundred feet above the sea.   From
this the view extended forty or fifty miles south, over
hopelessly level ground.   It seems that the course of
Gregory was one of the very best for the examination
of the northern limits of the tableland, and the features
that it presented on its route were extremely interesting.
The heads of the rivers were in an especial manner
attractive.   Thus, on the 20th August, they reached a
place where deep gullies took their rise on the south-
east slope of the high land, and rapidly increased by
their junction until they formed the head of the Nicholson River.   The ridges of upraised sandstone were very
rough, so that the valley was crossed with difficulty.
Granite was found below.   The river soon entered the
sandstone ridges to the east, over whose barren summits
the party toiled for three days without being able to
find even sufficient grass for the horses.   Following
.down the stream, the country became more level and
the banks grassy, but the greater portion of the land
was worthless until they came within thirty miles of the
Albert River, where the Plains of Promise commenced.

They crossed, on the 30th August, a fine running
creek, which joined the Nicholson, in lat. 17° 53', after
which the river turned to the north.   Three miles further east brought them to a stream of running water,
with grassy open plains upon its banks.   Its course was
nearly east for four miles, when it was joined by a small
creek from the south, forming a fine reach of water,
which they recognised as part of the Albert River of
Stokes, and the Beames' Brook of Leichhardt.   This
was the rendezvous of the *Tom Tough*, and she had not
arrived.   There were no signs of any visits, except that

of Her Majesty's ship *Torch*, the name of which had
been cut upon a tree. Mr. Gregory thought it better
not to wait, so he buried a letter of instructions, and then
proceeded upon his journey.

On the 3rd September they left the Albert River,
and traversed the level open country to the south-east.
Two days' journey brought them to a river, a hundred
yards wide, but with water in it now, only in detached
pools. This was the stream which Leichhardt had mistaken for the Albert, and as it had not been properly
named, it was called after the explorer who first crossed
it. The Leichhardt has since become remarkable as the
stream by the means of which M'Kinlay travelled down
to Carpentaria from the interior. In crossing it, Gregory's party was suddenly attacked in a very bold
manner by the natives. In the early part of the conflict the chief was killed, but after the first surprise was
over, small shot was found quite sufficient to repel the
attack.

From the Leichhardt the course was nearly east, the
country consisting of low sandstone ridges, very thickly
timbered, and nearly destitute of grass. It improved
again as the Flinders River was approached; and when
they crossed that stream, the grassy plains extended
nearly twenty miles back from the channel on both
sides. Beyond, the land became level and worthless,
though covered with small trees. In the attempt to
cross it to the eastward, they were repulsed several
times for want of water, and at last had to travel north,
to lat. 17°, where they reached the Gilbert. It was a
broad sandy stream, coming from the south, and certainly of more importance than Leichhardt considered
it to be. They stopped two days, while they killed a
horse and jerked his flesh, for the want of fresh meat
began to be much felt by the men, and this was their
only substitute. The general flow of the Gilbert was
from the south-east, and this enabled them to resume
their course with great facility, though several miles
often intervened between the water-holes in the channel.
The level of the surrounding plains was so uniform that
only one range of hills was seen until they reached lat.

18° 20′, long. 143°. This was on the 27th September, and the level of the river was then seven hundred feet above the sea. It was not a fertile tract in any part of its progress. Grassy flats extended for one or two miles along its banks, but beyond the country was poor and scrubby. Low ranges of hills now succeeded with improved vegetation. They had, for a time at least, left the sandstone formation, and the rocks were granite, gneiss, porphyry, and slate. This was near the head of the eastern branch of the Gilbert; and when they reached that, another horse was killed and jerked, while Mr. Gregory went in advance, to examine a path across the ranges.

On the 11th they began to cross the mountains. These were the spurs of a part of the great Australian Cordillera. In lat. 18° 45′, long. 143° 50′, they were two thousand five hundred feet high, and the travelling was difficult and dangerous. The party were, however, upon country previously explored, and this was a great help in choosing a road. They soon reached the southern branches of the Lynd River, which was here fifteen hundred feet above the sea level. The ranges rose very abruptly on the west side, but the east was formed by a gradually rising sheet of basaltic lava, which separated it from the valley of the Burdekin. This portion of the country was well grassed, yet from the porous nature of the rock, retained no surface water. But in spite of this and many other obstacles, the party descended into the valley of the Burdekin, on the 14th October, in lat. 18° 57′. The channel was here about fifty yards wide, with a small stream of water trickling along its sandy bed. The valley was well grassed, but the broken and almost mountainous country of the higher ranges was very poor and stony. Except in the bed of the stream itself, water was very scarce indeed, and so, perforce, they had to keep along it to the south-east.

The remainder of Mr. Gregory's narrative is so condensed that it is impossible to give the reader more than the merest outline of the progress of the expedition. In fact, the concluding portion of the report is

inserted almost word for word. In any case, full details
would not be necessary, because the party was now
almost upon the tracks of Leichhardt, and the country has
been described before. Below the junction of the Clarke,
they found a great improvement in the land, especially
near the larger tracts of basaltic soil. South of lat. 20°
granite and trap rock prevailed, forming fine open grassy
ridges, timbered with ironbark. This continued to
lat. 28° 40'. The junction of the Burdekin and Suttor
Rivers was attained on the 30th October, in lat. 28° 31',
long. 146° 50'. They followed the Suttor, as there was
some doubt of the course of that stream. This led
them into dense scrubs of Brigalow Acacia, which gradually extended over the whole face of the country,
and impeded their progress considerably. At about
lat. 21° 30' they found that the Suttor was joined by
the Belyando of Sir Thomas Mitchell. This, it will be
remembered, is the river which Sir Thomas Mitchell
discovered in 1846, and which he was prevented from
exploring very far, because of the dense scrubs which
lined its banks. Owing to the heavy rains which had
recently fallen, it was now running, and this enabled
Mr. Gregory to follow it up as far as lat. 22°. He
then left it and steered to the south-east, in the hope of
finding a more open country; but after crossing a low
ridge of sandstone hills, he entered a vast plain, covered
with Brigalow scrub. This continued to lat. 22° 40',
long. 147° 10', when they crossed a range of mountains,
and descended to the Peak Downs on the 12th November. Before they left the western range, they could see
that these downs extended sixty miles, in gently undulating plains of well-grassed, rich black soil, separated
by hills of scrub. Of course, the origin of such a soil
was volcanic, and, like most basaltic plains, retained no
water. This latter peculiarity obliged the party to
skirt the south-west side of the downs, amid a great
deal of scrub and disagreeable travelling.

On the 15th November they reached the Mackenzie
River, about fifteen miles above the junction of Comet
Creek. Being now nearly in the latitude of Port
Curtis, they steered an easterly course, and reached a

tation on the Dawson River on the 22nd November.
From this Mr. Gregory proceeded by himself to Mount
Larcom, to connect his survey with the east coast, and
when he returned they proceeded through the settled
districts to Brisbane, which they reached on the 16th
November, 1856. Thus the expedition terminated.

There can be no doubt that this was one of the
finest, most extensive, and yet most expeditious explorations which had ever taken place in Australia. In less
than half the time taken by Leichhardt to reach Port Essington, Mr. Gregory had explored a much larger tract
of country. It is true, a great deal of labour was
curtailed by the knowledge of where Leichhardt had
previously found water, but only a comparatively small
portion of the explored route was made use of, and the
greater part of the line was a perfectly new tract. It
was concluded from this journey that the whole northern
interior, from the river Victoria to the 140th meridian
was a vast tableland of sandstone, of an average height
of eight hundred feet above the sea. Along the edge of
this, a number of small rivers take their rise, which only
water the small space which lies between the edge of
the tableland and the ocean. The end of the tableland
was the origin of all the rivers flowing into Carpentaria,
except the Flinders and the Leichhardt, whose limits
were unknown. Their sources form an interesting
portion of subsequent discovery; but it may be mentioned that they rise from ranges in the interior, which
Burke and Wills called the Standish and M'Kinlay
Ranges. Mr. Gregory corroborated Stokes' report of
the Plains of Promise, and explained that Leichhardt
had given such an unfavourable account of them because
he had mistaken their locality.

The *Tom Tough* arrived safely in Brisbane, but so
much out of repair that the rest of the party went on in
another vessel to Sydney. In closing the account of
this journey, one cannot help regretting that the more
lengthy details of it have not been given to the public.

CHAPTER XV.

LAKE TORRENS AGAIN.

Gold search—Babbage at Blanchewater—M'Donnell's Creek—Campbell discovers Beda and Elizabeth Creeks—Goyder's discoveries near Lake Torrens—Colonel Freeling at the same place—Crossing-place of Lake Torrens—Hack on the Gawler Ranges—Springs amid the ranges—Warburton's explorations—Lake Gairdner—Swinden at Lake Torrens.

WHILE Mr. Gregory was still toiling on his journey from Carpentaria to Brisbane, the people of Adelaide were making a great stir in the matter of exploration. It was the people, not the Government, that initiated the movement. Not for the sake of geography, however. What the South Australians wanted was gold, and to search for this an engineer of Adelaide, named Babbage, had been sent to explore the colony. The gold search was not successful; and when Mr. Babbage had examined all the settled districts, he turned his attention to the country further north, which had not been examined much since the time of Eyre and Frome. The discoveries he made were not very extensive, nor contributing in any way to the important possessions of the colony; but they are remarkable as being the first of a series of explorations which led to the elucidation of what were the true features of Lake Torrens, and showed how erroneous were the popular ideas about its horseshoe form.

Mr. Babbage left Mount Serle on a three weeks' journey; and when he had quitted the spaces and offsets of the Flinders Range, he found himself, as all his predecessors in this country had done, on a large plain, bounded by ranges on all sides, except the north.

which appeared to be the basin of Lake Torrens. The
plain was covered with quartz fragments, besides specular iron and ironstone. Upon its opposite side he found
two low, rugged hills of quartz rock, with loftier ones
among these of slate and limestone. Among the hills
he found a gum creek, with permanent water in pools,
and in following the creek towards Lake Torrens, he saw
several very fine sheets of water, the largest of which
he named Blanchewater. Eyre, in his journey, must
have passed very close to these reservoirs, and yet, by a
singular fatality, he missed them all, and reported this
country as being utterly destitute of permanent water.
Beyond the tableland described by Eyre, the creek was
found to empty itself into a sandy plain. It was called
M'Donnell Creek, after the governor of Adelaide.

From Blanchewater, Mr. Babbage moved in a
south-east direction for about ten miles, when he came to
another large creek, whose sources were near M'Donnell
Creek. A remarkable isolated hill, about seven hundred
and fifty feet high, was near this channel, about twenty
miles to the south of Mount Hopeless ; and in returning
from it over well-grassed limestone country, some
excellent springs of fresh water and another creek were
found. The creek flowed to the eastward, and the
natives told Mr. Babbage that by following it down he
would arrive at a crossing-place, where there was but
little water, and the ground was hard. Though this
was said of a place near which Messrs. Poole and Brown
looked in vain for a crossing-place, in 1844, in Sturt's
expedition, yet it has since been found to be correct,
and that really Lake Torrens is here broken up into
two small lakes. Probably they are like the salt lakes
in the scrub of Western Australia, which have a communication in times of heavy flood. Mr. Babbage made
an attempt to solve this geographical problem ; but
having lost his horses, returned unsuccessful.

In January, 1857, there was another small increase
given to the knowledge of the Adelaide territory. Mr.
Campbell, an old settler, made some explorations on
Lake Torrens, but in a direction quite different from the
course of Mr. Babbage. He went round by the west

side from the Port Lincoln crossing-place, and there
discovered some good country, and a creek named Beda
Creek. This was salt, but at some distance further
north he crossed a fine large watercourse with abundance of fresh water in it; and when he visited it again.
in company with Mr. Swinden, in an expedition to be
spoken of just now, he called this stream the Elizabeth.
In returning to the settled districts he came upon Lake
Torrens, about fourteen miles to the eastward, and only
one small flat-topped range intervened between it and
the watercourse. The lake extended very much in a
westerly direction, beyond which there appeared a long
low peninsula. At the head of the Elizabeth, Mr.
Campbell found a water-hole, which, from its size, appeared to be permanent; but with this exception the
whole of the country seemed to be destitute of any but
salt water. No particulars of this journey were ever
published, though the knowledge obtained by it served
as a basis for all future operations.

The next news of explorations in Australia was from
Lake Torrens; but not until the year 1857 was pretty
well advanced. In April of that year Mr. Goyder, the
deputy surveyor-general of South Australia, was despatched to the north for the purpose of making a trigo-
nometrical survey in the neighbourhood of Blanchewater,
and the country discovered by Mr. Babbage. He returned in the early part of June of the same year.
having penetrated to the south side of the lake, about
latitude 29°. From this point, Mr. Goyder had a view
of about thirty miles of lake Torrens; and when he
returned he gave a most surprising account of what he
had seen. His journey was first to M'Donnell Creek,
and then to an elevation named View Hill. From this
summit it seemed to Mr. Goyder that the cliffs on either
bank of the creek were solely the result of denudation
from the stream, though the intervening valley was
from one to four miles wide. There was no appearance
of Lake Torrens, but five long creeks could be seen
converging to the eastward. Mr. Goyder crossed these
channels. The first two were dry, but the third contained water, which was considered to be salt, because of

he incrustations on the edges. He was just going
ɔ leave it when his horse stooped down and drank of
; readily. The water proved to be fresh, and the in-
rustations on the edges were natron or nitrate of soda.
'his natron, Mr. Goyder considered to be ammonia,
rom its smell, and was much surprised at the extraor-
.inary nature of his discovery. His hasty conclusion
ɔ this particular is an instance of the way in which he
llowed his senses to get the better of his judgment in
vhat followed.

He continued to the eastward, about fifty miles from
Ʋiew Hill, crossing other watercourses, until he reached a
ɔool about half a mile north of Blanchewater. Two
niles north of this he met another lagoon with an abun-
lance of springs bubbling out of the ground. These
vere named the Reedy and Rocky Springs, from the
aature of the locality in which the two largest assem-
blages occurred. About half a mile north of them there
was an isolated hill, named Weathered Hill. From its
summit, Mr. Goyder saw, or thought he saw, a belt of
gigantic gum trees in the distance, beyond which
appeared a sheet of water, with lands on the opposite
side, apparently increasing in elevation. There also
seemed to be a large lake about ten miles to the *east*; but
as this was in the road he had just passed over, the appearance of water he knew must have been the effect of
refraction. From Weathered Hill he descended in a
north-easterly direction to the M'Donnell, following its
source down about seven miles, and passing several
large water-holes, which appeared permanent. This
was in the country of the Werta-Werta tribe of natives,
and the water-holes were named after them in consequence. Following down the creek, Mr. Goyder came
at last upon Lake Torrens, in latitude 29° 13'. He
found the water quite fresh, and the enthusiasm with
which he described the scene before him is worth noting
here. Contrasted with the descriptions of Eyre and
Sturt, it shows how the aspect of this strange country
changes according to the season in which it is viewed,
and probably according to the observer.

"From the spot where my observations were taken,"

he says, " the lake stretched from fifteen to twenty miles
to the N.W., forming a water horizon from north by
west to north-west. The south portion terminated by
high land running south towards Weathered Hill, at
once explaining the cause of the various creeks running
to the eastward. An extensive bay is formed inside
this promontory, extending southward and westward,
when the land again runs to a point approaching, and
passing me by a gentle curve to the east, inclining gradually to the south-west, and ultimately disappearing in the
distance. The north portion of the horizon is terminated
by a bluff headland, round which the water appears
to extend to the north. This land passes thence to the
east, and forms the north boundary of the visible portions
of the lake, and from a higher elevation appeared to
extend round to the eastern wing. Its shores were
apparently about five miles distant, their perpendicular cliffs were very clearly discerned by the aid of
a telescope.

"From the first, I had anticipated finding large
lakes of fresh water at the termination of the various
creeks, or one large lake, into which a number of them
discharged their waters. But in such I should have
discovered flood-marks indicating the rise and fall of the
waters; and even supposing them to have attained their
maximum height, the vegetation in some portion of
the surface inside the water's edge would have revealed
this fact. But in this case there was an entire absence
of such marks, the water's edge being clearly defined,
and the bed changing its character so suddenly from an
alluvial soil to blue loam, covered by an inch of fine
silt, renders it almost *beyond the possibility* of a doubt
that the *surface water is subject only to the most trifling
variations of level,* and the absence of deltas in · the *em-
bouchures* of the creeks tend to show that there is no
reacting force (!) ; but that the waters in times of flood
flow uninterruptedly elsewhere, and I am inclined to believe in a generally north-west direction."

A certain portion of this description is marked in
italics, not to show how much Mr. Goyder erred, but to
give an instance how appearances in a particular locality

nay combine to deceive. Undoubtedly, the explorer was
rather too positive in his assertions, too careful, in fact,
to close every avenue of escape in case he should prove
to be wrong. In his reiteration of the proofs why it
was impossible for him to have been deceived, he reminds one of the gentleman who secured his cellar by
nailing it up from the inside. For any mistake in inter-
preting appearances, we can excuse Mr. Goyder; but
we can hardly excuse him for the glowing description
of the scene, when he must have known how large a
portion was due to refraction. For he says immediately afterwards, " We then proceeded due west for
twenty miles, to obtain a view from the summit of the
high land running from the north-west point of
Weathered Hill, crossing on our way those creeks at
ten and thirteen miles' distance. The first we named
Duck Pond Creek . . . . . . and the second, Mirage
Creek, from its forming the boundary of an imaginary
lake, which we supposed we were approaching, but
which disappeared as we neared the elevated land. It
would be useless to repeat the number of times we were
deceived by mirage, and surprised by the enormous refraction produced by these plains. Some idea of it may be
obtained from the fact, that the large gum trees seen
from Weathered Hill to the north, proved to be bushes of
from two to four feet high; and a large hill seen from
the summit of Mount Serle, by the aid of a powerful
glass, and which we estimated at least three thousand
feet, dwindled down to sixty." It would be well to have
borne this in mind when describing the cliffs at Lake
Torrens.

With the knowledge he had obtained, Mr. Goyder
returned to Adelaide, and published his account of the
wonderful country he had seen. The discovery caused
a good deal of excitement, for this region had been previously regarded as a desert. The Government was
besieged by applications for squatting licences; but
they very prudently, or imprudently as it turned out,
resolved not to sell good land too cheaply. They determined first to send the surveyor-general out to examine
the country, and report upon its extent and value. The

whole thing is an amusing episode in Australian exploration—a subject which, amid its usual sombre horrors of suffering and privation, affords few such sun-lit passages. It may be conceived, as already said, that the matter created a great stir in Adelaide and the neighbouring colonies. There was a movement in all directions, and the newspapers were crowded with pas-sages headed, " Northward Ho ! "

The surveyor-general, Colonel Freeling, R.E., set out with his party, and most anxiously was his report awaited. It came at last; but, oh, what a change came over the bright dream of lakes, and cliffs, and grassy plains! A note was received in Adelaide about the end of September, 1857, which dashed down all hopes, raised to the highest degree of expectation by seeing Colonel Freeling depart with a large boat, with which he was to have sailed about the ornamental water of Lake Torrens. The public were disappointed, but the surveyor-general was indignant, for he wrote as follows :—

" I much regret that what I have to relate is deci-dedly unfavourable to the extension of discoveries in the direction mentioned, and by the means proposed. The extensive bays, described in Mr. Goyder's report, the bluff headlands, the several islands between the north and south shores, the vegetation covering them, and their perpendicular cliffs, have all been the result of mirage, and do not, in point of fact, exist as represented. The conclusion drawn in that report, that the lake is subject only to the most trifling variations of level, is also proved to be an erroneous deduction."

This was clear enough, and as a summing up of evi-dence quite sufficiently judicial to secure an immediate verdict from the public, in its wrath making probably too little excuse for Mr. Goyder. What Colonel Freeling saw was, however, more than sufficient to justify what he said. He arrived at the lake on the 2nd September. He had observed a marked change in the country after leaving Mount Distance ; the ranges merging into hum-mocky hills, sometimes isolated, and having extensive plains, all of alluvial nature, rapidly opening into

issures under the sun's heat. There was very little
perceptible fall towards the north. For miles over these
plains there was abundance of drift timber; and this
showed that at times a vast body of water must come
down to the lake through the M'Donnell and the other
creeks. These indications led, at the very commencement, to a very strong suspicion that Mr. Goyder's lake
was merely an accumulation of flood-waters. The
party arrived on the 3rd at the exact spot where the
lake was observed, and one of the men who had been
with Mr. Goyder stated that the water had already
receded half a mile. For six miles round the country
was nearly a dead level, though apparently covered occasionally with water, probably one foot deep. The
soil was coated with salt, and was a mixture of clay and
sand without stones. The water was almost fresh.
The Mount Hopeless Range was visible to the south,
distant twenty miles. To the north there was the appearance of islands and cliffs, with vegetation upon them,
but their aspect was so peculiar that their true nature
could not be inferred.

On the 4th, the boat was brought up, as well as a small
folding iron punt, which had been provided in case of their
meeting shoal water. Both had been dragged thus far,
with the greatest difficulty, and it was quite marvellous
how they had come whole and sound through all the
passes in the ranges. But now that they were
brought to the lake, neither of them would float. The
punt was dragged a quarter of a mile through the mud,
in which the men sank, as they worked, up to the calf
of the leg; but after all there was scarcely water enough
to float a shoe. Continued observations of the land and
islands opposite were made. One of the islands showed
the perpendicular cliffs described by Mr. Goyder, but
on looking over the level plain which they had ridden
across, and which beyond a doubt they knew to be
nearly level, and not to have cliffs upon it, they saw
the appearance of the islands reproduced. This, at least,
furnished strong evidence that the aspect of the land
south was not to be relied on.

Being anxious to settle the question beyond any

possibility of dispute, Colonel Freeling, with a gentleman named Hawker, and three men, started on an attempt to cross the lake on foot. The walk was both fatiguing and dangerous. No water of more than six inches was met with, and so they had to wade through mud and slush, which every moment became deeper and deeper. Two small islands covered with scanty vegetation afforded them resting-places; but even with this help they barely accomplished three miles, and the cliffs seemed as far off as ever. Two of their number, more adventurous than the rest, made a further journey of two miles, but the fatigue endured by one of them was so great that it was with difficulty that he returned to the camp. Finally, Colonel Freeling closed his account by stating that the whole country round the lake was of the most desolate description; and thus the pleasant dream inspired by Mr. Goyder was dispelled.

It remains to be asked how are we to account for the water in such quantity and so fresh, seen by Mr. Goyder? There were many reasons for it which were not known to exist at that time. The Barcoo has been found to drain into Lake Torrens, and the sources of that river are far away, as we are aware, amid the basaltic table-land of the east coast. That year the whole of the eastern ranges were visited by extraordinary rains and floods, and a great portion of them were found next year by Gregory to have drained into the Barcoo. There were also heavy floods in March upon the Mount Serle Ranges; and M'Donnell Creek carried down a great deal of water. Thus it was, the lake was then fresh at a place where, nearly twenty years previously, Eyre and Frome had pronounced it to be more salt than the sea. It is rather curious, however, that no refraction was observed by Mr. Babbage when the country was comparatively dry. Probably moisture has a great deal to do with a phenomenon by which explorers in Australia have so often been deceived. Grey saw it on the coast, and so did Eyre; but I cannot recall any instance where it has been seen away from the influence of moisture.

Mr. Babbage had been of opinion that Lake Torrens

would be found passable in dry seasons, about the spot
where Freeling tried to cross. He thought that there
was a spur of granite from the Barrier Ranges, crossing
the lake, and uniting with the granite on M'Donnell
Creek. For this opinion, at least as far as the granite·
is concerned, there does not appear to be any foundation; but the lake has been crossed near the spot indicated when the season has been dry. A surveyor named
Ball crossed at this place on two occasions, and took two
horses with him. He described the crossing-place as
marshy, and without any surface rock. Of course, the
possibility of traversing a morass would prove nothing,
but it has since been found that the lakes are disconnected,
and that there are moderately high and dry banks of
sand between them.

About this time the South Australian colonists began
to take the most lively interest in the subject of exploration, and several expeditions were set on foot. People
began to see the folly of trusting to the first impressions
of early explorers, and to act as if they had not been
infallible in every case. Shortly after Mr. Goyder's
report, a party was sent to the westward of Lake
Torrens, under the command of Mr. Stephen Hack.
The party consisted of five men with twelve horses, a
dray, and six months' provisions. They first proceeded
by sea to Streaky Bay, and there a depôt was formed;
and subsequently explored to the north. This course
would take them into the Gawler Range, and it was
hoped that among those hills, which had only been
seen at a distance by Mr. Eyre, good country would be
found.

Mr. Hack's first camp was at Parlā, about thirty
miles nearly east from the depôt. Here he found some
small holes in the granite rock, which were the only supplies at all visible thereabouts. The summit commanded
an extensive view, but by no means a cheerful one.
All around the country appeared covered with scrub,
with here and there a granite hill projecting. He
could see the Gawler Range to the northward, and as
that seemed the only chance of better soil, he went
towards it with Mr. Miller, a volunteer, Mr. Harris, the

surveyor, and an aboriginal native as a guide. Travelling north-east, they reached the range upon the second
day, at a gap seen from Parlā. It was about seventy
miles from Streaky Bay. They found there a spring of
·fresh water at the foot of the granite rock, and Mr.
Hack considered it to be permanent; but that we
may reasonably doubt, from what will be told subsequently.

From the spring, Mr. Hack steered a little to the
east of north for another remarkable granite hill which
stood in the midst of a circle of similar elevations, and
was thence called Mount Centre. The road lay through
a very scrubby country, utterly destitute of any useful
vegetation. As they toiled along it they could see salt
lakes extending to the north-west as far as the eye
could reach, and there seemed to be very few crossing
places on them. From the top of the mount they could see
a mass of ranges to the north. But nothing showed them
that the country was likely to improve, or to be found
better provided with water. From the mount, Mr. Hack
returned to Parlā; he found as he went the tracks of
Major Warburton and his party going to the westward,
on an expedition, of which an account will be given
further on. Fifteen miles north of Parlā, he found a
considerable extent of grassy country in bold downs,
and it was seen from the top of a hill that the same
tract extended some distance east, and to the north-west
about eight or nine miles. It was run through at places
by belts of scrub, but Mr. Hack said there was about
a hundred square miles of good country. This was the
only result of the first examination of the country, which
was completed by the end of June.

It was not until the 6th July that the party were
again moved forward. On the 7th they reached a
rockwater, thirty-four miles from Parlā. They would
have continued on from hence, but the native guide
became so ill that Hack left the camp, and went on to
examine the ranges about Mount Centre. When he
returned, the black fellow was still very bad, so he
was sent back to Streaky Bay, and two other natives
engaged to guide the party on. These arrangements

so detained them that it was not until after the 22nd
that the whole party were got to Ponàra, the water-
hole under Mount Granite. They left this on the 23rd,
and kept outside Mount Granite, passing through
twenty miles of scrub. Then they came to a well-
grassed plain. About six miles from this, they camped
at Warroonà, a permanent water-hole in a creek coming
from the eastward. It was dry, but water could be
easily got by scraping in the gravel at the bottom; and
the natives said this was the case even in the driest
season. The country all around was salt bush and
grass, without any scrub. To the north-east there was
a fine range, twenty-five miles away, running east and
west.

On the 27th they moved through a similar country
to a spring, named Koondooléa, eight miles away. Mr.
Hack then left his party, and rode about ten miles to
Yālbinda, another spring. All the land was good for
at least ten miles more, and at that distance he could
see the last portion of the Gawler Range running out
as low detached hills. Beyond these there was none
visible for at least fifty miles. The natives said that
there was no water to be found upon a north course,
but that to the east of north there was a very large
salt lake. This would be about the direction of Lake
Torrens, and Mr. Hack therefore thought it better to
choose that route. From Koondooléa the party went
to a rockwater, named Kŭrahkildē, and from thence to
Yāna, a creek with surface water. From Yāna they
went to Wānea, a distance of twenty miles, through
very indifferent salt-bush country and scrub. And
thus for some few days more they journeyed on from
spring to spring, or from rockwater to rockwater,
through either a dense sterile scrub or salt-bush plains,
until they came to an immense salt lake, which the
tracks of Major Warburton showed had been visited
previously. It was very shallow, and surrounded for
a long way from the water by a white crust, like
glittering snow. To the north, as far as they could
see, the horizon was a mass of salt, with no high land
visible. There are strong points of resemblance be-

tween this country and the scrubs so frequently described in the expeditions about Western Australia.
Everything corresponds. The scrubs, the vacant plains,
the granite hills, and the rocks with surface water,
are very similar in both places; and when we come to
the immense salt lakes, with sheets of salt extending to
the far distant horizon, the resemblance is quite complete. It has not been ascertained whether the South
Australian scrubs are on a sandy tableland, nor, if so,
what height they are above the sea. But if there are
plains of any considerable elevation, one must conclude
that the peculiarities of the Australian flora and climate
lead to scrubs, salt lakes, &c., wherever elevated sandy
land is found.

From the lake, Mr. Hack found that the country
began to improve, until he came to a spring named
Colàmirrika, one of the names given by Messrs. Oakden and Hulkes, as belonging to the country discovered
by them in 1851. It was a spring of water in a deep
rocky creek, in a high range. The party were now
only a few miles from Mount Granite, and the country
was in general good. It will be needless to mention
all the springs and watercourses which were found on
the Lake Gairdner side of the Gawler Range in the
course of this expedition. They were very numerous,
and the country round of middling quality. The whole
of Mr. Hack's time was taken up in going from spring
to spring, and from hill to hill, in the Gawler Ranges,
and were the reader to follow his journal, it would be
merely an uninteresting record of names. The extent
of country which was thus minutely examined was
scarcely sixty miles square, and by the time that the
principal creeks and mountains were named and
mapped, Mr. Hack's provisions were exhausted, and
it was time for him to return. He made for Port
Augusta, by the head of Spencer's Gulf, and found no
permanent surface water between the gap of Baxter's
Range (where Mr. Eyre found water) and the most
easterly portion of the country he had been exploring;
but this was only a distance of twenty miles.

Mr. Hack's report of the result of the expedition

was very favourable. Unfortunately, the details are
imperfect, and he does not give the latitude and longitude of any point of his route. He had, however,
rounded the northern spur of the Gawler Range, which
runs from the neighbourhood of Streaky Bay, towards
the head of Spencer's Gulf.

The above journey has been mentioned before that
of Warburton, though the latter was the first to discover some of the country just described. Unfortunately, no detailed account of the journey was published,
nor, as far as I am aware, were any maps of the route
made. This has obliged me to mention Hack's
journey first; but the difference in point of time was
very slight indeed. It was in June, 1857, that Major
Warburton traversed the Gawler Ranges from east to
west, his course from the southern portion of Baxter's
Range being west-north-west until he reached Lake
Gairdner. After this, he proceeded northwards for
thirty miles, then, turning west and south, emerged on
the chain of salt lakes west of the ranges. During the
whole of this journey neither Major Warburton nor
any of his party found a single spring of running water
nor any supply which could be called permanent. Two
small holes were found in shallow watercourses, but
with this exception, all the rest was the produce of
showers which the Major had been obliged to wait for
before he started. Neither was he much more fortunate
in discovering pasture than water. Patches of country
were found which would be tolerably grassed at the
most favourable season of the year, and at the eastern
end of the range there was a long and narrow strip
of pasture land, with some very pretty grassy valleys;
but, on the whole, Major Warburton's account of the
Gawler Range was decidedly unfavourable, and quite
the reverse of that given by Mr. Hack.

Now, which was right? If one or two circumstances
are borne in mind, it will not be very difficult to decide.
Mr. Hack, as an old squatter, was, no doubt, a better
judge of pastoral country than Major Warburton; but
the question turns upon the water. If there was no
water, the country must be considered unavailable for

any purpose. Now, Major Warburton found none before the winter rains had set in, and begun to tell upon
the ground; and Mr. Hack found plenty when the
same rains had just concluded. The inference is obvious. All that the later party found was shallow
surface water; and we must still adhere to the account
given by Eyre, and confirmed by Warburton, that
unless water should be procured in wells, the Gawler
Range, even in the best parts, will be found uninhabitable.

In July, this same year, another exploration of the
country to the west of Lake Torrens had been undertaken. The party consisted of Messrs. Swinden, Campbell, Thompson, and Stock. They travelled on horseback, lightly equipped, and their supplies were carried
on two pack-horses. They crossed the head of Spencer's
Gulf on the overland crossing-place to Port Lincoln;
and on the 1st August had made about twenty-five
miles northerly through a scrubby country. On the
next day they reached Beda Creek, which had been
discovered by Campbell in the preceding January, as
already mentioned. There was plenty of water in the
creek at this time, but the horses would not touch it, so
they had to continue their journey. They went on,
steering north-west. At six miles, they struck Lake
Torrens, or an arm of it, running in a westerly direction. They crossed it. Nine miles to the west, the
country became very scrubby, and for the next ten
miles was nothing but heavy sand hummocks. There
was abundance of salt water in all directions, but none
fresh, and the horses were now evidently flagging for
the want of it. This was, it must be admitted, very
like the country of Western Australia, and not at all
like the fertile tracts described by Hack. But there
was better than this. After leaving the scrub, and
passing over some open ground, they reached a large
creek, and some excellent water, at a hole called by the
native Pernatty. This was about seventy-five miles
from Port Augusta.

On the 4th they descended the creek for about four
miles, but as it turned too much to the southward, they

left it, and at two miles came to another. This also
contained water in a fine sheet, called by the natives
Yanaherry. Next day they went towards a remarkable
flat-topped hill to the northward, which they had
named Bonney's Bluff. It lay close to other hills, and
when they had passed them, they came upon the
Elizabeth. At first, the holes on it were salt, but as
they traced it down they came upon plenty of fresh
water. It was a fine stream, and, according to the
explorers, far more entitled to be called a river than
the streams about Adelaide, such as the Torrens or
the Light. What little further examination they could
afford increased their opinion of its importance; and
then, as their provisions were almost exhausted, they
set out on their return. In their homeward journey,
they crossed several other creeks, but all salt, so that
their horses suffered a good deal for want of water ere
they reached the settled districts. One remarkable
discovery of theirs deserves especial mention. The
crossing place between the head of Spencer's Gulf and
Lake Torrens used to be over a narrow portion of a
morass, which was considered to be the old line of
junction between the two waters, and that no better
crossing could be found. Our explorers, however,
found a dry elevated strip of land between the lake and
the gulf at least a quarter of a mile wide.

Mr. Swinden started again in August, with three
companions. He reached Pernatty on the 23rd, and
they explored down the creek to which it belongs,
finding abundance of fresh water. The next day he
steered west, until he came to a large water-hole, named
Yaltacowie. From this he followed up a creek three
miles, and then steered north for some bold hills.
These proved so stony that he was obliged to leave
them, but the same night he reached, on a nearly north
course, a fine water-hole on a creek within sight of Lake
Torrens. On the 25th he went to the eastward, over
stony hills, finding some fresh water-holes close to a lake
named Andemorka. From this point he returned to
the south, and after crossing a brackish creek, reached
Beda again. There were many other water-holes found

near Lake Torrens, besides those spoken of above.
The most of them seemed permanent. It will be remarked that these explorations speak of nothing but
the water. The squatter looks principally for a locality
to which he can remove his flock, so that water is the
first consideration, and the other physical characters
remain undescribed. We know, however, enough of
this tract to be able to say that it differs in no respect
from salt lake country described elsewhere, except,
perhaps, that the scrubs are more open. The sand is
red, the scrub is Acacia, and there is a great quantity of
spinifex grass.

The tract thus discovered was called Swinden's
country, and it was visited during the month of September by two or three parties. Fifty miles north of
Swinden's furthest, Mr. Campbell found an excellent
pastoral country, with abundance of fresh water in
lakes, some of which he said were five or six miles in
circumference, and several feet deep. In one of the
lakes a prodigious quantity of emu bones were found.
A narrow ravine near the lake appeared to be a trap
into which the birds had been driven by the natives,
and then eaten where their bones were found. It was
supposed that the available country beyond Campbell's
furthest must have been a considerable distance, for the
natives did not know anything of the tribes to the
north. Swinden's country, it will be seen, lies a great
deal to the north of the Gawler Ranges, Andemorka
being in lat. 30° 40', long. 137° 10'.

In the same year, about the month of October,
Messrs. Miller and Dutton made an exploration at the
back of Fowler's and Denial Bays. They went out
with a native guide, with three horses, very lightly
equipped. The first stage was to Beelemah, in Denial
Bay, a waterhole used by Mr. Eyre in 1840. It is a
large swamp, and the hole opened at that time was now
a spring bubbling over. After travelling thirty miles
through alternate plains and low scrub, they stated
that they came to water, which, however, was not permanent. More open country next succeeded, with
patches of scrub, until they came to large plains

destitute of trees stretching beyond the range of vision to the northward. This was about forty-five miles due north of Fowler's Bay. Thence they travelled south-east ten miles to a rockwater, and then due east through scrub and occasionally open country. All the land was tableland, at least after a certain distance from the coast; but there was no water upon it, nor was any found until they returned to Streaky Bay. It is due or right, however, to state, that the accounts of these gentlemen have been called in question; and though their description of the physical features is substantially correct, it has been denied that they ever penetrated so far inland as their diary asserts.*

---

* A controversy has since ensued as to the character of the grassy plains north of Fowler's Bay. Major Warburton, who saw the ground at its worst, describes it so as to bring forcibly to mind the naked plains in some parts of the Sahara. Captain Delisser, on the contrary, asserts that the land could not be better for the purposes of pasture, except from the absence of trees of any kind. Yet, in spite of this opinion, recent attempts at forming a settlement have failed for want of water. A well has been, I believe, sunk, but no water found at over 100 feet in depth. These immense arid plains form a large and curious feature in the physical geography of Australia.

CHAPTER XVI.

THE DISCOVERIES OF BABBAGE, WARBURTON, AND
F. GREGORY.

Babbage explores near Lake Torrens—Mistake in his instructions—Warburton succeeds him—Warburton's exploration—Opening up of the path
which led Stuart to the centre—Parry—Geharty—Burt—F. Gregory's
explorations along the Murchison—The Gascoyne—The Lyons—The
Edmund.

In 1858, the Parliament of South Australia voted a
sum of money for the purpose of equipping a party to
continue Hack's explorations to the northward. A
party of eight men were engaged by the Government,
and the command given to Mr. Babbage, who has
already been spoken of in connection with his explorations near Lake Torrens. Mr. Harris was the second in
command, and to act as surveyor, in which capacity he
had been out with Mr. Hack. The stores provided were
three drays, a tank cart, sixteen horses, a hundred and
eighty sheep, and eighteen months' provisions. It was
intended that the party should proceed northward very
rapidly, but the instructions given by Mr. F. S. Dutton,
the Commissioner of Crown Lands, were not compatible
with this intention. In his letter he told Mr. Babbage
that the primary objects of the expedition were the
thorough exploration, as far as practicable, of the
country lying between the western shore of Lake
Torrens and the eastern shore of Lake Gairdner, and
thence northwards; the surveying and mapping of
the western shore of Lake Torrens, so as to remove any
doubts as to the extent, direction, and outline of the

lake; surveying and mapping of the eastern and the northern shore of Lake Gairdner in like manner.

It will be easily seen that the objects of the expedition were, after these instructions, principally confined to surveying. Eighteen months would be barely sufficient to perform what is here set down, and that was the extent of the rations supplied to the party. Unfortunately, neither Mr. Babbage nor the public viewed the instructions as they should have done, and the consequence was that everyone regarded it as an exploring expedition. By-and-by, when very little advance was made by the party, people began to murmur, and were loud in their complaints about the waste of time and money which was apparently going on. Much to Mr. Babbage's surprise, the Government took up these complaints, and the blundering commissioner who had written the letter of instruction now reprehended Babbage severely for his delays. The manner in which this was done was somewhat singular. It may be observed in the letter quoted above that the word northwards occurs once, but that the directions to survey the shores of the lakes were without reference to any point of the compass. Taking advantage of this point, Mr. Babbage was greatly blamed for coming to the southwards with his survey. Mr. Babbage, however, was to blame. Not only did he come southwards, but he reappeared in the settled districts; and this certainly was not in accordance with any portion of his instructions, nor what was due to himself.

Having mentioned this, in order that too much might not be expected from the expedition of Babbage, admirably equipped as it was, I now proceed to relate the discoveries which resulted from it. On the 1st April (the date is important) the party reached Beda; and nearly fourteen days were occupied in looking for water in the neighbourhood and surveying the hills around. Mr. Babbage made a short exploration on foot towards Lake Torrens, and from an eminence near had an extensive view of the Gawler Range to the south, and the Flinders Range to the east. Some days were also lost in searching for a young man named Coulthard,

who had been lost in searching for a sheep-run to the
west of Lake Torrens.* It would be hard to describe
how the party was employed until the 8th May, but the
duties performed were mostly in camp. On the 9th,
Mr. Babbage made another expedition, proceeding westward, with one companion. He found a salt lagoon
near Oakden's Table-topped Hill, which he named Lake
Windabout. The country he examined was generally
scrubby, with salt lakes; and until 29th August the
time was spent among them, surveying, according to
instructions, the shores of Lake Torrens and Lake
Gairdner. Of the salt lakes, Hart, Hanson, Young-
husband, and Red Lake were the principal, but some
of these had been previously discovered by Messrs. A.
M'Farlane, T. Seymour, and Dugald Smith, who, in the
latter part of 1857, had been out here in search of
country available for squatting purposes.

Thus Mr. Babbage continued mapping and surveying, making a small expedition here and another there,
until the 29th of August, at which time he was at Port
Augusta, taking a rest after his labours. This was
a queer kind of exploration, beside which the tedious
delays of Leichhardt look like a forced march. When
Mr. Babbage arrived at the township, he heard to his
surprise that Mr. Harris was on his way down to
Adelaide with a great many of the horses and drays.
The leader immediately started in pursuit, and overtook
his men about one hundred and sixty miles from town.
Here a new surprise awaited him. He heard that the
Government had sent on Mr. Charles Gregory as his
second in command, in place of Mr. Harris. He learned
also that Mr. A. C. Gregory had just arrived in Adelaide,

* The melancholy fate of this poor fellow is a specimen of what sort of
dangers are run by the first settlers upon a newly discovered country. He
had gone with one companion in search of some pastoral country, but soon
became much distressed for want of water. He then separated from his companion in search of it, and was never afterwards seen alive. When his
body was found, his tin canteen was scratched with a brief record of his
horrible sufferings from thirst. He had killed his horse for its blood, and
then had gone forward on foot under a burning sun, searching for water in
every hollow and crevice. The record then becomes straggling and difficult
to read, and the sentence which is left unfinished, shows a terrible struggle to
maintain the powers of life while he wrote his dismal story.

after tracing down the whole course of the Barcoo; and
as this had been done with the aid of horses alone, the
Adelaide authorities were of opinion that Mr. Babbage
should send back his drays, and confine himself to horses
alone for carrying his baggage.   Of course, he was very
much annoyed at this change in his plans, and he was
still more annoyed on reaching his camp and finding a
very strong reprimand from the commissioner for doing
almost what he had been told.   Yet as he must have felt
that a part of the rebuke was deserved, he merely wrote
a remonstrance, and set to work exploring in earnest,
even though nearly six of the best months were gone.
He asked Mr. Gregory to accompany him to the north
for three months, but that gentleman declined, as he
had not agreed to remain with the Adelaide Government for so long a time.   He therefore returned with
the stockkeeper, and Mr. Babbage started on the
28th September, with four men and six months' provisions.

His first stage was to a water-hole, named Smith's
Main Waterhole, which had been previously discovered
by him.   The water was five feet deep, and promised to
hold out for a long time, though the large lake found
by Mr. Campbell, which they passed next day, was
perfectly dry.   By the aid of such surface-water, in
creeks and in water-holes, he continued to advance to
the northward, sometimes over scrubby sand-hills, and
sometimes over stony, salt-bush plains, until he had
reached the limit of his previous explorations.   He then
halted the party three days, while he went to examine
the country further north.   The camp was at a water-
hole, and there was no creek from it, as in the case of
most of the others, but it seemed to draw its supply
from many swamps in the plains around, which all,
even at this time, contained water.   From these the
party were moved up twenty-one miles north-east, to
another large water-hole, supplied in a similar manner
to the last.   Then ensued low sand ridges, with salt
bush upon them, and higher ones, crowned with pine
trees, and occasionally wide, open valleys.   The next
water-hole was distant eleven miles, and barely ten

more to one beyond that. The last was at the head of
a creek, already visited by Messrs. Stuart and Forster,
who had set out to the north-west while Babbage was
surveying about Lake Gairdner. Their expedition will
be spoken of presently. The creek was called after
Stuart, but the latter had already named it after Mr.
Chambers—a name which it still preserves. The
native who had accompanied Babbage as a guide thus
far, now left him; but before doing so took him to a
creek with water-holes, about sixteen miles from their
last camp. On their way they passed several water-
holes in the cliffs of a detached table-topped hill. From
the top of one of the cliffs they could see a range of
hills on the other side of Lake Torrens, running north
of the position of Mr. Eyre's Mount Norwest, and they
gave this the name of the Hermit Range, on account of
its isolated character. They followed Horseshoe Creek
to its junction with Stuart's Creek, but though water
was found in its course, several of the holes were salt.
It was different with Stuart's Creek, which was traced
down to a large salt lake, which was named Lake
Gregory.

From the lake, Mr. Babbage made an excursion
across to the Hermit Range, the nearest portion of
which was about twenty miles west of his position. At
the distance of sixteen miles he found a gum creek,
with salt water, but liable evidently to considerable
floods at times. On ascending the range, he could
distinctly trace the shores of Lake Gregory trending
northwards, but to the west and north-west, where he
expected to see Lake Torrens, he saw no sign of a lake,
nor anything except an extensive plain. To the south-
east there were hills, and to the south several isolated
salt lakes, amid extensive plains of sand ridges and
scrub. The height of this hill, Mr. Babbage considered,
was about three hundred and sixty-three feet from the
plain, and, in consequence of the view from it, he subsequently expressed an opinion that Lake Torrens did not
extend thus far (lat. 29° 37'), or that if it did it must be
as an inconsiderable channel. Mr. Babbage did not,
however, state this early enough to put it beyond a

doubt that he and no other first discovered that Lake
Torrens did not extend like a horseshoe of salt lakes all
round the Flinders Range. Mr. Eyre did not see this
portion of the imaginary circle, except at a great distance, and then the salt lakes scattered here and there
might have made him imagine that they were continuous. What he saw was that large lake called now
Lake Eyre, but which Mr. Babbage had not as yet
recognised as Eyre's Lake Torrens, and had named Lake
Gregory. There is a very broad strip of high land,
between the latter and the salt lake which reaches
down to Spencer's Gulf, and now retains the name of
Lake Torrens. That lake is a long, narrow sheet of
water, extending nearly parallel with the Flinders
Range, while Lake Eyre is a broad, irregularly shaped
sheet of salt marsh, of immense size, whose northern
boundaries are as yet completely unknown. Of all the
facts lately discovered about these singular features in
the geography of Australia, we cannot give Mr. Babbage
credit for more than a suspicion of the truth, which
could hardly have escaped the observation of any
explorer in the same locality. To Major Warburton
undoubtedly is due the discovery of the most part of
what is now known.

On returning to his camp, Mr. Babbage started
northwards, and in about ten miles found a singular
hot spring about four and a half miles west of Lake
Gregory, or Eyre, as we shall in future call it. This
spring was the first of a series of such features found in
this country, which is the only point of distinction
between it and the salt-lake territory of Western Australia. The spring was a basin formed by a sand-hill,
about twenty feet high, and covered with reeds. The
area enclosed was thickly overgrown with rushes, amid
which water was bubbling up and running over in
several channels. These united in a stream which
flowed through a break in the sandy basin, and from
thence into a reedy swamp below, which drained into a
salt creek. The water was too hot for the hand to
bear even for a minute, but it was quite fresh, and
yielded about 175,000 gallons daily. It did not appear

to be affected by the rains. Such a discovery in such a
place very much surprised the explorers, and how to
account for so great a supply amid a country where the soil
was principally sand, and the water principally salt, was
a mystery to them as it is to us. Of course, the discovery
removed the most of Mr. Babbage's apprehensions, for
he now knew that he could carry on his explorations
without any fear of not having water to fall back upon.
He called the basin, Emerald Springs.

From this point Mr. Babbage endeavoured to trace
the shores of Lake Eyre before returning to his depôt
camp on the Elizabeth. He found a branch of the lake
running up to the north-east, corresponding exactly
with the position of the most northerly point where Eyre
visited his Lake Torrens. This branch opened into a
larger portion of the lake basin, which had no shores
visible to the north or north-east. A long arm, running
south from the western side, obliged Babbage to double
back upon his course in order to round it, and he then
followed up its western side until he got into a country
void of water, and was therefore obliged to return. In
crossing Stuart's Creek, he noticed fossils in the banks,
which, he said, resembled the fossils in the Murray
cliffs. At any rate, the stone was much of the same
character.

In the meantime, the Government in Adelaide had
become so disappointed at hearing that Mr. Babbage
had been seen at Mount Remarkable that they had sent
out Major Warburton to supersede him. The latter
did not reach the camp until Mr. Babbage had already
started from the depôt on the Elizabeth. The water
was getting very scarce, but the Major thought it better
to follow Mr. Babbage as soon as possible; and after
writing one or two letters to Adelaide, in which Mr.
Babbage's conduct was reflected upon very unfavour-
ably and harshly, he started in pursuit. He found Mr.
Babbage at Lake Eyre on the 5th of November; and
having sent him back with some of his former companions, the Major continued the explorations. It is
not my intention to trouble my readers with a record of
the unseemly disputes which ensued between the two

explorers as to the priority of certain discoveries.
After patiently wading through the whole correspon-
dence—and I assure my readers it does require patience
—I am convinced that Mr. Babbage discovered no more
than is here set down to his credit. When Major
Warburton arrived, Mr. Babbage asked for one man
and rations to assist him in ascertaining the fact of the
division between the salt lakes. Of course, in refusing
this, the Major was not to blame, because his instructions were to supersede Mr. Babbage, and not to assist
him in finishing his explorations. Yet not only did he
refuse his request, but he stated in his official despatches
that Mr. Babbage only obtained the idea of the crossing-
place from him, the Major; and, moreover, he insinu-
ated that Mr. Babbage had never been at the Hermit
Range at all. True or not, this was an abrupt way of
putting it. No doubt, Major Warburton was a more
active and enterprising man than Mr. Babbage, and
probably more fitted to conduct the expedition, but he
seemed then unfit to conduct the discussion with an easy
good-temper. Mr. Babbage, though hampered by his
instructions, was unfairly treated by the Government,
though quite unfit for such a position; and after saying
this, such matters had better be left to oblivion.

In searching for Mr. Babbage, Major Warburton had
made many valuable discoveries. On the 24th October,
he crossed Margaret Creek, and then turned north,
towards a prominent hill. In making for this, he
traversed the channel three times, and found some very
good water-holes in its bed, and also a salt creek coming
from the north-west. The hill was called Mount Hamilton, and near it were some fine fresh-water springs.
These, and many others which the Major found
on his explorations, were generally at the foot of hills,
rising out of salt pans, with reedy or limestone mounds.
Some of them were running strongly, and all, apparently, into reedy swamps. The country round them
was boggy, and well supplied with vegetation, and they
were generally so much alike that a description of this
one found at Mount Hamilton will suffice for the whole.
It was a conical mound of limestone, measuring two

hundred and fifty yards round the base, and sixty at the top. It rose to the height of forty feet out of a flat salt pan, and the cone was covered with a wreath of reeds, eight or nine feet high. These concealed a circular basin of water, about fifty feet in diameter, and ten or twelve deep, and from this the overflowings of the spring ran out over the face of the rock in strong streams.

From the springs, Warburton struck west of north over ten miles of very good country until he reached a salt creek. Altering his course to west, he came, at ten miles more, to a chain of ponds, named Pasley's Ponds, and here he camped. The scene was very different from the previously received notions of the country round Lake Torrens. The ponds there were found in a short creek, and were, even at that late season, fine sheets of water. There were hills near, named Beresford Hills, with another batch of springs. The water was good, the country around excellent, and the game was so plentiful that the party obtained an abundant supply of wild ducks. As the 27th was wet, they camped, but on the 28th they travelled seventeen miles north-west, towards a remarkable collection of little hills, which proved to be another batch of springs. They were named Strangway's Springs. The salt creek they had previously crossed ran westward, and Major Warburton followed its course for some distance, through a well-grassed valley; and when it led to an inferior country he struck north again. He crossed the creek with difficulty, as there were many quicksands in it. Well-grassed sand-hills and valleys succeeded for the next seventeen miles, and the whole party camped together at a small water-hole.

All this time the Major was advancing in a north direction, keeping a little to the west, in order to travel parallel with Lake Eyre. The creeks, therefore, that he crossed came from the higher land to the westward, and, for the most part, ran into the lake. As yet the country had been good, but very uniform. They were evidently coming to a change, for on the 30th they could see the distant looming of a high, rugged range,

some distance to the north. Of course they made
towards this at once, for not only was a range unexpected at this side of the lake, but it was also the first
glimpse of the truth that the interior of Australia was
not the desert which Sturt had described it to be.
Major Warburton directed his companions to make for
the highest hill in the range before them, named Mount
Margaret, while he explored down a large gum creek,
named the Douglas, which they crossed on their route.
He traced the stream for several miles, and found a few
water-holes, but no permanent supply. Having satisfied
himself of this, he turned to the range, which he now
named after Mr. Samuel Davenport. Owing to some
mistake, he did not meet his companions, and was
obliged to encamp without food or water. The range,
according to the Major, was most interesting and picturesque, rising at least one thousand feet above the level
of the plains. There were immense cliffs of white
quartzite in it, exposed in high bluffs along the southern
face, and they gave the hills a grand and imposing
appearance. Several gum creeks ran from it to the
eastward, but they did not contain any water. It should
be noticed that this range, if really of quartzite, would
probably belong to the system of rocks in the Flinders
Range, and would differ altogether from the mountains
of granite, quartz, greenstone, or gneiss found in the
salt lake country of Western Australia.

The next day, the Major returned to his companions,
and they set about retracing their steps to seek for Mr.
Babbage, as they were very much to the north-west of
that gentleman's furthest. It is a pity the Major did
not continue his explorations into the Davenport Range;
but he considered it paramount to send Mr. Babbage
back, even though his own labours could be carried on
but little further, in consequence of the delay. Owing
to this, Major Warburton missed making the discoveries
which afterwards fell to the lot of Stuart; but it must
never be forgotten that the former gentleman opened
up the way which made a passage to the centre of
Australia comparatively easy.

In returning, the Major varied his tracks, finding

the country still good, and discovering some more
springs, named after Corporal Coward, who accompanied
him.   When Babbage was found, and sent back to the
Elizabeth, Major Warburton sent all his stores and
companions back also, intending to take two men
only with him and explore the country between the
lakes.   He started across Stuart's Creek, and travelled
to the north-east over eight miles of open country.   It
might be considered good land, for it had small
watercourses amid its slaty hills, and only very light
scrub.   On the 9th November, he came upon a fine
creek running south, with plenty of water in it.   It was
named the Gregory.   There were two other creeks
further on, and the last was broad and salt, running at
the foot of the Hermit Range.   Very likely these
streams do no more than drain the range just named,
but it is possible they may form a channel of communication between the salt lakes in very rainy seasons.   At
the foot of one of the hills in the Hermit Range, there
was another batch of springs, decidedly the finest they
had yet discovered.   One of the basins was twenty feet
deep, and the water one hundred and fifty feet long by
one hundred wide.   They were named Finnis Springs,
and were so numerous that the Major thought he
could see hundreds, with the water flowing from them.

On leaving the Hermit Range, they ascended a
tableland, over which they travelled for twenty-one
miles.   The country was pretty good, but very level,
with the exception of one well-watered valley, which
crossed the tableland, about two miles and a half wide
and fifteen or twenty miles long.   At the end of the
twenty-one miles, no signs of Lake Torrens lay before
them, and then Major Warburton became convinced
that he had accomplished his object, and had no further
occasion to look for the lake, so he turned to the
southward.   He kept south-east, and on the 10th reached
what had been apparently the former bed of the lake.
It was bounded on the western side by broken cliffs, and
on the eastern by a long range of high land.   The cliffs
on the west may have been the effect of refraction, and
the depression may not be always dry ; but at any rate,

it is very likely to be the channel of communication between the lakes in times of flood. The country around was covered with salt bush, and was slightly boggy, but certainly not barren.

Major Warburton was upon the tracks of other explorers, now to be mentioned, and therefore we leave him, only remarking that this terminated the bungling expedition sent out at so great an expense, the partial failure of which was shared as much by the Government as by the gentleman at first in command.* Before proceeding further, however, let it be mentioned how much these discoveries altered the map of Australia. Lake Torrens had always been represented like an immense sickle, wrapping round the range, and drain-ing by a marsh into Spencer's Gulf. It was now proved that a complete separation existed between the most southerly part of the lake and the gulf; that the lake was divided into many great salt-water basins, and that a great portion of the intervening land was of fair quality, and well supplied with fresh water. No doubt, these views were a considerable relief to those who imagined that such an immense tract of country was a salt marsh. What a change it was from the prevalent opinion, may be gathered from a description of the lake by Colonel Gawler, when lecturing before the Royal Geographical Society. "Picture to the mind," he said, "the dimensions of that lake. Let us place ourselves on Highgate Hill, near London, and if it were possible to carry the eye to Gravesend or Chatham, that would be the breadth of it near its south-western extremity. Carry on this breadth from London to Newcastle-on-Tyne, diminishing the width to twelve miles; then turn that line into something like a horseshoe, and you have an idea of what we know of Lake Torrens." Now,

* I regret to add that the Adelaide Parliament showed itself in a most unenviable light in rewarding Major Warburton's exertions; only £100 was voted to him which, of course, did not clear his expenses. Next year, to indemnify the country for such an extravagant piece of generosity, £100 per annum was taken off his salary when the estimates were passing, and he has been receiving this reduced rate ever since. Surely such parsimony puts a bar upon energy and active enterprise in the public service. It was certainly a lucky thing for Columbus that he had not an Adelaide Parliament to deal with.

though the truth is something near this, the lake is
not that barrier to the interior which it had been
formerly considered, and large breaks in its length, such
as those just described, give great hope of the country
in which it occurs.

In July, 1858, Mr. Parry, a Government surveyor,
had been sent out to map the territory between the west
side of the Flinders Range and Lake Torrens.   On the
27th of the same month, he got well out on to the
plains, within what was formerly called the Horseshoe.
The country was very rough, the whole surface being
broken by projecting peaks of vertical clay slate, from
one to fifteen feet in height.   He camped that night
upon Frome Creek, which was dry, even though this
was the season, if any, that it should contain running
water.   The next day he proceeded a little north
of west to a fine water-hole, named Shamrock Pool,
which had been previously discovered by Mr. McFar-
lane.   Within a few hundred yards of it, there was a
singular piece of tableland, about fifteen feet high.   It
was about a mile long, and of irregular figure, and the
banks were nearly perpendicular.   It was composed of
gypsum, and for about one hundred yards all around the
ground was nearly destitute of vegetation, but cracked
in all directions, like dried mud.

Mr. Parry's course for some time after was over
stony, yet soft ground.   The land appeared to rise, and
they crossed the bed of an extensive lake, running north
and east.   The land then broke up into hills, but not
above the plains, for they seemed as if they were cut
down into the tableland, as their summits seldom rose
above it.   The bluffs abutting on to the lake, and the
dip of the clay-slate strata, were towards the water, and
perfectly level ridges of slate formed its bed.   The
area was about twenty miles by five.   A little beyond
it, the land suddenly dipped to a lower level, and then
succeeded a succession of sand-hills, about five hundred
feet high, with a little surface water here and there, but
only very little.   One or two large ponds were met
with, containing abundance of fresh water; and near
these there were creeks, dry, of course, and having

polygonum bushes in the bed, as if the water had not
run for ages.   There were thousands of pigeons round
the water-holes; and in this, as well as in many other
respects, the country resembled the land found by
Sturt in the neighbourhood of Strzelecki's Creek and
the Barcoo.   The country was very poor, with large
patches of pebbles imbedded in sand; but at times these
were replaced by clay plains, rent and fissured if dry,
and boggy if still retaining moisture.   The only vegetation was salt bush and large shrubs.   The horizon
was broken occasionally by peaked or table-topped hills.
One large creek was crossed.   It contained deep reaches
of water, and seemed permanent.   It was called The
River; and after five miles of good country beyond it,
sand-hills were reached, which succeeded each other like
waves of the sea, all about five feet high.   It was easy
to say what this would lead to; and in a short time they
came upon the Lake Eyre.   It was covered with salt,
and very boggy.   As Mr. Parry returned, he discovered
other pools of fresh water; and in reading his account
one cannot help being struck with the resemblance this
country bears to that called the Central Desert by Sturt,
and as it is known for how small a distance any of the
features found by Mr. Parry continued, we may readily
imagine the same for those found by Sturt.   Parry's
experience with regard to the refraction on these plains
was the same as that of previous explorers in the same
locality.

Before turning to Mr. Gregory's expedition down
the Barcoo, there are one or two little explorations
made about this time which it is more convenient to
introduce into this part of the work.   A police trooper
named Geharty was sent, with one companion, from
Streaky Bay, to examine the country described by
Messrs. Miller and Dutton, north of Fowler's Bay, and
to report upon it.   He reached Hack's Yalbinda
Spring on the 23rd June—that is, on the grassy plains
marked in the map of his journey.   Geharty was not,
however, so well satisfied with the locality as Mr. Hack
had been, and stated that with the exception of half a
mile of grassy land close under the hills, dense scrub

upon sand-hills was all that met the eye on every side.
The spring was not worth mentioning, being only the
surface drainage from the hill.   From this point
Geharty made several journeys to and fro in Hack's
country, and gave a most unfavourable report of all the
land in the vicinity of the Gawler Range, thus confirm-
ing the accounts of Eyre and Warburton.   The range
itself was described as being quite unworthy of the
name of a range.   At a distance, certainly, the hills
looked grand and imposing, but a nearer examination
showed them to be only granite peaks, quite barren, or
with a very little grass upon them of a useful quality.

Geharty explored also in the neighbourhood of Lake
Gairdner, or at least what he imagined to be that lake;
but as he had nothing to guide him but the descriptions
of others, this fact alone makes his accounts liable to
suspicion.   It might have happened that he did not
examine the same country as Hack; and at any rate
there is no means of ascertaining whether their springs
were identical.   But he must at least have passed over
a good deal of Hack's discoveries, and these he reported
as barren and useless.

He also went to find those fine plains described
by Miller and Dutton, north-west of Fowler's Bay.
He could find none of their grassy flats, stretching
beyond the range of vision, nor anything better than
the most desolate and arid scrub.   In returning he
made every search for the tracks of the former explorers,
but without success.   This led to an inquiry, from
which there appeared a strong probability that those
gentlemen had very much miscalculated their distance
from Fowler's Bay, and that the grassy country must
have been some level scrub seen from a long distance.
The result of all these journeys seemed to be that the
country around the Gawler Range was hopelessly sterile
for a long distance, and differing very little from the
arid scrubs in Western Australia.   It is true that sometimes explorers gave a different version of its nature,
but its true character has been asserted by the absence
of any settlement upon the land, and the subsequent
accounts of other explorers.

When Major Warburton started to take command of Babbage's expedition, he sent Corporal Burt to Mount Norwest to meet him there, having formed a very just idea that a passage would be found across Lake Torrens. Corporal Burt made a number of journeys over the ground of Parry's discoveries, but in other respects did not add much to the knowledge already obtained of the localities. Yet these expeditions were having one important effect, and that was to render this territory quite familiar to the public, and pave the way for discoveries much further beyond.

In the same year as all the explorations recorded in this chapter, discovery was still going on in Western Australia, and fortunately now, at last, with important and useful results. Mr. F. Gregory made a journey up the Murchison towards the Gascoyne, and what he explored in that direction has been a prelude to a very valuable series of discoveries on the north-west coast, which have quite taken away the reproach of sterility from this part of Australia. It will be remembered that the Gascoyne had been first seen by Grey in his terrible expedition in 1839. The Gascoyne empties itself into Sharks Bay, and had never been further explored; while the Murchison, which has its *embouchure* in Gantheaume Bay has been mentioned many times already. It will be also remembered that Mr. Austin, in trying to reach Sharks Bay, came upon many tributaries of the Murchison, near Mount Welcome, and having subsequently returned to the main stream, traced it down to the Geraldine Mine.

In 1858, then, Mr. F. Gregory started on an expedition from the Geraldine Mine, about the 16th April, at the time that his brother was journeying down the Barcoo; for there was a perfect *furor* this year on the subject of exploration. Mr. Gregory arrived on the 24th April at Austin's furthest northern point, near Mount Murchison, where two tributaries of the river had been named the Impey and the Roderick. Both streams came from the east-south-east, and the tableland at their junction was about eleven hundred feet above the level of the sea. Proceeding up the river

T 2

until the 28th, Gregory found the land on either side to consist of plains, as usual in the tableland, but more open, and less scrubby. Yet there was no grass, except in narrow strips upon the banks; and no water, except in small shallow pools in the channel, which was only about fifty yards wide.

But the elevation was increasing, and soon attained thirteen hundred feet. On the 29th, Gregory struck to the north-east for some granite rocks, and then, as these proved unimportant, north-west, over the several sandy scrubs and dry watercourses. One of these, much larger than the rest, was seen on the 1st May. It was twenty yards wide, and, to the astonishment of Gregory, had a due north course, showing that he had passed the watershed, at least between the northern and western waters. Of course, he followed such a promising feature, and on the 3rd it brought him to the Gascoyne, coming from the eastward, in a running stream, about sixty yards wide. At the junction the river changed its course to the north.

Overjoyed at the discovery, and being now without fears for water, Mr. Gregory made a rapid journey down the river. It ran through open grassy plains, fringed with granite rocks in the distance. One of these, on the west bank, was named Mount Puckford, and another further on Mount Stere. The latter was fourteen hundred feet above the level of the sea. On the 5th, two considerable tributaries were passed; one from the east, and another from the south; and next day the main stream, which had been keeping an average north-west direction, turned suddenly west, and then south. It kept this course for about thirty-five miles, in a direct line, and then wound about to the west and north-west again, through an uneven sandstone country, quite destitute of grass. At last it reached the junction of a fine river from the north-north-west. This was named after Admiral Lord Lyons by Gregory, who reached it on the 12th May.

The Gascoyne now preserved a westerly course, making straight for Sharks Bay. On its north side there was an extensive stony valley, with scanty feed, evidently the gradual descent of the sandstone tableland. The level of the country had been getting lower as they went to the westward, and at the junction of the Lyons it had only been five hundred feet above the level of the sea. The end of the Kennedy Range could now be seen above them, to the northward, showing that they were leaving the higher regions. They kept descending until the flat between the range and the sea was attained, and reached the mouth of the river in Sharks Bay on the 17th of May, or one month after leaving the Geraldine Mine.

Gregory now retraced his steps to explore the river Lyons. On the 24th, he reached the junction again, and then commenced his journey up the new stream. At first it was found to run through barren plains, which became gradually undulating and stony, until it passed through a deep gorge. On the further side of this there was a broken country, and open, grassy plains. The river contained only water in pools, and preserved a course slightly to the east of north. The open flats were pretty well grassed, and interspersed with large gum trees. On the 29th May, a large tributary from the north, named the Alma, was passed. It was about ninety yards wide, with water in pools in its bed; and before coming to it, other tributaries had been seen, but none of any considerable importance. Near the junction were two large mountains, named Mounts Thompson and Agamemnon, about nine hundred and twenty-seven feet above the sea level.

Beyond the junction of the Alma, the Lyons took an easterly course, and in fifteen miles was joined by another tributary from the north, named the Edmund. It was one hundred yards wide. After this, there were several other tributaries, until the Lyons took a more southerly course, and the country to the north seemed broken by thinly grassed granite hills. Keeping through open, grassy plains, and subsisting on the pools in the bed of the stream, Gregory reached a part of it close to a very high mountain, which he visited. This he named Mount Augustus. It was three thousand four hundred and eighty feet above the sea. From its summit he was able to sketch the course of the river

for more than twenty miles further, and it appeared as if
its tributaries took their rise from ten to one hundred miles
still more remotely to the eastward. The country to the
north-east seemed to improve, until the view was inter-
cepted by bold ranges of trap and granite; but to the
south-east the ground was not so promising, and appeared
like the terrible scrub of the tableland.

Altogether, this discovery was a very satisfactory
one to Gregory, and seemed likely to lead to most
important results. Such a high mountain in this place
was quite unlooked for. Fancy the feelings of a man
discovering Snowdon, and looking down from its
summit on the view around, as hitherto untrodden by
the foot of civilized man. The view from Mount
Augustus was probably not quite so encouraging; but
it was very different from what explorers had been
accustomed to in Western Australia, and promised a
new future for that struggling colony. Having been
so successful hitherto, Gregory now determined to leave
the Lyons, and examine the country to the southward.
He left it on the 3rd June, and passed over first a
grassy flat, and then a short scrub, with many watercourses, in an undulating stony country. On the 5th,
he arrived at some low granite ridges, where he
encamped on a stream which ultimately proved to be
a tributary to the Gascoyne. This was the commencement of a regular series of tributaries, one of which was
the main channel, for it was running, and probably
came from a great distance beyond. Near this stream
was Mount Stere, ascertained to be seventeen hundred
and forty-three feet above the sea.

From the mount, Gregory proceeded over extensive
grassy plains, without water, to a stony country and low
granite ridge. Stony plains, low quartz rises, with
many watercourses, and occasional grassy flats on sandy
land, ensued for nearly thirty miles, when a hill, named
Mount Gould, was reached. This was about two thousand feet above the sea level, while the level around
was at least sixteen hundred and thirty. From the
summit, the plain was perceived to the north-east, as far as
the eye could reach, and the Murchison could be seen

coming from it, running, as Gregory thought, for probably one hundred miles further. He was thus disappointed in his expectation of reaching, as he hoped, the sources of that river; and as the limit of his journey was now exceeded, he proceeded down the channel to the Geraldine Mine. He arrived there on the 22nd June, and thus this important journey terminated.

Many valuable facts are contained in the above recital. The number and the importance of the streams from the tableland, and the excellence of the country to the north, were all circumstances previously unknown and unsuspected. But one important fact disclosed should not be lost sight of, for it contains a problem for future explorers to work out. The sources of some of the rivers have since been discoverd; but the sources of the Murchison have not; neither consequently have we as yet seen the highest part of the sandstone tableland. If the Murchison goes on for one hundred miles beyond Mount Gould, the tableland must be nearly three thousand feet high; and if such lands have a western watershed, they must have likewise an eastern one. Are there then, it may be asked, large streams which flow into the interior, where the evaporation prevents their reaching the coast? Such things happen to streams coming from the eastern watershed, and why not from the western. One cannot yet help thinking that such streams exist, and that by their aid an advance across the continent from the westward might be made in favourable seasons.

CHAPTER XVII.

A. C. GREGORY EXPLORES THE BARCOO.

The Barcoo—The Alice—The Thompson—Journey up the Thompson—Great dryness of the season—Return to the Barcoo—Sandy Desert—Strzelecki's Creek—Lake Torrens—The L marked trees.

AFTER so many explorations about Lake Torrens, readers have to take their attention to a different field— where more fertile, picturesque, and varied scenery occurs, and where salt lakes and sterility are not the rule. A search for some traces of Leichhardt had been organized in Sydney—not, of course, with the hopes of finding him alive, now that ten years had elapsed ; but with the hope of ascertaining something about the route he had fol- lowed, and whether any traces of the missing party or their papers might yet be recovered.

On the 15th January, 1858, Gregory proceeded to Moreton Bay, but it was not until the following March that the expedition started. It consisted of nine men, including the leader; and they were provided with forty horses. The provisions for the journey need not be enumerated, but each horse carried about 150 lbs. weight. The men were armed with double-barrelled guns and revolvers, and the tents were of the lightest description of calico, capable of accommodating two per- sons in each. On the 29th March, they reached Scott's Creek, a small tributary of the Dawson River. Their general course was west-north-west, through a country with rich grassy valleys and dense scrubs of Brigalow Acacia on the higher ground. This tract of land has been described in connection with other explorers, and need not be further alluded to. Gregory had resolved

to take Kennedy's track direct to the Warrego. He
reached the watershed which separates its waters from
the head of the Nive on the 16th April, and on the
next day emerged upon the rich open downs of the
Barcoo.

These were very different in appearance from what
they had been when Mitchell first arrived upon them.
They were so withered for want of water, that the
country around appeared like a desert. The bed of the
river was there only ten yards wide, and perfectly dry,
so that water was found with difficulty. This was the
splendid stream of which Mitchell spoke so enthusiastically; but in comparing his account with the
appearance now, we must remember that the scene,
dry and withered as it was, did not differ much from
many districts which are considered fertile even in the
summer, when artificial means of procuring water have
been resorted to. We must however, at this season,
dismiss from our minds the glowing picture drawn by
Mitchell, of the swelling green meadows through which
the river wound into the hazy distance, amid a shady
line of stately gum trees.

As the party were now upon the line of route which
Leichhardt was supposed to have taken, the men were
divided so that both sides of the river were examined
in all probable positions; but as the high floods of the
previous year had inundated the country for nearly a
mile on each side, every track which might have existed
had, of course, been obliterated. In place of water,
now there was not even moisture; the vegetation had
quite disappeared, leaving nothing but very deep fissures
upon the surface. When, however, they attained the
junction of a large creek there was a fine pool of water,
and a slight improvement in the grass; but the back
country was a dense scrub. There were some few
natives about, who, contrary to the character of these
tribes on the Barcoo, seemed inclined to hostilities; but
they did not venture very near the explorers. In lat.
24° 25', long. 145° 6', they found a tree marked
with an L on the east side, and near it there were the
stumps of some trees cut down with an axe, and one

marked as if at one time it had supported the pole of a
tent. This was thought by Gregory to have been one
of Leichhardt's camps, but no other indications were
found at that time. Others have been found since,
however, but the fact of their being traces of Leichhardt
is still disputed. The reasons on both sides cannot be
given here, but they have been inserted in an appendix
which will be found at the end of the volume.*

When Gregory arrived upon the Alice, it appeared
to him to be so small that he could not believe that it
was that river. He traced it up a little way before he
discovered his mistake, and as it was perfectly dry, it
certainly looked a very insignificant stream. But it
was not the Alice alone that was dry and unimportant at
this time. The whole party soon found that their
position became extremely critical. The continued
drought had dried up the water everywhere, except in
the deepest hollows of the Barcoo. The smaller vegetation and even the trees on the back country were
destroyed, and their dead branches rendered the country
almost as impracticable as the absence of water. Only
in the moist bed of the river was there any grass, and
that was barely sufficient for the horses. Knowing how
much more scarce the grass would become as the
Barcoo was followed down, Gregory resolved to strike
to the north-west when he came to the Thompson, in
the hope of meeting a more practicable route : for
in a far more favourable season Kennedy had found no
feed for his animals, and the water entirely failed ; so
it was not to be expected that it would be possible now to
get any, much beyond the junction of the Thompson.
Besides this, it would assist him in the object of his
journey, for there was every probability that Leichhardt had taken that course.

Fortunately, on the 2nd May, there was a heavy
fall of rain, which relieved all their apprehensions for a
time ; but even this was not without its inconveniences,
for had the channels been flooded, the camp, which was
between them, must have been swept away. As it

* See Appendix A.

was, the plains were inundated, and the ford, which
before was cracked with deep fissures, was now a succession of deep channels and boggy gullies, which the
party had to flounder through, and in which the horses
narrowly escaped suffocation.   To add to their dis-
comfort, there were natives about, who were very
troublesome, and kept the men constantly on the alert
to prevent a surprise.

Gregory thought that his movements would be more
free after the shower of rain, so he left the Barcoo and
tried to steer west to the Thompson.   He was soon
driven back from this by barren plains and a dense scrub.
A week or two later, and the plain would have been
covered with grass, and as for the scrub, we know now
that it would not have been an impediment for any
great distance, so that it is a pity Gregory could not
have advanced in that direction.   This was the second
time that the watershed of the Flinders was nearly
discovered.   At any rate, he had to return to the river,
and on the 8th of May, as he went down it, he found it
trending to the west, and contracted to the width of one
or two miles.   The plains were firmer, and the grass
more abundant.   Salt bush began to be plentiful, and
they saw the commencement to the great hills of red
drift sand.   They were in the position at this time
where the surface drainage began to tell upon the bed
of the stream, so that they frequently met the fine long
reaches or lagoons described by Sturt and Kennedy.
As usual, the blacks abounded; but it was very singular
that they were not then as friendly as they previously
and since then proved themselves to be.   A large
party of them were surprised at one of the lagoons, and
they fled away in great alarm.   Subsequently, however, they returned, and appeared to be most amicably
disposed; but that night they tried to sneak upon the
camp.   A few shots were fired over their heads, but
that had no effect; so a charge of small shot was sent
among them into the bushes, and it is surprising with
what alacrity they decamped.

The Thompson was reached upon the 10th of May.
It was flowing, probably, from the effect of the recent

rain. The same showers had had, apparently, no
effect upon the vegetation, for it was quite devoid of
grass and almost of any sort of growth.   They
had to travel twelve miles up its banks before they
found sufficient grass for the horses, and, even then,
what they found was by no means plentiful.   And this
barrenness continued. Except a few trees which grew
on the immediate bank of the river, there was scarcely
one that was not withered, while the plains were mere
baked clay—nothing else; not even a useless plant.
At the distance of seventeen miles from the junction,
they came upon the low ridges of red drift sand.   Its
well-known features were painfully familiar to Gregory.
It had baffled him before on the Victoria River; it had
baffled Sturt and Kennedy near this very place ; and
now, said Gregory, it seemed so much in keeping with
the season and the place, that it cast a red glare into
the sky above. But he kept on, nevertheless.   In lat.
24° 40', low sandstone hills or tableland approached
both banks of the river, and gave rise to gullies which
helped to supply the stream.   They were dry now, and
so indeed was the main channel. In spite of the aridity,
Gregory kept on as far as lat. 23° 47'. At this place
there was no water nor grass, and the channels of
the river spread out so that it was almost impossible to
trace it through the plain. So Mr. Gregory and his
party returned. It is evident that the aspect of the
Thompson had a very depressing effect upon him.
The reader should bear his description in mind until he
comes to the explorations of Landsborough, when he
will find the Thompson described as one of the most
charming rivers in Australia. Both were right; but
both their experiences were the extremes of seasons in
this singular country.

There were now two courses open to Gregory :
either to proceed to the head of the Barcoo, and then
go north to the Belyando or Suttor; or to follow down
the stream and see whether it really were a portion of
Sturt's Cooper's Creek, or a tributary of the Darling.
In the former case, he might still be following Leichhardt's tracks, or he might not ; but the latter seemed

preferable, as it was possible that the lost explorer
might have been driven to the south-west. That was
the course then that Gregory resolved to adopt.   He
returned down the right bank of the Thompson, but
only one small creek and some inconsiderable gullies
joined it on that side; nor was the country of a better
character than that upon the left bank, being, in fact,
nothing but barren plains liable to inundation, and
rocky scrubby ridges.

On the 23rd they reached the Barcoo, and continued
travelling down it.   The channel still contained water,
but nothing could be more desolate than the banks,
which were an unbounded level, without vegetation of
any kind.   The horses, in consequence, suffered very
much.   They were reduced to eating decayed weeds,
and, in their hunger, would even devour the thatch
on the deserted huts of the natives.   On the 27th, they
had nearly reached Kennedy's furthest point; but the
animals were evidently failing.   The dry mud was so
deeply cracked and fissured, that they were continually
falling into crevices which were wide enough to contain
them, and deep enough to do them injury.   This added
very much to their fatigues, and at last one had to be
abandoned, for he could not be got along.   They
reached one of Kennedy's camps upon the 28th.   The
marks upon the trees were as perfect and as fresh as if
they were only made the day before—showing the dryness of the climate, and the slow growth of the trees.

On the 29th, they had to toil through thirty miles
of dried mud, as in all the distance they could not find
a place on which to encamp.   At the end of their
journey they found a small patch of grass, but it was so
small, and the horses were so very hungry, that by the
next morning it looked no different from the surrounding plain.   Three miles lower down they found another
little patch of herbage, and so important had such scrub
vegetation become, that they were glad to halt upon it,
even after such a short journey.   The peculiarities of
the river were now such as are met in no other stream in
the world.   There can be no doubt that the Barcoo
drains an immense area, and that if it were always flow-

ing, would be a most important feature. Its valley is
of immense width, sometimes more than ten miles wide,
and the actual stream-bed where it can be traced, or
where it does not subdivide into three or four channels,
has the proportions of a noble river. But with all these
characters, it is never running for any length of time,
and the grass on its banks is as scarce as the water itself.
It is like the ghost of a river that had been formerly
splendid and important; and because extremes meet in
its features, there is often an inundation overspread-
ing the country from the channel, and the country also
looks in places as if it had been fertile once. The consequence was, that the diary of the party under Gregory
was as monotonous as their journey was wearisome.
One day they passed over barren clay plains, and the
next they found fine deep reaches of water, with a perceptible current of the water in them. But it was not
always easy to trace the stream. It was lost occasionally in sandy plains, and it seemed as if the water
flowed no further.

On the 4th June, they reached where the low sandstone tableland approached the west side of the plain,
and the muddy space between was so very stony that
the horses suffered much in going over it. This tract,
Gregory said, resembled Sturt's Stony Desert, which
was at least two hundred miles to the westward; and if
the cause I have assigned for that feature be the correct
one, this was a similar place. In point of fact, such
stony plains may be expected whenever the sandstone
occurs. Wherever the red sand becomes disintegrated
by the surface decomposition, the lighter portions will
be blown away into shifting ridges of red drift sand,
and the heavier stones will remain behind upon the
plains. At this place, however, the tableland approached
so near the channel that the water was collected into
long and fine reaches, and the sand disappeared.

By following the western limits of the plains, they
reached lat. 27° 30' on the 8th June. There the
sandstone plateau receded, leaving a boundless mud
plain before them, without one tree, or any other
vegetation except atriplex and polygonum. A day's

journey below this they reached a large lagoon. There
were, singularly enough, signs of a current in this towards
the north-west in times of flood; but there was evidently
a westerly trend in all the creeks, showing that they
were likely to merge into the Cooper's Creek of
Sturt. The sandstone soon closed in again on both
sides, and, as a consequence, the different channels of
the Barcoo were collected together again, and formed
fine reaches of water. The soil of the intervening
plain was much firmer, but displayed the saline nature
which so often attends the development of the upper
sandstone in Australia. Grass became abundant again,
and the horses improved rapidly from their emaciated
condition.

They were soon actually upon that part of the
Barcoo which had been discovered by Sturt, and which
has since attained such a mournful celebrity in connection with the explorations of Burke and Wills. The
river takes here a new course, and flows down into a
portion of the country which had never yet been
explored. Readers no doubt remember that when
Mitchell discovered it, the flow was to the north-west,
and he thought that it would lead to Carpentaria.
Kennedy found, subsequently, that it turned to the
south-west, and afterwards kept a south course. Where
Sturt found it, the channel trended due west, and even
a little north of west. Yet it was supposed to empty
itself into Lake Torrens, which was still to the south,
and this was the problem that Gregory had now to
solve.

On the 12th June, when they were approaching the
141st meridian, which is the boundary of the province
of South Australia, stony ridges closed in both banks of
the stream, forming almost a natural division. Here
Mr. Gregory says he noticed the only instance he ever
saw of natives trying to remove natural obstacles from
their paths. The loose stones from the ridge were all
removed from their track and piled on one side, as
though they sought here to make a permanent road.
After passing the stony valley, the hills receded suddenly
both to the north and south, and the whole country to

the west seemed a succession of low ridges of red sand.
and level plains of dry mud, evidently liable to inundation. Shortly before reaching the branch of the Barcoo,
called Strzelecki's Creek, the tracks of horses were
seen, and these were imagined to be from the animals
abandoned by Sturt in 1845.

Strzelecki's Creek was found to separate at nearly
right angles from the main channel, and appeared to
convey about one-third of the Barcoo waters nearly
south, thus connecting it with Lake Torrens. They,
however, continued to follow the channels which trended
west, for there was just a chance that it might lead far
towards the centre of the continent. They proceeded
for thirty miles, but large branches continually broke
off to the south and west, and at length the whole was
lost in the plains of dry mud between the sand ridges.
Gregory now thought that there was no chance of
either water or grass to the west, and so on the 16th
June he turned to the south. It is a great pity that he
did so. His previous experience of the way in which
the Barcoo disappeared and reappeared so frequently
might have encouraged him to push his investigations a
little further. It would have been satisfactory to know
whether the river does flow further west. I am convinced that it does, and that the final receptacle of the
waters of the Barcoo will be found in the immense salt
basin of Lake Eyre. If this should be proved, it would
be a most important fact. It would show that large
salt lakes are always connected with fresh-water drainage, and probably fresh-water rivers; and we might
then look to the north-west side of Lake Gairdner as
the receptacle of some great system of drainage, possibly from the tableland of Western Australia, which
feeds the Murchison River.

For fifty miles after leaving the Barcoo, the journey
of the party was through a desert. Low ridges of sand,
from ten to fifty feet high, running parallel with each
other in a north and south direction, surrounded them
on every side. Little puddles of rain-water were occasionally found between the ridges, and with these and
the weeds which late rains had caused to spring up,

the horses managed even to improve in so desolate a
region.

They reached Strzelecki's Creek on the 21st June,
in lat. 28° 24'. It was still a fine and fertile creek, and it
was easy now to guess its destination. Its course was
south, with a little west, through sandy ridges. In lat.
29° 25' it turned west, and shortly afterwards Gregory
found himself upon the edge of that feature which
had baffled Eyre and Sturt, and stood so long like a
plague-spot upon Australian maps—Lake Torrens. This
was one termination, then, of the Barcoo, and also of
many a pet theory of amateur geographers. This was
the end, too, of the Victoria—Mitchell's highway to Carpentaria—the splendid north-west river. Fortunately, to
indemnify us for such a disappointment, we are obliged
to have a better opinion of the basin of Lake Torrens.
Gregory was destined to add another cheering fact with
reference to it. He passed between the north-eastern
arch and, what had been hitherto considered, the eastern
arm. Where he crossed—which, be it remembered, was
at no very great distance from Blanchewater and the
scene of Goyder's dreams and Freeling's flounderings—
he tells us, triumphantly, that the passage between the
lakes was a level space, about half a mile wide. It was
sandy, and covered with *Salicornia*, without any connecting channel or creek of any kind. This may have been
the passage described to Mr. Babbage by the Werta-
Werta natives.

From Lake Torrens, Mr. Gregory proceeded to Mount
Hopeless, and as he was amid the settled districts, there
is no need to pursue his explorations further. Of course,
the news he brought was considered of the utmost importance; but what excited the most comment was the
L marked camp which he had found. I have already
alluded to the discussion on the subject, and have referred the reader to the Appendix for an exposition of
the question. What Gregory said is now given. He
pointed out that if the camp were one of Leichhardt's,
there could have been no truth in the report of Hely
that he was murdered by the natives; indeed, very little
reliance can be placed upon the story, even apart from

any discoveries. If Leichhardt's party had camped there, Mr. Gregory was of opinion that they had left the Barcoo about the junction of the Alice, and that then, when far advanced—finding, as they would have .done, that water was unobtainable—they made an ineffectual effort to retreat, and perished for want of water. Of course, this theory depends upon his having found the same aridity as Gregory did in the extraordinary season of his journey. In other cases, the Alice would have been found well supplied with water, so that the shadowy probability of Gregory's theory becomes very dim, indeed.

The general description of the Barcoo given by Mr. Gregory was decidedly of an unfavourable character. He stated that though fertile spots might occasionally be met with, the uncertainty of rain, and the light character of the vegetation, would always render it an unsafe place for stock. Of the country near Lake Torrens he gave a similar description. The geological character of the tract passed through was remarkably uniform. Carboniferous shales and sandstones, with occasional beds of coal, and superincumbent hills and ridges of basalt, extend from the Darling Downs to the 146th meridian. At that point the rocks are covered by horizontal sandstone, with beds of chert and water-worn pebbles. The latter formation seemed to extend as far as the slates of Mount Hopeless.

The last result of this expedition was the final extinction of any hopes which might still have been entertained that the interior of the continent would be found to be depressed into a lake or reservoir of some kind. This notion had been somewhat revived by Gregory's discoveries on the northern side of the continent beyond the sources of the Victoria River. But the explorer himself entertained a very different opinion. He argued that even large lakes or accumulations of water would not be found; for, said he, if Lake Torrens is the receptacle of such a large river as the Barcoo, as well as the drainage of the Stony Desert, and the other streams that are known to the westward—and if, in spite of all this drainage, it does not flow into the sea, but is, on the contrary, only a succession of shallow lagoons—*à fortiori*, the evaporation of the interior would dissipate a greater drainage. It will be seen, however, that a part of this opinion is founded on an imperfect knowledge of the nature of the Lake Torrens basin. The lake receiving the waters of Strzelecki's Creek was not the same as Lake Eyre, a gigantic basin, whose existence Gregory did not know of at the time he wrote the report. I have quoted his idea more than his words, and possibly I may not understand his meaning correctly; but a portion of Sturt's idea of the central lake seems to me to be true. Lake Eyre and Lake Gairdner are a part of the result of the depression of the interior, and it yet remains to be seen how much they are affected by a drainage which is yet unknown to us. For my own part, I do not think it a bit more unreasonable to expect a large river flowing into the north-west side of Lake Gairdner than to expect that a Queensland river like the Barcoo should terminate in such a basin as Lake Eyre.

In conclusion, I cannot take leave of this last exploration of Mr. A. C. Gregory without praising, in the highest terms, his eminence as an explorer. He it was that set the example of rapid and expeditious movements; he it was that gave the key to larger explorations, by showing what could be done if proper means were selected; and with all this his observations are so concise, so clever and ingenious, that it is a matter of great regret that they have been so brief, or that he has not published them in a more extended form.

CHAPTER XVIII.

STUART'S FIRST JOURNEYS.

WHILE Mr. Babbage was slowly working his way from Beda Creek to the Elizabeth, and Gregory was making his rapid march down the Barcoo, another explorer had appeared in the field, who was destined to do more for Australian geography than any man who had preceded him. A creek has been mentioned in the account of Babbage's explorations, which that explorer had named Stuart's Creek, because there were tracks upon it that it had been previously visited by Stuart. This was Mr. John M'Douall Stuart, who had been out with Sturt in 1845, as draughtsman, and who had now started on his own account, with only one companion, besides a native, and five horses.

He reached Mr. Babbage's camp, and then went to the Elizabeth on the 16th June, and camped there for a day. He then moved on to the north, over the usual sandy, scrubby country, with many angular flint stones covering the surface. It is not my intention to weary the reader with the record of more than the results of this journey, for though they afford the most complete guidance to any person travelling over the same tracts, to say the least, they enter most drily into detail. Mr. Stuart kept a most accurate diary—so minute, indeed, in its detail that it is difficult, amid such a number of facts, to collect the general results of his journey. The reader should be now well acquainted with the country through

which Stuart passed in the first part of his journey : it was that explored by Babbage, Campbell, Warburton, and Swinden, on the west side of Lake Torrens.

On the 22nd June, Stuart came in sight of the lake, and could see, as he thought, Mounts Norwest and Deception inside, with the Flinders Range in the distance. From this his course was over sand-hills and tableland, and stony plains, all poorly supplied with water, but evidently forming a part of the great sandstone tableland in which Lake Torrens might be considered a wide gorge. Stuart was making for a tract of country, called by the natives Wingilpin, which was a large area, as they declared, lying to the north-west. Their reports could not have been made from actual observation, for their guide was now evidently out of his own country, and so bewildered as to be of no use to the explorers. They met other natives, however, and one was surprised before he could escape. He was in the most abject state of terror, and could give them no information, so that Mr. Stuart was quite at a loss what to do. He finally determined to move towards the west, for they were evidently not out of the country which dipped to Lake Torrens.

The first part of the journey, on the 26th, was over an undulating plain, with low sand-hills and wide valleys between, all thickly covered with salt bush and grass. The last part was, however, very bad—less grass and salt bush, and more stones. There was a high tableland to the west, and several tent-shaped hills to the east. One of these was of a very peculiar form. It seemed as if a white tower had been built on the top of a conical hill, with a black ring near the top, which came to a point. The termination of their journey was at a very fine creek, which, as Mr. Stuart thought, equalled any of the South Australian rivers. It was named Stuart's Creek by Babbage; as already stated, Stuart called it Chambers's Creek—a name which it has since retained.

Stuart moved up this watercourse. The stony nature of the country had so crippled his horses that he could only get along slowly. To the north and south the table-topped hills seemed to get higher as he came to the

which Stuart passed in the first part of his journey : it was that explored by Babbage, Campbell, Warburton, and Swinden, on the west side of Lake Torrens.

On the 22nd June, Stuart came in sight of the lake, and could see, as he thought, Mounts Norwest and Deception inside, with the Flinders Range in the distance. From this his course was over sand-hills and tableland, and stony plains, all poorly supplied with water, but evidently forming a part of the great sandstone tableland in which Lake Torrens might be considered a wide gorge. Stuart was making for a tract of country, called by the natives Wingilpin, which was a large area, as they declared, lying to the north-west. Their reports could not have been made from actual observation, for their guide was now evidently out of his own country, and so bewildered as to be of no use to the explorers. They met other natives, however, and one was surprised before he could escape. He was in the most abject state of terror, and could give them no information, so that Mr. Stuart was quite at a loss what to do. He finally determined to move towards the west, for they were evidently not out of the country which dipped to Lake Torrens.

The first part of the journey, on the 26th, was over an undulating plain, with low sand-hills and wide valleys between, all thickly covered with salt bush and grass. The last part was, however, very bad—less grass and salt bush, and more stones. There was a high tableland to the west, and several tent-shaped hills to the east. One of these was of a very peculiar form. It seemed as if a white tower had been built on the top of a conical hill, with a black ring near the top, which came to a point. The termination of their journey was at a very fine creek, which, as Mr. Stuart thought, equalled any of the South Australian rivers. It was named Stuart's Creek by Babbage; as already stated, Stuart called it Chambers's Creek—a name which it has since retained.

Stuart moved up this watercourse. The stony nature of the country had so crippled his horses that he could only get along slowly. To the north and south the table-topped hills seemed to get higher as he came to the

CHAPTER XVIII.

STUART'S FIRST JOURNEYS.

Stuart starts northward—Chambers's Creek—Good country to the north-west—
Stuart's Range—Mulga Creek—Dense scrub—Mount Finke—Fowler's
Bay—Streaky Bay—Crawford on the Barrier Ranges—Holroyd—Stuart
again—The mysterious journey—Governor M'Donnell—Stuart—The
Springs—Lake Torrens—Tolmer.

WHILE Mr. Babbage was slowly working his way from
Beda Creek to the Elizabeth, and Gregory was making
his rapid march down the Barcoo, another explorer had
appeared in the field, who was destined to do more for
Australian geography than any man who had preceded
him. A creek has been mentioned in the account of
Babbage's explorations, which that explorer had named
Stuart's Creek, because there were tracks upon it that it
had been previously visited by Stuart. This was Mr.
John M'Douall Stuart, who had been out with Sturt in
1845, as draughtsman, and who had now started on his
own account, with only one companion, besides a native,
and five horses.

He reached Mr. Babbage's camp, and then went to
the Elizabeth on the 16th June, and camped there for a
day. He then moved on to the north, over the usual
sandy, scrubby country, with many angular flint stones
covering the surface. It is not my intention to weary
the reader with the record of more than the results of
his journey, for though they afford the most complete
guidance to any person travelling over the same tracts,
they, at the least, they enter most drily into detail. Mr.
Stuart kept a most accurate diary—so minute, indeed, in
its detail, that it is difficult, amid such a number of facts,
to collect the general results of his journey. The reader
would be now well acquainted with the country through

which Stuart passed in the first part of his journey: it
was that explored by Babbage, Campbell, Warburton,
and Swinden, on the west side of Lake Torrens.

On the 22nd June, Stuart came in sight of the lake,
and could see, as he thought, Mounts Norwest and
Deception inside, with the Flinders Range in the distance. From this his course was over sand-hills and
tableland, and stony plains, all poorly supplied with
water, but evidently forming a part of the great sandstone tableland in which Lake Torrens might be considered a wide gorge. Stuart was making for a tract of
country, called by the natives Wingilpin, which was a
large area, as they declared, lying to the north-west.
Their reports could not have been made from actual
observation, for their guide was now evidently out of his
own country, and so bewildered as to be of no use to the
explorers. They met other natives, however, and one
was surprised before he could escape. He was in the
most abject state of terror, and could give them no information, so that Mr. Stuart was quite at a loss what to
do. He finally determined to move towards the west,
for they were evidently not out of the country which
dipped to Lake Torrens.

The first part of the journey, on the 26th, was over
an undulating plain, with low sand-hills and wide valleys
between, all thickly covered with salt bush and grass.
The last part was, however, very bad—less grass and
salt bush, and more stones. There was a high tableland
to the west, and several tent-shaped hills to the east.
One of these was of a very peculiar form. It seemed as
if a white tower had been built on the top of a conical
hill, with a black ring near the top, which came to a
point. The termination of their journey was at a very
fine creek, which, as Mr. Stuart thought, equalled any
of the South Australian rivers. It was named Stuart's
Creek by Babbage; as already stated, Stuart called it
Chambers's Creek—a name which it has since retained.

Stuart moved up this watercourse. The stony nature
of the country had so crippled his horses that he could
only get along slowly. To the north and south the
table-topped hills seemed to get higher as he came to the

CHAPTER XVIII.

STUART'S FIRST JOURNEYS.

WHILE Mr. Babbage was slowly working his way from Beda Creek to the Elizabeth, and Gregory was making his rapid march down the Barcoo, another explorer had appeared in the field, who was destined to do more for Australian geography than any man who had preceded him. A creek has been mentioned in the account of Babbage's explorations, which that explorer had named Stuart's Creek, because there were tracks upon it that it had been previously visited by Stuart. This was Mr. John M'Douall Stuart, who had been out with Sturt in 1845, as draughtsman, and who had now started on his own account, with only one companion, besides a native, and five horses.

He reached Mr. Babbage's camp, and then went to the Elizabeth on the 16th June, and camped there for a day. He then moved on to the north, over the usual sandy, scrubby country, with many angular flint stones covering the surface. It is not my intention to weary the reader with the record of more than the results of this journey, for though they afford the most complete guidance to any person travelling over the same tracts, to say the least, they enter most drily into detail. Mr. Stuart kept a most accurate diary—so minute, indeed, in its detail, that it is difficult, amid such a number of facts, to collect the general results of his journey. The reader should be now well acquainted with the country through

which Stuart passed in the first part of his journey : it was that explored by Babbage, Campbell, Warburton, and Swinden, on the west side of Lake Torrens.

On the 22nd June, Stuart came in sight of the lake, and could see, as he thought, Mounts Norwest and Deception inside, with the Flinders Range in the distance. From this his course was over sand-hills and tableland, and stony plains, all poorly supplied with water, but evidently forming a part of the great sandstone tableland in which Lake Torrens might be considered a wide gorge. Stuart was making for a tract of country, called by the natives Wingilpin, which was a large area, as they declared, lying to the north-west. Their reports could not have been made from actual observation, for their guide was now evidently out of his own country, and so bewildered as to be of no use to the explorers. They met other natives, however, and one was surprised before he could escape. He was in the most abject state of terror, and could give them no information, so that Mr. Stuart was quite at a loss what to do. He finally determined to move towards the west, for they were evidently not out of the country which dipped to Lake Torrens.

The first part of the journey, on the 26th, was over an undulating plain, with low sand-hills and wide valleys between, all thickly covered with salt bush and grass. The last part was, however, very bad—less grass and salt bush, and more stones. There was a high tableland to the west, and several tent-shaped hills to the east. One of these was of a very peculiar form. It seemed as if a white tower had been built on the top of a conical hill, with a black ring near the top, which came to a point. The termination of their journey was at a very fine creek, which, as Mr. Stuart thought, equalled any of the South Australian rivers. It was named Stuart's Creek by Babbage ; as already stated, Stuart called it Chambers's Creek—a name which it has since retained.

Stuart moved up this watercourse. The stony nature of the country had so crippled his horses that he could only get along slowly. To the north and south the table-topped hills seemed to get higher as he came to the

CHAPTER XVIII.

STUART'S FIRST JOURNEYS.

Stuart starts northward—Chambers's Creek—Good country to the north-west—
Stuart's Range—Mulga Creek—Dense scrub—Mount Finke—Fowler's
Bay—Streaky Bay—Crawford on the Barrier Ranges—Holroyd—Stuart
again—The mysterious journey—Governor M'Donnell—Stuart—The
Springs—Lake Torrens—Tolmer.

WHILE Mr. Babbage was slowly working his way from
Beda Creek to the Elizabeth, and Gregory was making
his rapid march down the Barcoo, another explorer had
appeared in the field, who was destined to do more for
Australian geography than any man who had preceded
him. A creek has been mentioned in the account of
Babbage's explorations, which that explorer had named
Stuart's Creek, because there were tracks upon it that it
had been previously visited by Stuart. This was Mr.
John M'Douall Stuart, who had been out with Sturt in
1845, as draughtsman, and who had now started on his
own account, with only one companion, besides a native,
and five horses.

He reached Mr. Babbage's camp, and then went to
the Elizabeth on the 16th June, and camped there for a
day. He then moved on to the north, over the usual
sandy, scrubby country, with many angular flint stones
covering the surface. It is not my intention to weary
the reader with the record of more than the results of
this journey, for though they afford the most complete
guidance to any person travelling over the same tracts,
to say the least, they enter most drily into detail. Mr.
Stuart kept a most accurate diary—so minute, indeed, in
its detail, that it is difficult, amid such a number of facts,
to collect the general results of his journey. The reader
should be now well acquainted with the country through

which Stuart passed in the first part of his journey : it
was that explored by Babbage, Campbell, Warburton,
and Swinden, on the west side of Lake Torrens.

On the 22nd June, Stuart came in sight of the lake,
and could see, as he thought, Mounts Norwest and
Deception inside, with the Flinders Range in the distance. From this his course was over sand-hills and
tableland, and stony plains, all poorly supplied with
water, but evidently forming a part of the great sandstone tableland in which Lake Torrens might be considered a wide gorge. Stuart was making for a tract of
country, called by the natives Wingilpin, which was a
large area, as they declared, lying to the north-west.
Their reports could not have been made from actual
observation, for their guide was now evidently out of his
own country, and so bewildered as to be of no use to the
explorers. They met other natives, however, and one
was surprised before he could escape. He was in the
most abject state of terror, and could give them no information, so that Mr. Stuart was quite at a loss what to
do. He finally determined to move towards the west,
for they were evidently not out of the country which
dipped to Lake Torrens.

The first part of the journey, on the 26th, was over
an undulating plain, with low sand-hills and wide valleys
between, all thickly covered with salt bush and grass.
The last part was, however, very bad—less grass and
salt bush, and more stones. There was a high tableland
to the west, and several tent-shaped hills to the east.
One of these was of a very peculiar form. It seemed as
if a white tower had been built on the top of a conical
hill, with a black ring near the top, which came to a
point. The termination of their journey was at a very
fine creek, which, as Mr. Stuart thought, equalled any
of the South Australian rivers. It was named Stuart's
Creek by Babbage ; as already stated, Stuart called it
Chambers's Creek—a name which it has since retained.

Stuart moved up this watercourse. The stony nature
of the country had so crippled his horses that he could
only get along slowly. To the north and south the
table-topped hills seemed to get higher as he came to the

source of the waters, but the country seemed to improve,
for many small tributaries joined, and there was abundance of game. He left the creek on the second day,
and went slightly north of west for nearly thirty miles.
The travelling was better, owing to rain which had
softened the ground, but it was sadly stony and barren.
Stuart thought it very much resembled the Stony Desert
which he had seen when out with Sturt. It had a similar bleak appearance, without any vegetation of any
kind; and, according to the views already expressed, we
may consider it to be one of the very same features, as
the desert. When they left it they had the tableland
upon their left for eighteen miles beyond, but the country became more open, and, except in the direction of
the plateau, stretched out like an immense plain dotted
with flat-topped hills; they were, in fact, crossing between the head of the watershed and the lake, thus
passing many creeks near their sources, and meeting
with a rather better grassed country.

At the end of the immense plains they could see a
high range before them to the north-west; but as the
rain came down copiously for a day or so, they could not
reach it as soon as they wished. The rain lasted for
several days, making the creeks run so that they had
no apprehensions about the water, though they moved
on more slowly as the ground became boggy. The
range showed them a finely wooded country to the north
and east, which offered a very favourable contrast with
what they had passed through. Yet they were not yet
off the tableland, neither had they come to any change
in the nature of the rocks.

There was another range still before them to the
north-west. It seemed higher than any seen hitherto,
and they moved towards it with eagerness, across many
creeks, which were not only well watered, but even
boggy. They ascended the highest point of the hills,
and looked eagerly at the prospect. The view to the
north-east was over an immense stony plain, with broken
hills in the distance. To the north, also a plain, and
distant table hills, and to the north-west there was the
termination of the range they were upon, distant about

ten miles. This was the furthest point north, in lat. 28° 20', long. 134° 10'. The range was not of great elevation, and yet it was certainly a watershed. Most of the creeks upon the north side ran northward down very plain gullies : on the south side the dip was not so perceptible. It seemed, on the contrary, like the gradual slope of a tableland. By consulting the map readers will see the system of water subsequently discovered by Stuart in connection with the north side of this elevation. The country on the south—or more correctly, perhaps, upon the summit—was good, yet very stony, if the two qualities are compatible. The refraction of the atmosphere was so great that the smallest bushes appeared at a distance like gum trees, and the whole country before them like a sheet of water. There was no timber, and water was so scarce that they had to camp the first night without it. The stony plain, like the other desert, seemed to continue a long way to the south-west, but there was no telling with certainty, as the refraction was so great.

Stuart now turned to the southward. He had satisfied himself of the practicability of going further to the north than he had done, and he now wished to examine the country to the south and west. His principal object had been to look for the available tract named Wingilpin by the natives, and as he had long ago passed what must have been the northern limits of their geographical knowledge, he thought that the place, if it existed at all, must exist to the south and to the west of Lake Torrens. If he had been exploring, he could have gone further north-west, for though the Stuart Range had been traced nearly to its termination, yet all the creeks he had passed were only the sources of streams running down from the tableland, and as the rains had set them all running he could have followed any one of these ; but his object on this journey was a different one, and he contented himself with ascertaining the practicability of further explorations to the north.

In moving to the south, he passed over stony plains, and traced one or two creeks ; but, as might be expected, the stony plains soon terminated in red sand-hills,

which were almost impenetrable to horses so fatigued
and emaciated as those of Stuart.   Seeing that there
was no likelihood of a change for a long distance, Stuart
crossed to the south, and then to the south-east, for a
point about one hundred miles north of Swinden's Lake
Campbell. By this course he would ascertain the nature
of the country south-west of his route.   For five days
subsequently his journey was as monotonous as one can
imagine.   At first, the plains were open, but by-and-by
the scrub got thicker and thicker, with nothing else to
be seen all around.   The soil in this shrubby forest was
of course sand, and there was no surface water.   One
day a creek was met with, but this was the only watercourse flowing down along the tableland.   For the other
days they fortunately found a few puddles left by the
rain.

On the fifth day Stuart saw some hills to the north,
and he fancied that they might be a part of the table
range he had explored at his furthest point.   As they
approached one the country became better grassed; but
the view from its summit was not encouraging.   All
around was scrub, and the range he was in search of
was seen in the distance. Fortunately, there were grassy
patches here and there, so that Stuart could hope to
continue his journey.   On the 21st, he got over twenty
miles of good country, with scrub and grass in patches.
It was, he says, the finest grass and salt-bush country
he had travelled over, but there was no water.   The dip
of the country was evidently to the south-west.   On the
22nd they crossed an exceptional feature in this country. This was a limestone range, which bounded a
large p ain from north-west to east.   It was very
good country, though stony, with a few sand-hills at
intervals.   Some distance beyond this, he could see
the table range to the north, which has since been named
after him, and the intervening country seemed not different from what he had hitherto examined.

Stuart's wanderings from this point were almost
towards every point of the compass, so thoroughly did
he explore the land around.   When he lost sight of
Stuart's Range, he went towards the north-west side of

Lake Gairdner, over the usual undulating stony plain,
with narrow sand-hills at intervals, and lagoons. The
country was still good, and the native tracks numerous,
but still no signs of permanent water. It is about here,
that I would suppose, the drainage into Lake Gairdner,
from the western tableland takes place. It is no evidence against its existence that Stuart did not see any
such stream. We have seen that in the course of the
Barcoo there are many places where its course could not
be traced, and at the junction with Lake Eyre especially.
The same thing happens at Lake Gairdner. The occurrence of salt lagoons shows at least there is a depression,
and the native tracks and the good country must likewise be connected with fresh water somewhere near. It
should be remarked that the salt lagoons are marked in
Stuart's map as a line going as far as he could see in a
north-west direction.

It will not be necessary to follow Stuart's journey
further on this occasion. From the map, it will be seen
that after many windings he steered for Fowler's Bay.
Not one interesting feature met him in that long course,
except perhaps Mount Finke. This was a granite mountain, much above the usual height of such rocks in the
scrub, and commanding an extensive view. Stuart
named it as above, and from its summit he had a very
extensive view, but not a cheering one. All around was
a dense scrub, with patches of open plain, without water.
Stuart says the desert near the mountain was a far worse
desert than the one found by Sturt in the interior, because there was at least salt bush on that, but here there
was absolutely nothing but spinifex. But yet there was
a good deal of fair grassy country upon this tableland,
though such tracts are invariably so dry that no use can
be made of the grass they contain. Taking it altogether, I should say, from the descriptions of explorers
in both places, that the tableland of sandstone on the
peninsula, between Fowler's Bay and Port Lincoln, is
not so utterly barren as that of Western Australia.

But whatever interest this journey lacks from the
nature of the country passed through, is more than
compensated by the heroism of the little band which

made it. Their sufferings and privations are almost
beyond belief. Their provisions were not calculated to
last more than half the time of their actual absence, and
even this small stock had been much lessened by wet
and damage. Yet, by dint of careful management, and
very small rations, Stuart contrived to make them last
until they reached Lake Gairdner. At that time the
last ration of flour was served out. Yet, in spite of
their prospects, Stuart kept on exploring, and even
going further from where alone he would get assistance.
As soon as provisions became scarce the native guide,
deserted them, as a matter of course; but this diminution of their number rather lessened than increased
their means of support. How they existed after that
it would be difficult to tell. Sometimes it was an
opossum, sometimes a crow. Very rarely, indeed, could
they get so large an animal as a wallaby, and their last
supply was mainly a kind of marsupial mouse. But for
the abundance of those small creatures, the danger of
starvation would have been very imminent. When
they reached Beelimah, they lived on shellfish, until
they came to Streaky Bay, where there was a settlement,
and there they rested for a time.

But their troubles were very far from being over.
Long suffering and starvation entailed, as a natural
consequence, a serious illness, and it was not until the
3rd September that they were able to move forward
again. When they did, travelling soon brought on a
relapse, and only enabled them to make very short
stages. Still, Stuart managed to travel along Hack's
tracks, seeking in vain for the good country described
by that gentleman. Weak, ill, and exhausted as they
were, he and his companions managed to cross over to
the Freeling Range, and camped for a night there,
without water. At last, on the 11th September, they
reached Thompson's Station, at Mount Arden, after
having accomplished, in exactly three months, on the
slenderest resources, more than any previous explorer
had ever done in twice the time, with double the means.
Praise would be superfluous for such deeds.

The effect this journey had upon public opinion was

very great. It taught, first, a valuable lesson, in showing
what small resources could accomplish; and proving
that the best exploring expeditions were by no means
those best equipped; and, secondly, it gave an entirely
new turn to the notions about the interior. Instead of
there being nothing but desert beyond Lake Torrens,
and north of the Australian Bight, there was an extensive tract of country with grass and water, stretching
far to the northward. This was truly good news, and
the colonists began to ask each other whether they had
not been too premature in concluding, that because
Sturt and Gregory had met desert in the interior, at
places widely apart, that therefore all was desert
between. But there was no disposition to inquire
further into the matter just then. The public were rather
tired of exploring expeditions. Babbage's was not home
yet, and it had almost proved a failure; and there had
been too much excitement on the subject not to cause a
powerful reaction—so the subject was dropped.

But Stuart started again. Notwithstanding colonial
apathy on the subject, he was not tired. It is supposed
that he crossed the Davenport Range on this occasion, and
it is known that he found the main river into which
drainage from it and from Stuart's Range flowed. This
river he named the Neales. It was a very fine, large
stream, with important tributaries from the north-west,
named the Hugh, the Finke, &c. In some of them the
water was salt, but fresh water was easily obtained, and
grass on the banks of the creeks was abundant and
good. The Neales flowed into Lake Eyre, and is the
main channel for more drainage than is yet known.
Stuart explored a great deal of it, and of the good
country on the Davenport Range, first discovered by
Warburton. What was however the nature of the
exploration, or how long it took, is not known. The
journal never was published. On his return to
Adelaide, Stuart offered to let the Government have his
maps and plans of the country for a fourteen years'
lease of fifteen hundred square miles of the country,
for a pastoral occupancy; the first four years to be rent
free. The proposal was submitted to the Adelaide

Parliament, who rejected the offer. During the discussion of the proposal, many members seemed to wish to send Stuart out again, to cross the continent, with a properly equipped party. But the truth was, people were tired of this kind of thing; and after a long discussion, it was agreed that the public should take no further action than to offer a reward of ten thousand pounds to the person who should first, at his own expense, cross the continent from sea to sea, in a north and south direction. Readers may possibly think that the colonial legislature did not act very generously to Stuart, because, in consequence of the little encouragement given to him, he, in disgust, declined to give up his journals. They are little likely now ever to see the light. I am sorry to add, too, that, when the continent was crossed, the ten thousand pounds was not paid; on the ground, I believe, that the offer was only available for a certain time.

While the Government were discussing the advisability of acceding to Stuart's demand, he made a further attempt to explore the country discovered by him, and to survey it in two blocks, for pastoral occupation. The journal kept by him on that occasion has been submitted to the public, and will be alluded to just now. It may be mentioned, however, that the peculiarity of bubbling springs of water, such as those found by Babbage and Warburton, was found to extend to the Davenport Range, and along the banks of the Neales. The number of these rocky basins found was truly astonishing, and quite sufficient to remove any anxieties about the water supply, in case this country should be settled upon. They were all like those at first described by Babbage and Warburton, but seldom any were so hot as the Emerald Springs. It is probably, as yet, useless to speculate upon the origin of these strange basins of water, but they may be the drainage from the western elevated tableland, which runs between the sandstone and the underlying rock, coming to the surface near the lowest level. If Australia may be described as an immense tableland, tilted up at the east and west sides, we might expect immense springs along the trough or cylindrical axis of the centre of the continent. The vast drainage from the slopes at both sides must accumulate in basins, under as well as over the rocks, and of course would seek an outlet at the surface, as they were filled. The depth from which they come would account for the heat of some of them.

It is not often that the governors of colonies brave the danger and inconveniences of a bushman's life, for the sake of extending the geographical knowledge of the country they govern. Governor Fitzgerald, we have seen, was one exception to the rule ; and Sir R. M'Donnell, of South Australia, was another. He had become so much interested with the account of the north-west country, that he determined to examine the locality in person, and try to push discovery a little further. He started in October, 1859, with three companions and three mounted troopers, besides about eighteen horses, amply equipped. The first part of his journey lay amongst the Mount Serle Ranges. He then crossed the head of the only lake to which now the name of Torrens is applied, and passed by the springs of Babbage and Warburton. The season was one of extraordinary dryness, and the party suffered very much in consequence, for want of water. The governor, however, in spite of every inconvenience, reached the Davenport Range, and visited some of Stuart's Springs. He confirmed the reports of that explorer as to the value of the country around, but, with the exception of some trifling features round about, he did not make any discoveries of importance. It is believed, however, that but for the remonstrances of some of his companions, he would have made a regular exploration to the northward, though probably not without a good deal of suffering, at that period of the year.

During this time, several other minor explorations had taken place in South Australia. A search for gold had been made in the Barrier Ranges, which, it will be remembered, was the first range crossed by Sturt, after leaving the Darling, in 1844. From that time until

the expedition now to be described, no further examination of these ranges had been made, except in 1855,
when Messrs. Williams and Stone got as far as the
Coonbaralba Range, but were obliged to return subsequently for want of water. The expedition of 1859
was placed under the command of Captain Crawford,
but it led to no important results. A chain of hills,
named the Tiyano Range, was discovered. It runs
parallel with the Barrier Range, at about twenty-five
miles' distance, though sometimes apparently much
nearer. It was not laid down by Sturt, but it must
have been seen by him. The tracks of the latter,
though made fifteen years previously, were still quite
visible, showing what a little rain must have fallen
upon these hills. Mr. Poole's grave was found undisturbed. Water was, however, even scarcer than when
Sturt crossed this inhospitable region, so that the party,
after a hasty and cursory examination, were obliged to
turn homewards. No traces of gold were found in the
hills. The Barrier Ranges consisted of slates, schists,
and granite, with ironstone and quartz veins. The
Grey Ranges are almost entirely composed of quartzite,
with magnetic iron ore, and a white trap rock, of varying appearance.

In August, 1859, in consequence of a murder and
robbery by the blacks, in the neighbourhood of Streaky
Bay, Inspector Holroyd was sent with four troopers to
try and arrest the delinquents. They travelled over a
good deal of the country explored by Mr. Eyre, and
even found his tracks, though made twenty years previously. A little of the back country was seen, and
its aspect only tended to confirm the reports of previous
visitants. It was unexceptionably barren and arid.
North of Fowler's Bay a large tract of what Mr.
Holroyd called splendid sheep country, was found, but
notions about good country depend so much upon the
individual opinions of explorers, that first reports are
generally unsatisfactory.

It was in November, 1859, that Stuart made the
journey already alluded to, for the purpose of surveying
the country discovered in his second expedition. At

that time he made a visit to the western shore of Lake
Eyre, and this was one of the few features of the
exploration worth recording. When he came in sight
of it there was a large bay, but from the northern side,
and all round to south, there was nothing visible but
the horizon. There was a large island visible, in shape
much resembling Boston Island, at Port Lincoln, but
the shape was the only point of resemblance, and for
the rest, it formed a worthy portion of the dreary scene.
There were other islands here and there, and round
them, as well round the shore, a glittering white beach
seemed so dazzling and frothy looking, that one would
have thought it was the surf, beating in from the blue
water beyond, but that the stillness and the silence
showed it to be an emblem of the desert. The lake, in
fact, was another dead sea. Stuart got up the day
following before daybreak, to ascertain if there were
any land upon the horizon; but even with a powerful
telescope he could see none. He then went two and a
half miles north to examine the shore, and found it to
be a sort of concrete, formed of salt, lime, and ironstone
gravel. He considered, that when the lake was flooded,
the water would be about three feet deep, at about fifty
yards from the shore. Finding the ground too soft for
a horse, he walked towards the water. On the way he
found a number of small fish, all dried and caked in
salt. They seemed to have been left by receding
waters, or driven on shore by a storm—at least, so Stuart
thought, but probably they were destroyed by the
increased saltness of the water, caused by evaporation.
They were like species found in the fresh-water rivers;
and if we suppose them to have been brought down by
the Barcoo, by a flooded state of its waters, we can easily
understand how they would perish in the saline waters
of Lake Eyre. They were lying in great quantities
along the shore, in a belt about twelve yards wide; and
in whatever way accounted for, the fact is worth the
notice of geologists.

In trying to proceed beyond, Stuart was stopped by
the softness of the clay, which lay in thick ooze under
the salt, at a depth of three inches. As his horses were

at this time distressed for want of water, he returned
that night to Emerald Springs. Singularly enough,
these were found to contain fish, and amid the hot water
basins one was found comparatively cold. Stuart proceeded subsequently in his explorations about the
Davenport Range. This was found to consist principally of granite rocks, both red and grey, but it differed
in one respect from the granite jutting up in mountains
amid the sandstone of the western tableland. It was
flanked by slates and schists, and bore marks of being
an older range, and more fertile, than any other granite
hills.

It has already been mentioned, that this journey of
Stuart, like the preceding one, was remarkable for
the number of springs discovered. It would be an
almost endless work to particularize them. Some
covered an extent of five acres of ground. The
William Springs were upon a hill one hundred feet
high. The lower part was red sand, with a course of
limestone higher up, and on the top was a black soil.
In the latter there was a pool of water, one hundred
feet long, and from the abundant tracks of natives and
emu about, it was evidently the great resort for fresh
water for a long distance around. The Primrose
Springs, near Mount Charles, were hot. The hill upon
which they were was a very remarkable one, and from
the west side would be taken for a mere sand-hill, with
scrub growing upon it. The springs are not seen until
the top is reached, and there the hot basins were placed.
The colder ones were half-way down upon the east side,
which were covered with reeds.

When Stuart had finished his work of survey, he
went to examine the place where the Neales empties
itself into the bed of Lake Eyre. This river was the
recipient of all the drainage from the tableland to the
westward, and was a very important stream in its
lower part. It spread out over the plain in numerous
channels, altogether occupying a space of about four
miles wide, but the main channel alone had water in it,
in holes, sometimes salt, and sometimes brackish.
There was plenty of green feed on its banks, and fine

gum trees lined the sides. Fresh water could easily be obtained by digging. From these features it will be seen that the river was very much like all Australian streams, and not very different from the Barcoo, which joins Lake Eyre on the other side. But near its termination a very great change occurred. The channels were broad, and the main one had abundance of water, but quite salt. There was a creek which flowed into it, a little above the mouth, and this was supplied by brine springs, so strongly saturated with salt as to crystallize upon every object it flowed over, and incrust it quite white. This was the termination of the river; but the flood marks upon the banks, and the large drift wood in the bed, showed that it sometimes contained a flood of fresh water which even the birne springs could not contaminate. The lake into which it emptied could not be certainly pronounced as Lake Eyre, and as soon as his surveys were completed, Stuart went to settle this point. He got a view of the lake close to the Neales, from whence he could see the island before described as being like Boston Island. This was decisive of the point, but in any case there was evidence clear enough of the character of the lake he saw before him. To the eastward he could see nothing but the distant appearance of land, looking, even with the aid of a powerful telescope, like a thin, dark line, upon the blue horizon. To the north, the horizon bounded the view. Stuart rode down to the beach, and found it to be sand and gravel, quite firm close to the shore, but very soft beyond. In spite of the softness, he tried to advance on foot, but at two miles further was obliged to retreat, without having reached the water. The quantity of salt was not so great here as where he had examined first.

Returning from the lake, Stuart searched down a creek, named the Davenport, for water, but could find none. He remarks that he could never find any springs, cold or not, to the east of the hot springs. Another creek, named the George, was found on this expedition, with water in it, and with this discovery all the more important portions of Stuart's journey have been enumerated.

In the same year, and about the same time, Mr. Tolmer organized an exploring party in Adelaide. He hoped to be able to cross the continent by a rapid march, made by a well-mounted expedition; and with this view he left Adelaide, about September 20, 1859. The expedition was unfortunately nothing but a series of disasters, after it had left Spencer's Gulf, in consequence of the rapidity with which the movements were made. By the 6th October, four of the horses were dead, and all of them more or less incapacitated. Shortly afterwards the party was broken up, and its object abandoned. This was long before they had reached the unexplored districts. Strictly speaking, such attempts require no mention in this history, but the instance is given to show that though much has been done with small means in Australian exploration, failure and loss have always resulted from imprudence, whether the means were large or small.*

* It should be mentioned that one reason why the Government did not accede to Mr. Stuart's proposal for a lease of the country he had discovered was, because it did not appear that there was any large quantity available for pastoral purposes, and probably not sufficient for what Mr. Stuart demanded for himself.

CHAPTER XIX.

STUART AT THE CENTRE OF AUSTRALIA.

WHEN Stuart found that the Government would neither grant him a reward nor give him a lease of part of the country discovered, he determined to try and gain the reward offered for crossing the continent. He was not long before he started again. In March, 1860, he left Chambers Creek, with thirteen horses and two companions, Mr. Kekwick and Benjamin Head. The exploration did not commence, properly speaking, until they had reached the Neales; but one incident in the early part of their journey deserves mention, as it is a good specimen of life among the natives of Australia. When encamped at Beresford Springs, they found the corpse of a native in a place where there had evidently been a fight. The body was that of a tall man, lying on his back, with his feet to the north-west, and the hands gone. His skull was broken in three or four places, and the flesh was nearly devoured by crows and native dogs. On the rising ground near were three or four native huts, round which were waddies (clubs), spears, boomerangs, and a number of broken dishes. There was also a singular mark near the huts, which seemed placed there as a sort of superstitious rite in favour of the murdered man. It consisted of a handful of hair torn from the skull of the corpse, and a bundle of emu feathers placed close

x 2

together, the hair to the south-east, and the feathers to
the north-west. They were placed between two pieces
of wood which had been burned, but extinguished before
the feathers and hair were placed between them.

The little party reached the Neales on the 17th of
March. It was then a fine stream, for the rain had been
heavy. The great difficulty now was to find fords over
the numerous creeks and tributaries which joined the
Neales, for the country was boggy, and the sands in
the bottom of the streams very treacherous. Of course,
the first intention of Stuart was to follow up the river as
far as it would lead him. The rains made him quite easy
as to the water supply, and as the drainage came from
about north-west, it was just in the direction he wanted
to go. The country passed through may be easily described. As the Neales runs down from the tableland to
Lake Eyre, its channel, as also that of its tributaries,
are a series of gorges, varying in size, through the
sandstone level. And yet the surface of the tableland
was a good deal varied; generally, it was of a light
brown colour, with stones on the surface, and plenty of
vegetation ; but sometimes the soil showed gypsum
underneath, and often it opened out into fine grassy undulating country, of a dark red colour, slightly covered
with scrub. There were, besides, a good many sand-
hills, and the land was diversified by hills, because a
range, named Heed's Range, was seen to the south-
west on the 24th. Altogether, there was a good deal
of scrub to be got through, which damaged their packs
exceedingly, so that on the 25th they were obliged to
camp for one day to refit.

While they were repairing the damages, Stuart
went to a neighbouring hill to see the nature of the
country in advance. The view told him nothing. To
the east and west there were sand-hills and a good deal
of scrub, and to the north there was a range and scrub
too ; but there was nothing whatever to teach him what
he had to encounter in his further journey. On the
28th, on getting through the scrub to the northward,
they were led to some low sand-hills, and, though no
high land was visible ahead of them, a range could be

seen to the north-east. To this, therefore, they journeyed, and after thirty-five miles of grassy Mulga scrub, reached the junction of three creeks, all coming from the north-west. The most northerly was running, and Stuart supposed it to be the upper part of a tributary of the Neales, which he had named the Frew. The country between the creeks and the range was stony, and when some hills were reached, they showed an open country to the northward. The Frew wound round the northern base of the range, and there were still some fine water-holes, with the remains of a large native encampment. Their winter habitations were upon the side of the creek, and there was a native grave near, composed of sand, earth, wood, and stones, about four and a half feet high, round, and about eight yards across ; but it was not very different from other native tombs. The range hills to the north-east could be seen, but they dropped into low table-hills at a short distance ; while, to the north, the country seemed so open that Stuart thought it best to keep on in that direction. There was scrub at first as he journeyed, but the scene soon opened into fine flats as fertile as most of the sandstone plains to the south.

On the 30th, they continued their northerly course, deviating slightly to the westward, to some flat-topped hills. At sixteen miles they crossed a large gum creek, named the Ross, running to the east and south. It spread out over a flat, between rough hills, half a mile wide. The bed was sandy, and the water certainly not permanent ; but it proved to be only a small tributary of a much more important stream. This was the Stevenson, which was reached immediately after crossing a low volcanic range, probably not much different in character from the volcanic hills amid the tableland of Western Australia. The main river was very broad, and its banks were splendidly grassed, while the mussel-shells, and the small fish and crabs in its bed, seemed to indicate that it was likewise permanent.

Such a stream was quite unexpected at this place, but its easterly course could leave no doubt of its sources or ultimate direction. Like the Neales, it rose in the

tableland, to the eastward, and, like it, flowed down
into Lake Eyre. Stuart could still see a water haze to
the eastward, and imagined that it was a continuation·
of the lake ; but whether or no, the receptacle of such a·
large amount of drainage must be very nearly as important a basin. The Stevenson, of course, had other
tributaries, and these were crossed in journeying towards
some distant hills to the northward. At six miles, they
struck the first, with large gum trees, but no permanent
water. At ten miles they found another running, between
rugged banks, to the east-south-east, amid a mass of
hills. Two miles beyond this there was a valley, a
quarter of a mile broad, through which ran a gum creek,
with abundance of drift timber upon its banks. This
was found subsequently to be the tributary of a more
northerly watercourse than the Stevenson, and, together
with the next seven courses that were met, to flow down
to the east, probably to the same lake basin. The land
they watered was generally scrubby, and an ironstone
soil, with some white flint occasionally.

The range turned out to be principally gypsum,
quartz, and ironstone, very much like the hills of the
Grey Range found by Sturt, or the termination of the
Flinders Range on Lake Torrens. The highest part of
it was named Mount Beddome, but from its summit no
great difference could be seen in the country beyond.
All around there were flat-topped hills of various elevations, and of deep red colour. There was a hill to the
north, to which they journeyed, giving their horses a
drink at a pool of surface water, for they had had none at
their camp on the range the night previous. Thus
they were advancing slowly towards the interior. As
yet, they had met with no difficulties, and water
had been abundant. The country had not changed
very much in appearance, so that the mystery of the
interior seemed likely to prove no mystery after
all ; but they were still within the influence of the
watershed of Lake Eyre, and there might be a great
change once the limits of that basin were passed.

The tablehill was named Mount Humphries. They
ascended it at break of day, upon the 4th, and found its

composition a little varied from the others. It was a soft, white sandstone this time, and on the top was water-worn quartz, cemented into large masses. The view from it showed scrub to the south and west, and more open country northerly; fortunately, again in the direction they wished to take. About two miles from the camp, they came upon a splendid creek, with abundance of grass upon excellent soil; in proof of which, game was most plentiful. The stream was named the Finke, after one of the most liberal promoters of all Stuart's expeditions. Stuart says of this watercourse, that he had not passed over such splendid country since he had been in the colony. The channel went to the east, but upon the next journey it was found that it soon joined the main stream, which flowed almost due south, to the other tributaries already spoken of, and thus it could be seen by the waters that they were passing the northern limits of the Lake Eyre depression.

On the 5th, as they advanced, a change commenced in the appearance of the vegetation. A new *Casuarina* was observed, growing large, with a rough, thick black bark, and a very dismal appearance. The other vegetation was a variation between spinifex and grass, with a decided prevalence of the former. In the far distance to the south-west a long range was visible, with scrub and sand-hills between, and with few intermissions the prospect round to the east was a mass of table-hill, of every size. The main channel of the Finke was crossed, and Stuart said it was the largest gum creek he had yet discovered. It seemed to come from the south-west, but the sand-hills and *Casuarinas* were so numerous, that it was very difficult to make out its true course. They had great difficulty in crossing the bed, for it was full of quicksands. When they were nearly across they saw a black fellow among the bushes, and Stuart pulled up and spoke to him. At first he seemed at a loss to know from whence the sound came, but when he saw the horses he disappeared in a moment. The upper part of the Finke runs through high red sand-hills, with very thick spinifex grass: as we may suppose, something like that part of the Thompson where Gregory

turned back from it. It is astonishing what various
effects these red hills of drift sand had upon different
explorers. They used to dismay Sturt; but Stuart was
so used to them that he would have travelled for days
through them without looking upon the country as a
desert.

They continued through the sand-hills for ten miles
further, until they came to the remarkable hill named
Chambers Pillar. This was a pillar of sandstone,
standing on a hill upwards of 100 feet high, and itself
105 feet high, 20 wide, and 10 thick, with two peaks
upon the top. * Round the elevation were a number
of remarkable hills, which had the appearance of old
ruined castles. This reminds us of Leichhardt's Ruined
Castle Creek. The pillar is not unlike Tower Almond,
and the hills round, described by Mitchell, at the head
of the Belyando: the latitudes of the two places differ
very slightly.

On the 8th, the party moved north-east over low
sand rises and fine grassy plains, lightly sprinkled with
Mulga Acacia and the new *Casuarina*. They were
moving now towards a set of hills, named the James'
Range, which, for a wonder, was not flat-topped, though
it was red sandstone, and had huge blocks of the same
rock lying on its side. A creek, named the Hugh, took
its rise near at hand, but it was dry, and of no more
importance than for speculation as to where it came from
and whither it went, for they seemed to be altogether
out of reach of Lake Eyre now. To the east there were
red sand-hills and ranges beyond, and to the northward
a high broken range, standing out boldly with two very
remarkable bluffs in the centre, and altogether
very different from the hills met with hitherto. Of
course they steered towards it, hoping that now, at least,
they were to meet with a complete change in the
character of the scenery. The sand-hills, alternating
with grassy flats, continued meanwhile, and at sixteen
miles the Hugh appeared to come from that direction
through a smaller range south of the principal line of

* It was named after Mr. Chambers, the great promoter of Stuart's explorations, who died in 1862, before he could see his work completed.

hills. It was nearly perpendicular, with huge masses of sandstone upon its sides. They had experienced much difficulty in crossing James Range, but this was a far greater obstacle, which it cost them infinite time and labour to overcome. They had to keep down it for miles before they could get a crossing-place, not alone because of the rocks : there was an immense quantity of dead scrub, and when they moved aside to avoid a precipice they were always met by the thicket, which opposed them like a wall. Torn and harassed, they were nearly naked when they arrived at the further side of the hills. At eight miles further they reached the head of the Hugh, and were obliged to encamp for a day to repair their damages. One of the horses was seriously lamed by a splinter of dead scrub.

On the 10th, they reached the furthest range, which was found to be divided into two chains of hills, amid which the Hugh still ran between perpendicular rocky gorges. The valley around was rich, and the grass plentiful. The ranges were named after Mr. Waterhouse, at that time chief secretary in Adelaide. At eight miles beyond them the explorers again crossed the Hugh, which now came from the east, and for the first time in the country they met with pine trees upon its banks. There seemed to be a spring in the water-hole when they encamped.

The next day they entered the lower hills of the range, and travelled through a splendid grass country. At eight miles they struck upon the creek coming from the westward ; and at twelve miles met with a number of springs in the range. As they approached a bold high bluff in the foreground, their route became very difficult. They could not go up the bed of the creek, because of the precipices on either side, and to get another path was a very difficult matter. They were obliged to turn in every direction, so that it took them the whole afternoon to reach the foot of the bluff, and then it was too late to think of ascending. They camped beside a good spring, surrounded by a new species of vegetation, which told them of the gradual advance they were making to the unknown country. The foliage was very graceful; for among the trees was a remarkable palm, whose leaves hung over the tree-top like a plume of feathers. The leaves were light green, broad and sharp-pointed, and about eight inches long. The fruit had a large kernel, which was like a potato when roasted, but not in its effects. It made the explorers very ill when they had eaten a small quantity. In this respect it was like the pandanus.

Here, at last, there was some variety from the monotonous tableland. The range, says Stuart, was the only real range he had met with since leaving the Flinders Range, and like it it had granite and gneiss among its rocks. It ran east and west, and was named the M'Donnell Range, after the governor of the colony. The bluff in front was named after Major Brinkley, and Stuart tried to get a view from it next morning. The day was very hazy, but even if it had not been so, a hill named Mount Hay shut out a good deal of the view to the north-west. A wooded plain and another range were visible to the north. To the north-east there was the end of another range from the south, and this was named after Mr. Strangways. Beyond this there was the luminous haze of water, but none could be seen, and it is very unlikely that there can be any very large area of water in that direction. After descending the bluff, which was a frightfully perilous task, Mr. Stuart made for one more to the westward. At ten miles he reached it, and encamped at a permanent water-hole. The day following was entirely taken up in crossing the range, a distance of only five miles, and when they had passed it, the creeks were found to run to the north, with springs of fresh water in them; so that Stuart might consider that he had now fairly passed all the limits of the southern waters. The M'Donnell Range has not been explored further to the east or west. As a range of metamorphic rock it might be considered very important, but when we know that it divides the northern from the southern waters, and that in width it occupies no less than five miles, its western prolongation must be certainly worth exploring.

Before leaving the hills, a better view was obtained of the surrounding country. To the north-west, between the range with the conical hill and the Strangways Range, there seemed nothing but an open scrubby plain, into which the creeks from M'Donnell Range seemed to empty themselves. This was not a very encouraging commencement after leaving the watershed; but Stuart did not hesitate one moment. He was now within the tropics, and on a fair way to the centre; and as water had never entirely failed him hitherto, he had good hopes of finding, at least, the small quantity he should require for his party. Of course, he must have had some misgivings, for if the desert existed at all in Australia, he might reasonably expect to meet it near the position he then occupied.

On the 10th April he journeyed through twenty miles of an open plain, often scrubby, and sometimes well grassed. He met with no water after leaving the range, and so he camped without it. Next day, at eighteen miles, they saw to the west two prominent bluff hills, and two or three small ones about ten miles off, but they did not reach them until sundown. They had to go two miles in search of a watercourse, and when at last they reached one, it was dry. This was the only stream bed since leaving M'Donnell Range, and Stuart began to fear that he should, in spite of himself, he obliged to turn back. He passed an anxious night in suspense, but the morning brought him relief. On ascending the range ne saw, to his inexpressible delight, a little creek bearing to the east. He found, too, that the highest point of the range was still thirteen miles ahead, while the country to the west and north-east seemed a mass of hills. To the south-west there were high broken ranges, and to the east, scrub and the tops of distant hills.

In the meantime, Mr. Kekwick had found some water in the southern creek; but Stuart determined not to leave the range until he procured a permanent supply, for the country had an arid, parched appearance in the north, as if rain had not fallen upon it for many years. The range was still gneiss and granite rock.

It was named the Reynolds Range, and the hill from which the view was taken was called Mount Freeling. On the 19th, they moved to the east side of the mount, where Stuart had seen the pool. They were obliged to go a long way round to get to it, as the hills were rough with sharp rocks, and quite impassable to the horses. There was abundance of grass, however, and at ten miles' distance they found a further supply of excellent water. This was in a branch creek a little higher up, and amid the ledges of rock they found two very large reservoirs quite full. This was decisive of the question of further progress. They could now move forward in safety.

Thus, they were slowly working their way onward; and still as they advanced their prospects seemed to improve. When they crossed the range, they found on the other side a large creek, with water upon the north-east bank. Besides this, there were others, and with these cheering indications of moisture, there was good grass and many new and beautiful flowers. In such a country, the three intrepid explorers found many means of palliating the scurvy, from which they now slightly suffered. On the 21st, they travelled over seven miles of beautifully grassed open scrub; but, after this, the scrub became very dense, with many dry watercourses in a red sandy soil. To make the resemblance to the tableland of Western Australia more complete, there were two granite rocks. After a journey of thirty-six miles, they camped by a little pool of rain-water in a dry creek, which ran towards the north-east.

The day following this was an important one in the history of Australian exploration. When Stuart took his observations, he found that he was in the centre of Australia, and thus realized his fondest hopes. It certainly was a position of which he might be proud. Leichhardt, Sturt, Eyre, and Gregory had all striven, and striven in vain, amid fearful suffering and disappointment; and here Stuart stood, having found a clear and unobstructed passage to the long-desired object. About two and a half miles from the camp there was a high mount. It was not in the centre; but was the

only one at all near it ; so he chose it as the spot of his
triumph. Everyone will envy him his feelings, as he
unfurled the flag of his country, and firmly planting
the staff, called it Central Mount Stuart. The little
party then gave three cheers, and buried a bottle containing an account of their discovery. This was a prudent though a sad precaution ; for who could tell, now
that they had penetrated so far, that a single one of
these weakened famished men would ever return to tell
what they had accomplished ? The mount was at least
two thousand feet high, and the view to the north
extended over a large plain, with watercourses running
through it. The large gum creek upon which they had
camped, and which they had named the Hanson, ran
round the hill, and at ten miles to the north-east was
joined by another. Central Mount Stuart was the commencement of a new sandstone range which continued
northward ; and all around the country the soil was a
red sand, without stones, but well grassed.

And yet in spite of the grass and the aspect of the creek,
the country to the north looked dry and discouraging.
Even if it had appeared more favourable, Stuart thought
that his best way now to cross the continent would be
to make for the sources of the Victoria River, and so he
turned to the westward, towards a peak visible in that
direction, where he hoped to find a better country for
travelling. To the north and south there were a number of isolated hills, principally composed of granite ; and
at ten miles or so, came upon three watercourses, with a
little water in one of them. Leaving these, they
crossed much scrubby country with a good deal of grass
and watercourses, but no water, though they went on in
hopes of it for thirty-eight miles. Two mountains were
near the camp, named respectively, Mount Denison and
Mount Leichhardt. In searching near these water was
found, while the ground round the base of the range
was covered with luxuriant grass and vegetation.
Signs of natives were numerous, some of them very
recent, which was rather embarrassing to the explorers,
though it showed the favourable nature of the country.
In order to explore as rapidly as possible, Stuart and

Kekwick had both to be away in different directions, leaving the camp under the protection of one man. None of the savages were seen, however.

Mount Denison was climbed by Stuart on the 28th. It was the highest mountain he had been upon hitherto in his explorations, and it took him eight hours to reach its summit. He first led his horse up a rocky creek, and, passing through a precipitous gorge, came upon a fine water-hole. Two hundred yards beyond this he was stopped by a perpendicular precipice, over which a spring trickled into a shady reservoir. He had to take to the hills to accomplish his purpose; and thus, by scrambling over peaks and down gullies, he reached the top. The view from such an elevation repaid him well. To the south were broken ranges and wooded plains, with a high mountain in the distance : more to the westward, a number of ranges seemed to terminate, until they faded into distant high land, and then all beyond was a boundless plain covered with patches of scrub. The next range bearing nearly west, was named the Barkly Range (after the governor of Victoria). There Stuart intended to go next, but the level to the north-west was very discouraging. While he rested himself, and gazed with admiration at the vast untrodden fields which lay around him, uniform in colour, and tinging even the sky with a portion of their hue, he became uneasy about the signs of life which he suddenly saw beneath him. He had been obliged to leave his horse tied to a tree, about half-way down the mountain; and now he could see, to his horror, smoke rising very near the place. He descended rapidly, as well he might. His horse was safe, but the natives had been very near. These risks seem almost incredible. Fancy tying one's horse to a tree while toiling for hours up a mountainside, in a wild country of savages, while the only help for thousands of miles is two men out of sight and hearing !

Leaving Mount Denison, they crossed eighteen miles of spinifex plain without grass. This brought them to Mount Barkly. They camped without water; and though on the north-east side of the hill, a scanty supply was obtained; it was the result of surface drainage, and not to be depended on for any length of time. The country in advance seemed, if possible, still more unfavourable, but they kept on their north-west course. At six miles, they came upon a many-channelled gum creek; dry, of course, but with a small native well in its bed—so small, indeed, that the rest of the day was spent in watering the horses from it. The soil around seemed to be derived from Mount Barkly, which was a hard red sandstone. The creek was named the Fisher, after the president of the Legislative Council. Thirteen miles beyond this, they came upon some hills; but as these were without water, they turned more to the westward, in the hope of finding some. That day passed without any indications of even a native well. The country from Mount Denison had been a dead level, except at Mount Barkly, consisting of loose red sand, covered with spinifex. They went eighteen miles further, through this arid plain, which seemed as if, even in wet weather, it could not retain water. The only change which occurred was in two unimportant hills which they passed, named Mount Turnbull and Arthur's Hills; and then, as the country seemed to get worse instead of better, they turned back. Their turning-point was in a tract more fertile, apparently, than Stuart's Central Desert; but even worse off in regard to water. It was very deceitful to the view, and looked at a distance much more pleasing than it really was. One native track was seen in it, rather different from the tracks usually made by the natives; in fact, more like that of a white man; but this was the only indication of the nature of the aborigines in this singular desert.

The horses were brought back with great difficulty; but they found a native well on their return, which enabled them to regain the Fisher. The animals were but poorly supplied, and only then by the party sitting up all night to collect the water as it flowed into the basin. On reaching Mount Denison, they were detained three days by illness, caused by their late exertions.

On the 12th of May, they moved from Mount Denison in a direction slightly east of north, thinking that they might be able to pursue their object in that direction at least. For twenty-seven miles, this course took them through very thick Mulga scrub, gum flats, and spinifex. They camped without water, of which the country was not only destitute, but seemed incapable of retaining it for a single day. The next day, they kept more to the east, in order to cut the creek they had passed on their journey to Mount Leichhardt. It was found at three miles, but was quite as dry as the country around. They then passed through another scrub, and at ten miles reached the northern termination of the range proceeding from Mount Stuart. It gave a most disheartening view over the surrounding plains of red sand and scrub. Hard as it seemed to Stuart to retrace his steps, there was no resource but to do so now; at least as far as the Central Mount. This would bring him to the sources of the Hanson; by following which to the north-east he might be more fortunate in his discoveries of water.

They reached the centre again on the 14th of May. The horses were very much exhausted for want of water, and poor Stuart was really ill, partly from scurvy, and partly from a very severe fall from his horse in the scrub. We may judge of his condition by the following extract from his journal :—" The horses are very bad." (Some had nearly given up on the journey back). " Yesterday, I rode in the greatest pain, and it was with difficulty I was able to sit in the saddle. My hands are a complete mass of sores which will not heal. I am nearly helpless. My mouth and gums are so bad that I am obliged to eat only boiled flour and water. The pains in my limbs and muscles are almost insufferable. Kekwick is suffering also from bad hands; but, as yet, has no other signs."

While Stuart took a few days' rest, which he needed so much, he sent Kekwick to the northward, with directions to devote two whole days to a search for permanent water. He thought, that if he could only get one hundred and twenty miles further, there would

be a chance of his getting to the opposite coast; but the
weakness of the horses was his greatest difficulty. For
himself he did not care; and though later he describes
the scurvy as turning his limbs black, still, he says,
that he was determined not to give in. Considering his
state, and how well he might have been satisfied with
what had been done, it is a wonder that he persevered
any longer.

But Kekwick returned with cheerful tidings. He
had found a small quantity of water in the Hanson,
fifteen miles further north. By the aid of this the party
were able to advance; but only very slowly, because
Stuart was too ill to travel far or even to move every
day. The channel was traced until it spread out into the
valley of a salt creek, and then formed a lagoon at the
foot of some sand ridges, twenty-five miles from Mount
Stuart. On the east there was a large dry lagoon, at
least five miles long, and this was all that could be seen
of the course of the Hanson. Like many other streams
in Australia, this failure of the channel may be only
temporary; and, possibly, all these creeks may form
the head of a larger watercourse running to the north
from the mount. However this may be, Stuart found
another creek in a gum plain, a little way beyond the
lagoon. At two miles it ran out; but at two miles
further they struck it again; and to their joy, as great
as it was unexpected, found it full of water. Some natives were encamped near it, but they ran away in the
greatest haste, only allowing the explorers to see that
they had no hair on their heads.

The creek was named the Stirling, and came from a
range a short distance away to the north-east. It was
soon reached, and from its summit hills of red sandstone could be seen all round them. This was very
encouraging, especially as to the north-east there was a
range with a valley between, which gave every promise
of water. The further range was called after Mr.
Crawford, and the one they were upon, after Mr.
Foster. Due north of them, in the Crawford Range,
there was a fine hill, named Mount Strzelecki. In
moving towards the latter, they found abundance of

water in a creek, and thus reached the mount with a full supply.

Thus far they had succeeded in getting a long way beyond Mount Stuart; but not without much labour. Stuart was ill again, from ascending Mount Strzelecki, so that we have no statement of the view obtained from its summit. The journal is rather defective in this portion; but he accounts for it, by saying how ill he was, which now rendered his share of the labours of the party quite incompatible with much writing. He adds, with touching simplicity: "It is terribly killing work." We know, however, from the summit of the mount a range was seen in the far distant north, as a point to which they could proceed. It was called the Davenport Range; and the intervening country held out very small hopes of water. Its looks did not mislead. For forty-eight miles, they travelled over undulating plains of red sand, with scrub and various other kinds of timber; but not the smallest sign of water. Occasionally, they met with plains which seemed as if they had been flooded; but only one creek, and that was dry wherever they searched. The range, when reached, was the usual hard red sandstone. On its further side, there was a little pool left by the rains in the rocks, and there was no improvement in the prospect of the country before them.

To turn back now, when they had come so far, would have been hard; but unless the country improved, there would be considerable danger in advancing beyond with such scanty supplies. They camped one day at the pool, and Kekwick was sent on to look for water. Stuart was better, and wished to finish his maps; but when night came there were no signs of Kekwick's return. There were many tracks of natives about, and Stuart became very uneasy. In great anxiety and suspense he passed the night, for the lives of the whole depended upon the safety of each one. With the light, Kekwick returned. He had found abundance of water in advance, but had been very ill on his return, and even then was so poorly, that they had to encamp another day. They could afford a day

or two now, for the water in advance of them was
in abundance.

On the 1st of June, after crossing five miles of
Mulga scrub, and passing two considerable creeks, they
came upon a large and splendid watercourse, having
fine deep reaches of water, and fish four or five inches
long. Its course was to the west-north-west, with perpendicular banks well grassed, and lined with gum
trees. The bed was nearly seven hundred yards broad;
in fact, it was a large and important river, in the Australian sense of the word. It was named the Bonney.
It had tributaries; one of which, named the M'Laren,
was nearly as important as itself; and when both had
been crossed, the explorers reached a low range of trap
rocks. Stuart was too ill to ascend this the next day;
so on the day following they kept round to some more
distant ranges on the north-west. They were reached
on the 5th of June; the intervening country being the
usual grass and scrub without an object of interest of
any kind. From a summit, Stuart saw a number of
broken ranges before him, with no appearance of
water; but yet fortune favoured him, for a few miles
beyond, he came upon a splendid hole of water in
a watercourse, which he named Goodiar's Creek. It
was deep and permanent; but, unfortunately, there was
no grass for the horses near it.

These passages in Stuart's journey make the proceedings of one day so very like another, that one pauses
frequently to rest, as it were, in following him over this
monotonous tableland. Had Stuart been more scientific
or more observant than he was, it was impossible for
him to vary his narrative much in crossing this tedious
country. It was a range, a creek, a barren plain, or a
scrub; but all on red sand, and all equally destitute of
points of interest. Fortunately, we are coming now to
a change in the narrative, otherwise it would be necessary to summarize the journeys very briefly, or else
altogether weary the reader.

On the 6th of June, after crossing numerous creeks
and stout spinifex grass, through which they had great
difficulty in driving the horses, they crossed a gum

creek at five miles, with good grass and water, so they
encamped. Before they reached this, they passed a
number of marks much resembling the tracks of horses.*
Next day, they passed amid a number of huge, broken
granite rocks, about three miles from their camp, from
which a few small watercourses seemed trending to the
eastward. They then encountered a thick scrub. In
crossing through this towards a range, they came upon
another creek with water, evidently a place of great resort by the natives. The aspect of the country was now
changing very much. The creeks were more numerous,
but the scrubs were thicker, and of a more tropical
character. Bishop's Creek was followed through
scrub and plains until it emptied itself into a large gum
plain.

Twelve miles beyond the termination of the creek
the range was reached. It was found to be tableland,
composed of ironstone, granite, quartz, and red sandstone. It was very difficult to ascend, and when they
got upon the top, they had to go along its surface two
miles, and then camp without finding water. This range
was named after Dr. Short, and seemed to run to the
north-west, parallel with one visible in the distance,
named after Sturt. The tableland continued for two
miles further; after which they descended into plains,
sixteen miles of which were scrubby, and thirteen miles
beautifully grassed. But the grass was too good to last.
When they left it, the scrub became very thick indeed,
and all signs of water disappeared. This was their
first bold push for the Victoria River, so Stuart held on,
tearing his horses through the scrub, and hoping to find
creeks at every sandy rise. It was so very tempting to
have the sources of the Victoria scarcely three hundred
miles away from him, that he was determined not to
give up until he had made every effort. But what
efforts could succeed in such a country? Stuart at last
saw that it was no use, and so, very reluctantly, he
turned back. The scrub was utterly impenetrable, even

* Were these Leichhardt's tracks? Supposing him to have gone up the
Flinders, and to have reached the watershed found by McKinlay, had he
struck then to the westward, he may have crossed about this latitude.

had there been water; for the want of which the horses
had begun to show great signs of distress. Instead,
however, of falling back direct to Bishop's Creek, Stuart
foolishly resolved to try a south course. In this direction, the country was even worse, and when they had
got so far as to render a speedy retreat impossible, one
of the horses became mad for want of water, and the
others began to give in. In the hasty march they had
to make, three had to be abandoned, and the rest were
much exhausted. This journey told as much upon
the men as upon the animals; not only because of the
thirst, but by the fearful anxiety, lest they should not
succeed in bringing back a single horse alive. This destroyed all Stuart's hopes of reaching the Victoria
River.

They rested now for a time at Bishop's Creek.
While they were encamped there, four natives made
their appearance. They seemed more angry than
alarmed; and, making frantic gestures, they approached
the explorers, as if about to throw their spears. Stuart
came peaceably towards one of them, and so far succeeded in disarming their rage, that a conference was
obtained. It led to nothing. The natives did not, or
would not, understand the signs, and gave no information about the water further north. One of them was a
powerful fellow, six feet high, with a red net upon his
head; but this was the only clothing any of them possessed.

Stuart was not yet inclined to resign his plan for
crossing the continent. He had been beaten back in
one direction, but he resolved to try others before he
relinquished all hopes. He was much better in health,
so he started again on the 18th, in a direction slightly
east of north. There was a very encouraging prospect
in this direction. At ten miles they came upon a fine
creek, named the Phillips, with plenty of water. Next
day, the journey from this was over the spurs of Short's
Range. This fringed a large plain to the east, which
at fourteen miles was well watered with swamps and
pools of water. These were named Kekwick's Ponds.
From these they went more to the east, as the country

to the north did not look favourable. But it was certainly no change for the better. After passing one more creek, they entered the thick scrub again. Still they kept on. From some granite hills on their course they could see a few red sand-hills and a lake ten miles further, and other lakes with sand-hills around; but though this was promising, they had to camp that night without water. The next day the lakes turned out to be large grassy plains of rich alluvial soil, and the sand-hills proved to be rocks of ironstone and granite. A persevering search for water was made, but it was quite unsuccessful, and as the weakened horses could not stand a longer abstinence, without the risk of losing some of them, Stuart was reluctantly obliged to fall back upon Kekwick's Ponds.

While resting here, the natives visited them again. They were peaceable in their disposition, but very much inclined to steal. Two powerful young men were among them, one of whom had a head-dress exactly resembling a helmet. There was an old man also, who was very talkative, but Stuart could get no information from him. After talking for some time to the young men, he turned to Stuart and gave him a masonic sign. The explorer looked at them steadily, and the three natives then repeated the signal. Stuart returned it, which seemed to please them very much. The old man then patted him on the shoulders, and stroked his head, and, departing, made friendly signs; but they did not repeat their visit.

On the 25th, Stuart again moved to the northward: he steered now for some distant hills, hoping, as a last resource, that he might be able to reach the watershed of Carpentaria. At two miles he crossed a watercourse, and at fourteen miles another, with abundance of water. There were fish in the ponds, and altogether it seemed such an important stream that Stuart determined to follow it down. It soon turned in a northerly direction, with long sheets of water and very steep banks. While searching in the neighbourhood of the creek for some indications of a favourable route to the north, they saw some natives, evidently watching their movements.

They took no notice of this at the time, and went on
with their explorations. Towards evening the savages
made a sudden and determined attack upon them, and
Stuart thus recites the encounter :—

" Putting the horses towards the creek, and placing
ourselves between them and the natives, I told the men
to get their guns ready, for I could see that they were
bent upon mischief. They paid no regard to the signs
of friendship I kept constantly making, but were still
gradually approaching nearer. I felt very unwilling to
fire upon them, and continued making signs of peace
and friendship, but all to no purpose. The old man,
the leader, who was in advance, made signs with his
boomerang for us to be off. This proved to be a sign
of defiance, for I had no sooner turned my horse's head,
to see if that were what they wished, than we received
a shower of boomerangs, accompanied by a fearful yell.
They then commenced jumping, dancing, yelling, and
throwing their arms in all sorts of postures, like so many
fiends, and setting fire to the grass. Still I felt very
unwilling to fire on them, and tried to make them
understand that we wished to do them no harm. They
now came to within forty yards of us, and again made
a charge, throwing their boomerangs and spears, one of
which struck my horse, and the rest came whistling and
whizzing past our ears. I then gave orders to fire,
which stayed their mad career for a little."

It is needless to tell the rest of the story. The
pack-horses were frightened by the firing, and bolted,
and the natives tried to cut them off from the explorers.
They, however, kept out of reach of the guns, and thus
Stuart was enabled to get rid of them and return to his
camp of the previous night. This encounter was, however, fatal to his plans. It would have been madness
now to try to proceed further with so small a party.
Moreover, two-thirds of his six months' half rations
were now expended; and unless he thought of retiring
now, he might never get back at all. Most reluctantly,
at length, did he resolve to return; and thus, with
success almost within his grasp, he was obliged to
retrace his steps, with half his work undone. If he had

not been so wonderfully fortunate, one would pity him more ; but considering that he had done more than it had ever fallen to the lot of an explorer to perform before, and remembering that he had almost solved the problem of the Australian desert, one can find no room for pity in such a triumph.

It will be scarcely necessary to give more than a mere outline of the return journey. Their marches were, of course, more rapid, because they knew the nature of the country they had before them. One of the most interesting features of their outward course had been Bonney's Creek; and when Stuart came back to it he resolved to explore it further, and perhaps, by its means, reach the Victoria River. But he was unable to do so. After waiting six days for a fall of rain, which seemed threatening every day and yet did not come after all, he relinquished the idea, as the watercourse was far too dry to attempt its exploration. When they reached the Hanson, near Central Mount Stuart, they were pursued by a tribe of natives; but there was not much trouble with them, as they kept a respectful distance from the explorers. With this exception, their journey scarcely possessed any interest. The water in the holes they had passed was nearly dried up, and the Hugh and Finke had scarcely any fresh water in them at all; but to make up for this they found some new water-holes, and neither the horses nor men suffered much in this respect. But they did in others. Stuart was very ill again, for all his scurvy symptoms returned. He was obliged to delay the others at times, and could only sit on horseback with the greatest difficulty. Kekwick and Ben had also their share of suffering; and at last it was almost impossible to move them along. But in spite of all these drawbacks, they reached the settled districts by the 2nd September, very much exhausted, it is true, but with no more serious injury than what rest and good food would remedy.

And thus ended the most marvellous exploration ever made in Australia. Not only must the smallness of the resources be considered, and the gigantic importance of

the discoveries, but also the immense tract of land traversed, and carefully explored.   Thus was one portion
of the veil of mystery raised from the centre of Australia.
It had already been proved that the red sandstone plateau
extended throughout a great portion of the continent ;
and as it had been met with principally in connection
with a desert, it was thought that it would be always so
found.   But the sandstone plateau had been crossed ;
and instead of a desert, a uniform, scrubby, and moderately grassy country was seen.   It had been thought,
too, that there could be no hills, except in connection
with an extensive mountain range, and these the shores
of Australia declared did not exist.   And yet here was
a succession of small, isolated ranges, with no constant
direction for any one of them.   And lastly, it was
imagined that because there were no rivers to be seen
upon the coast, that there were none in the interior.
But plenty were found.   Where they all went to might
be, and is still, a problem ; but there they were, and
Australia was shown not to be the arid desert it was
supposed, nor its map a huge blank for imagination and
conjecture to fill up.

CHAPTER XX.

STUART'S SECOND JOURNEY.

Warburton—The head of the Australian Bight—Stuart starts again—Many
new creeks discovered—Traces down the Bonney—Whittington Range—
Morphett Creek — Tomkinson's Creek — Mount Primrose — Carruther's
Creek—Various attempts to cross the Victoria River—Ashburton Range
—Other unsuccessful attempts—Newcastle Water—Encounter with the
natives —Final attempts—Return.

Of course, Stuart was received with acclamation by
his fellow-colonists, who were quite as much astounded
as delighted at the news he brought. Of course, too,
there was no difficulty now in equipping a party, for
every one was anxious then to solve the rest of a
problem thus so happily begun. Before, however, the
narrative of his adventures is continued, it is necessary
to describe a small expedition which started from
Adelaide about this time. Towards the close of the
year 1860, Major Warburton explored for some distance
beyond the head of the great Australian Bight. As
the locality had been visited previously by Mr. Eyre,
the only result of the journey was to confirm the reports
of that explorer. His tracks were still visible, or rather
there were still signs of the places where he had dug
for water. The Major had many difficulties to contend
with ; but, of course, having the benefit of Eyre's
knowledge, besides three men and eleven horses, he
was not in such a position as the first explorer. He
managed easily to reach eighty-five miles beyond the
head of the Australian Bight. The country was remarkably barren and desolate. Two journeys were
made from the coast to the northwards, in each of
which three days were given to the examination of the
country. The first was from the head of the bight, and

the course was first northerly, then east, and then south-
west, making a kind of triangle. During the whole of
the first and second day's journey they travelled over a
dreary waste, extending as a level plain as far as the
eye could reach, and wholly destitute of wood, water,
or even stones. There was no perceptible inclination
of the country one way more than the other. Rain had
recently fallen, and here and there a few blades of
grass were springing up; but, says Major Warburton,
evidently for no purpose but to be scorched up and
swept away by the first blast that came across these
plains. He also inferred that rain seldom fell in this
locality; but where it did, was immediately absorbed
by the thirsty soil. The only creatures seen were a
few bustards and a variety of snakes. Altogether, one
is very strongly reminded of the Libyan Desert on reading this description of the Major's.

He started to make another attempt to explore from
the head of the bight by a north-west course. The
first six miles was through open scrub, and when this
was passed he entered the great plain upon which he
travelled before. Here it was a little better. There
was more grass and of a stronger quality. The ground,
too, was not quite so level, for there were little depressions where rain might collect. But this improvement
was only temporary. In a very short time the desert
resumed its old character, and, for the thirty-two miles
traversed the first day, did not change in the least.
The next day they continued for twenty-seven miles,
making in all more than sixty from the coast, and as
there was no alteration, Major Warburton returned. He
had thus failed twice in an attempt to ascertain the
termination of the plains; and when so intrepid an
explorer gave the matter up, we may well regard it as
hopeless. In pursuing the inquiry he had suffered
many privations, but returned in safety to Adelaide
about the end of the year.

How far this desert may extend can only be a
subject for conjecture. If the red sandstone must be
considered a recent tertiary rock, then the level tract
can only be broken by table ranges. From analogy

with other parts of the coast, we might suppose this
would be a distance varying from one hundred to two
hundred miles; but this would be no more than a supposition, and of little value. The resemblance of this
tract to the Libyan Desert is very striking. The surface
of the latter is not covered with sand, but consists of
immense plains of horizontal sandstone, as level as a
bowling-green, and without the least furrow or depression, until it terminates in a pebbly gravel, furrowed
by ravines and glens.

We return now to the prosecution of Stuart's discoveries. The Government of Adelaide was not long,
as we have said, in equipping an expedition under
Stuart's command to follow up the discoveries he had so
well begun. In the meantime, an expedition had started
from Melbourne, whose importance is so great in connection with his history, that I prefer to disturb the
chronological arrangement, for the sake of rendering
the narrative more complete in each part. I allude to
Burke's expedition. The tidings brought by Stuart
were sent after Burke, to guide his movements, and then
no time was lost to learn the rest of the story so pro-
vokingly interrupted at Attack Creek. The party was
to consist of eleven men, with Mr. Kekwick as second
in command.

They started on the 1st January, 1861. Of course,
it will not be necessary to do more than to indicate
the new features met with on their outward route. At
Loudon Spa, or the hot springs, in the first stages,
five horses were left, and the party reduced to ten men,
with thirty weeks' provisions. The weather was fearfully hot here, and Stuart was so ill that it was not
until the 4th February that they reached the Lindsay, a
new creek to the north of the Stephenson, in lat. 26° 10'.
From this point they passed a good deal to the east of
their former track, discovering many tributaries of
creeks formerly crossed, and meeting with natives
which they had not seen before. At Mount Humphries
other fine springs were found, and more as they went
along the Finke; but a few were springs of salt water.
Near the Finke, also, some of the horses were taken ill,

as if they had eaten a poisonous plant. One died in
consequence, but the others recovered. The month of
February was spent in very slow journeys, because the
water was so scarce; but Stuart hoped that when the
equinoctial rains set in he would be able to proceed
much more rapidly. The Hugh was found to be
better supplied, and there was a batch of springs in the
Waterhouse Ranges; but by the time they got to the
northern side of M'Donnell Range, they were delighted
with a heavy shower, which set all the creeks running.
As usual, such an advantage was counterbalanced by
difficulties. The ground became so soft that their
progress was stopped until the 26th March. A good
deal of the delay was caused by their losing the
horses.

They reached the Bonney on the 12th April. It
was now running, and had abundance of green feed
upon its banks. Stuart thought this a good opportunity
to trace its course. He found that some stony hills lay
across his path; and when he reached the west side of
these, saw a creek which he considered to be the
Bonney. But as there was an appearance of another
channel further on, he continued towards that. After
passing over some low limestone hills, with small flats
between, he arrived at the same kind of country which
had turned him back from beyond Mount Denison in
the preceding year. He therefore returned to where he
had crossed the Bonney, which still contained plenty of
water, though it was so small that he could scarcely
believe that it was the river. The country near it was
well grassed, with granite and sand-hills around. On
the second day, Stuart went west for a few miles, and
then turned more to the north, in the hope of finding
the M'Laren—a creek he had seen north of the Bonney,
on his first journey. Three miles from his starting-
place he found that the latter had spread out over a
large grassy plain, covered with long grass, and a great
number of ants' nests, putting one in mind, says Stuart,
of walking through a large cemetery. In many places
it was very boggy. He followed it up, notwithstanding, for ten miles, but it continued the same, until the

scrub and the growth of gum trees became so thick that he could scarcely see a yard before him. This was all he could learn of the creeks; and though they were interrupted, like most Australian rivers during a part of their course, in clay flats, yet it must be considered that their ultimate course has not been ascertained.

By the 24th April the party had reached Attack Creek, and from that point the explorations commenced in earnest. There were many traces of natives about where the encounter had taken place; but none were visible now, and the strength of the party made it a matter of indifference whether they appeared or not. The creek took its rise from a range a short distance to the westward, which ran north and south. Stuart's first care was to ascend this, and then make a new effort to reach the Victoria River by a north-west course. Water seemed likely to be their least difficulty, for shortly after starting they met with a winding watercourse, and numerous well-filled holes. The range from which it proceeded was a picturesque line of hills, very different from any previously met with, because it had tall gum trees upon its summit. It was named the Whittington Range. The view to the east and south-east extended over a thick and dense scrub, but to the north-west the country appeared more practicable, for there was a gap in another range, through which he imagined the creek would flow. He went therefore towards it, but was disappointed. The country inclined to the south more than to the west, and, at any rate, there was no water, so he had to return to Morphett Creek.

He now kept northward along the grassy slopes which led up to the range, for it was clearer travelling, and there was more chance of water in that direction than in any other. When he had crossed the last spur, he met with another watercourse, on a large plain covered with grass and a few bushes. But it was quite dry, and no search that they could make would detect even moisture in its bed. Stuart was very much disheartened at this. The day's journey had been very rough and stony, mostly over the spurs of the range,

which were covered with spinifex and scrub. The
drainage from the hills seemed to run down into grassy
plains and there was lost, and there was not a drop of
surface water to be had in any direction. Hard as it
seemed to Stuart, there was no course open but to return if he did not find water on the following day,
because, owing to the delays which had occurred, the
horses were very weak, and it was doubtful whether
even now all could be brought back again.

On. the day following, Stuart found a temporary
relief to his anxiety. When he had crossed the grassy
plain, he found a creek with plenty of water in it. It
was named the Tomkinson, and the whole party were
brought up to it without delay. There was evidence
now that they were coming into a very different kind
of country. The plants and flowers were new and
beautiful; the trees were large, with a fine luxuriant
foliage; and amid many new kinds of fruit there was a
species of wheat which produced a strong grain.
Stuart camped on the stream during the 28th April,
while one of his men examined its course. It was
traced for nine miles in a westerly direction, and then
emptied itself into the plains, and became quite dry.
The camp was on the north side of Whittington Range,
with plenty of grass, and game abundant. Two of the
horses which were too weak to travel were left here,
and Stuart intended to take them as he returned.

From the Tomkinson the journey was not far to
the next watercourse, named Carruthers Creek. Like
the former, it was a western stream, flowing down into
plains from a range running north and south. There
was a detached hill near, from which Stuart got a view,
but it was not extensive. Native fires could be seen to
the west and south-west, with high ranges and innumerable hills in the same direction, but to the north
the view was shut out by the range, except a few
peaks, which showed that there were elevations still
further beyond. These, like the most of the country,
seemed covered with thick scrub. As long, however, as
the range continued, Stuart knew from experience that
he need be under no apprehension about the water, and

the only drawback now to his advance was the scrub
and the stony nature of the soil.

A little beyond the Carruthers they met Hunter's
Creek. This was a more important stream, and contained plenty of water. Stuart followed it for a time,
as it went to the north-west, and he had a faint hope
that there might be a passage in that direction. The
stream wound very much, and crossed their track no
less than thirteen times in the course of their journey,
and then it suddenly ran out in a large grassy plain.
Not finding the creek or the least indication of moisture,
and the scrub being very thick, Stuart changed the
course to north. At three miles, they entered a very
thick scrub of a new kind of tree, rather graceful in
appearance, but an awful impediment to the explorers.
Three miles beyond this again they were obliged to
camp without water. It was evident that they could
not pursue their course further in such a country, and
so the next day they were obliged to retrace their steps
to Hunter's Creek, keeping more to the eastward to
intercept any channel which might flow down from Ashburton Range. For about nine miles they passed over
a splendidly grassed plain, with trees. It was a great
disappointment to leave such good soil as impracticable,
but Stuart did not do so until he saw that there was
no chance whatever of a watercourse. At his most
westerly point upon the plain, he sent one of the men
up a high tree to look for rising ground to the westward; but there was none; and that discovery extinguished all hopes of finding water. If it had only
rained, they might have managed; but though it seemed
threatening every day, none fell.

On the 3rd May, Stuart again tried a due north
course. At nine miles, he came upon a creek, which
furnished a little water. This led to the east of north,
so he moved along it. For the first ten miles, the
course was open plain, into which the creek emptied.
It was covered with long high grass, and splendid in
appearance. The explorers had to expiate such a
luxury by six miles of hard scrub on the other side,
which gave great trouble and annoyance to both men

and horses. Gradually, however, the gum trees became thinner and thinner, until they terminated in an immense plain, without anything but grass upon it. Stuart thought that this plain, like the others, must be the receptacle of a large creek from Ashburton Range, which though low, and now near its northern termination, seemed to be the watershed of very extensive drainage at some seasons. He accordingly went among the hills to find the source of the stream. They were not high, but the level of the country around made the prospect extensive. It was over boundless plains to the westward, well wooded to the foot of the range, but supporting only grass further on. Two creeks were found, as Stuart anticipated. Both contained water, but the more northerly one, named Hawker's Creek, had a very large supply.

Next day, Stuart advanced to the north-west to cross the plains, and at eleven miles reached a hill which had been seen from the range. It turned out to be what had once been the banks of a fine fresh-water lake. It had, says Stuart, small iron and limestone gravel in the bed, with sand and a great number of shells worn by the sun and atmosphere to the thinness of paper, plainly indicating that it was many years since the water left, though there were marks to show that it had once been twelve feet deep. They proceeded twenty-one miles across this dried lake bed, but it was terrible work. The ground was covered with dwarf *Eucalyptus* and thick grass, which concealed the soil, and this was fissured into gaping mud-cracks and very deep holes, into which the horses fell at every step. They threw their riders occasionally, and Stuart thus got a very severe fall. Of course, there was no water in such a country as this, and from the highest tree no change was visible in advance. The latitude was 17° 49'. They were consequently very near the Victoria River, but were obliged to turn back. Stuart said if he could have seen the slightest hope of a termination of the plain, he would have proceeded, and have risked everything; but as it was, the horses were already far spent, and one had to be abandoned before they returned.

But Stuart was far from resigning all hope. On the most westerly part of the plain, as already stated, no change in the country could be seen from the top of the highest tree, but still, with the aid of a powerful telescope, and the refraction of the atmosphere, it was thought that some high land was visible very far in the distance. Stuart thought that he might possibly reach this by striking towards it from a more northerly portion of the range. He therefore took with him two companions, seven horses, and a week's provisions, and started on his journey on the 9th May. But it was to no purpose. The country was richly, and even beautifully grassed for twenty-three miles from the range, and then the plains terminated. A desolate change ensued. They entered upon a red sandy soil, with a scrub which gradually became thicker and thicker. After six miles of this, they camped without water, and, as a matter of course, not the slightest chance of getting any. The next day they reached the elevations seen to the westward. They were dismal, scrubby, red sand-hills, which stretched out far beyond the range of vision. The first was about two hundred feet above the plains, but further west they were lower, and became like all the red sand ridges in the tableland. Had there been water here, Stuart would have continued for sixty miles further, and that would have enabled him to cross to the good country of the Victoria River. But there was no water; no, nor any vegetation that could not subsist on the few scanty drops of moisture that fall at times from the heavens. There was no help for it; back they must go. They did not retreat one minute too soon, for the horses had scarcely strength enough to reach the water.

Stuart was now obliged to rest for a time, as all his animals were quite exhausted; but on the 13th he again advanced along the range to the north. At the distance of five miles he crossed a large creek from the hills, named Fergusson's Creek. Some other creeks were seen further on, but the ominous red sand reappeared, so he returned to the first creek and camped. The next day a journey to lat. 17° 45' brought his party to another creek, named Lawson's Creek, with abundance of water and native camps. On the 15th, they went twelve miles along the range, and then descended from it, crossing a wooded plain liable to inundation, but then retaining no moisture. Neither did they fare better as they advanced. Red sand alternated constantly with scrub and barren plains, until they desisted from their search, and camped without water. Stuart was very ill next morning, so he sent one of the men to some rising ground to look at the nature of the country in advance. The hill was only a small sandy elevation, with dense scrub all round. This news caused Stuart to cross the range and turn to the east; but this was the worst course of all. At two miles he was completely baffled by the dense scrub he met with. Very reluctantly, he was obliged to return again to Lawson's Creek, in a direct course, for the sake of the horses. In doing so, he found that the open parts of the plain consisted of black alluvial soil, so rotten and cracked that the horses sank in it up to their knees. It was covered with long grass and polygonum, just like all the flooded plains in the south; and no doubt Stuart was right in fancying that water could be easily obtained there by digging. The scrub from which he had returned was the densest he had ever met with, and had so roughly handled the clothes and baggage of the party, that three days were spent in refitting.

On the 20th, Stuart started with two men and seven horses 'in a north-east direction. This was on a different side of the range; and though Stuart's Plains seemed to be represented in that direction, but more arid and desolate, it was thought that an effort should be made on every course before the route should be given up as impracticable. It is needless to give the particulars of this journey. Forty-two miles brought them again to the scrub, which was perfectly impenetrable, as formerly. There was no water, and Stuart thought that, with the aid of his telescope, he could ascertain that for sixty miles all round there was not the slightest appearance of any rise or watercourse. On the 22nd, they returned to Lawson's Creek, with

z 2

their horses much exhausted, for they had travelled for eighty miles without a drop of water.

But even this was not enough to satisfy Stuart, who chafed like a wild bird in a cage at the thought of being so near the north side of the continent, and yet unable to reach it. On the 22nd, he started once more, with two men and seven fresh horses; again to the north, but on the west side of the range. The first ten miles was over a rich deep soil, full of the usual fissures and cracks. In the midst of these, they came upon a magnificent reach of water, very wide, and extending further than they could see. They named it Newcastle Water. The more they examined it the more important was it found to be, both in length and breadth; and yet in the journey of May 16th the whole party had passed within a mile or so of it without even suspecting its existence. Of course, such a discovery changed Stuart's plans at once, and he went back without loss of time to bring the rest of the party up to the new-found treasure.

On the 25th, the men were moved some twenty-nine miles along the water, and Stuart went four miles beyond, to the northward, to get a view from some rising ground. It was a patch of stony sandy table-land, and showed very thickly wooded hills about twenty miles to the north-west. After getting this view, Stuart returned to his party, and they rested for one day. For the first time, they saw natives about this place; and while the men were scattered, the savages succeeded in separating one from his companions. He easily escaped by firing his gun point-blank into the face of the nearest native as he was in the act of cutting him down with his boomerang. This was the only encounter which took place, though there could be no doubt that, like all the tribes on the north coast, these were very hostile.

Stuart moved down Newcastle Water to the north-ward, but though the river conducted him much further in that direction than he could have anticipated, it terminated at last like all the others, in flooded plains. Finding this, the camp was moved back to the most

northerly water, and then Stuart advanced to the northward with three men and nine horses. They followed
a native track for five miles, and then struck out into
the plains in a more westerly direction, through seven
miles of a very dense scrub. This was succeeded by
plains, and then scrub again, until they had advanced
twenty-eight miles, and were obliged to camp without
water. Next day, another ten miles brought them into
the thickest of the scrub, and from a high tree a more
dense track was seen to lie before them. Added to
this, the red sand reappeared, and left no hope of
water. Though now only one hundred miles from Gregory's camp upon Campfield Creek, they were obliged
to turn back. It was very hard to see hopes when near
fulfilment thus so rudely destroyed, but we have witnessed many such instances in the preceding pages.
Again, it was a difficult matter to get the horses back.
As they returned it was found that the natives were
watching them, and had tracked their footsteps backwards and forwards.

Three days were spent in recruiting the horses, for
Stuart determined to make one more effort to the westward. Of the east he quite despaired, for the country
there was so very dry and arid. But while he was
deliberating it began to rain, and though, as usual, the
country became boggy, the wet raised his hopes of
proceeding further. The natives reappeared meanwhile, and made warlike demonstrations, but they were
easily dispersed by firing over their heads. Owing to
the wet, and other causes, it was not until the 10th
June that Stuart was able to continue his investigations.
He started with three men, nine horses, and fourteen
days' provisions, and his course on this occasion was
five degrees north of west from a point a good deal
south of his last effort. The first five miles was over
a very soft grassy plain, the horses sinking up to their
knees in the soil. It soon, however, became sandy, and
at fourteen miles they gained the top of a sand-hill,
which seemed to be the termination of the range Stuart
had turned back from on his first journey to the west,
early in May. From hence, until their day's journey

terminated, the scrub was very thick—thicker, indeed, than any previously met with. The horses could scarcely face it, especially as the ground was very soft and yielding. The latter circumstance will show what small hopes they could have of water. Still, on the 11th, Stuart pushed on a little further. Two miles beyond, the country became open, and splendidly grassed, and again revived his drooping hopes; "but, alas!" he says in his journal, "it only lasted about two miles," and he again entered a forest thicker than ever. At eleven miles it became so dense that it was nearly impenetrable. "I saw," says Stuart, "that it was hopeless to face through any further. Not a drop of water had we seen, although the ground is quite moist, the horses sinking above their fetlocks." The soil was again the fatal red sand which had baffled Stuart before now, and seemed to haunt him here, as it did Sturt. Thus ended all Stuart's hopes of reaching the Victoria River on this expedition, though he made another attempt before he left.

In consequence of the rain, Stuart thought he might reach the Gulf of Carpentaria by crossing Sturt's Plains to the eastward. He did not, however, get much beyond where he had reached on the 22nd May. The scrub, as usual, was thick, and water absent. Both men and horses were very weak, and now thoroughly spiritless. The rations had been latterly reduced to four pounds of flour and one pound of dried meat each per week, and starvation began already to set its gaunt stamp on the faces and frames of the party. Much against his will, all hope was resigned by Stuart. Grieved and disappointed as much as any man could be, he turned his steps homeward.

There was only one resource now left, and he was resolved to try it. This was, when he got far enough to the south, to endeavour to get round the south end of the terrible array of trees which had hitherto barred his progress to the westward. On the 23rd June the whole party reached Tomkinson's Creek, and it was from this point that the attempt was to be made. On the 24th, Stuart took three men, ten horses, and four-

teen days' provisions, and again started on a course
20° north of west. At fifteen miles they ascended a
stony rise, and saw that the creek emptied itself into an
open grassy plain. The country became stony and
scrubby, and after a day's journey of twenty-eight miles,
they camped without water. Again, the next day, the
red sand glared before their faces like a horrid vision.
They continued, however, twenty-seven miles, and then
were obliged to yield. There never was so inhospitable
a country. Where there was water there was scrub,
and where the scrub was absent there was no water,
except when there was red sand; then sometimes
neither scrub nor water was to be found.

Stuart returned to Tomkinson's Creek; the horses, as
usual, exhausted, having come one hundred miles without water. He would not return even now without one
more attempt in the direction of Carpentaria, and another
final and last effort to the north-west. He was delayed
a good deal before he could start, principally in searching for one of the men, who had been lost three days
and two nights. After seeing the man restored from
the effects of exhaustion, he started, with three companions, on a course 36° north of east. At eleven miles
he reached the top of a high hill. The view was not
extensive, as the hill (Mount Hawker) was only eight
hundred feet high. He descended, and crossed a creek,
named the M'Kinlay, and at five miles reached another
hill, named Mount Hall. From this the view was most
extensive, over a vast expanse of white, grassy plains.
The terminations of other spurs of this range were
visible fifteen or twenty miles south-east, but beyond
them nothing but plains. These were of the same
description as all Sturt's plains. It seemed madness
to go further into them without water, so Stuart returned. As they came back, Loveday Creek was found,
and it had a little water in it. They remained here one
day.

On the 4th July, Stuart made the last attempt to
reach the Victoria River, on a course a little more
northerly than his last. He left with three men, ten
horses, and a month's provisions. At three miles, they

left the plains, and proceeded over stony rises for two miles more. The land then became sandy, with thin scrub. At twenty-five miles, having come to a little grass, they camped, and next day found a creek of water five miles beyond. This was called Burke's Creek, after the celebrated explorer. Having followed this eight miles, they camped on the last water-hole. Three miles beyond, it disappeared altogether in the usual grassy gum plain, so they changed to their old course, with very feeble hopes of finding any more creeks. The plain continued for three miles, and then became sandy, with scrub. At the further side of a low sand-hill there was another flooded plain, inundated occasionally from Hunter's Creek, which trended towards it from Ashburton Range. At two miles they came to the top of a sandy tableland, with patches of thick scrub. It was a terrible country to travel through. The first day and two-thirds of the next were occupied in tearing their way through it; but every exertion was made, for it was their last and final effort, and Stuart was determined not to give up without a severe struggle. Contend as he would, however, he was defeated in the end. The country was positively impracticable. They dug for five feet at their furthest point: there was no water; the ground at that depth was not even moist. They turned back at last; and no one can say that Stuart did not make every effort before he renounced the hope of crossing the continent on this expedition. He had started with thirty weeks' provisions, and had now been out twenty-six of those; nor could they hope to reach the settled districts in less than ten weeks. There was nothing now left but to return as soon as possible.

Until the 11th July was occupied in shoeing the horses and repairing the saddles, bags, &c. They had run out of everything. Their clothes were nearly all gone, and they were barefoot. This would not have mattered so much if the men were in good health, but starvation was telling sadly upon them. "I had no idea," says Stuart, "in starting, that the hills would terminate so soon, in such extensive level country, without water, or I should have tried to make the

river when I first saw the rising ground from Mount
Primrose. These are the sandstone and ironstone
undulations passed over on my southern and most
westerly journey. Before I went to Newcastle
Water they completely deceived me, for, from the top
of the hills, they had the appearance of a high range;
which I was glad to see, thinking that if the range I
was following up (Whittington Range) should cease, or
if I should not find a way to the river further north, I
would be sure to get in by that distant range, which
caused me to leave the Newcastle Water country sooner
than I should otherwise have done; and now I have
not provisions to take me back again. From what I
have seen of the country west and south of the Newcastle country, I am of opinion that it would be no use
trying again to make the river, for I believe that no
water can be obtained by sinking. The country is a
sandy tableland, on which not a drop of water remains,
and there is not a blade of grass. To the west and
north-west the country is apparently lower, and I think
that water could be obtained at a moderate depth.
It is the shortest distance between the waters, but
the greatest difficulty would be in getting through a
dense forest and scrub. That, I think, could be overcome."

On the 12th July, they started on their return.
On the 19th, they crossed the M'Douall Ranges, and
found that the rain had not fallen so far south as this
since they had left. This made their homeward supply
precarious and doubtful. A large quantity was still
found in Anna's Creek, in the Murchison Ranges. In
the Bonney, also, a considerable spring, affording a
never-failing supply, but the water was all gone from
Mount Morphett, and they only obtained some on the
third day's journey by digging. Had they not found
some, the weaker horses would have been abandoned.
This was their worst privation on their return, though
other occasional inconveniences for want of water
occurred. As they came southward, the signs of the
winter rains began to show themselves, but the Neale
was nearly dry; probably because it only flows when

the other tributaries have accumulated. Many new
springs were discovered.

On the 15th September, they reached the settled
districts, and thus Stuart's second expedition terminated,
after an absence of nearly eight months. It was successful, if we properly estimate the importance of the
discoveries.

CHAPTER XXI.

THE CONTINENT CROSSED AT LAST.—BURKE AND WILLS.

Exploration in Victoria—Kyte's munificent donation—Party equipped—Start for Menindee—Burke proceeds with Wright—Wright sent back to bring up the other party—Burke and Wills start—Stony Desert—Final departure—King's Creek—Other creeks—Standish Ranges—Cloncurry Creek.

WHILE Stuart was making the wonderful journeys just recorded, an exploring party had been fitted out by another colony. It had even started before Stuart's second expedition; and had accomplished its disastrous work before he returned; but in order not to interrupt the sequence of the explorations which it gave rise to, and which were not terminated until 1862, the chronological arrangement of this history has been slightly disturbed.

During the previous three or four years the desire for discovery had taken a great hold on the colonial mind, and the mystery of the interior parts of the continent was being rapidly dispelled. The fatal journey about to be recorded is, however, the most important of all that was done, not only in the great and unexpected results achieved by it, but in the subsequent explorations to which it gave rise. We have, without doubt, to deal with the most glorious era in the history of Australian discovery, and no period can even remotely compete with it for the number of expeditions sent forth or the vast amount of territory whose geographical features it made known to the world. And all this was mainly initiated by the colony of Victoria. This is a fact worthy of remembrance. Of all the colonies, Victoria had least to gain by exploration. The boundaries of that colony were within districts thoroughly explored, and, therefore, no new discovery would affect it. The equipment of an expedition by that Government showed a noble disinterestedness in the cause of science which must excite admiration. The people of Victoria have, besides, displayed as much anxiety as any to solve the problem of the interior of the country; from which, however, they had nothing to gain. It is true that some were found to blame the manner in which these designs were carried out. This was when the bulk of the party had returned, and the expedition regarded as a complete failure. But when great and unforeseen results had been obtained, when, in less than a year, the continent had been crossed four times, and more knowledge of the interior obtained in that time than that arising from the explorations of the preceding thirty years, then Victoria obtained the meed of praise which is never denied to success. Let us hope that all the colonies will do as much for Australian geography within the next ten years.

But if the colony of Victoria deserves praise, how much more is due to those colonists who were mainly instrumental in stimulating the public to the undertaking? Foremost among these stands Mr. Ambrose Kyte, who offered to give one thousand pounds towards the exploration of the interior, provided another two thousand pounds were raised by public subscription. What made the offer more disinterested and more noble was, that it was made anonymously, and Mr. Kyte did not let his name appear until his generosity had produced the splendid results above alluded to. There never was a better illustration of the proverb, "Cast thy bread upon the waters;" and Mr. Kyte, who has risen by his own industry from a humble sphere to wealth and independence, has the satisfaction of knowing that this one act of his has done more for Australia than ever has been performed by one generation before.

The offer of one thousand pounds soon produced activity. The project was taken up by the Royal Society of Victoria, and as early as 1859 the sum of three thousand two hundred pounds was raised. Then the Colonial Government gave assistance. At a cost of three thousand pounds, camels were procured from India, and a supplementary grant of six thousand pounds was made by the Legislature. The camels provided were from Peshawar, twenty-four in number, of the fleet and heavy species. They were brought over by Mr. Landells, who was named second in command of the expedition. For a long time it was undecided who was to be the leader. Mr. A. Gregory was written to, but declined, though he offered some useful suggestions, one of which was that a permanent depôt should be established at the Barcoo, and all expeditions to the interior be made therefrom. This was agreed to by the Exploration Committee. Major Warburton was recommended by Mr. Gregory, but there were many difficulties in the way of this. At last, the appointment was given to Mr. Robert O'Hara Burke, one of the superintendents of the Victoria police, and previously connected with the Irish constabulary and Austrian cavalry, in all of which careers he had distinguished himself. This appointment was an unfortunate one, and but that the committee was composed of men who (with one exception) knew little or nothing about exploration, it would have been inexcusable. Burke was not a bushman, knew nothing of the practical duties of a surveyor, had not been many years in the colony, and, as far as can be gathered, had not had his attention especially directed to Australian geography or exploration.

William John Wills, of the Melbourne Observatory, was appointed astronomical and meteorological observer, and third in command. This young gentleman was truly the hero of the expedition. It will be seen how, as this narrative proceeds, but his former career deserves some special notice now. He was a medical student, and the son of a medical man in Devonshire. He had always shown a great taste for science, and his attainments had procured him, shortly after his arrival in the colony, a situation, first in the Survey Department, and, subsequently, in the Observatory. Such was his zeal for exploration, that it is related of him that, in 1856, he had walked a distance of ninety miles for the sake of

upon their management, they should have acknowledged their incapability, no matter what the position, influence, or notoriety they would thus sacrifice.

The party, as I have said, started late in August. They were enthusiastically cheered as they left Melbourne, and their reception throughout the settled districts was all that men engaged in so perilous an undertaking for their fellow-colonists could expect. No doubt their hearts swelled with pride at being connected with such a fine array of camels, horses, and baggage. In truth, it was a fine, imposing sight to see them start. It was still fresh in the memory of the colony when news arrived which made the recollection a very bitter one. People shuddered at recalling the scene when, in thirteen months, the tidings spread that the expedition was a failure; that Burke and Wills had started for three months, and had not returned at the end of four; and that those who had returned were broken down by disease, and had already buried four of their number in the desert. The narrative is fresh in the minds of those who have taken an interest in geographical subjects, but probably not as a connected story. The news did not come in regular order, neither were the details received except in small instalments. Now, however, the events can be taken in the order in which they happened, and set down as a plain history. This will be done in the succeeding pages, as far as the broken details left by Burke and Wills permit it.

The instructions given to Burke upon his leaving were of a very general nature. He was to make a depôt near Mount Macpherson, on the Barcoo, and then to push forward to the Gulf of Carpentaria, avoiding Leichhardt's track to the east, and Sturt's to the westward. This was in the event of his not being able to connect his route with that of Stuart; but, in any case, though some minor directions were given to him with regard to the examination of the country to the right and left, he was not to be absolutely tied down to any particular route when once he had established his depôt on the Barcoo, and a line of communication between it

and the Darling. How these directions were first carried
out will be soon told. It is not my intention to enter into
the details of little squabbles between some members of
the expedition. Such as they were, they led to some
changes when the party had reached Menindee.* All
that need be said is to be found in what follows.

The progress to the Darling was very slow, owing
to the amount of the baggage. There were disputes
between Burke and some of his officers. Mr. Landells
and Dr. Beckler wished to leave the party. The season
was far advanced, and some of the camels were unfit to
proceed immediately, so Burke, tired of the delay,
decided on advancing, with Mr. Wills and six men, as
far as the Barcoo. He took some of the camels with
him, and the rest were to follow slowly with the
heavy supplies. A Mr. Wright, of Menindee, had
offered to show the party a direct and well-watered
track to the Barcoo, instead of following the arid and
winding course adopted by Sturt. Burke, of course, was
glad to avail himself of such assistance, for he knew
nothing whatever of the country before him.

The first despatch received from Burke was dated
Torowotto, the 29th October. It stated that he had left
Menindee on the 19th October, with five horses and
fifteen camels. They had travelled through two hundred
miles of fine sheep-grazing country, with creeks and
water-holes, some of which seemed permanent. They
had never been obliged to go for more than twenty
miles without water. On the previous day they had
come from Wannomatēa to Paldrumāta Creek, over
splendid grazing country, and the camp, Torowotto,
was a well-grassed creek or swamp. In sending Mr.
Wright back with this despatch, he had instructed him
to act as third officer, and to follow up as soon as possible
with the remainder of the stores and an extra supply of
salt meat.

On the 30th January another despatch was received
from Burke. He had left Torowotto on the 31st October, and had arrived on the Barcoo on the 11th

---

* This township, it should be stated, is near Mitchell's Laidley's Ponds on
the Darling.

November. This portion of his journey had been easily accomplished; the first half being over good country as far as a watercourse named Wright's Creek; and the second over very stony ground, but by no means impracticable. On arriving on the Barcoo, Burke went slowly along its banks, in order to recruit his animals, and look out for a suitable camp at leisure. A depôt was fixed upon on the 20th, but it was found to be so infested with rats that it was soon given up. They then moved two camps lower down the stream, and there a permanent depôt was established. As far as the feed and water were concerned, the locality was good enough, but the flies, mosquitoes, and rats made it anything but a pleasant residence.

Once established, frequent excursions were made, in order to find a route to the north between Gregory and Sturt's tracks. The knowledge thus obtained was not encouraging. Mr. Wills, on one occasion, travelled ninety miles to the north without finding water. He would have gone further but that his camels escaped, and he and his companions were obliged to return on foot. Fortunately for them, they found a pool of water as they came back, or their lives would have been much endangered. The three camels were not recovered, but they subsequently made their way to the settled districts. A few days after this journey, Burke, Wills, and King went seventy miles to the northward, but could not find the water discovered previously by Wills. The latter, with King, went a third time, and found the water again, and they succeeded in bringing back the saddles and other things left behind when the camels were lost. On this occasion they got into a stony desert. There were ranges about two or three miles to the east of them, but in other respects the country around was quite level and covered with stones.

Meanwhile, Wright had not arrived with the rest of the party, although nearly six weeks had elapsed since he returned from Torowotto, and the whole distance between Menindee and the Barcoo had been accomplished by Burke in twenty-two days. Much time had been already lost, but every preparation was made for a start

directly he should come. The horses were shod, and
two were killed and dried for food. Every part of the
outfit was rendered fit for service, and thus the time of
inaction was not quite thrown away. But when all was
completed, Burke got tired of waiting. In an evil hour
he resolved still further to divide the party. He determined to push on, with three months' provisions, to
explore towards Carpentaria. Four men, with six
camels and twelve horses, were to remain at the depôt,
while Burke and Wills, with two others, were to form the
exploring party. The men left were to employ themselves in constructing a stockade while waiting for
Wright, and when he had arrived they were to occupy
the time in seeking a more available and direct route to
the Darling.

On the morning of the 16th December, Burke told
all the men to fall in, and the command of the depôt
was given to one named Brahé, until Wright should
arrive. He then shook hands with them all, and bade
them good-bye. One of the men, who afterwards died
of scurvy, had known Burke since he was a boy, and
he shed tears at saying farewell, for he was very fond
of his old master. The latter said, with a kind of presentiment of his fate, "Patten, you must not fret. I
shall be back in a short time. If I am not back in a
few months, you may go back to the Darling." There
was much dash and energy about Burke; perhaps a
little too much of it. In one of his letters to his friends,
just at the commencement of the journey, he said that
baggage should never ruin his expedition. For his
own sake, it is a pity that it did not. And yet, in
seeing him leave on what we now know to have been
his march to the grave, one cannot help admiring his
bold and manly courage. He was a generous man; so
much so, indeed, that he gave away his clothes, right
and left, to the natives. When he was taking his fresh
supply, before leaving, he was heard to say, that, provided he crossed the continent, he did not care if he had
only one shirt on when his journey ended.

On Sunday, December 16, 1860, the devoted little
band started, three out of four of whom were destined

never to see their companions any more. King, the
survivor, has given us an account of how they proceeded. At first they rode, but after a short distance
they walked. Burke and Wills walked on ahead, each
carrying a rifle and a revolver. Wills made notes and
examined the country, while Gray and King followed
behind, leading the horse and the six camels. Wills
also carried the compass and took astronomical observations every evening, and then wrote his diary. Burke
sometimes wrote, but not often. He considered it sufficient to hear Wills read his journal, and he made such
alterations as he thought necessary. Their provisions
were a pound of flour and a pound of meat daily, with a
little rice occasionally. They camped out every evening
without tents. No doubt this self-denying mode of proceeding was very heroic and courageous, but was it
necessary ? It certainly does seem a pity that after the
great care taken to equip the party adequately, that its
main work should have been done by a feeble party,
badly provisioned, and subject to the disadvantage of
crossing the country on foot. The work was done, it is
true, but done in an imperfect way. No one could expect
four poorly-fed men, to manage six camels, to force their
way through untrodden scrubs, and yet keep a journal
and make observations. No one could expect it, and it
was not done. The journal left is most incomplete, and
to this day several portions of the route are still matters
of dispute.

For the rest of this sad history we have only the
imperfect journal of Burke and Wills, and the statements of King. It will be almost needless to say that
the materials could not be more meagre for the description of such a journey. In order that the narrative
may be clear to the reader, one or two words of explanation may be offered. It will be observed, by consulting the map, that Burke's party crossed the Stony
Desert between the most northerly and the southerly
track of Sturt. From this they made for Eyre's Creek,
but in their way met with a fine sheet of water, which,
at first, they thought was the stream they looked for;
but it was not. It will be remembered, doubtless, that

Sturt found on the west side of the desert a mud plain, without stones or even grass, looking, in fact, as if the ground had been ploughed, harrowed, and then well rolled. There were creeks in this coming from the north and east, but with a general trend towards the Stony Desert or, probably, Lake Eyre. These may be regarded as part of the drainage from the west bank of the Barcoo, which all explorers agree in saying was a high tableland, and to which the mud plains stand much as the same kind of plains at the head of the Australian Bight stand in relation to the sandstone tableland of the whole continent. Whence they are derived, whether from the mud drainage from the creeks, or the decomposition of a more argillaceous portion of the sandstone rock, it is impossible to say, or to give a reason why such tracts, like the Libyan Desert, should be deprived of any kind of vegetation. At any rate, Burke found them now clothed with the ephemeral verdure of recent rains, and as the first creek they met had water in it, they followed it up for a time, and then struck north over the tableland. The preceding chapters will have been read to very little profit if one cannot tell what the journey over the sandstone was like. The whole may be easily described. Moderately fertile grassy plains, much interrupted with red sand-hills clothed with spinifex or scrub. Watercourses run hither and thither, often containing drains of nearly permanent water-holes. When these creeks run they empty themselves into plains thickly covered with gum trees, but well grassed, and sometimes supporting shallow swamps of water. Towards Carpentaria the creeks become more numerous and better watered. We know that the sandy plateau terminates somewhat abruptly before reaching the Gulf of Carpentaria, but as Burke reached a tributary of the Flinders, in all probability the long distance of the fall towards the coast made the descent less precipitous than at other places.

The above, then, is the explanation of the journey we have now to follow. The little band, with their train of camels, were, however, utterly ignorant of what was before them. They knew nothing from actual experience, and what they could have learned from others, would, in fact, give them only false impressions. So they slowly wended their way, with doubt and anxiety, towards the reputed deserts which had already baffled so many. Considering how many, there is something admirable in the attempt being made by so weak and inexperienced a party—something wonderful in its success—something very mournful in its fatality. To be successful, and then to die, as men do in battle, might be an enviable lot; but to be successful and then perish by such a death as that of the explorers! well may we pity them as they go down into the desert with their little train of camels and their small resources.

The movements of the party from the Barcoo to the Stony Desert are easily described. This is the tract whence the main body of the river drains into Lake Eyre, and so it is very well watered. Sturt found plenty of lagoons and grassy flats even in the dreadful season of his exploration, and so Burke was even better off. There were red sand-hills, of course, and abundance of natives, but the feed was good, and as for game, the air was darkened by the immense number of Sturt's pigeons which fed by the side of the lagoons. Sturt mentions these birds, and indeed they have attracted the notice of all the explorers in this locality, not only for the beauty of their plumage, but for the enormous numbers in which they occur The sand-hills were the two tracts of desert hills—passed also by Sturt—to the south and to the north of where Burke now was. They were loose and shifting, and so honeycombed by rats that the camels fell on them very frequently. No doubt, these drifts are derived from the light portions of the decomposed sandstone of the desert, as already stated, and this origin is a proof that it will never be found in extensive tracts. It was not so here, at any rate, and Burke soon found himself standing on the edge of the desolate Stony Desert, and saw it stretching out as a horizontal plain, almost beyond the range of vision.

They struck across the desert in a west-north-west direction, and at four miles and a half came upon a sand ridge, from whence they turned again to their course north-west by north. At fifteen miles they crossed another sand ridge, with plenty of grass and salt bush round it. On the other side of this there was an earthy plain, with a soil exactly like slaked lime, and full of small creeks, sometimes evidently full of water, for there was a large hole, now dry, and a number of native huts. By following the flight of some pigeons, they came upon a creek at nine miles, which was found next morning to contain an abundant supply of water. This was named after one of the men, Gray.

On the 25th they left this and proceeded to cross the rotten clay plains in the direction of Eyre's Creek. At nine miles small watercourses commenced, and then one with a good deal of brackish water in its bed. A camp of natives was near. The blacks followed them, and seemed to wish the explorers to go to the north-east. But they kept on their course, and soon were rewarded by meeting with a magnificent creek coming from the west of north. It was thought to be Eyre's Creek, but as it was traced up to the north for a crossing-place, its course was too much from the north to be Sturt's stream. But how that explorer could have missed it seemed very incomprehensible. He certainly crossed to the south of this point, but the stream might have taken a more westerly bend at that time, and as an instance of the fatality which seemed to attend poor Sturt, it can now be seen that if he had pressed on in his second attempt to cross the Stony Desert he would have found this channel. By turning back when half-way he left a triumph for others which was within his grasp.

Burke followed up this creek from point to point of the bends. Its banks were steep and covered with trees, bounded by high red sand-hills, and to the north and south by an extensive plain. Its general course was north at first, but at six miles a sand ridge closed in upon it, and it turned north-west, and became dry and shallow, on a bed of limestone and clay. Near this another water-hole commenced, and the stream kept more to the north. To avoid a large bend, they crossed the channel and steered northwards, following up the stream from the 26th to the 30th. By this time its trend was considerably to the east, and it became necessary to think of trusting themselves once more to the northward and stand their chance of finding water. They loaded their camels with ten days' supply, and made for some stony ranges which were visible to the north. On the last day of the year they travelled thirteen and a half hours over alluvial earthy plains, and camped without finding water. This, according to King, was their first and last privation of the kind. Next day they found plenty at a creek named after Wills, and for the next three days there is a blank in the journal. We know from King that the journey meanwhile was through a desert, and where the diary of Mr. Wills recommences there is an entry which states that the country was improving, and that a few blades of grass were beginning to appear.

On the 7th January their camp was within the tropics, and thus far all was well. They were steadily accomplishing their work, and, as far as water was concerned, they were now under no anxiety whatever. But within the tropics the change for the better in the country was most marked and permanent. They first entered immense plains of firm argillaceous soil, liable to inundation from the innumerable creeks which coursed through them. The latter were lined with gum and box trees. The grasses and other vegetation were splendid; and as for game, the entries in the journal of pigeons, wild ducks, &c., show these plains to be of no ordinary fertility. Mr. Wills says that the richness of the vegetation did not arise from any chance thunderstorm, for the trees and bushes on the open plains were healthy and fresh looking. The grasses were numerous, and there were besides several kinds of vetches, portulac, and salsolæ.

These rich plains and creeks continued until the 12th. They then entered a series of low slaty sandstone ranges, among which were some well-grassed flats and plenty of water in the main gullies. The more stony portions had Mallee and porcupine grass upon them, while the large ant-hills showed that they were

coming to the north coast. There was a continuous
rise perceptible all the way in crossing the ranges, and
from the highest portion there was a good view of the
country in advance. There was a large range to the
northward, and to the west a mass of broken sandstone
ranges. To the east there were ranges too, but higher
and more distant. The intermediate country in advance
was a continuation of the ranges already passed through.
They were called the Standish Ranges, and contained a
number of well-watered creeks. We must suppose that
the passage through these continued with very little
variety, for there is no entry in the journal for the next
five days, and the map is marked ranges.

On the 19th the journal is again continued. It
appears that on that day they got clear of a portion of
the Standish Ranges, which rose to a great height in
Mount Forbes. They passed to the north-west of this,
across a fine and well-grassed plain, and kept a north by
east direction. At the distance of three miles the plain
became everywhere very stony, and scattered over with
loose quartz pebbles. A little further on they went
to low quartz ranges, the higher portions of which
were covered with porcupine grass, but the valleys
clothed with coarse rank vegetation. Amid this a
large creek (Green's Creek) took its rise. Crossing the
range at the head of the creek they came upon a gully
running north, but as this trended to the east they left
it, and soon reached another. This they followed down
for a short distance.

The next day, we learn from Burke's diary that
there were terrible ranges to cross, but from Wills'
journal we learn nothing at all, nor is there any entry
until the 27th January. By that time they had reached
Cloncurry Creek, one of the sources of the Flinders.
Whether or no this was found in the gully just mentioned, there is no fact to guide us. The creek probably
passes the M'Kinlay Range, found by the explorer
whose name it bears, and there it is a wide and fine
watercourse, with stony country upon its banks. This
is all we, as yet, know of its character. Water was
abundant in every part, but there was no appearance

that the creek had flowed for a considerable time. The land, Wills says, appeared green and fresh. Palm trees were numerous, and these gave a picturesque and pleasing aspect to the scene. One of the camels got bogged in the channel, on the 28th, and they were obliged to abandon him, for the natives were very numerous, and they dared not delay nor divide the party.

From this point there is a deplorable *hiatus* in Wills' journal. The next entry which occurs is Sunday, February, 1861. This must have been either the 3rd, 10th, or 17th February. Most probably it was the 10th, because the camp of the 30th January is marked 112, and this was camp 119, which would give four days' rest between the two places. Such a delay is easily accounted for, because we know that the rains were heavy and frequent, making the ground almost impassable. King stated subsequently that he and Gray were left by Burke and Wills on the 9th of the month, and that they returned on the 12th. Wills' journal goes on to say that the ground was in such a state from heavy falls of rain, that the camels could scarcely be got along. It was decided at length to leave them at camp 119, while Burke and he proceeded towards the sea on foot.

They started with three days' provisions. The first difficulty was in crossing Billy's Creek, where it entered the river a few hundred yards below the camp. The horse got bogged in a quicksand, and they only succeeded in getting him out by digging close to him on the water side. This was in one respect a fortunate circumstance. It left behind a mark on the sand which gave a clue to the track which they had followed. After getting the horse out they proceeded down the river which bent about from east to west, but kept generally a north course. But it was not easy travelling. A great deal of the ground was so soft and rotten that the horse could scarcely walk over it, especially as he was extremely weak. Finding that the river bent too much, they struck due north and soon came to some tableland, where the soil was gravelly, and clothed with

box and flooded gum trees. Beyond this was an open
plain covered with water up to the ankles; but as the
surface was uneven, this frequently became knee deep.
After wading through several miles of such country,
the water disappeared. Further on they came upon
some natives, who immediately decamped upon seeing
the explorers. The savages had left some yams behind
them in their hurry, to the great comfort of Burke and
Wills, for sharp hunger now made them very indis-
criminating in the nature of their food. A small distance beyond they reached a salt marsh, which was
filled by the ocean tide. Such a forest of mangroves
lay northward that they could not get a view of the
sea. Yet they made an attempt to do so. The horse
was too weak to advance further, so they left him
hobbled and walked on. But they were not able to
attain the beach. This, however, did not distress them
much. They had crossed the continent and reached
within the limits of the tide, and that was all they hoped
to do, or what their fellow-colonists would expect from
them. With feelings which all may envy them, they
left a record of the glorious accomplishment of the
expedition, and left the sea-shore to return to their
companions:

CHAPTER XXII.

FATE OF BURKE AND WILLS.

The Flinders River mistaken for the Albert—The continent recrossed—Great sufferings—Death of Gray—Reach the depôt and find it deserted—Wills' diary—Journey down the creek—Camels killed—The water fails—Obliged to return—The last camel killed—Starvation—Wills returns to the depôt—His gradual decay and death—Death of Burke—King is taken by the natives and fed.

IT was a moment of great triumph for Burke and Wills when they resolved to return. They had, with their small means, succeeded in crossing a continent which for many years had defied all efforts to explore it. No matter what privations they had suffered, or what they had still to endure, their victory was gained. They believed that they had crossed the continent to the Albert River of Stokes—for that was the stream they had steered towards—but it was the Flinders they had journeyed down, and this river was destined to become thenceforth remarkable as the basis of nearly all the discoveries which were made in North Australia for some years subsequently.

And now the little band set out upon their return. Their provisions were sadly reduced. The whole commissariat consisted of 83 lbs. of flour, 38 lbs. of meal, 12 lbs. of biscuit, the same of rice, and 10 lbs. of sugar. How four men were to exist on this for two months, was more than problematical; but yet they were all in good health except Gray, and if the worst came to the worst, they would eke out their provisions with the horse and a camel. It is true that these animals were weary and reduced, but their loads were light, and as each part of the route was known, and also where water could be found, it was hoped that they might even improve.

On the 21st February, they set out to return. The rain fell incessantly for the first part of their journey, deluging the ground, and delaying the progress very much. Yet matters went on pretty well. Besides, the effect of the rain was very partial, and as they went south, they would make a more rapid advance over the dry ground. Very little, however, is known of the return journey, nor how the explorers managed to keep well so long as they did. But their exertions began to tell on them at last. Sickness commenced with Gray, who never had been very strong, and then Burke became very ill. Poor Gray, it appears, appropriated during his sickness more than his share of the rations, and Burke chastised him for it; but we know that hunger drives men to desperate deeds, and it is hard to reproach these poor sufferers with infirmities or selfishness which stern necessity had brought upon them. First, one camel was killed, and then another; and thus their provisions were eked out. Both Burke and Gray got a little better in the dry country, but it was not for long. While they were suffering, the rain came down heavily again, and the ground became so soft that one of the camels could not be brought along. On the 6th of March he was left behind, and this was the commencement of their losses.

On the 20th March, 60 lbs. of baggage was abandoned; and it was on the 25th, that Gray was found eating some of the provisions. He was ill at the time, though his companions thought that he was shamming; but certainly, he could hardly be well, for their rations now were a quarter of a pound of damper, with twelve small sticks of dried camel's flesh, assisted by as much portulac as they could manage to gather. The latter was a vegetable which, when boiled, made a very good article of food; but unfortunately, it was not always obtainable. On the 30th they killed another camel, and on the 10th April they killed the horse, who could scarcely be got along; and as the explorers could scarcely crawl themselves, it was useless to try to bring

him further. They were all now nearly exhausted.
Wills was still cheerful, though suffering; but the
others were kept alive by the hope that they were near
help. Burke spoke continually of the assistance they
were to get. There was a party, he said, coming to
survey the country up to the Barcoo, and he was sure
of aid from Melbourne, because he had requested this
so often from the Exploration Committee. Indeed, he
expected to meet assistance long before he reached the
depôt, because he had left directions that he was to be
followed up. But in spite of hope they became weaker,
and Gray much worse than the others. He could not
walk, and to get him along they had to strap him on
the back of a camel. Up to this time, fortunately, they
had never been a day without water; but on the 13th
April, they came back again to the Stony Desert, and
were two days without reaching a creek. This was the
last effort poor Gray was able to make. He managed
to travel seven miles on the 16th, as usual, strapped to
the back of a camel as emaciated as himself, and then
he could go no further. They camped at a polygonum
swamp, and tried to mitigate his sufferings; but he was
then so far gone that he could scarcely speak. He
knew that he was dying. Some days before, he had
requested that a friend of his should be informed of his
death, and gave some directions about his little property. That evening he could say nothing, so they
covered him over and left him for the night. Next
morning they found him dead. Little did Burke and
Wills think that they saw their own fate in the terrible
spectacle of Gray's slow death. They buried him in the
desert, and then camped for a day. . That small delay
cost them their lives.

When they moved away from Gray's grave they
had abandoned everything except the two camels, their
firearms, and a little meat. They did this in order that
they might ride and travel as fast as possible. They
hurried on, sometimes followed and threatened by the
natives, and sometimes across the dreary succession of
sand-hills which had so discouraged Sturt. On the 20th,
they made a tremendous effort by travelling all night.

They had restored themselves somewhat by shooting and eating crows, so they continued longer on the camel's back; Burke riding one, and Wills and King the other. All day long, with great exertion, the poor animals were urged on. At last, when they had travelled thirty miles, Burke, who was in advance, called out, "I see tents ahead!" for his eager expectation made him imagine everything he hoped for. It was a cruel disappointment to find that he was mistaken. The camp was reached at last, and no tents were seen. Burke "coo-ed" several times and called the names of some of the men, but only the echo of his own voice came back to him. The truth broke upon him at last—the depôt was deserted!

It needs no minute description to realize the awful position of these three men abandoned to starvation in the desert. It is a tragedy of stern and bitter reality, and the simplest details will serve to show its frightful features. Mr. Wills was the first to overcome the excitement which the awful disappointment had caused. He soon found a tree, marked—"Dig three feet westward." Wills and King at once dug down, for poor Burke was too utterly overcome by the misfortune to do anything. They soon came upon a chest, which they opened in a fever of expectation. It contained provisions, and a letter stating that the depôt party had left *that very morning!*

Could disappointment have been more bitter? To be so near help and yet unable to follow; and to remember that all would have been avoided had they only pushed on the day that they buried Gray. It was very hard to bear. Had the depôt party said that they were weak or unwell, the explorers would have made every effort to overtake them; but the letter stated that the men and animals were in good condition, and one day's journey would put them utterly out of reach. It was proved afterwards, that Brahé's party were both weak and unwell, and only made a very short stage that day. It is a pity that the explorers did not, as Mr. Wills wished, follow down their track. They were camped within a few miles of each other, and either

party would have sacrificed everything to know that
the others were so near. But pity and regret are useless. The explorers knew nothing but the fact of their
desertion. They sat round the small collection of provisions which Brahé had left, deliberating on a plan of
action. It is easy to imagine the intensity of their
feelings, at least in part, but to realize them all, one
must have stood like them—face to face with a horribly
lingering death. It was long and anxiously argued by
Wills, that they ought to return the way they came;
but his sensible advice was not taken. It was an evil
day for all when Burke's counsels prevailed, and they
decided to keep Gregory's track down to Mount Hopeless, where they hoped to reach a cattle station about two
hundred miles away. For the rest of the narrative we
have to depend on the diary of Wills. Up to this time he
had kept no regular journal, but now his notes were
made every day. It is a record which shows him in a
most amiable light. Suffering as he was, he wrote with
words full of hope and even cheerfulness, and in rising
from the perusal of its pages, one cannot help concluding that the greatest disaster the colony suffered from
this ill-fated expedition was in losing such a hero as
William Wills.

The plan, therefore, now was to reach Mount Hopeless by slow journeys. This they thought their provisions would easily enable them to do, provided that they
could find water. They had 50 lbs. of flour, 60 lbs. of
sugar, 60 lbs. of oatmeal, 20 lbs. of rice, and 25 lbs. of
jerked meat. In fact, they had nearly double what
they had had when leaving Carpentaria, with five times
the distance to accomplish, and four persons to feed
instead of three. Thus their chances did not seem bad if
they could only find water. And so, having collected
what baggage they thought necessary, they rested one
day at the depôt, and then commenced moving slowly
down the Barcoo. The new supplies of provisions
raised their spirits, and after the first flush of the disappointment was over, the warm weather, the pleasant
scenery, and the thought they were only such a very
short distance from Mount Hopeless, raised a little of

the despair from their minds, and made them hope for the best. Their first adventures, too, tended still further to elate them. They met some natives, who, in exchange for a few straps and matches, gave them about twelve pounds of fish. This was certainly a valuable addition to the rations, but what made it an especial matter of congratulation was that the natives would have obtained the same articles for nothing at the old camp. Next day, the savages returned and brought more fish, and seemed inclined to accompany the explorers. They appeared very well behaved, and could be so useful that Burke made no objection, and thus everything seemed to aid them in the journey.

· The river took a south-west course about this place, and was found by Gregory to flow out towards the upper part of the supposed horseshoe of Lake Torrens, before it was finally lost in the sand-hill. Burke meant to follow down Strzelecki's Creek. It was easy travelling. Here and there were patches of strong ground and points of rock jutting out into the channel, but they were not numerous. The water was abundant. Long clear reaches continued to give a charm to the scenery, especially as they were fringed with splendid trees, and covered with water-fowl. Their journeys were, at first, necessarily very short, for they were weak and feeble; but Wills was very sanguine. He says, in his journal, that they were getting stronger and stronger every day, and that in a week's time he hoped to be able to undergo any fatigue. The comparative rest and change of food had worked wonders, and their only sufferings were at night. This was because their clothing was now reduced to a few rags which afforded a very insufficient covering in the chilly evenings. Their greatest discouragement must have been to look upon each other, remembering how different their appearance was when starting, compared to the three haggard men with the faces and clothing of beggars, creeping slowly along by the side of their camels, and almost tottering under the weight of their firearms.

Their first misfortune occurred on the sixth day

after starting. One of the camels got bogged in a water-hole, and after spending two days in trying to extricate him, they were obliged to shoot him and preserve what flesh they could get at. It took one day more to dry the meat, and then having loaded the camel with all he could bear, they each had to take a small quantity of bedding upon their shoulders and move down the river again. On the 2nd of May they met another camp of natives, who were most liberal in their offers of fish and a kind of cake. The explorers were glad to get anything, and probably, their supply on this occasion was owing to their forlorn appearance, which was enough to move the heart of even a savage. A little beyond the camp they met the southerly branch of the Barcoo, which they followed. They had misgivings about its character at first, but it soon widened out into a broad stream with fine reaches of water. The cliffs were very steep, but what made it difficult for the party was the scrub upon its banks. Towards evening, its channel began splitting up into small water-courses, and was finally lost in the sand. The explorers made an unsuccessful search for some other water, but were obliged to return to the last reach. Their prospects commenced to look a little gloomy. They could not advance to the south, and the camel began to give in. He had been trembling very much all day, and at night seemed quite exhausted. A faint effort was made to lighten the load by doing away with the tea, sugar, and a few tin plates, and then they returned to the main stream. But no better success awaited them there. After travelling a short distance, there was a repetition of the features of the other branch, and the water failed again in a kind of desert. The soil was cracked and loose in places, as if rain had not fallen for months, and when the arid ridges of sand disappeared the country was a wide expanse of dreary plains, covered with box trees and no water. It was a cheerless place. If its aspect made Sturt gloomy, provided with resources as he was, what must it have seemed to these poor fellows who felt that their lives depended on getting through it?

In truth, they were almost in despair at their prospects. Their rations were rapidly diminishing, their clothes, and especially their boots, were gone to pieces; and their camel could scarcely crawl along. Wills supposed at the worst now, that they would have to live like the blacks for a few months. Alas! even that consolation was denied them. On the 7th May, the camel could not be got to rise. After making every attempt to get him up he was left to himself, and Burke and Wills went down the river to examine the country closely. At eleven miles they came again to some natives, who gave them some fish. Poor Wills would have gladly shown his gratitude by giving them something, but he was almost as destitute as themselves. However, he tore off two pieces of his mackintosh, and Burke gave one and he the other. They then went to the camp and were treated with food until they positively could eat no more.

On the 8th of May, another attempt was made to trace down the river. It was quite unsuccessful. There were plenty of fine water-holes near the camp, but not a drop of water further, though Wills went on for seven miles. He could not go further, so he returned to his native friends. They treated him as usual with hospitality, though their means were confined to the rough fare the country afforded. Wills was too hungry and emaciated to be nice, and he relates, with seeming relish, how he enjoyed the rats they cooked for him. When he returned to Burke and King, he found that their last camel was dead, and all hope of reaching the settled districts was destroyed. They did not, however, despair of being able to live, for they had found that the blacks seemed to exist well on some seed, which abounded on the flooded flats, and that if they could find the plant they could manage to live until some assistance was sent out to them. But Wills at first could not find the seed. It was called by the natives nardoo (a cryptogamic plant, *Marsilea quadrifida*), and as it grows in little tufts close to the ground, it is not surprising that he could not discover it. Burke and King, therefore, went down the creek to find out all particulars from the

natives, and Wills was left to jerk the flesh of the
camel. He seems to have been as cheerful as ever, and
writes confidently of being able to entrap birds and
rats. Yet there must have been a dash of sorrow
amid all his efforts at cheerfulness, for he drops a
word or two of regret at such prospects, after having
made so gallant a trip to Carpentaria.

Burke and King were unable to find the natives.
They had moved from their camp, and the poor explorers were at a loss what to do: they could neither
advance nor retreat, and to sit down until they had
eaten their meat was only to stave off the evil day for a
time. Burke thought that it would be better for one to
remain with the things, and feed on the flesh of the
camel, while two went in search of the blacks and nardoo. Accordingly, Wills was left in the camp, while
the others took four days' provisions with them, and
went to look for the natives. They returned after two
days, utterly unsuccessful. Burke would not go further,
for he thought that an effort might be again made to
reach Mount Hopeless—anything, in fact, was better
than starvation in the desert; and if the attempt was to
be made with any chance of success, no more time should
be lost. They resolved to start at once. The few unnecessary articles — and these were very few—were
buried in the sand, and they commenced their forlorn
journey. They had not gone very far before they were
obliged to bury some more articles, for they were too
weak to carry much, even of provisions. It seemed like
burying their hopes to have to leave so many things in
the sand; and no doubt the ominous name of the mountain to which they were journeying was not without its
significance, when they saw how rapidly their chances
of reaching it were fading away. Yet they did not
complain. Wills continued to make his meteorological
notes, giving great prominence to the coldness of the
weather, and the keen chilly winds of the morning and
evening. Poor fellow! no doubt he felt it bitterly.

But there was room for hope even yet. On the 17th
May they found out the plant which bears the nardoo
seeds, and, what was better still, discovered that the

2 B 2

flats were covered with it. This was a great relief to
the poor sufferers, and they rejoiced at it just as if their
lives were thereby secure. They considered that they
were now in a position to support themselves for a long
time, even supposing that the natives gave them no
assistance.

After the date of this discovery no entry occurs in
Wills' diary for seven days. This fact is very significant, and the next entry explains it. He tells us that
picking the nardoo seed was a very difficult and much
slower process than they had expected In fact, the
small size of the plant, and the way in which each seed
grows upon separate stalks, must make it almost a day's
work for one man to collect sufficient for two meals.
When collected, it was necessary to pound and clean it,
and this also must have been a work of time and
patience. At first, the explorers would not be great
adepts at the process, and so we may imagine it took up
all their time to get sufficient sustenance. Thus we see
the cause of the blanks in Wills' note-book; and it
points very plainly to the struggle for life which was
now commencing, which threw every other consideration into the background. It is mentioned, as a curious
circumstance by Wills, that while he and King were on
their knees picking nardoo they distinctly heard an
explosion, as if of a gun at a considerable distance. On
returning to Burke they found that he had not even
heard the noise. Such melancholy sounds are not uncommon in the desert. Sturt noticed them, and so did
Mitchell; and they appear to be in some mysterious way
connected with large mounds of drifting sand, in almost
every climate.

It was now determined to send Wills back to the
depôt to deposit a notice of their state, and implore
assistance. On reaching the sand-hills below where the
camel was bogged, he met with some natives collecting
nardoo. It was very abundant there, so much so, in
fact, that the ground was black with the seeds. The
poor savages received the starving traveller with the
greatest kindness. It goes to one's heart to read how
these wild children of the desert surrounded him and

overwhelmed him with favours. How one insisted on
carrying his spade, another his bundle, and all in the
most friendly manner pressing his return to the camp
for food and rest. It is a very different spectacle from
those fearful scenes of savage warfare which have been
so often chronicled in these volumes, where the sight of
civilized man seemed to make these untutored beings
ready for any deed of blood. But for a different sort of
disposition among these tribes, the fate of the explorers
would have been decided long before.

When poor Wills had rested some time with his kind
entertainers, he went on towards the depôt. For the
first time we find him complaining of ill-health, and
stating that the rough food seemed to have an injurious
effect upon him. This must have been the nardoo, but
there was no help for it, as nearly every other kind of
ration was gone. As he went along, however, he found
some crows fighting for a fish, which he added to his
rations; and even such a questionable kind of nourish-
ment as that seems to have been a relief to him, and
made him a little more cheerful. He reached the depôt
on the 30th May. Brahé and Wright had been back to
it meanwhile, and had noticed no traces that it had been
visited by Burke. Wills now saw no signs that it had
been visited since he had left. There was a strange
fatality in all this which is very difficult to account for.
He dug down, and left his diary in the *cache*, together
with some letters, and requests for assistance. He then
returned towards his companions.

Sickness and famine now commenced its work upon
his frame, as he toiled back. He could not get along
now half so quickly as usual, and on the first day he became so weak and tired that at a few miles he was
obliged to lie down under some bushes, and share with
the desert animals his bed for the night. The next
day's journey was but little better. He thought to have
got back to the native camp, but he was too weak and
exhausted. It was as much as he could do to cross the
numerous gullies of the river, and was at last obliged to
make another lonely bed amid the desert bushes. Next
morning he reached the camp, but the natives were

gone. He tells this circumstance with a plaintive simplicity, as if it were not of much consequence, but it
must have been a bitter disappointment.   He sat down
by the deserted camp fires and ate a few fish-bones which
he found, for this was all the refuse that the savages had
left.   He then went on again.   One can fancy the pleasure which came over his gaunt features as he found two
dead fish in a water-hole further on.   He said that a
certain amount of good luck always stuck to him.
Alas ! who could bear to look upon that wan face, that
sunken eye, and still think so. His bed was again under
a bush.

Next day he met the natives.   They called to him
directly he came in sight, and seemed very glad to see
him again.   It was with the greatest difficulty he
ascended the sandy path which led to the camp, for
famine had nearly completed its work upon him.   The
chief conducted him to the fireside, and fed him with
fish and nardoo cake until he could eat no more, while
the other savages stood round looking with the greatest
delight on the pale, weak man satisfying his cravings.
So anxious were they that he should eat plenty that
Wills could scarcely believe that the pile of fish they
placed upon the fire was all for him. It seems a mockery
to call these people savages.

Such treatment made Wills very grateful.   At first
he declined their invitations to remain, but on reflection
he thought it better to return to them and learn a little
of their mode of life.   He stayed with them four days,
and then went to fetch Burke and King, so that they
might live with them for the future.   His companions
readily agreed to go back and adopt the native mode of
life for a time.   It was their only chance of life, if there
was a chance at all, for they were so weak and enfeebled
that they could scarcely move. Packing up such things
as they required, they made for the native camp. They
did not reach it on the first day, because they could not
get far with the things they carried. Wills had the
lightest load—barely thirty pounds—but he could hardly
carry it a mile without a long rest. With the greatest
fatigue and difficulty they reached the camp.   It was a

miserable disappointment to find that the blacks were gone. They were too weak to try to follow them, so they took possession of the best hut, and tried to live upon nardoo.

And now commenced the last act in this sad tragedy. The daily records in the diary become shorter and shorter, and always reveal some new feature in their fearful sufferings. Burke and Wills staid in the huts pounding and cleaning the seed which King collected for them. It appears that King was still the strongest, though too weak to walk steadily; while Burke was very feeble, and Wills not able to go out. He tells us that he cleaned the seed meanwhile, and his note-book shows that the intervals were occupied in calmly watching the changes in the clouds, or noting the wind and weather. The nights were generally tranquil, but cold, and that is a fact which is so often mentioned that no doubt he had good reason for bearing it in mind. He must have suffered very much, and yet his mind seems to have been tranquil and unruffled, like the many nights he notes down, when he must have lain awake silently watching the changes in the heavens. Sometimes a crow was shot, and sometimes circumstances aided them in getting a little extra supply of nardoo; but it was no more than staving off hunger, making the death more lingering. On the 20th June, Wills says he was completely reduced by the effects of cold and starvation, and could not blow the dust from out of the seed. Finding the sun a little warm, he tried to sponge himself, but his weakness made the process a slow one, and he became more cold. But amid all this, he wrote clearly and sensibly of his position. "Last night," he says (on the 21st), "was cold and clear. I feel much weaker than ever, and, unless relief comes in soon, cannot last more than a fortnight. It is a great consolation, at least in this position, to know we have done all we could, and that our deaths will be rather the effects of the mismanagement of others than any rash act of our own. Had we come to grief elsewhere, we could only have blamed ourselves; but here we are returned to Cooper's Creek, where we had every reason to look

for food and clothing, and yet we have to die of
starvation."

The weather now began to help on the ravages of
starvation upon the persons of the explorers.   The days
became sultry and still, and amid the lonely valleys of
the sand drifts the distant booming of thunder could be
continually heard.   In the night the wind blew, and the
cold was so intense that Wills said it almost shrivelled
him up.   His wardrobe at this time consisted of a
merino shirt, a regatta shirt without sleeves, the tattered
remains of a pair of flannel trousers, and a waistcoat.
His state was truly pitiable, but he lay there without
complaining.   He seemed to regret not being able to
witness some astronomical phenomena, of which he
attempts an explanation.   But evidently his mind was
beginning to fail.   Errors in the dates commence in
his notes and two days are repeated.   It must have been
a harrowing sight for those who were a little stronger
to look upon him stretched there without being able to
afford him any assistance.   But what could they do?
They did not like to leave Wills alone, and they could
not find the blacks unless they did so.   At last, they
proposed the plan to him, but with great reluctance, and
stated that if he objected they would stay and take their
chance together.   Wills consented at once.   He had no
fear of being left alone, for he could have no hope of
recovery if left as he was.   Burke and King prepared
to get a supply of water and nardoo to leave by his side,
and then to leave him.   The prospect satisfied, and even
pleased him, as an effort to escape.   The day before they
started, he wrote in his note-book, "I am weaker than
ever, although I have a good appetite, and relish the
nardoo much, but it seems to give us no nutriment, and
the birds here are so shy as not to be got at.   Even if
we got a good supply of fish, I doubt whether we could
do much work on them, and on them alone.   Nothing
now but the greatest good luck can save any one of
us, and as for myself I may live four or five days, if the
weather continues warm.   My pulse is at 48, and very
weak, and my legs and arms are nearly skin and bone.
I can only look out, like Mr. Micawber, for something

to turn up, but starvation on nardoo is by no means very unpleasant, but for the weakness one feels and the utter inability to move oneself; and, as far as appetite is concerned, it gives me the greatest satisfaction. Certainly, fat and sugar would be more to one's taste. Those seem to me to be the great stand-by in this extraordinary continent; not that I mean to depreciate the farinaceous food, but the want of sugar and fat in all substances obtainable here is so great, that they almost become valueless as articles of food without the addition of something else."

These were the last words the poor fellow ever wrote. It seems wonderful to find such cheerfulness and such courage at the very last moment, but his was no ordinary character. The day after this entry brought the last scene in this sad drama. Having collected and provided seed to last him eight days, and having left wood and water within his reach, Burke and King bade him adieu. They told him still that they would not go unless he wished it, and under no circumstances would they leave him unless to get him further assistance. But he repeated his request, as he looked upon it as their only chance. He gave Burke a letter for his father and a watch, and they buried the journals near the hut. He asked King, in case he should survive Burke, to be sure and see his last wishes fulfilled.

Further than this we know nothing. He could write no more, as his journal was buried. One can imagine the last sad farewell of his companions, as they left him stretched upon the pile of rags in the hut, never expecting to see his wan and emaciated features any more. One can imagine his calm tranquillity while the daylight faded into evening, like the ebbing away of his own life.

His night was passed without any sounds, except his own weak breathing. He may have watched the changing clouds, the fitful breezes, or the stars, as his journal tells us he had done before. Their faint light brought some comfort to his glazed eyes, and one can fancy how his whispering sighs would echo round the hut as the weary hours passed on. A few days more—three at

the most—and even that sound was gone—poor Wills
had passed away.

From the first day of travelling, Burke seemed very
weak, and complained of great pain in his legs and
back. On the second day he could only go two miles.
With great exertions King got him to go a little further,
but only a very little. It was the end of a long and
sorrowful journey. He abandoned everything he had,
and dragged himself to a few bushes, where he lay
down for the night. King collected some nardoo, and
shot a crow, but the end was too near to be averted.
After his supper, he said he felt convinced he could not
last many hours, and he gave his watch and pocket-
book to King. He then said, he hoped King would
remain with him until he was quite dead, for it was a
comfort to know that some one was by. He wished to
be left unburied as he lay, and to have a pistol placed in
his right hand. These were his last requests. That
night he spoke but little, and next morning he was
speechless. He died at about eight o'clock. Thus
Burke and Wills terminated their noble careers.

King now wandered about in the most forlorn and
lonely condition. He was, as it were, the last man in
the desert, and every scene reminded him of his lost
companions. In searching about the native huts he
found a bag of nardoo, enough to last him a fortnight,
and he clung to every means of prolonging his life with
extraordinary tenacity. He went back to where he had
left Wills five days previously, and found him lying
dead in the hut. The natives had been there meanwhile, and had taken away some of the clothes. King
buried the corpse in the sand, and then went to look for
the natives. His search was a long one, but he managed
to subsist upon hawks and crows until he found the
camp. The blacks treated him very kindly, and gave
him food, but did not seem anxious to keep him. By
shooting birds, however, he secured at last their good
opinion, especially by rendering some medical services to one of the tribe, and so they treated him as
one of their tribe, and gave him daily supplies of nardoo and fish. They were very anxious to know where

Mr. Burke lay, and one day King took them to the spot.
On seeing the body, remembering well how he was the
leader of the party which came some time before to the
place, they wept bitterly, and covered the body with
branches. After this, says King, they were much kinder
to him than before, and he took care to explain to them
that when his white companions came to search for him
they would be rewarded for their kindness. He looked
confidently forward to the time of his delivery, which
happened as described in a future chapter. Leaving
King, therefore, the only survivor of this fatal expedition, under the care of his native friends, we must now
turn to the circumstances which led to the abandonment
of the depôt.

CHAPTER XXIII.

Why Brahé's party left the depôt—Wright's delays—A party sent out to over-
take Burke—Returns unsuccessful—Wright starts at last—His delays—
Torowotto—Poria Creek—Bulloo—Attacked by natives—Death of some
of the party—Brahé's return—Wright goes to Cooper's Creek—Return to
Menindee—Consternation at the news—Parties equipped—Howitt—
Walker—Norman—Landsborough—M'Kinlay.

WHILE all these things were going on, it will naturally
be asked, What became of Mr. Wright? who, it will
be remembered, had been sent by Mr. Burke back to
Menindee to bring up the main party to the Barcoo.
He had never done so, but remained losing time about
the Darling, thus being, indirectly, the cause of all the
disasters we have just related.

It is, of course, in my readers' recollection that
Brahé had been left in charge of the depôt until
Wright's arrival. It has not, however, been explained
why he had deserted his post before Burke and Wills
returned. The facts are easily told. Wright did not
come up. From day to day, and from week to week,
Brahé had impatiently expected him. The men worked
hard at first, building stockades, and providing for the
animals, until the blacks became troublesome. They
were thus more confined to camp, so that looking out
for Wright became their only occupation. By-and-by
the men began to sicken, and complain of scurvy. They
had no medicine, and knew not what was the matter
with them. Four months at last elapsed, but Wright
did not come, neither were there any signs of Burke,
and the provisions of the party were getting very low.
Sickness continued, and return began to be talked of.
There was, no doubt, some little risk in remaining much
longer, and their fears probably magnified it. At last,

on April 21, 1861, exactly four months and four days since Burke had proceeded to the north, they gave up all hope of ever seeing him again, and left the Barcoo. One cannot blame Brahé very much for this. He was a working man, and never intended to have any command in the party. It was not unreasonable that he should have believed Burke to have perished, since he had so much exceeded the time for which he had taken provisions. But for two things he should certainly be blamed. The first was, for leaving so small a quantity of provisions; and secondly, that he did not state the truth as to the condition of the party. Had he said, " My men are much weakened by scurvy, and will not be able to travel far," Burke would have followed, and the lives of the explorers been saved.

But what had become of Wright meanwhile? I now proceed to answer that question. According to his statement, Burke had told him that he was not to leave Menindee until his nomination had been confirmed by the Exploration Committee. Now, this can hardly be true, because it does not tally with Burke's despatch, and such an enormous delay seems to have been a preposterous idea, when the whole party were only equipped for twelve months. Besides, Burke's letter says distinctly: " Mr. Wright returns from here to Menindee. I informed him that I should consider him third officer of the expedition, subject to the approval of the committee, and I hope that they will confirm the appointment. *In the meantime*, I have directed him to follow me up, with the remainder of the camels, to the Barcoo, and to take steps to procure a supply of jerked meat." This, at any rate, contradicts Wright.

But he had another excuse. Shortly after returning to Menindee, despatches were sent containing an account of Stuart's discoveries, which were to have been forwarded to Burke as soon as possible. He sent forward one of his men with a trooper to carry on the despatches, and wrote to the committee these words: " I have the honour to inform you that, pursuant to a *previous understanding* with Mr. Burke, it was my intention to rejoin that gentleman." He then goes on to state that the horses and camels were not in a fit state to travel on to the Barcoo.

Some days after the departure of the men and a native with the despatches for Burke, the black fellow returned with a piece of paper, signed by his companions, imploring assistance to rescue them from immediate starvation. This was on the 18th December. On the 19th, Dr. Beckler hastened out, and found them about one hundred and ninety miles from Menindee, subsisting on the hospitality of the natives. After receiving the confirmation of his appointment, Mr. Wright was in no hurry to move. Not until the 26th January did he make a final start from Menindee. I need not detain the reader with his reasons for this last delay, as they are as absurd as those alleged for not following Burke immediately.

The party was in good health, and the stock in sound condition; and, provided expedition was used, and energy displayed, there was no reason why they might not yet be in time to do good service. One thing, however, it is quite impossible to understand. Mr. Wright left the greater portion of his stores and equipments behind him at Menindee, and only started with six months' provisions for himself and his party. One might have had patience with him up to this, but such a step is beyond endurance. What, in the name of common sense, was the use of the party starting at all, if they only provided themselves with provisions for three months' journey out, and three months' return? How could they possibly expect to be of the smallest assistance to Burke, even if they reached him? It is true, Wright intended to send back for the remainder; but this excuse is unbearable nonsense. The manner in which this march of folly was conducted was well worthy the contriver. The first day's journey is a specimen. "Saturday, January 26. — Packing stores until eleven, a.m., when the camels were sent on under charge of Dr. Beckler, with instructions to camp on the west side of Pamamaroo Lake. Owing to the unruly disposition of the horses, it was one o'clock before they started with four; five more started at two, p.m., and four more at three. The afternoon was occupied in packing and unpacking, nearly every horse throwing his load, and the party becoming separated in consequence. One part of the expedition was not able to find Dr. Beckler's camp, and two horses broke away, and remained all night in the polygonum, with their packs on them. The whole distance made was only five miles."

A part of their journey was over country quite destitute of water; so, on the 1st of February the packs and saddles were left behind, while a rush was made with the camels to the Motanie Ranges (the Daubeny Ranges of Mitchell). They then camped until the 7th, while journeys were made backwards and forwards to recover the packs. This delay might perhaps be excused. On the 7th, they moved on to a creek named Nuntherunge Creek, eighteen miles from the range; and thence, on the 8th, twenty miles over heavy country, to Yeltawinge Creek. There was a small range visible to the north-east. They travelled very slowly. Not only are the distances just enumerated very short stages, but on the 10th they only went eight miles down the creek. On the 11th, they left the creek, travelling over clay plains, with cotton bush and salsolaceous plants, for twenty-two miles, when they came to a water-hole in Paldromata Creek. On leaving this next day, they passed to a salt lake, and camped that night at Torowotto Swamp. This is one of the many mud or gum plains into which the surface water of the surrounding country drains. It was abundantly covered with nardoo. At Torowotto, Wright rested for two days, but does not state for what cause. There were natives about, who were inclined to steal, but not otherwise troublesome. On the 15th they left, passing over barren clay plains for eighteen miles, and camping on a sand-hill whose summit showed them plainly that there was no water to be obtained in advance. They remained here, while a search was being made, until the 19th. They then proceeded to traverse the plain until they reached, towards evening, some water which the previous day's excursions had enabled them to discover. There were abundance of rats there, and this circumstance obtained for the camp the name of Rat Point.

Beyond this position there was no permanent supply of water to be had. Searches were made in every direction, but none found. It was then determined to send back the horses and camels to Torowotto, while a more systematic search was being carried on. In this way they consumed the time from the 20th February until the 12th of March. It appears from the diary that Mr. Wright did not spare his own exertions during the time, and took every precaution to send the animals backwards and forwards to Torowotto. They thus became very poor and exhausted ; and, what was worse, four of the party, Dr. Beckler and three of the men (named Stone, Purcell, and Smith), became seriously ill with the scurvy. All the search of Mr. Wright had only resulted in the discovery of a small supply in the mud and saltbush plains, and then, further on, but with a considerable interval of desert, a large supply in Poria Creek. On the 19th, Wright reached this position with the horses, but the exertion cost two of them their lives ; and on the 20th, the camel party came up. Some of the men were now very ill indeed.

In order to restore them, Mr. Wright stopped until the 29th at this place ; but the men did not improve. Their greatest enemies during all this time were the rats, which abounded in these plains. Not only did these animals gnaw through everything within their reach, and do considerable damage, but they even attacked the men, and were as ready to approach them as domestic animals. On the 29th there was a heavy fall of rain, which caused a creek, named Koorliatto Creek, to run, and they camped upon its banks. Dr. Beckler, Purcell, and Stone were very bad with scurvy, and quite unable to move, even when carried about on camels. A tent was put up for them at this place.

The creek they were upon was a tributary of Poria Creek, running from east to north-west for seven miles, and skirting the south-west base of a range named the Bulloo Range. There was much more timber on this range than on the Poria, and excellent feed for the cattle.

Finding it impossible to move the sick men, Mr. Wright determined to move on to the Barcoo with a small party, as, he informs us, he was sure Burke's provisions must by this time have needed replenishing. He therefore left the sick in charge of Dr. Beckler, and crossed the creek with difficulty. After passing the sand-hills bordering the creek, he came upon an extensive plain, with watercourses and innumerable rat-holes. At twenty miles from Koorliatto, he reached Bulloo Creek, which at the camping place contained a reach of water five miles long, from one hundred to two hundred yards wide, and in some parts sixteen or twenty feet deep. From this place Wright made an excursion to the north-west to try to reach the Barcoo, a distance of between seventy and eighty miles; but he states that he was unable to do so in consequence of the hostility of the natives. Readers who have seen in the preceding pages what other explorers have done under similar circumstances will hardly admit such a plea. At any rate, Wright finding that he could not advance, sent word to Dr. Beckler to take his sick men back to Menindee, and having left them there, to bring back others in their places, so that they could go on to the Barcoo with the whole strength of the party. In the meantime, Wright was to entrench himself at the Barcoo, and wait for assistance. One may ask, if Wright was not afraid of the natives at Bulloo, where he would have to camp for the long period of Dr. Beckler's absence, why should he be afraid of advancing eighty miles further? However, Dr. Beckler protested so strongly against the removal of the sick to Menindee that the order was countermanded, and they were removed with care to Bulloo. All these things occupied until the 21st April, which was the very day on which Burke arrived at the depôt, and found it deserted. On the day following, while all but two of the able men were away from the camp, searching for the camels, an attack was made by the natives, who moved away, however, on being threatened, after stealing a great

many things. While this was going on, one of the
men (Stone) died. The next day the party erected
a stockade, and the day following another of the
men (Purcell) died. Shortly after this another party
of natives came down. They went to Stone's grave,
and one of them taking a dead rat, made a long
harangue over it, and then threw it towards them, inti-
mating by this gesture that there was not much time
for any of them to live, but that they would all be buried
like Stone, the dust of whose grave they threw in the air.
They then left them. On the 27th, however, they came
down in great numbers, and then at last it was necessary
to fire upon them, when they were easily dispersed.

On the 29th, the party were much surprised at
seeing an extensive cavalcade of horses and camels
approaching them. This was Brahé and his party.
His story was soon told. Burke had left nearly five
months previously, taking with him provisions for three
months, and he had not been since heard of. They
had given him up for lost; and as three of the men were
suffering from scurvy, Brahé thought it best to remove
towards the Darling as soon as possible. He at once
placed himself under Wright's authority. The evening
of the same day witnessed the death of Dr. Beckler; he
was buried next day.

Wright now resolved to return to Menindee as soon
as possible, and give information of Burke's disappearance,
so that if he had not turned up at some other place, a
search in aid might be instituted at once. Accordingly,
he moved from Bulloo to Koorliatto, on the 1st May.

When he reached that place, it struck him that it
would be as well, before finally leaving, to ascertain
that Burke had not been to the depôt during Brahé's
absence; and so he directed his party to remain in the
encampment while he and Brahé went back to the
Barcoo. He arrived there on the 8th of May, exactly
sixteen days after Burke, Wills, and King had left,
and proceeded down towards Mount Hopeless. Both
Wright and Brahé state that the things were undisturbed, and they did not dig down to see if any of
the things had been removed. This is a most unfor-

tunate circumstance. King states expressly, that if
they had used their eyes they must have seen that
Burke had been there, for they placed many marks and
signs about, to show that the place had been disturbed.
But it seems that Burke and his party were doomed.
At the very time that Wright and Brahé stood within
a few inches of what would have told them the whole
truth, Burke and his companions were thinking of
wending their way back, after having found it impossible
to find water to take them to Mount Hopeless. It would
seem very probable, that had Wright found Burke's
letter, he could not have done much to aid him. To
have gone down the creek with his scanty supply of
provisions seemed impossible, and to have returned for
assistance to his companions, who were already so
reduced by scurvy, would have given time to Burke
to get so far from him that he could no longer be sure
of finding him. But one thing we may ask; why did
not Wright bring with him a fresh supply of provisions,
to be left at the depôt? He knew that the supply left
by Brahé was miserably small, and it was downright
madness to leave such a quantity as a means of subsistence for the party, had they returned. We may
certainly say that the neglect shown in this particular
is inexcusable, whatever may be said of the rest—if
that mild term will suffice to qualify that which led to
such sad results.

Had Wright brought a fresh supply of provisions
to bury, all the lives might have been saved. In
digging to place them they would have found Burke's
record, and rescued him, or at any rate they would have
provided a new resource against starvation for Wills,
when he returned to the depôt, as he did, on the 30th
May. No more need, however, be said, about Mr.
Wright's shortcomings. I am unwilling to add to the
bitterness of what his regrets must be by any further
remarks. The facts are besides, so plain, that few
readers will hesitate as to what conclusions they should
draw. When Wright and Brahé returned to Koorliatto,
they made all haste to return with the party to the
Darling. Some of the men improved on the journey

down, but their progress was very slow. Patten, however, sank gradually, and died near Torowotto on the
6th June.

On the 18th June, they reached the Darling, and
sent on their despatches in great haste, begging that aid
might be sent to Burke, if he had not since been heard
of. This was only a few days before Burke and Wills
both died of starvation in the desert.

It need scarcely be told what a deep feeling of
dismay and disappointment filled every mind when the
return of Wright was reported, with the dismal news
he brought. A fine expedition, so splendidly equipped,
was thus proclaimed a failure, having cost the lives of
four of the party, and probably the two leaders. Two
men had perished without accomplishing anything more
than rushing on to their own destruction. The disappointment was universal, and nearly every one had something to say as to the various causes of the failure : but
such opinions would have been useful only beforehand.
One sentiment was, however, universal, and that was
that something should be immediately done to rescue
the unhappy explorers still unaccounted for. The
activity shown on this subject forms a very pleasing
portion of colonial history, for not only was the most
earnest desire to assist Burke displayed by the Melbourne Government, but every one of the other colonies
evinced the same anxiety. In the first place, the Exploration Committee were able to send off a succouring
party without the least delay, for a small party was just
equipped when the news came. The fact was, that the
committee were alarmed at the length of time which
had elapsed since the starting of Wright without their
hearing any news of him, and therefore had despatched
A. W. Howitt, with three companions, as a sort of con-
tingent party. He was to proceed as far as he could by
the mail, and then to purchase horses for himself and
companions, who were to start as lightly equipped as
possible, along Burke's tracks. This Mr. Howitt is the
son of the celebrated William Howitt, of good bush
experience, and fit to be an explorer.

Mr. Howitt having met Wright, returned to Melbourne with Wright's messenger. His party was immediately doubled, because of the news from Wright about the hostile character of the Bulloo natives, and he again started from Menindee, with the object of proceeding at once to the Barcoo, with such of the men, horses, and camels as might be sufficiently recovered. He was then to track Burke. He was accompanied by Mr. Walsh, a surgeon, who had been out with Stuart on one of his explorations.

This, however, was not all that was done. It was thought probable, from a suggestion made by Mr. Wright, that Burke might have found his retreat cut off, and then advanced with his party towards the northern coast, upon which he might be now endeavouring to subsist. The Exploration Committee applied to the Government for the aid of the steam-sloop *Victoria*, in order that she might go round to the Gulf of Carpentaria, and examine the coasts in its vicinity for traces of the expedition. Unfortunately, the *Victoria* was then under repairs, and though the Government at once acceded to the request, the vessel could not be placed at their disposal for three weeks' time.

In the meantime, it was determined that a party should be despatched overland from the northern settlements of Queensland to the head of the Gulf. A gentleman of the name of Walker was strongly recommended to the committee for the purpose. He had been formerly a superintendent of the native police, but was now employed at the head of a band of his former men in discovering and taking up country for the squatters. His services were immediately accepted.

The committee were still anxious that a second land party should go round by sea with the *Victoria*; but as the funds at their disposal were now exhausted, and the Parliament was not in session, it was not decided upon until Queensland had agreed to give two thousand pounds towards the expenses of the journey. This party was to proceed in the *Victoria* to the Albert River, and then to search for Burke downwards, towards the south coast. As this expedition was more immediately under the control of the Queensland Govern-

ment, its preparations were made under the superin-
tendence of Mr. A. C. Gregory. The command was
given to Mr. Wm. Landsborough, a gentleman of very
considerable bush experience. He was to be accompanied by three Europeans and four natives (two of
them native troopers), selected by himself; and he was
furnished with thirty horses, and a requisite supply of
provisions. The instructions to both Walker and
Howitt were prepared by the Victorian Government, but
the general command of them was given to Captain
Norman, of the *Victoria*. The latter vessel was to
remain six months at the Gulf of Carpentaria, and was
to be accompanied by a transport.

Another specimen of the activity of the Melbourne
Government in this matter must be mentioned. A
little steamer of fourteen tons, named the *Hotham*, was
despatched by her owner at his own private expense,
to ascend the Albert River, and see if it could be of
any assistance to Burke.

In addition to all this, the Government of South
Australia had agreed to defray the cost of an expedition
to search the continent from south to north. The
command of the party was given to Mr. John M‘Kinlay,
and consisted of six men, twenty-two horses, four camels,
and twelve months' provisions.

Thus, it will be observed, that there were no less
than five exploring parties sent out in search of Burke.
They were Howitt's, Walker's, Landsborough's, Norman's, and M‘Kinlay's. All these could not fail to
lead to an important increase to our knowledge of the
continent; but as the reader must bear them in mind,
with their several objects, in order to have a clear idea
of their movements, and the wonderful discoveries they
led to I will therefore repeat their destinations.
Howitt was to search the Barcoo from Menindee;
Walker was to go to the Gulf of Carpentaria, from
Rockhampton; Landsborough was to go with Norman,
in the *Victoria*, to the Gulf of Carpentaria, and then
to examine the coasts, while Norman waited for him and
Walker for six months; and M‘Kinlay was to start for
the Barcoo by way of Lake Torrens.

Howitt started early in July; Norman sailed from
Queensland with Landsborough, on August 24; Walker
started on the same day from the furthest out-station,
near Rockhampton; and to the credit of the prompti-
tude of the Adelaide Government, M'Kinlay left on
the 14th August.   Now we will take these parties
separately, commencing with the expedition of Howitt,
which was the first to start, and really was the only one
that succeeded in finding facts about the fate of Wills
and Burke.

CHAPTER XXIV.

HOWITT RESCUES KING.

Stokes' Range—Finding of King—Burial of Wills and Burke—Reward to the
Natives—Committee of Inquiry—M'Kinlay—Finding of Gray's body—
Encounter with the natives.

MR. HOWITT'S first journey was to Poria Creek, on a
direct course for Stokes' Range (of Sturt), and thence to
the Barcoo, leaving Wright's track from Poria considerably to his right hand. In order to understand this
and the other tracks, I must mention some facts connected with the geography of this locality. When
Sturt, in 1845, and Crawford, in 1859, went from
Menindee, they struck north-west, to the Barrier Ranges.
From thence Sturt went north to the Barcoo, which, it
will be seen by the map, winds at a great distance round
the head of the Grey Ranges. In going north, readers
will remember the range was found to become gradually
lower until it disappeared entirely, and then a small
low range, named Stokes' Range, was seen by Sturt to
the eastward, and that was the only elevation until the
Barcoo was reached. Before Sturt left the Barrier
Ranges he made an expedition to Mount Lyell, which lay
between him and the Darling, and first seen and named
by Mitchell, in 1833. Now the course kept by Wright
was from Menindee to Mounts Lyell and Daubeny,
leaving Mitchell's Stokes' Range to the east, and thence
north, by the aid of the watercourses from the Grey
Range, making an immense and wide sweep round to
the east before reaching the Barcoo. Howitt's course
was similar up to Poria Creek, when he made for
Stokes' Range, and thence across the plains to the
creek.

His journey may be described in a few words. Up to Stokes' Range was sand-hills and scrub, with open gum clay plains between, in which the nardoo grew abundantly. These plains were interrupted with occasional watercourses, and were, apparently, liable to inundation. In fact, if one were to write volumes upon the country it would all result in the same description. When there are not sand-hills there are plains, through which small creeks run in very wet seasons. The country is so level that they soon run out on flats, in which shallow swamps consequently occur. This description, it will be seen, differs nothing from the country passed through by Sturt and Burke, except that near the Barcoo there are no ranges, beside the Stokes' Range, and these are very stony, low hills, with thick scrub, and about eight hundred feet high. Below the range the plains were frightfully stony.

Mr. Howitt had much difficulty in penetrating across these ranges, more especially as it was now September, and the dry season was setting in. He found their summits to be composed of large masses of crystalline stone, white in colour, and grouped into irregular columns. He says this was the same stone which was strewn all over the country, and of which, and a coarse sandstone and conglomerate, the ranges were principally formed. From the Stokes' Range, a country succeeded exactly like the Stony Desert.

Mr. Howitt came on Brahé's track (Brahé was with him) on the 6th September, and found no water the first two days, except what they carried with them. On the 7th it rained, and this detained them one day. On the 8th, they reached the Barcoo, about nine weeks after the death of Burke and Wills. The river was very low, no rain, apparently, having come down it for the preceding two seasons. The ground upon its banks was much cracked and fissured, and the most of the water-holes dried up. Yet there were flood marks, which showed that the river was sometimes only confined by the stony rises, and these were at least two miles apart. Some of the water-holes were very salt. The feed was miserable, except on sandy ground, where it was a shade

better, but the general aspect of the Barcoo at this time
was wretched.

At first, Mr. Howitt saw many natives as he journeyed
up the river to the eastward. Some were frightened,
and made off, while others were communicative and
inoffensive; but none as yet seemed to know anything
about the explorers. On the 13th, he reached the depôt,
named Fort Wills. Strange to say, he did not dig
down to see if anything had been disturbed. Brahé
told him that things were just as he left them, and as
Mr. Howitt did not want provisions, and would only
have been encumbered with these if he dug them up,
he did not disturb the *cache*. It is singular what a
fatality there was about this depôt. Since Brahé had
first visited it, Burke had been there, Brahé and Wright
had been there, Wills also, and now, finally, Howitt,
and yet each thought that the place was quite undisturbed. Mr. Howitt, however, noticed that the things
were carelessly buried, but Brahé assured him that
they were just in the state in which they had been left.

On the 14th September, Howitt went down the
river, crossing several branches which went out south,
and formed a reach of water before reaching the main
channel. Here the rocky ridges of the stream both
closed in, and the water had, consequently, forced a
narrow, deep channel through a perfect wall of rock,
forming below a splendid deep reach of water, several
miles long and five hundred yards wide. While going
down this, Mr. Howitt noticed camel tracks, where
Brahé assured him the camels never before had been.
As there were no foot tracks near, they began to think
they were the tracks of the camels lost by Wills on his
first journey northward; but next day the signs began to
be more significant and mysterious. Mr. Howitt thus
tells the story: "Camp 32. September 15. Lat. 27° 44',
long. 140° 40'.—On leaving this morning, I went ahead
with Sandy to try and pick up Mr. Burke's track. At
the lower end of a large water-hole, found where one or
two horses had been feeding for some months; the
tracks ran in all directions to and from the water, and
were as recent as a week. At the same place I found

the handle of a clasp-knife. From here struck out south for a short distance from the creek, and found a distinct camel's track and droppings on a native path. The footprints were about four months old, and going east. I then sent the black boy to follow the creek, and struck across the sandy country, in a bend, on the north side. No tracks here; and coming on a native path, leading my way, I followed it, as the most likely place to see any signs. In about four miles this led me to the lower end of a very large reach of water, and on the opposite side were numbers of native wurleys. I again came on the track of a camel going up the creek. At the same time I found a native, who began to gesticulate in a very excited manner, and to point down the creek, bawling out, 'Gow, gow!' as loud as he could. When I went towards him he ran away, and finding it impossible to get him to come to me, I turned back to follow the camel track, and to look after my party, as I had not seen anything of them for some miles. The track was visible in sandy places, and was evidently the same I had seen for the last two days. I also found horse tracks in places, but very old. Crossing the creek, I cut our track, and rode after the party. In doing so, I came upon three pounds of tobacco, which had lain where I saw it for some time. This, together with the knife-handle, the fresh horse tracks, and the camel track going eastward, puzzled me extremely, and led me into a hundred conjectures. At the lower end of the large reach of water, before mentioned, I met Sandy and Frank looking for me, with the intelligence that King, the only survivor of Mr. Burke's party, had been found. A little further on I found the party halted, and immediately went across to the blacks' wurleys, where I found King sitting in a hut which the blacks made for him. He presented a melancholy appearance, wasted to a shadow, and hardly to be distinguished as a civilized being but by the remnants of clothes upon him. He seemed exceedingly weak, and I found it occasionally difficult to follow what he said. The natives were all gathered round, seated on the ground, looking with a most gratified and delighted

expression. Camped where the party had halted, on a
high bank, close to the water. I shall probably be here
ten days, to recruit King before returning.

"Camp 32, September 16.—King already looks
vastly improved, even since yesterday, and not like the
same man. Have commenced shoeing horses and preparing for our return. Wind from south-west, with signs
of rain. The natives seem to be getting ready for it.

"Camp 32, September 18.—Left camp this morning
with Messrs. Brahé, Welsh, Wheeler, and King, to
perform a melancholy duty which has weighed on my
mind since we camped here, and which I have only put
off until King should be well enough to accompany us.
We proceeded down the creek for seven miles, crossing
a branch running to the southward, and followed a
native track leading to that part of the creek where
Mr. Burke, Mr. Wills, and King camped after their
unsuccessful attempt to reach Mount Hopeless and the
northern settlements of South Australia, and where
poor Wills died. We found the two gunyahs pretty
much as King had described them, situate on a sand
bank, between two water-holes, and about a mile from
the flat where they procured the nardoo seed on which
they managed to exist so long. Poor Wills' remains
we found lying in the wurley in which he died, and
where King, after his return from seeking for the
natives, had buried him with sand and rushes. We
carefully collected the remains, and interred them
where they lay; and, not having a prayer-book, I read
chapter v. of 1 Cor., that we might at least feel a
melancholy satisfaction in having shown the last respect
to his remains. We heaped sand over the grave, and
laid branches upon it, that the natives might understand by their own tokens not to disturb the last repose
of a fellow-being. I cut the following inscription on a
tree close by to mark the spot:—

> W. J. WILLS,
> XLV. Yds.
> W.N.W.
> A. H.

The field-books, a note-book belonging to Mr. Burke, various small articles lying about, of no value in themselves, but now invested with a deep interest from the circumstances connected with them, and some of the nardoo seed on which they had subsisted, with the small wooden trough in which it had been cleansed, I have in my possession. We returned home with saddened feelings; but I must confess that I felt a sense of relief that this painful ordeal had been gone through. King was very tired when we returned, and I must, most unwillingly, defer my visit to the spot where Mr. Burke's remains are lying until he is better able to bear the fatigue."

The 19th and 20th were occupied in shoeing horses and sending off four carrier-pigeons they had brought from Melbourne. The latter did not carry the news as they were expected to do. Two of them must, however, be excused, as they stopped on the way from the camp to make a meal for some kites which were near. The others were not heard of again. We now resume Howitt's narrative; here mentioning that the diary of every day need not be given, as some were merely occupied in waiting for King's recovery, which was now happily progressing rapidly, though it was dangerous to think of removing him as yet. Where they found him was not far from the bodies of Burke and Wills, who died at no great distance from each other.

"September 21.—Finding that it would not be prudent for King to go out for two or three days, I could no longer defer making a search for the spot where Mr. Burke died; and, with such directions as King could give, I went up the creek this morning with Messrs. Brahé, Welsh, Wheeler, and Atkins. We searched the creek upwards for eight miles, and at length, strange to say, found the remains of Burke lying among tall plants under a clump of box trees, within two hundred yards of our last camp, and not thirty paces from our track. It was still more extraordinary that three or four of the party, and the two black boys, had been close to the spot without noticing

it. The bones were entire, with the exception of the
hands and feet, and the body had been removed from
the spot where it first lay, and where the natives had
placed branches over it, to about five paces distant. I
found the revolver which Mr. Burke held in his hand
when he expired, partly covered with leaves and earth,
and corroded with rust. It was loaded and capped.
We dug a grave close to the spot, and interred the
remains, wrapped in the union-jack—the most fitting
covering in which the bones of a brave but unfortunate
man could take their last rest. On a box tree, at the
head of the grave, the following inscription is cut :—

R. O'H. B.
21 | 9 | 61
A. H.

"September 23.—Went down the creek to-day in
search of the natives. One of the party accompanied
me, and we took two days' rations, in case it should be
necessary to prolong our search. Two days after we
camped here the natives left, and have not been seen
since ; and I could not think of leaving without showing
them that we could appreciate and reward the kindness
they had shown to Burke's party, and particularly to
King. For three miles we travelled over alluvial flats
along the creek, timbered with box and large gums, and
dotted with bean trees, orange trees of large size, but at
present without fruit, various kinds of acacias, and
other bushes. To the right hand, level flats and sand
ridges, apparently tolerably grassed. We then came
on a large reach of water, where four or five natives
had just been fishing ; their nets were lying on the sand
to dry, and the fire yet burning. Not seeing any one
about, and getting no answer to a cooey, we went on.
At three miles more we passed the first feeder of
Strzelecki's Creek, going to the southward, and at a
large reach of water below found the natives camped.
They made a great commotion when we rode up to
them, but seemed very friendly. I unpacked my
blanket, and took out specimens of the things I intended

giving them—a tomahawk, a knife, beads, a looking-glass, comb, and flour and sugar. The tomahawk was the greatest object, after that the knife, but I think that the looking-glass surprised them most. On seeing their faces, some seemed dazzled, others opened their eyes like saucers, and made a rattling noise with their tongues expressive of surprise. We had quite a friendly palaver, and my watch amused them immensely. When I gave them some of the sugar to taste, it was absurd to see the sleight of hand with which they pretended to eat it; I supposed from a fear of being poisoned, which I suppose general, as our black boys are continually in dread lest the 'wild black fellows' should poison them by some means. I made them understand that they were to bring the whole tribe up next morning to our camp to receive their presents, and we parted the best of friends. The names of the principal men are Tohukulow, Mangallee (three in number), Toqunuter, Pitchery (three in number, one a funny little man, with his head in a net, and a kite's feather in it; another a tall man, with his beard tied in a point), Cruriekow, and Borokow.

"September 24.—This morning, about ten o'clock, our black friends appeared in a long procession, men, women, and children, or, as they also call them, picca-ninnies; and at a mile's distance they commenced bawling at the top of their voices, as usual. When collected together on a little flat, just below our camp, they must have numbered between thirty and forty, and the uproar was deafening. With the aid of King, I at last got them all seated before me, and distributed the presents—tomahawks, knives, necklaces, looking-glasses, combs—among them. I think no people were ever so happy before, and it was very interesting to see how they pointed out one another who they thought might be overlooked. The piccaninnies were brought forward by their parents, to have red ribbons tied round their dirty little heads. One old woman, Carrawaw, who had been particularly kind to King, was loaded with things. I then divided fifty pounds of sugar between them, each one taking his share in a union-jack pocket-handkerchief, which they were very proud of. The sugar soon found its way into their mouths; the flour, fifty pounds of which I gave them, they at once called 'white fellow nardoo,' and they explained that they understood that these things were given to them for having fed King."

After having discharged this duty, Mr. Howitt thought it better to return, for though the temptation to explore further was very great, so well equipped with provisions and necessaries as they were, yet he had accomplished the object of his journey, and the news he had to bring was of too great importance for delay. He therefore bent his course homeward. He need not be followed over this oft-trodden ground; suffice it to say that he arrived with King safe at Poria Creek on the 9th of October, 1861, and here his journal ends.

Deep grief prevailed through all the colonies when the sad story was revealed. In Victoria the sorrow was very great, and as the only way of showing their gratitude to the explorers who were no more, it was agreed that Howitt should go back and bring down the bodies for a public funeral in Melbourne. It should also be mentioned that honours of a more substantial kind were not forgotten. A large sum of money was voted to the nearest relatives of Burke and Wills, and to King a grant was made which ought to suffice to put him in easy circumstances for life.

But while rewards were being distributed, blame was not forgotten. It was agreed on all hands that no life need have been lost had proper precautions been used. Who was to blame? was asked by every one, and the Government determined to sift out the truth. A committee was appointed for the purpose, and its management given to General Sir T. Pratt, K.C.B., Sir F. Murphy, M. Hervey, Esq., T. F. Sullivan, Esq., and E. P. S. Sturt, a brother of the celebrated explorer. The committee sat for a period of two months and a half, examining all the persons in any way connected with the expedition. They then delivered their report. With that report every sensible man must concur. Having carefully read through all the evidence, not once, but some portions many times, and I must say it would be impossible to give a fairer exposition of the impression to be gained from its perusal. The report ran as follows :—

"In conformity with the terms of Her Majesty's Commission, we have made inquiry into the circumstances connected with the sufferings and death of R. O'H. Burke and W. J. Wills, the Victorian explorers.

"We have endeavoured to ascertain the true causes of this lamentable result of the expedition, and have investigated the circumstances under which the depôt at Cooper's Creek was abandoned by Mr. William Brahé. We have sought to determine upon whom rests the grave responsibility of there not having been sufficient supply of provisions and clothing secured for the recruiting of the explorers on their return, and for their support until they could reach the settlements, and we have generally inquired into the organization and conduct of the expedition."

Then, after further preamble, the following report is added :—

"The expedition having been provided and equipped in the most ample and liberal manner, and having reached Menindee, on the Darling, without experiencing any difficulties, was most injudiciously divided at that point by Mr. Burke.

"It was an error of judgment on the part of Mr. Burke to appoint Mr. Wright to an important command in the expedition without a previous personal knowledge of him, although doubtless a pressing emergency had arisen for the appointment from the sudden resignations of Mr. Landells and Dr. Beckler.

"Mr. Burke evinced a far greater amount of zeal than prudence in finally departing from Cooper's Creek before the depôt party had arrived from Menindee, and without having secured communication with the settled districts, as he had been instructed to do; and in undertaking so extended a journey with an insufficient supply of provisions, Mr. Burke was forced into the necessity of overtaxing the powers of his party, whose continuous and unremitting exertions resulted in the destruction of his animals, and the prostration of himself and companions from fatigue and severe privations.

"The conduct of Mr. Wright appears to have been reprehensible in the highest degree. It is clear that Mr. Burke, on parting with him at Torowotto, relied on his receiving his immediate and zealous support; and it seems extremely improbable that Mr. Wright could have misconstrued the intentions of his leader so far as to suppose that he ever calculated for a moment on his remaining for any length of time on the Darling. Mr. Wright has failed to give any satisfactory explanations as to the causes of this delay, and to that delay are mainly attributable the whole of the disasters of the expedition, with the exception of the death of Gray. The grave responsibility of not having left a larger supply of provisions, together with some clothing, in the *cache* at Cooper's Creek, rests with Mr. Wright. Even had he been unable to convey stores to Cooper's Creek, he might have left them elsewhere, leaving notice at the depôt of his having done so.

"The Exploration Committee, in overlooking the importance of the contents of Burke's despatch from Torowotto, and in not urging Mr. Wright's departure from the Darling, committed errors of a serious nature. A means of knowledge of the delay of the party at Menindee was in the possession of the committee, not, indeed, by direct communication to that effect, but through the receipt of letters from Drs. Becker and Beckler, at various dates up to the end of November, without, however, awakening the committee to a sense of the vital importance of Mr. Burke's request in that despatch, that he should 'be soon followed up,' or to a consideration of the disastrous consequences which would be likely to result, and did unfortunately result, from the fatal inactivity and idling of Mr. Wright and his party on the Darling.

"The conduct of Mr. Brahé, in returning from his position at the depôt before he was rejoined by his commander, or relieved from the Darling, may be deserving of considerable censure; but we are of opinion that a responsibility far beyond his expectations devolved upon him; and it must be borne in mind that, with the assurance of his leader, and his own conviction he might each day expect to be relieved by Mr. Wright, he still held his post for four months and five days, and that only when pressed by the appeals of a comrade sickening even to death, as was subsequently proved, his powers of endurance gave way, and he returned from the position which could alone afford succour to the weary explorers should they return by that route. This decision was most unfortunate; but we believe he acted from a conscientious desire to discharge his duty, and we are confident that the painful reflection that twenty-four hours' further perseverance would have made him the rescuer of the explorers, and gained for himself the praise and approbation of all, must be of itself an agonizing thought, without the addition of censure he might feel himself undeserving of.

"It does not appear that Mr. Burke kept any regular journal, or that he gave written instructions to his officers; had he performed these essential portions of the duties of a leader, many of the calamities of the expedition might have been averted, and little or no room would have been left for doubt in judging the conduct of those subordinates who pleaded unsatisfactory and contradicted verbal orders and statements.

"We cannot too deeply deplore the lamentable result of an expedition undertaken at so great a cost to the colony; but while we regret the absence of a systematic plan of operations on the part of the leader, we desire to express our admiration of his gallantry and daring, as well as the fidelity of his brave coadjutor, Mr. Wills, and their more fortunate and enduring associate, Mr. King; and we would record our feelings of deep sympathy with the deplorable sufferings and untimely death of Mr. Burke and his fellow comrades."

This report was signed by all the members of the committee. It is, probably my readers may say, not eminently grammatical or well constructed; but of its singular justice and good sense no one can entertain a doubt.

Before turning to the exploration in the north,

2 D 2

under the direction of Norman, Landsborough, and Walker, it is necessary to mention a portion of Mr. M'Kinlay's explorations, which created at the time a good deal of mystery.

Mr. M'Kinlay left Blanchewater for a lake named Lake Pando, on the 24th September. They arrived at the lake on the 6th October, after passing very nearly along Gregory's track from the Barcoo to Lake Torrens, over much good pasture land, which was here and there well watered. From Lake Pando they proceeded by way of various creeks and lakes to where it was rumoured among the Lake Torrens blacks that white men had been seen. In this part of their journey large numbers of well-fed, healthy-looking blacks were met, who, from many circumstances, appeared to have been in communication with white people before. This country was to the west of the Barcoo, and similar to what had been described by other explorers in this locality—namely, gum flats, with fresh-water swamps and dry watercourses. The natives now seen had some articles of European manufacture, and everything led M'Kinlay to imagine that he was on the traces of Burke, who he was confident had been murdered by natives. Acting under this impression he caught some further evidences of the death of the party, and what he found is thus related in his diary :—

"October 20.—Reached Lake Kallhi-View. Found plenty of water. Watered the horses (the camels some distance behind, unable to keep up), and at once proceeded northward, along the side of a large, beautifully timbered grassed, and clovered swamp or creek, about one and a half mile across, to ascertain the fact as to the presence of a European, dead or alive, and there found a grave lately formed by the natives, evidently not one of themselves, sufficient pains not having been taken, and from other appearances, at once set it down as the grave of a white man, be he who he may, and returned to Lake Kallhi-View to await the coming of the camels, which was not until about five, p.m. Determined in the morning to have the grave opened and ascertain its contents.

" Whilst I went to the top of the sand-hills, looking round me, Mr. Hodgkinson strayed a short distance to some old deserted native huts near, and by-and-by returned bearing with him an old flattened pint pot, no marks upon it; further evidence that it was a white man's grave. Plenty of clover and grasses. Whole distance travelled about eighteen miles. Kept watch as usual (did not intend doing so). Just as we were retiring we thought some of the natives had followed us, or some others came to the lake—rather a strange matter, after dark. It soon after disappeared, which made us more certain still that it was natives. Intend spelling the camels for a few days to recruit them. One on arrival was completely done up, and none of the others looked very sprightly.

" October 21.—Up in good time. Four starting for the grave ; went round the lake, taking Mr. Hodgkinson with me, to see if the natives were really on the lake. I did not intend saddling the camels to-day if there were no natives here, intending to leave our camps unprotected, as hands were short, and the grave was out of sight. Found no natives round the lake, but some of the trees were still burning. We started at once for the grave, taking a canteen of water with us, and all the arms. On arrival we removed the earth carefully, and close to the top of the ground found the body of a European enveloped in a flannel shirt with short sleeves, a piece of the breast of which I have taken. The flesh, I may say, completely cleaned off the bones, and a very little hair but what must have been decomposed. What little there was I have taken." Then followed a description of the body, which need not be given, because it is nearly certain that the grave found was that of Gray. The latitude was about 27°, and the long. 139° 50', or forty miles from where Wills died, and this was the place where Gray was buried, who, according to King, was dressed as above described.

M'Kinlay goes on to say, that a small tree immediately south he marked " M'K., Oct. 21, 1861."

Immediately this was over, they commenced questioning a native they had with them on the subject of

the white man. The statement made is useful, as it
shows how utterly impossible it is to rely on the smallest
circumstance related by the blacks in Australia. He
said he was killed by a stroke from what the natives call
their sword. He showed also where the whites had
been camped and attacked. M'Kinlay saw lots of fish-
bones, but no evidence on the trees that whites had been
there, and he imagined that the camp was a very bad
one, as it was in the centre of a box scrub, with native
huts near.

"On further examination we found," says M'Kinlay,
"the tracks of camels and horses, evidently tied up a
long time ago. Between that and the grave we found
another grave, evidently dug with a spade or shovel,
and a lot of human hair of two colours that had been
decomposed. I fancy they must have been all murdered
here. Dug out the new-found grave with a stick, the
only instrument we had, but found no remains of bodies
except a little bone. The black accounted for this in
this manner: he says they had eaten them. Found an
old fire-place, immediately adjoining, with bones very
well burnt, but not in any quantity. In and about the
last-named grave a piece of light blue tweed, with fragments of paper, and small pieces of the *Nautical Almanac*
were found, and an exploded Eley's cartridge. No appearance on any of the trees of bullet marks as if a
struggle had taken place. On a further examination of
the blacks' camp, where the pint pot was found, there
was also found a tin canteen, similar to what is used for
keeping naphtha. Native says that any mems. the
whites had are back on the last camp we were at, and
as well as the ironwork of saddles, &c., which we mean
to recover on our return.

"October 22.—The natives appeared this day, but fled
on seeing the whites. With much difficulty one was
taken, in order to gain something from him about the
circumstance of the grave." On taking him back to the
camp he led them to an old camp, and then took up a
quantity of baked horse-hair for stuffing saddles, which
King stated had been left where they buried Gray.
He told them that everything of the saddlery was

burned, the ironwork kept, and the other bodies eaten. He stated that there was a pistol north-east of them and a rifle. This was doubtless the rifle left in a hollow tree by Wills, who was unable to carry it further. M'Kinlay sent the native to fetch it, and then marked the tree at the spot. There were tens of thousands of pigeons there ; in fact, since they came north of Lake Torrens, they had been very numerous, and, at the same time, very wary. The native who had left had the marks of many wounds, which he bore upon his person, which M'Kinlay thought evidently caused by shot and two bullets. If this was the case, it could not have been from any contest with Burke. It might have been one of the natives fired on by Wright, at Bulloo, or else one of the Cooper's Creek tribe, which Gregory was obliged to fire on with shot. He did not return that night, and signal fires were seen burning round the party after dark, so that we are not surprised at finding the following entry in the diary : " October 23, 4 a.m.—Just as we were getting up, when it was not| very clear, about forty natives came down, headed by the fellow that was sent for the pistol. They were armed and had torches, and shouted with a good deal of noise, evidently endeavouring to surround us. I immediately ordered them back ; also telling the native that was with me to tell them that if they did not keep back I would fire upon them, which they one and all disregarded. Some were then within a few paces of us, the others at various other distances.

"I requested Hodgkinson and Middleton to be ready with their arms, and fire when desired, seeing nothing else left but to be butchered ourselves. I gave the word "fire." A few of those closest retired a few paces, and being encouraged on to the attack, when we repeated our fire, until several rounds were fired upon them (and no doubt many felt the effects) they did not wholly retire. I am afraid the messenger, the greatest vagabond of the lot, escaped scatheless. They then took to the lake, and a few ran round the westward side of it southwards, whom we favored with a few dropping shots to show the danger they were in by the distance the rifles would carry on the water. They then cleared off, and we finished with them. I then buried the memo. which follows :—

"To the leader of any expedition seeking tidings of Burke and party. Sir,—I reached this water, Lake Massacre, on the 19th inst., and by means of a native guide discovered a European camp, one mile north on the west side of flat; at or near this camp the tracks of camels, horses, and whites were found. Hair apparently belonging to Mr. Wills, Charles Gray, and Mr. Burke or King was picked from the surface of a grave by a spade, and from the skull of a European buried by the natives; others less important, such as a pannikin, oil can, and saddle stuffing have been found. Beware of the natives, upon whom we had to fire. We do not intend to return to Adelaide, but proceed west of north. From information, all Burke's party were killed and eaten."

Thus for M'Kinlay. The mystery about these statements has not been entirely cleared up; but there can be little doubt that the body was that of Gray.

M'Kinlay being satisfied that he had found as much of Burke's party as there was to find, proceeded to fulfil the second part of his instructions, which was to proceed to Lake Eyre, and then to Central Mount Stuart, and carefully to examine the country intervening between Burke and Stuart's tracks. He was to examine the shores of Lake Eyre for indications of gold, and he was to return along Stuart's track to Finnis' Springs, where a depôt of fresh provisions should be established for him.

This party will be returned to when Walker, Landsborough, and Norman's expeditions have been described. The reader must now turn to Western Australia, where, meantime, the work of discovery had been going on.

CHAPTER XXV.

F. GREGORY ON THE NORTH-WEST COAST.

Nickol Bay—The Nickol—The Maitland—The Fortescue—Bad travelling—Desert country — The Hammersley Range — The Ashburton — The Hardey—Capricorn Range—Mount Samson—Mount Bruce—The Sherlock—The Yule—The Strelley—The Shaw—The De Grey—The Oakover—Sandy Desert—The Davis—Breaker Inlet—Return.

THE explorations made in connection with the expedition of Burke and Wills threw every other discovery into the shade, so that it was a long time before the colonial public recognised that most important researches into the geography of the north-west coast had been made about the same time by Mr. F. Gregory. This was the same explorer who, in 1858, had traced the Gascoyne down from the tableland, near the sources of the Murchison, and in doing so had discovered the Edmund, the Lyons, and the Alma, coming from some elevated land to the north-west. The existence of such large rivers, in a country hitherto supposed to be the empire of barrenness and desolation, excited both interest and surprise. No one imagined that there could have been two opinions about that tract. King had explored to the bottom of Exmouth and Cambridge Gulfs, and had left a dreary picture of the country. The narrative of Stokes was not more encouraging, and it was concluded, as a matter of course, that inside the dreary coast-line an absolute desert extended, waterless, arid, and quite destitute of trees. The beach was low and sandy for miles, and there were no rivers of any kind. This was the report of Dampier and the Dutch, and it remained to F. Gregory to remove the erroneous prejudices of two centuries.

It was not, however, until 1861, that the Government of Western Australia were able to follow up these discoveries, by an examination of the country to the north. It was decided, in the first instance, to send a party round by sea to the north coast, and that they should proceed southward and make an examination of the interior. The expedition, commenced under the joint authority of the local and imperial Governments, and aided by private subscriptions, was placed under Mr. F. Gregory. It was to consist of nine men, with twenty horses, and provisions for eight months. On the 23rd April, 1861, the *Dolphin*, a bark chartered for the purpose, sailed from Perth, and after some stoppages at Champion Bay, arrived on the 7th May at North-west Cape. On the 10th they anchored under the south end of Delambre Island, and next day moved to the south-western side of Sloping Head. In passing down the shore, they found that the promontory extending to the north of the Head was an island, and it was called after the vessel.

After a preliminary and rather perilous examination, the vessel was taken to the southern head of Nickol Bay, and then Gregory landed to look about for a good place to disembark the horses. He and his companions walked through mud and coral to a belt of mangroves, and next to a sand-hill just behind. From this to the foot of a range of rugged sandstone hills, there was a loamy plain, about half a mile wide, covered with grass and shrubs. Ascending the range they saw a tidal inlet to the eastward, terminating in a salt marsh. On the second day they went to the south-east, over a grassy plain of light brown loam. At five miles they reached a deep stony watercourse, containing only brackish water. It was an unimportant stream, and did not seem to have a longer course than twenty miles. It was named the Nickol. They now turned westward, recrossing the plain more to the south, and passing several clay-pans, which were all dry and well-grassed. Not meeting any water they returned to the ship.

In the meantime, a very eligible spot was found in the south-west corner of the bay, in a sandy cove, a few

hundred yards behind which was a well of good water,
and abundance of green grass. On the 16th they commenced landing the horses, two at a time, by swimming
them ashore. On the arrival of the first pair, Mr. Hew-
son, the mate of the vessel, was seriously wounded by the
accidental discharge of one of the muskets. Fortunately,
the wound did not prove dangerous, and, with the exception of the delay it caused, resulted in nothing very
grave. The guns were kept loaded because of the
natives, for since their arrival in the bay, several parties
of them had visited the ship. Their conduct at first was
friendly, but one of them was detected aiming his spear
at a horse, and he was fired at. After this they had
become friendly again, but it was necessary to be very
cautious. They had seen white men before, and knew
the use of tobacco.

It was not until the 21st that all the horses were
landed, and by the 25th the party started. Their first
care was to cross the marsh, or salt-water inlet to the
eastward, and then they resumed the southerly course.
Their journey was over an extensive low grassy plain,
of a red loam, with some small watercourses. On the
second day they reached one much more important than
the others, named the Maitland. It was sixty yards
wide, with beautiful grassy banks. It came from
the south-east, through plains very liable to inundation,
terminating in some ranges which lay before them.
In order to cross any stream which might come down
from these hills, the party proceeded to the westward of
south. They soon crossed a dry stream bed, sixty yards
wide, coming from a granite range to the southward,
while at every step the country became more barren.
In the afternoon of the 27th it began to rain heavily,
just after they had crossed a watercourse, and as the
rain continued, they camped at another a little further
on. The rain flooded this so rapidly that their camp
fire was swept away by it, and before the explorers
could remove anything there was a foot of water in the
tent. Such rapid floods show the very transient nature
of the drainage, and is a pretty good proof that the
ground is too barren to support much grass or timber.

The day after this storm was nearly occupied in drying the stores, so that they did not get beyond the next watercourse they met. Beyond this there was a plain extending as far as the eye could reach to the north-west, and covered with spinifex and stones, in fact, with a painful family likeness to all the deserts of the interior of Australia. It was utterly unfit for any purpose, and especially for travelling, because the spini- fex grass made the horses suffer severely. At thirteen miles they struck the channel of a considerable river coming from the south. It was about two hundred yards wide, and, apparently, at times a very important stream. As Gregory was now in long. 116°, he did not wish to go any further to the west, so he determined to trace up the new river to the southward. It was called the Fortescue, after the Under Secretary of State for the Colonies.

· Soon after starting, on the 30th, they came upon a camp of natives, who fled precipitously, and would not hold any parley; but it was at any rate a good sign of the country that there were inhabitants. Five miles beyond, the river turned abruptly to the north-east, through a precipitous rocky defile. It was far too rough a road for the horses to face, if a better could be found, and some little time was lost in making the search. But after being involved for some time in im- practicable ravines, they were obliged to return to the stream, and follow up its bed. This was a very difficult road. Not only was the bed very stony, but it was blocked up by large stones which greatly impeded their progress. The general course was east and south, but extremely winding. The banks were rocky and pre- cipitous, and bore flood-marks thirty feet above the level of the water, which was running in a channel thirty yards wide, while the river valley was at least a quarter of a mile. As they went up, the country im- proved, the valley being diversified by beautiful new shrubs and flowers. But the travelling, was still very bad for the horses. It was useless, however, to think of quitting the valley, for except in its immediate vicinity, the land was destitute of grass and water, or trees of any kind. Hills of sandstone frequently jutted out into the river bed, and as they neared the sources, these began to hem them in on every side. By the 5th, the channel narrowed rapidly until it was walled in by perpendicular cliffs. Gregory did not like to go further up such a gorge, so he returned. During the previous two days they had caught sight occasionally of an elevated range of hills, about ten miles to the southward, extending parallel to the stream for a long distance. Gregory determined to go towards these hills, and he left the river and came to the top of the tablehills through which it ran. In ascending the sides of the valley, he found that the country for many miles was intersected by deep ravines, terminating to the south in a level plain, which extended to the base of the range. It certainly must have been a singular country, and these rocky gorges remind one forcibly of the rocky table-land of Africa and Arabia. When after four hours' toiling they reached the top of the plain, it was like the desert tracts of Western Australia. At first it was covered with Acacia, and stony, but it became better as they advanced, until the whole plains were thickly grassed. The surface was scattered over with the black seeds (about the size of a pea) of a small white convol-vulus, which grew abundantly. Near the foot of the range the ground became stony, and covered with spinifex, but with good grass in the ravines.

This then was the character of the plains up from the sea to the ranges they had now reached. There were sixty miles of poor open pastoral country, inter-sected by numerous small stream beds rising up in low stony ranges : then the Fortescue ran for seventy miles through a hilly, very stony sandstone country, and lastly, after ten miles of grassy plains, they had reached a fine range of hills, named the Hammersley Range. They pushed up one of the valleys to find a pass, but soon came upon steep and rocky masses terminating in cliffs five hundred or six hundred feet high, and extending, without a break, ten or fifteen miles along the face of the range. These cliffs were of sandstone, horizontally stratified, and in the form of their fortress-like escarp-

ments one would recognise the usual accompaniments of
tablehills already so well typified by Mount Cockburn
in Cambridge Gulf, and M'Adam Range on the Victoria
River. In fact, this character seemed to be one of
the marked features of all the ranges on the north
coast.

Finding that it was impossible to cross the range,
the explorers took a north-east course, and struck the
Fortescue many miles above the glen where they had
left it. The valley was again open and grassy, with
rich banks of black soil, well-grassed, and shaded by
handsome fan palms, with leaves eight or ten feet long.
The river had opened into deep reaches of water, and
the character of the country was evidently improved.
At five or six miles, however, it broke up all at once
into numerous channels in a well-grassed fertile forest
of white gum trees, and became lost in an open plain.
For a time the explorers could find no further trace of
the river, as it disappeared in open flats extending to
the base of the Hammersley Range. The waters
evidently spread out over these for miles in the rainy
season, leaving shallow pools and a rich deposit of
warp. On the 11th, a channel from the range seemed
again to offer the hope of finding a pass to the southward. They accordingly went up a rocky gully, clothed
with the terrible porcupine grass, and they had to make
what sort of a camp they could amid such an undergrowth in latitude 22° 12'. Next morning they were
stopped, at first by an impassable barrier of cliffs, but
on trying more to the eastward came upon the main
channel of the Fortescue, which led them through the
range at last.

But still it was not easy to follow the river. In a
very short time their progress was stopped again, but
this time by the deep and large pools of water in the
stream. While a camp was being formed at this obstacle,
Gregory ascended one of the highest summits of the
range, at an elevation of two thousand seven hundred
feet above the level of the sea, and seven hundred above
the river. There was a fine view to the southward
over an open plain, and Gregory observed that by fol-

lowing up a small dry ravine to the south-east, there
would be a fair prospect of getting to it. They reached
it on the 13th, after scrambling through the intervening
rocks, like so many goats. The plain appeared to be
much more elevated than those on the other side, and
was drained by several deep creeks in the range. As
they went south-south-west the land was at first stony
and covered with spinifex—that bane of the Australian
continent. Subsequently, however, the soil became
better, with fair pasture, and abundance of water in the
pools of a stream coming from the south-east. The
elevation of the land made the air clear and bracing,
and the nights cold. On the second day's journey the
plain was covered by rocky ridges, and the elevation
by the barometer was seen to be two thousand four
hundred feet above the sea. On the 14th June, night
overtook them in a rocky ravine without grass or
water.

They followed this gully on the 15th until the afternoon, but not finding water, turned more to the northward. This brought them to a small pool in a
streamlet, where the camp was pitched until the 17th.
On that day they resumed their south-west course, following the stream down to an improving country to
lat. 22° 51'. But they had to encamp without water.
There were hills to the east of their track, which rose a
thousand feet above the channel, consisting of metamorphic sandstone with shales, intersected by trap
dykes, and capped by red conglomerate. Nine miles
next day brought them to a patch of nice green grass,
upon which they halted, while Gregory, with one companion, went to a prominent hill six miles to the south.
From its summit they could see plains and detached
ranges to the southward. On their return to the party,
Gregory got the pleasing news that water had been
found during his absence. They did not move from
this next day, owing to the illness of Mr. Gregory,
who had been trying experiments as to the alimentary
properties of certain seeds he had met with.

By the 21st June the horses had become so distressed
for want of water, and from sore feet, that Gregory

formed a depôt camp, while he proceeded with a light party to explore the country between the range and the Lyons River. He left on the 22nd, with three men, seven horses, and fourteen gallons of water, and provisions for eight days. Travelling thus much quicker, they got through thirty miles of dry stony country, and then reached a large river, coming from the eastward. It was named the Ashburton, after the President of the Geographical Society. Gregory gave this name because—from the large extent of pasture land on its banks, and the extent from Exmouth Gulf to an unknown distance eastward—it seemed destined to become an important part of the province. The ordinary channel was only a hundred yards wide, with reaches of water in it lined with bamboo; but there were marks to show that during the summer rains the water was from four hundred to eight hundred yards wide, inundating the plains for more than a mile on either bank. Gregory followed it as long as it continued to the south of west, but it soon turned north-west, and appeared to flow towards Exmouth Gulf, joined by the Hardey, as the river at the depôt had been named.

From the Ashburton to the south the country became more rugged and mountainous. They kept up a stony ravine towards a range which was the same as one seen from the Lyons River in 1858. Gregory soon became involved amongst its sharp and steep ridges of slaty schist. He was obliged to camp that night in an awfully rugged country on a small tributary of the Ashburton. His situation was now upon the tropical line, and he therefore named the hills the Capricorn—a name not only due to its position, but also probably with special reference to the only animals for which such hills seem to be designed.

A rough ride on the 24th to the south-east brought the explorers to a watercourse sixty yards wide, and trending to the north-east. This contained water, and was traced to a deep gorge in a sandstone range. Next day, the country continued hilly for about ten miles, when they got to the summit of a granite and sandstone tableland, at the extreme sources of the watercourse

they had been following. From this there was a fine
view. They could see, eighty miles below them, the
summit of Mount Augustus, while more to the westward other portions of his former route could be discerned. The prospect, too, was a fair one. No longer
the desolate scrubs, the granite rocks, and distant trap
ranges of the rest of the western coast, but a series of
gently swelling green and well-wooded downs, smiling
under a blue sky and a brilliantly clear atmosphere.
There was only one range now between Gregory and
the Lyons, and there was a remarkable gorge in it,
which he went forward to examine. It was found to
be an almost perpendicular cut through a narrow ridge
three hundred feet deep, and not two hundred yards
long. From the summit of this pass the course of the
stream could be traced across the fertile flats of the
Lyons, until it was lost in its numerous channels.

Gregory having now connected his survey with that
of 1858, commenced to return to the depôt camp. He
kept more to the eastward on his way back, and then,
instead of going through the Capricorn Range, followed
the stream all the way to the Ashburton across a good
country. The junction was in lat. 22° 26'. South
of it, they passed easily round the end of the range,
in which they found a pool with fish in a rocky gorge.
They then crossed the Ashburton, and pushed across
open plains. They camped without water, seventeen
miles from the depôt, which they reached next day.

The whole party rested on the last day of June.
As the provisions were not much reduced, Gregory
would have gone eastward before returning to Nickol
Bay, but the pitiable state of the horses' hoofs prevented
this. They commenced marching back on their old
tracks, but when they reached the Hammersley Range,
Gregory determined to pass through the range, and
coming out on the beach to the east of the bay, follow
the coast-line to the ship. As they went back, several
of the most prominent peaks were ascended, and amongst
others, Mount Samson, a hill which gave a view over
seventy miles of the surrounding country. There was
one hill named Mount Bruce, which Gregory thought

was the most elevated in Western Australia. It was estimated to be about four thousand feet above the sea level.

When they re-entered the range, the country was of rather an inferior description for twenty miles. They then struck for the coast, intending to make it somewhere between Breaker Inlet and Depuch Island. On the 9th, they travelled across the plain to the foot of some low hills of trap and sandstone covered with spinifex, but with good feed in the valleys. Here they met a small tributary of the Fortescue, which they traced to its source in lat. 21° 41', and camped at a little pool of water. The country next day continued ascending gently for seven miles. The sandstone was replaced by boulders of trap, yielding a very rich soil and clothed with grass, but rather stony. In this respect the land always seemed to maintain a uniform character and the horses proportionally suffered. There were, however, abundance of small wild melons, edible, but bitter. When they had traversed the slope for some distance, the plain suddenly dropped to the northward, and they descended a rocky ravine with water and grass. It was the bed of a small stream. It flowed northwards for about ten miles, taking the explorers down a valley from two hundred to three hundred feet deep. For ten miles more it was diverted to the eastward by a cross range of black volcanic hills of loose rugged rocks, totally devoid of vegetation. Once past this, and the channel received several tributaries, becoming a succession of fine open pools of water, sometimes a hundred and fifty yards in width. There was very little grass upon this stream, which was named the Sherlock.

On the 12th the river resumed a course only a little west of north, and very soon led into an open sandy plain which absorbed it. There were, however, many flood channels, though widely separated, and all marked by a line of trees. Selecting the most promising of these, they journeyed down to lat. 21° 6', where a solitary pool of brackish water induced them to camp. Here they found some natives catching birds by means of neatly constructed nets—the only instance, I believe, of any such hunting contrivance among them. Next day the river turned west, through sandy and stony tracts of country for seven or eight miles, when it was joined by a fine channel coming from the south, and there were two reaches of water, with abundance of game upon them. While the party rested on this spot, Gregory and two companions walked, on the 14th, to the summit of a black range, one mile from the camp, on the western bank of the river. The hills were composed of rough scoriaceous sandstone, raised three hundred or four hundred feet above the plain, and quite barren. There were many deep fissures in the rocks, which were not volcanic. Beyond them, the Sherlock went over very stony country, with boundless plains to the north and east, interrupted only by occasional hills.

The land was so very stony all through that the horses suffered much, and one, whose hoofs were completely worn through, was abandoned. He was left in the midst of feed and water, but on returning, eighteen days later, the explorers found him dead on the spot where he was left. The country, for the last twenty miles, on approaching the sea, opened out into extensive grassy flats, occasionally inundated by the river, yielding, even at that dry period of the year a large quantity of fine pasture. The arable portion of this tract was estimated by Gregory at nearly thirty thousand acres, well watered by the river and several tributaries, which joined from the rugged volcanic ranges bordering the last forty or fifty miles of its left bank. When the party reached the sea, they were about forty miles from Nickol Bay, and as it was very doubtful whether water could be procured in that distance, Gregory determined on following up a leading valley of the Maitland. In the event of not finding water, he intended to pass through the heavy masses of hills which backed Cape Lambert, and by pushing round the heads of the river, to return by their outward track. This course they were, however, spared by finding water eighteen miles from their camp. After a desperate push through some stony country, which added fearfully to the sufferings

2 E 2

of the almost hoofless horses, they arrived at the ship
on the 19th July. They found that the mate of the
vessel had nearly recovered from his wound, and all
had gone on well during their absence.

On the 29th Gregory started again. As he had
now only nineteen horses, he could only take eighty-
seven days' provisions, at the rate of one pound of flour,
seven ounces of meat, and four ounces of sugar daily
per man. On the 2nd August they reached the camp
on the Sherlock, where they had left the horse; and
on the 5th they struck away from the river, taking
a south-east course over open plains, nearly all covered
with spinifex grass. At eighteen miles, they fell in
with stony ranges, in which but little water was found.
At one of the water-holes there was a native, who sig-
nified that they would find water to the southward, but
none to the east. Gregory was determined, notwithstanding, to try, but he had to camp one night in a
ravine of the ranges without water. The country
seemed so dry in advance that they went next day in a
south-west direction, and at four miles came upon a
south-east branch of the Sherlock, just at a point where
it emerged from the hills. They followed this up for
seven miles. It divided into numerous small dry ravines in the heart of an elevated range of granite,
capped by metamorphic sandstone.

Gregory now fell back upon a part of the stream
where there was water, and formed a depôt, while he,
with two companions, searched to the eastward for an
available route. Passing through the ranges, they
came upon a dry north-east watercourse. It was followed for fifteen miles, and then they went over twelve
miles of desert, camping at last in the midst of it, with
sandstones and spinifex all round, but no water.
Next day, however, there was better luck. An hour's
travelling brought them to a river, with a sandy bed,
about three hundred yards wide. There were a few
ponds of water in it, under a sandstone bluff, which rose
abruptly three hundred feet above the plain, adding to
the desert an appearance of ruin as well as desolation.
The river came through a gap in a granite range four

miles away. At this there was plenty of water and
grass, and as the river (the Yule) seemed to offer a
good chance of travelling to the south-east, they went
back to the depôt, and moved up the whole party on
the 13th.

On the 14th Gregory, with two companions, commenced travelling up the stream. As walking near the
bed was rendered very laborious by drift sand, they
steered direct for a pass in the range, about twenty
miles distant. This, however, was not the bed of the
river, and they had to turn south-west in order to reach
it. The character of the stream, when found, was still
the same. Its channels were numerous, and water was
easily obtainable by digging for a few inches. Giant
ant-hills were plentiful, and altogether the scene was of
a very tropical character. The river soon turned eastward, and had many tributaries. Towards evening,
on the 16th, they found that the main channel had
escaped them, and they were only on a small tributary,
which divided into numerous valleys. Water, however,
was still easily found by digging. There were many
natives seen about, which showed the good character of
the country; but they were extremely shy, and no information could be obtained for them. But the little
party had all they wanted, and water did not fail them
as they went on. Four hours' easy travelling on the
17th brought them well into a range where there was a
fine pool of water. It was above five hundred or six
hundred feet above the plain, and composed of the
usual sandstone or granite. There were some remarkably picturesque rocky glens as they descended, and,
what was still better, several springs and pools of water,
leading to a fine grassy flat. They camped there one
day, in lat. 21° 36', long. 119° 13'.

On the 19th they followed down the stream upon
which they were camped, although it trended slightly to
the north. In a few miles the valley widened, with fine
pools of permanent water, and abundance of game.
At eight miles it joined a wide valley from the south,
down which flowed a river divided into several
channels, containing pools still gently running from one

to another. The banks were well grassed, but very
stony, and the rocks full of so many clefts and
fissures that the horses had to jump from one to another
like goats. This was surely another Capricorn Range.
The river was named the Strelley. They left it on the
20th, for an easterly course, crossing many stream beds
well grassed, but the country remained hilly and stony.
At night they encamped in a romantic glen, hemmed in
by cliffs a hundred and fifty feet high, under which were
pools of water, and fish, which, from their shape, earned
the unromantic name of Glen Herring for the pass.
The whole of this locality, with its deserts, its streams,
its stony valley, and rocky glens, reminds one of the
descriptions of Arabia Petræa. Nothing could be more
solemn than the chasm in which the explorers camped,
whose dark, precipitous walls threw back the gleaming
of their camp-fire, and echoed the sound of their voices
with gloomy grandeur.

Glen Herring Creek carried them eight or nine
miles to the eastward, when it joined a fine river two
hundred yards wide, coming from the southward through
extensive grassy plains, the limits of which could not be
discovered in any direction. This river, says Mr.
Gregory, from its size and quantity, would have afforded a good opportunity of passing into the interior,
but the season was now too far advanced to admit of
their making the attempt without interfering with the
primary object before them—of penetrating far enough
to decide the question of the drainage of Central Australia. Naming the stream the Shaw, after the late
secretary of the Geographical Society, they pushed to
the eastward, up a considerable tributary, penetrating
into an elevated tableland. The ascent of this, on the
23rd, proved very distressing to the packhorses, more
especially as they had again to descend into rocky
ravines leading to the eastward. Once over the tableland, and they emerged into open plains extending to
the north. Gregory now determined to follow the
southern edge of the plain until a stream could be met
leading to the east. A few miles brought them to a small
watercourse running gently from some springs in the

plain, not, however, from the hills, but back into them.
There was plenty of grass about, so they rested one
day.

The stream they were upon led through the hills
and over plains until, on the 26th, they again found
themselves on the banks of a fine stream running to the
north-east. It was traced next day for ten or twelve
miles, receiving many tributaries. Altogether, it formed
an important river, and on account of the large extent
of good land found upon its banks, was named the
De Grey, in honour of the former president of the
Geographical Society. Leaving this stream for the
present, they again made to the eastward, passing on to
a precipitous tableland, with but little feed, though
water was obtainable by digging. They became much
involved in deep ravines before they got to the highest
level, and no sooner had they done so, than they had
to descend equally precipitous gullies to the eastward.
Two of the horses became disabled by the stony nature
of the soil, and, in easing their loads, three of the party
had to take their turn in walking. Five miles from the
range they reached a sandy stream bed, and then an
immense grassy plain succeeded, which they did not
finish crossing until the evening of the 29th. The
only elevations on this immense plain of waving white
grass were to the southward, and these were, as usual,
granite capped with sandstone. At the opposite side
of the plain was a river running to the northward, in a
channel two hundred yards wide. The explorer described
the scenery in the vicinity of the river as of most pleasing character. Undulating plains of long grass extended far away to the northward, while the banks of
the stream were overhung by a broad belt of cajeput, or
tea-tree (*Melaleuca*), whose rich foliage afforded them a
delicious shade during the many days they subsequently
followed its picturesque windings. It was named the
Oakover. The horses were too tired to attempt some
ranges to the eastward, so Gregory followed the
channel. At the end of two days, during which the
country had improved, and the game become very
abundant, it turned too much to the west to suit the

explorers. They camped for one day at the foot of a range to recruit the animals before again venturing to the eastward.

On the 2nd September they entered the range by a somewhat easy pass, and soon found a pool of water in a tributary of the Oakover, whose junction they had passed as they ascended. In the evening they got through the range. A new and far from agreeable prospect lay before them: all around, from north to south, they could see only open sandy plains of vast extent, nothing being visible but low ridges of red drift sand, nearly bare of vegetation. It was just such another scene as the Central Desert of Sturt, which he believed was unequalled in desolation by any other portion of the earth's surface. It was not, however, destitute of inhabitants, even if deprived of every other kind of life. A large party of natives were encamped upon the watercourse down which the explorers had descended into the plain. In order not to alarm them, Gregory camped below, amid abundance of grass, but destitute of water. Next morning it was found that the blacks had decamped, leaving behind them the most of their household (?) goods. Among the spoils was a helmet similar to that mentioned by Stuart as used by the natives of Northern Australia.

From their camp, Gregory made an effort to move over the red sandy desert, desolate and impracticable as it appeared. The reality was even worse than the appearance. The sand ridges were exactly like what has been so often described in connection with other desert explorations in Australia. The drifts, in this case, ran in parallel straight lines several hundred yards apart; the sand being thrown by the south-east gales into sharp ridges, thirty to sixty feet high. There was no vegetation upon them but spinifex and stunted gum trees, and, altogether, the soft sand, the tangled, distressing grass, and the perpetual ascending and descending, made it terrible work for all. After about eighteen miles of this travelling, Gregory halted. The horizon was still unbroken, except by the isolated granite hills, and there seemed to be not the slightest chance of water by pushing on. The horses, too, were much distressed. Very reluctantly, Gregory at last determined to fall back upon the pool of the preceding camp, and, having formed a depôt there, to examine the country for some route across the sand.

They returned to the pool on the 4th. Next day, while the horses were resting, Gregory walked round the plains at the foot of the range for ten or twelve miles, in search of a watercourse. He returned quite unsuccessful. Leaving five men in the depôt, with instructions to remain three days, and then, as there was very little water, to fall back upon the Oakover, he started with two companions and six horses, on the 6th. After keeping along the range for six or eight miles in a fruitless search for watercourses, he struck to the eastward between the sand ridges. At fifteen miles, the horses showed signs of failing. Distant ranges were now visible to the east, and a granite range about ten miles to the south. To go to the distant range would have been a great risk; while to go to the granite rocks would take them a most fatiguing ride across the sand ridges, with very little hopes of water at the end of the journey. The latter course, was, however, adopted. They only made four miles by nightfall, for the horses were very much distressed. At three miles, next day, one of them gave in. The others were nearly quite exhausted. Leaving the almost dying horse under the shade of the only tree they could find, the others were driven on by two of the men on foot, while Gregory proceeded in advance to search for water. Two hours' heavy toiling through the sand, brought him to the ranges; but there was no relief there. In terrible anxiety, he searched from one ravine to another all to no purpose. There was not a sign of moisture, and the awful aridity was like a sentence of death to the party. The heat was scorching, being over 100° F. By the time Gregory was joined by his companions, he was so exhausted that he could barely carry his arms and ammunition. The horses were in a pitiable state, and when the sad truth was told, the men camped with them upon a little patch of grass, with no water, except a small supply in the kegs. There was little time for deliberation; indeed, there was no need of it. The only chance of saving the animals now, was to abandon everything, and make all haste for the depôt, from which they were now thirty-two miles distant.

After a night of great anxiety, they started at dawn to return. At first, in the cool morning, they made some progress; but when the sun got up, the horses could be scarcely got along. They carried nothing but the saddles and the firearms, and yet they could scarcely stagger over the sand-hills. The explorers were little better. Mr. Gregory was so reduced from his journey of the day before, that he could not keep up with the rest. To add to their anxiety, they had no provisions, and it was feared that before they could reach the depôt their companions would have fallen back on the Oak-over River. In this case, their fate was sealed. They would then be certainly left in the desert to starve to death. To avoid such a terrible event, Mr. Brown (one of the party) was sent forward with the horses in the hope of reaching the depôt before their companions were gone. All now depended upon this effort. Mr. Brown soon got far ahead, and after a fearful march, Gregory and his companion reached within nine miles of the depôt by nightfall. All along the latter part of their track, they found the ground strewn with saddles, guns, and other accoutrements, showing how Mr. Brown had been obliged to sacrifice everything to get the horses a few miles further. At dawn, the two men moved on with little hope of travelling far, unless assistance were sent out to them. But help was near at hand. At four miles, they met Mr. Brown with fresh horses. He had reached the depôt the preceding evening with only one horse; the others having dropped behind, one by one, close to the end of his journey.

He now went back to recover the things left upon the track; but it was useless to attempt to rescue the stores, &c., left at the granite range. The whole party were soon again united at the depot; but two of the horses were never recovered. This trip convinced

Gregory of the impossibility of crossing the Sandy Desert with the means then at his disposal. This was very mortifying, as many circumstances convinced him that he was near some large river which emptied itself upon the north-west coast. He even supposed that the sand of the small desert he had just seen had been derived from water, and mentioned that the pebbles and *detritus* had a decidedly waterworn appearance. This latter circumstance will hardly, however, convince those who are aware that waterworn pebbles occur in far greater abundance in the African and Arabian deserts, which have certainly not been under water within the knowledge of man. But Gregory was probably right about a better country, and a river existing to the eastward, for he mentions having seen native fires in that direction. Finding it impossible to advance, they fell back to the tributary of the Oakover, named the Davis, on the 11th, and from thence to the main stream. The most promising route left open to Gregory, and in fact the only one now that a passage to the eastward was closed, appeared to be to follow down the Oakover to the northward. Accordingly, the party commenced its survey by easy stages, travelling through a very fertile country. The distance between the banks became gradually wider and the water more abundant, until in lat. 20° 36', when it was joined by the De Grey, coming from the south-east. The junction was reached on the 18th. The De Grey then came through a beautiful tract of level ground, with a broad belt of flooded gum trees growing on the sides. Passing through a river gorge about a quarter of a mile wide and a mile long, they came upon a camp of natives. But they could not communicate with them. As soon as the explorers were seen, the whole tribe dispersed in the greatest alarm. Two miles below their dwellings, the party camped upon the banks of a deep tributary from the southward. In the two days following no other streams were crossed; but the De Grey meanwhile ran nearly west, through about thirty-eight miles of open grassy plains of great extent, like the plains they had met with in the upper part of its course.

The channel was sandy, and contained abundance of water.

Shortly after starting, on the 21st, they crossed the bed of a tributary coming from the southward. It was a shallow sandy channel, draining, as Gregory thought, the high ranges between the De Grey and Shaw rivers. Distant ranges were visible to the north and south, while the river still kept a westerly course. Such good country was, of course, not without inhabitants, and many signs of the natives were seen. That evening, they surprised and frightened away a camp who were enjoying a rather miscellaneous supper. It consisted of fish, rats, beans, grass-seed cake, and a beverage made from some oily substance. There was variety there, at any rate. The natives resented the disturbance they had suffered in their luxuriant repast. Next day, they chased the horses and threw spears at them, so that they had to be scared away by firing a rifle over their heads.

Following the river, on the 23rd, it soon passed round the southern foot of a range four hundred or five hundred feet high; the country to the south being very fertile. At ten miles, they struck the Shaw River coming from the south-east, with a broad, deep, and well-defined channel, in which were many fine pools of water. Below the confluence, the De Grey widened out considerably, turning more to the northward, and seven miles further was joined by the Strelley, in lat. 20° 16', long. 119° 5'. The river was then turned to the northward by a rugged range of volcanic hills, and was now making direct for Breaker Inlet, from which it was only eighteen miles distant. Gregory ascended this range, which lay to the westward of his camp. The hills were only about five hundred feet high; but they commanded an extensive view. To the south, the glaring sun shone over a vast undulating plain, interrupted by detached granite and sandstone peaks; while narrow green lines of trees in various directions, indicated watercourses between the distant ranges and the sea. The course of the Strelley could be traced for many miles. To the

north, the De Grey could be seen, winding towards
Breaker Inlet; the position of which could be faintly
traced by the mangroves fringing the delta of the
stream. To the east and west the prospect was much
fairer than any explorer would have expected to find.
There was a wide expanse of fine alluvial flats, interrupted by detached forests of the never-failing flooded
gum tree.

As they traced down the lower portion of the De
Grey, it divided into two channels. They followed the
eastern one, and camped where it was brackish from the
ocean tides. A well was dug in the sand-banks at
the side, and fresh water easily obtained. The latter
part of the journey had been particularly heavy, in consequence of the numerous rat-holes, which completely
undermined the banks of the river for a quarter of a
mile back on both sides. In this respect, it was very
like the Barcoo; and it would be interesting to ascertain if the species were the same. In other respects, the
camp was not very eligible. In the morning, the water
in the well was quite salt, and they had to turn back to
the western channel. In doing so, they came to another
branch which joined again lower down, forming a large
alluvial island, named Ripon Island. When the party
were fairly on the fresh water of the western channel,
Gregory started with two companions, to examine the
mouth of the river. He found it to be, for the last
mile, between four hundred and eight hundred yards
wide, with depth sufficient to admit vessels of fourteen
feet draught, at full tide. Captain Stokes had been deterred from an examination of this inlet, in consequence
of seeing what he considered to be breakers. These
were, probably, waves caused by the in-coming tide
against the stream. Gregory had an illustration of
this; for while completing his observations, the roaring
of the rising waters warned him to return to his horses.
In spite of every haste, the muddy creeks filled so
fast, that he was barely able to reach the banks. It was
an oozy, dreary place. In addition to the mangroves,
the low coast, and the salt marshes, there was a rank-
ness about the fertility, which one would expect in such

a locality under the tropics. Gregory noticed abundance of fish rising with the tide, and among them one with long fins which could run along like a lizard on the mud banks, and take a leap of five or six feet.

When he reached the camp, Gregory went, on the 27th, to explore the plains to the eastward, towards a mountain which he had named Mount Blaze. For several miles after leaving Ripon Island, the country continued fertile, because liable to inundation from the river; when, however, that was left, the soil became lighter, with patches of spinifex and samphire. At twelve miles, he entered open grassy forest, but without water, and after turning northward in search of it, he returned.

He now thought of retracing his steps, and with this view, moved back the camp to the junction of the Strelley. He determined, before leaving this river for the Yule, to trace it up to its sources, or, at least, to the ranges from which it appeared to flow. In following it up, they found that, at first, the river spread through many channels, but gradually united to form a stream, one hundred yards wide. The country around was poor and barren. On the 2nd of October, they passed a considerable tributary coming from the southeast, but quite dry. It came from a bold granite range, ten or twelve miles to the southward, forming, as Gregory thought, a part of the main tableland; the plain they had been passing over being only a sea-flat, with a few detached ranges scattered over its surface. In this case, it would be fertile only on the banks of the rivers. As they skirted the ranges, they crossed several streams.

They came, on the 4th, to where the channel of the river divided; the main one coming from a deep gorge on the south-east; the western one leading to the Yule. The latter they followed. No water was found in its bed, and they soon traced it to its sources. They then struck westward for the Yule. The journey thence was a most painful one for the horses, for the plains were very arid and stony. But one large watercourse was passed, and the banks of this possessed the only fertile land that was seen. They rested two days at the Yule, and then made another push for the Sherlock, over twenty-five miles of waterless country. By making every exertion to carry water, this was accomplished in two days; and then, with some little trouble from the natives and the loss of one horse, they regained the ship on the 17th of October. This terminated their explorations. By the 23rd, all the horses, stores, &c., were re-shipped; and on the 9th of November the whole party were landed in safety at Swan River.

Mr. Gregory's opinions about the physical features of this part of the country are well worth insertion here, for their precision and value as generalizations. He considered that the territory which came under his observation consisted of a succession of terraces, rising inland for nearly two hundred miles, more or less broken by volcanic hills towards the coast. The first belt averages ten to forty miles in width from the sea, and is a nearly level plain, slightly ascending to the southward, with an elevation of from forty to one hundred feet. The soil varied according as it was derived from volcanic or granite rocks. Proceeding inland, for the next fifty miles is a granite country originally capped with sandstone, with an elevation of one thousand feet. This range terminates to the southward in level plains of good soil, produced from the next elevated terrace, and the south side is composed of dykes and the usual metamorphic accompaniments.

In about lat. 22°, they came upon another elevated range, having an altitude of two thousand five hundred feet above the sea, and trending to the south-east. This, unlike the last section, has a southern escarpment of about five or six hundred feet, and consists of horizontal sandstone and conglomerates. Its width is eight or ten miles; the southern flanks being bordered by fertile valleys of loamy clays, merging gradually to the southward in stony ridges and hills, some having an elevation of four thousand feet; the culminating point being Mount Bruce, in lat. 22° 30'. From this point, the country gradually falls to the Ashburton, the bed of which river is about sixteen hundred feet above the

sea, and the adjoining ranges about twenty-two hundred
feet, or the same as the country about the Lyons, Gascoyne, and Upper Murchison.

The greatest credit is due to Mr. F. Gregory for
the bold, intrepid manner in which this expedition was
conducted; during which, the extent of country explored, and the knowledge obtained of the rivers, was
far beyond what could have been expected from his resources. Of course, the discovery of so much good
land on the north-west coast was delightful news to the
colonists at Perth. Indeed, it made a great impression
in all the colonies, for it entirely altered the opinions
about that part of Australia. Doubtless, we shall see,
in a few years, a flourishing colony located there; since,
early in 1863, squatters had already commenced to
occupy it with their flocks and herds.

While F. Gregory was exploring on the north-
west coast, Mr. A. Dempster, with a small party, went
further to the eastward (in lat. 31°) than any previous
explorer. He found the usual succession of sandy
plains, scrubs, granite rocks, and salt lakes. Georgina's
range was one of the furthest points reached, and there
the country underwent a manifest improvement. The
soil was rich and the grass excellent, but the saline
basins increased to such an extent that a perfect chain
of them could be seen to the eastward from the mountains. In other respects this expedition did not alter
the impressions that previously existed with reference
to this part of the interior.

CHAPTER XXVI.

NORMAN AT CARPENTARIA.

The *Victoria* and *Firefly* proceed to Carpentaria—Wreck of the *Firefly*—Albert River—Landsborough starts—The Gregory—M'Adam's Creek—Premier Range—The O'Shannassy—Other creeks--Elliot Creek—The watershed—Southerly waters—Mary Lake—Herbert River—Douglas and other rivers—Return to the Albert—Walker arrives with tidings of Burke—Landsborough starts again.

AFTER having directed the reader's attention for a while to the north-west coast, we must now return to the all-absorbing topic in Australia at this time—the search for Burke and Wills. It will be borne in mind that a great many expeditions were to be sent from different colonies with a view to find some traces of the lost explorers. They have been already enumerated, but may be again briefly described here. Howitt was to search the Bar-coo, M'Kinlay was to start from Lake Torrens, Walker was to cross from Rockhampton, and Norman was to go round the coast to Carpentaria, and send Landsborough to the centre from the north side. The search of Howitt has been already described, and we now proceed to deal with that of Norman and Landsborough.

Captain Norman, having made the necessary prepa-rations at Brisbane, started in the *Victoria*, with the *Firefly* in company, on the 24th August, 1861. Their destination was the Investigator Roads of Flinders, and there two vessels, the *Gratia* and *Native Lass*, were to meet them with coals, and a further supply of provi-sions. The voyage from Brisbane to the Barrier Reef was very successful, having been made in eight days, and the explorers were congratulating themselves on their speedy arrival, when a fearful gale separated the two vessels. The *Firefly* struggled hard against the

gale for several days, and managed to work her course
through the intricate shoals and banks of Torres Straits.
After passing innumerable dangers, she anchored under
Sir Charles Hardy's Islands, but the sea was so high
that both her anchors parted, and she became a complete
wreck upon a coral reef. This was a very disastrous
commencement for the expedition. The cargo of the
Firefly was indispensable to the success of the undertaking. All Landsborough's party and provisions were
on board, besides the horses. Fortunately, twenty-
five of the latter were saved, and as the vessel was left
high and dry by the tide, the provisions were recovered. By the time that the party were safely landed
and housed under tents, the *Victoria* hove in sight.
Captain Norman thought it possible that the wreck
might be repaired sufficiently to get her afloat, and used
as a hulk at the Albert River. With this view the
crew were set to work, and soon put her into some sort
of repair. The loss of the stores and provisions through
the disaster of the *Firefly* obliged Captain Norman to
reduce the allowance of rations, and by that timely precaution the main objects of the expedition were in a fair
way of being still successfully carried out.

On the 12th September the wreck was got afloat,
and having reshipped the horses, the *Victoria* took it
in tow. On the 29th, they anchored in Investigator
Roads, and found the brig *Gratia* and the schooner
already waiting for them. Upon examination, it was
seen that the wreck could be got into the Albert River
far enough to land the horses. This was accordingly
done, and the animals brought ashore some twenty miles
up the stream. The vessel was then taken a mile and a
half further, and a permanent depôt was formed where
she was moored.

It was now determined to despatch Landsborough's
party to the south-west, hoping that in a course bearing
towards Stuart's Central Mount, Burke's tracks would be
found, if he had come so far to the northward. While
the outfit was preparing, Captain Norman made a preliminary examination of the river, so far as he could go,
in a boat. As he proceeded up, he found the track of

Gregory, made in 1855, but no record. He visited the Plains of Promise on the 8th November, and was as favourably impressed with their appearance as Stokes had been before him; but there was not much grass to be seen, for they had evidently suffered much from a recent drought. On the same afternoon he examined the division of the river, and named the upper branch the Barkly. He proceeded up this a little distance, but, like Stokes, he was soon obliged to stop, in consequence of the immense number of snags which lay in the bed of the stream. He then left his boat, and proceeded on foot, passing the junction of many dry streams, with abundance of ironstone pebbles and red sand in their beds. Every hundred yards or so he marked trees with a broad arrow and the letter V, with N under. This was to convey information to Burke, should he be still lost and wandering in that direction, as also to guide Walker, who was now daily expected from Rockhampton. Having taken these necessary precautions, Captain Norman returned to the ship.

On the 16th November, Mr. Landsborough started on his south-western journey. His party consisted of three white men and two native police—Jemmy and Fisherman—with twenty-five horses, to carry the provisions. Steering south-west they reached a large river on the 18th, which was a tributary of the Nicholson, from the tableland. As Gregory and Leichhardt had crossed below the junction, the stream had not been previously named, and it was called after Mr. Gregory. Near this they were visited by a number of natives, who watched their proceedings with silent wonder, but they did not attempt to interfere with the explorers, and whatever their impressions were they kept them to themselves. It was not until the 21st that Landsborough was able to cross the stream, and then it was only with much difficulty, as the bed was very boggy, winding amid thinly wooded and well-grassed plains. Leaving the Gregory, they kept across the plains for the tableland, but in their usual south-west direction. At first they were obliged to fall back upon the Gregory for want of water, but further on they met a watercourse,

2 F 2

which made them independent of the main stream,
though it only contained a very scanty supply. Landsborough hoped that by following this it would help
them for a long way towards Stuart's Central Mount, but
in this he was very soon disappointed.

On the 23rd, they steered in a south-westerly direction for about eleven miles, across thinly timbered
plains, on which the grass was quite dry for want of
rain. There they sighted the first hills which they had
seen since their arrival at the Gulf of Carpentaria. To
reach these they went to the south-east again, crossing
M'Adam's Creek, and arriving at the Gregory. They
camped near the end of a large reach of water, from
whence there was a rapid stream. The channel was
nearly a quarter of a mile wide, the dry portion being
thickly-wooded with fig trees, pandanus, and cabbage
palms, forming a luxuriant foliage of tropical aspect. In
following the river up to the south-west, they entered
the lower part of the tableland. There were high ranges
on each side of the stream, and the number of natives
about showed the favourable character of the country.
For the next three days they kept along the channel.
The season was very dry, and consequently the land was
barren; yet it might have been better in a rainy season,
for the soil was good. On the 27th, they came to a pass
in a basaltic hill, named Mount Kay. Here the channels of the river divided, and they were evidently approaching the sources of the stream. A creek, named
after Sir W. Stawell, had a slaty bed, and they crossed
this to the southward. At four miles they camped upon
a small stream, in the bed of the River Gregory, into
which one of the horses fell, and, before assistance could
be rendered, was drowned. Their camp was in lat. 19° 2',
long. 138° 52'.

On the 28th, while three of the party continued up
the stream, Landsborough and one of the native troopers
crossed the river, and went down to Mount King, to the
junction of a watercourse from the south. This had a
wider channel than the river, but was found not to have
much water in it. It was named the O'Shannassy. The
Gregory was the only stream they could now hope to

follow, but it wound very much through barren basaltic country, very unpleasant to travel over. However, they had to keep to its banks for the present, as their only resource for getting to the southward. Landsborough was unable to reach his companions that evening. Next morning he followed up the river, through a basaltic gorge, which took them in a direction slightly west of south, past the junctions of two watercourses, situate about two miles from each other. They were named Verdon and Balfour Creeks. Three miles beyond, they came upon the camp of their companions, on what was named Haines Creek. From this they went up the Gregory. Its scenery was now romantic in the extreme. The channel was confined by high basaltic ranges, forming singular cliffs and isolated columns of rock. The travelling was, of course, very rough, causing great distress to the horses, who were very rapidly losing condition. To add to the inconvenience of this, there was a prospect of the water failing. Their camp that night was on a part of the stream which was not running. Landsborough knew that in avoiding the banks of the main stream they must have left it, and followed some tributary creek. To ascertain this, he went next day across to where he supposed the larger river was. He found that he had been mistaken. The Gregory had hitherto been fed by springs, beyond the influence of which he had passed. It was satisfactory, at least, to know that there were springs from the tableland, but the prospects of the journey south were not very encouraging. Still he continued along the river, for it was far from being absolutely dry as yet. As they followed up its bends many dry tributary creeks came in, showing what a large body of water the channel must convey in favourable seasons. The windings went now in a west direction, and even north of west. One tributary, named Abbot's Creek, seemed to afford a chance of going southward. Mr. Landsborough followed it for five miles, almost due south, but finding no water in it he returned to his companions, whom he left at a water-hole a few miles below the junction. On the 5th, Mr. Campbell, accompanied by the native, Jemmy, went up the river in search of water, but returned in the evening quite unsuccessful. His course had been to the westward, and he found the country destitute of anything but spinifex, and very arid in appearance. There was now no longer any hope of following the Gregory further.

Next day, Mr. Landsborough went in search of water. He kept southerly. This took him seven miles up Fullarton's Creek, and then four miles over stony basaltic ridges overrun with desert spinifex. At length the gradual elevation brought him to a fine lightly-timbered tableland, with good vegetation. This was called Barkly's Tableland. In crossing it he found at eight miles some water in a stream, which had recently been flooded. This was named Pratt's Creek. It ran in stony basaltic country, thick with spinifex, but patches of good soil here and there. This did not seem a promising commencement for a tableland on which he hoped to reach the centre of the continent.

Landsborough brought his companions to Pratt's Creek on the 8th, and then again went forward in search of water. He was absent two days, but during all that time found only one water-hole, and that neither very large nor permanent. He went out again on the 12th, over rich tableland thinly timbered but well grassed. He journeyed a long way slightly west of south, and crossed a watercourse trending northerly, named Elliot Creek. Twenty-one miles on the same bearing brought him to another watercourse, named Herbert Creek, and on this he camped. In the day's journey he had found no water except in Pratt's Creek, about three miles above the depôt camp. He followed Herbert Creek for a little distance next day. At four miles he reached the junction of one dry stream from the north-west, but he could not go further. The horses were too much exhausted to advance, so he was obliged to return to the depôt. In going back he kept to the eastward, and found water at a channel named Clifton Creek. Here he camped. Still keeping to the east of north on his return, he thus crossed the O'Shannassy River, and then returned to the camp. It had been shifted three miles higher up the stream, as the water

was fast drying up. He now moved the depôt across
the rich basaltic plains to Clifton Creek, camping on a
fine little water-hole stocked with fish, at the junction of
a watercourse from the westward. From this, next day
they kept ten miles further to the southward, over the
same tableland plains. Two dry watercourses were
passed, but the prospects of the party were not improving. They were getting to the southward, it is true,
but as they did so the country was becoming more dry
at every mile, and their stages were necessarily very
short.

As no water was found, the party divided, three of
them going to the south, while Landsborough and one
native went to the east. The latter went first three
miles to a creek discovered by the native on the previous day. It was broad and deep, with coarse grass,
large trees, and high flood-marks, but then retaining
only a little water. Finding that in following it up he
was taken too much to the eastward, he left it and went
over the basaltic ridges back to the plains. Not finding
his companions where he expected, he went to a tributary of the Herbert, named Darvall's Creek, where he
found them encamped. They had been travelling all
day, but had found no water, except a little about three
miles further up the Herbert. To this the whole
party were moved on the 19th, in lat. 19° 28′, long.
138° 29′.

Landsborough had no option but to lose time in
making preliminary searches for water, as it would not
do to risk the safety of all by pushing on with the whole
party. He again started with two natives, and two
packhorses loaded with water, determined to go on
some considerable distance before giving up the search.
Two miles west by south took them down the Herbert to
the junction of a watercourse from the south-west, named
Turner's Creek. The journey was through long grassy
plains, beautiful and rich, if they were only better
watered. These plains continued for many miles more
in the direction of the country crossed by Landsborough
on the 12th, in his search for water. The fall of the
waters was to the southward, for they had crossed the

watershed of Carpentaria, and might reasonably expect
larger supplies further south; but to get there was the
question, for at the sources of the main channels of
drainage there was very little to be found. The precaution of some water-bags had not been very successful.
They had leaked so much that the horses had to be sent
back to the depôt, while Landsborough went down
towards the watercourse he had passed on his previous
journey. He found many dry streams joining from the
north-west, showing that a large body of water must
empty at times to the southward. Beyond the last of
them a fine water-hole, named Mary Lake, was found.
It was stocked with fish, crowded with water-fowl, and
evidently a favourite camping place for the natives.
This at last was something cheering for their prospects,
though it had been found rather late in the expedition.
The whole camp was at once moved up to it, and a depôt
formed in lat. 19° 54'.

Landsborough did not leave Mary Lake until the
26th, when he commenced to trace down the Herbert
River. He traced it in two days for thirty-three miles,
and found plenty of water-holes for the whole of the distance mentioned. Beyond that, however, it completely
failed. The rich plains on both sides of the stream were
well grassed, but much parched for want of rain. Yet
the flood-marks were numerous and high, showing that
the river spread by a number of shallow channels
through the plains, forming at times extensive sheets of
water. Lat. 20° 8' was the lowest part of the Herbert
reached by the explorers, who were obliged to turn back
for want of water.

On the 29th, after an ineffectual search for water,
Mr. Landsborough returned to the depôt on the Albert
River. The natives had become so numerous about the
neighbourhood of the Herbert, that he could not safely
divide his party while he made the necessary searches
in advance. The savages had not made hostile demonstrations, but they assembled in large numbers, and
were so well armed that it was deemed imprudent
to carry on the exploration further in that direction.
He therefore returned to Mary Lake, and rested one

day. After that they went to Clifton Creek, and thence
to the O'Shannassy River. This they followed down to
its junction with the Gregory, passing four considerable
watercourses. The explorers had come up on the north
side of the Gregory, and they returned on the south
side. In doing so they found another river joining,
named the Ligar. On reaching Beame's Brook· they
followed it down, and ascertained that it joined the
Albert River, and was, in fact, the junction or watercourse connecting the latter with the Gregory. On the
19th January, Mr. Landsborough returned in safety
with his party to the Albert, not having succeeded in
finding any trace of Burke as far as he went to the
south-west.

This insight into the tableland north of Carpentaria,
small as it was, showed very important results. It
proved that all the rivers did not owe their origin to the
sandstone tableland, but that a large proportion of those
mentioned by Leichhardt and Gregory, such as the
Albert, the Gregory, the Nicholson, Beames' Brook,
and some others, had their sources in basaltic hills very
near the edge of the plateau. It would appear as if all
the Carpentarian rivers took their rise from some elevation within the tableland, and, in some instances, a very
long distance to the southward. They all appear to have
basaltic watersheds, and this is the case with almost
every river in northern Australia. Supposing a line
drawn to connect these mountains, as far as they are
known, it would give the average length of the rivers
of Carpentaria, and the sources of the Gregory would be
one of the points on which it approaches nearest to the
coast. The fall of waters to the southward, in that instance, is brought very near to the sea, and offers, consequently, one of the best starting places for an expedition to the interior from the north. Reasoning from
analogy, we might expect a very important river in that
direction. The watershed of the Flinders gives rise to
large tributaries of the Barcoo. The watershed of the
Leichhardt, in all probability, sends streams in the direction of Lake Eyre, and therefore we may conclude that
the mountain sources of such rivers as the Gregory, the

Albert, &c., send also some considerable stream off on its southern side. Mr. Landsborough, it is true, says that the plains were level and the channels shallow, but that is the case at the head of every river commencing in a tableland, and their number shows that they must terminate in something important. Altogether, curiosity is much excited to know the rest of that country, so rich and fertile, of which but a glimpse has been obtained by Mr. Landsborough.

During the absence of the party, Captain Norman had not been idle. He had visited every place along the Albert, making continued searches for traces of Burke. While engaged in these searches, Walker's party arrived with the welcome news that he had found the tracks of the missing explorers on the Flinders River. As soon as he had given his report to the captain of the *Victoria*, he applied for stores and supplies to enable him to follow up his discoveries. Of course, none of them knew that Howitt had done all that was to be done; and though there was but little hope of finding Burke and his companions, still they hoped, in case of the worst, to be able to learn something about his fate. The party was soon equipped with all that was necessary, and they started on the 20th, Captain Norman agreeing to meet them upon a certain point at the Flinders River ere they turned to the south. All that Walker had done previously will be narrated in the next chapter; but in order not to interrupt his diary, what here refers to Norman and Landsborough will first be given. When the party started, Captain Norman hastened round in the steamer to the Flinders to meet it, as he had arranged. On arriving at the spot indicated, he found, to his great dismay, that it was on a part of the ground inundated at spring tides, so that it would be impossible for the horses to come down. After clearing a space in the timber and hoisting a flag, a search for Walker's trail was made, but without success. Burke's tracks were found, with those of a camel and a horse, but not a sign to indicate that Walker's party had gone back the way they came. On the 13th January, Captain Norman went up the river in a boat. At the

head of the Burial Reach of Stokes, the banks of the
river were rocky and precipitous, and the water very
shallow.   Shortly after the river divided, one arm going
to the south, and the other south-east.   Norman took
the latter, and in the space of four miles the boat had to
be carried over as many bars.   Finding at this distance
no indication of Walker, a tree was marked, and a
bottle deposited ; and as the time had long elapsed for
his appearance, all further search was given up, and the
Victoria returned to Investigator Roads.   It appears that
Walker had made a search for Norman, and was at one
time very close to him, but as he was supplied with
abundance of stores of every kind, he was not very
anxious about the meeting.

On the 19th, as already stated, Landsborough arrived, reporting that he had been two hundred miles in
a south-west direction, but had returned because of the
scarcity of water, and the danger of separating his party
in the presence of the natives.   On the 6th February
he came on board the *Victoria*, reporting his men all
well at the depôt, and no losses, except two horses, which
were drowned.   He was now anxious to go on a south-
east expedition in search of Burke—a course which had
not been contemplated by the Exploration Committee ;
but he did not ask for much to continue his explorations.
He only required tea, sugar, and rum ; but as Captain
Norman's crew had been on reduced rations for three
months, he had none of these articles to spare.   He informed Landsborough that it was not necessary for him
to return overland, and that he ought to return with
the *Victoria* to Queensland, in accordance with the instructions of the Royal Society of Victoria.   Landsborough, however, repeated his request, and then Captain Norman wrote to him stating that such other
articles as could be spared should be furnished, but that
if he considered his party in any way endangered by
going without the stores, the risk need not be run, as
there was every reason to believe that Walker's party
would do all that was possible or necessary in following
up Burke's tracks.   He added, however, that as
Landsborough had stated there was a possibility of

Walker losing the tracks, he had every sanction to proceed, if he thought proper, with all or any of his party, but that the *Victoria* would leave Carpentaria immediately.

Landsborough at once accepted the offer of continuing his expedition. Accordingly, stores were sent, and assistance rendered, in crossing to the eastern bank of the Albert. This completed the work of the *Victoria*. The guard at the *Firefly* hulk was removed. All the stores were taken away, with the exception of some deposited in an iron tank for the use of any party falling back upon the depôt, and then it was abandoned. On the 12th, the *Victoria* completed her coaling, and returned to Booby Island, where stores were left for any shipwrecked vessel which might be cast ashore upon this perilous coast. While Captain Norman was examining the country around, he narrowly escaped being speared by some hostile natives, to whom he had just before made some presents. This was the wind-up of the adventures; the gulf was left to the lonely dreariness of its solitary mangrove flats, and echoing sandstone hills. On the 16th February, the *Victoria* sailed, and after stopping at Moreton Bay, and other places, arrived at Melbourne on the 31st.

On the 10th, Landsborough had started from the Albert River. His courage, energy, and perseverance, cannot be too highly extolled. His expedition was now badly provided, and could have no hope of any assistance, unless he succeeded in crossing the continent. Yet, notwithstanding, he was most anxious to press forward when others would have been only too glad to have withdrawn in safety. Fortunately, the expedition turned out to be the most successful and brilliant that resulted from the search for Burke. Truly, Landsborough can claim nearly the whole credit of it to himself, considering the zeal with which he undertook the journey. His success will be narrated when Walker's expedition has been described, to which the reader must now turn, carrying his mind back to the start from Rockhampton.

CHAPTER XXVII.

WALKER'S DISCOVERIES.

WALKER started with his party from Rockhampton,
better known to the reader, perhaps, as Port Curtis,
first discovered by Captain Flinders, whose explorations
on this part of the coast are now fast fading into the
antiquities of Australian discovery. No journal was
kept by the party until they reached the head of the
Barcoo, because the ground had been already frequently
described. His course may, however, be briefly indicated. He crossed to the Dawson River, and thence to
the Albinia Downs. By many *détours* and windings
previously discovered by himself, he got through the
sandstone tableland at the head of the Claude, whose
magnificent scenery and picturesque ravines had inspired Mitchell with the names of Salvator Rosa and
Claude, as fit designations for the features he saw around
him. From these he crossed to the Barcoo.

Once on this river, Walker searched for the marked
tree which Gregory had found, and supposed to be one
of Leichhardt's camps. He found it, and seven miles
below found another. The distance of these camps from
each other very much strengthens the idea that they
were Leichhardt's, and Walker imagined that he had
struck to the north-west from somewhere about this
point.

On the 7th October, Walker having sent back his last
despatches, started from the Barcoo in a north-north-west
direction, determined, by leaving the river thus early,
to solve the question of the nature of the vast extent of
country between this point and Carpentaria.   The
track he proposed to follow would take him considerably
to the west of Leichhardt's first route, and the chances
of water were very slight, until he came to the sources
of the Alice.   The journey was very monotonous, more
so, indeed, than Leichhardt's, and with even less remarkable features to give it a hold upon the memory.   It
was at first open downs and plains, interspersed with
watercourses, but quite dry.   Then water-holes commenced to be seen, with scrub, until they crossed high
downs, supposed to be the line of separation between
the Alice and the Barcoo.   Beyond this there were
many small tributaries, forming an extensive drainage
from the north-east, so that it was very evident that the
Alice, which had never been explored, was the
receptacle of a large drainage, and was a very important
river.   The ground was generally poor, except in the
neighbourhood of the stream, always covered with coarse
wiry grass, and very often with thick scrub.   On the
10th, when they had ascended a tableland, and were
journeying across it, they reached a broad, sandy creek,
which had not long ceased running; this was called the
Patrick.   They followed it for some distance, as its
general direction was on their course, but as the ground
was heavy sand, and the day oppressively hot, they
soon camped near a fine reach of water.   The native
troopers this day found some tracks of horses, but
Walker did not see them, and he believed them to be
Leichhardt's.

Leaving the Patrick on the 11th, they only advanced
nine miles over fine downs, with belts of scrub, and
camped near some splendid grass, on a small creek.
Some ranges were visible to the eastward; they lay
about twenty-five miles away, and good country seemed
to intervene between.   Probably they were the sources
of the creeks they had crossed.   Fine high downs, with
many creeks, succeeded, as they kept on their north-

west course. On the 13th, they crossed the Alice. It
had plenty of water, and the view around was charming.
One splendid reach, in particular, seemed to be a
favourite resort for the natives. A little beyond the
Alice a thick scrub occurred. Making a small *détour*
to avoid this,.they came in four miles to the summit of
a ridge, which was considered to be the watershed
between the Alice and Thompson Rivers. The downs
continued for ten miles, and as they descended the
stony plains a beautiful river occurred, running nearly
to the westward. This was considered to be a tributary
of the Thompson, and was named the Coreenda. Mr.
Walker here states, in his journal, that he entirely
differed from Gregory's opinion, which supposed the
Thompson to emanate from some small watercourses at
its head, otherwise, he says, he never would have
ventured to where he then was. No doubt Walker
was right in this, and we shall have occasion to remark,
in other places, his singular shrewdness in matters
connected with the physical features of the continent.
The country here was very good, as far as its pastoral
capabilities were concerned, but the river had long
ceased running, and no opinion could be formed as to
its permanence. In advance of them there were many
signs of natives, who were burning the grass as they
went up what was apparently another stream. Next
day no progress could be made, because of the loss of
the horses, but in recovering them a large number of
very old horse tracks were found; so old, that they
were nearly obliterated. These were also considered to
be Leichhardt's.

On the 16th they advanced on their usual course,
over plains intersected with very thick scrub. Ten
miles brought them to a watercourse and some nice
lagoons, and the remainder of the day was over sandstone ridges, covered with spinifex. Four miles from
the lagoon they passed the tracks of a very large party
going to the west. They had been made in wet
weather, and consequently will be visible for years,
while, as Walker remarks, tracks such as his, made in
fine weather, would very soon disappear. At twenty-

four miles from the camp they came to the opposite
declivity of the sandstone ridges, and from thence saw
a high peak, which was named Mount M'Alister, and
another bluff mount was named Mount Horsfeldt.   Mr.
Walker, firmly believing the trail just mentioned to
have been Leichhardt's, says that he now perceived
why that explorer had been going west.   He had
camped upon the Coreenda, where the horse tracks were
first seen, and thence travelled parallel to Walker's
course.   Being higher up the ridges, he saw the peak
sooner, and turned off towards it.   It was a singular
circumstance, that the blacks seen here had iron tomahawks, and one had a broad axe.   But still it is
probable that Leichhardt did not make the marks here
described.   Mr. Landsborough says, distinctly, that
they were his.   They may have been, and at any rate
the matter must be looked upon as by no means conclu-
sive.   Landsborough had been out in this direction
previously, on a journey which will be alluded to presently, and as the tracks were only those of horses, and
Leichhardt had cattle with him, the probability is that
the former explorer made them.   There are, however,
some doubts, which have been fully treated of in the
Appendix, on the loss of Leichhardt.

On the 17th, in crossing a high ridge, they came upon
what Walker considered to be the head of the Thompson River, where old tracks of horses were again seen.
He then proceeded to the north-west, passing between
two basaltic ridges, which so hurt the horses' feet that
he was obliged to move more to the west, to get away
from them.   Other ridges, and the heads of other watercourses, succeeded, and amidst them all the tracks of
horses again, evidently made when the ground was very
wet.   At last, Walker got upon a high peak of the
rising grounds, and from its summit he could see displayed before him, to the westward, an endless waste
of plains.   From this view he supposed that Leichhardt
had taken to his old north-west course on finding he
was on the edge of what looked like Sturt's Central
Desert, but supposing the track to have been Leichhardt's, in such a wet season as the tracks showed, he

would not have found the plains either dry or impassable, and might have passed across them.

The ranges which Walker was now upon were of the greatest interest. He was evidently near the watershed of the streams flowing south, and it remained to be seen what waters they would give rise to upon their northern sides. This was the tableland sought for in vain by Mitchell. The drainage might lead to Carpentaria, but it was too early to conclude anything as yet, so Walker continued along it, feeling certain that he had made a great discovery. And so he had, but it was left to Landsborough to complete it. At present he continued along the spurs of the range, with no water except in a westerly creek, the pools in which were fast drying up. One ridge which he crossed showed him that he would have to keep a good deal to the west of north to clear the range. A large mountain was visible to the westward, with a remarkable gap in it, and in this he confidently expected to meet a considerable river. The country was very good since they had left the sandstone and got upon volcanic soil. Near the range the grass was thick, but as it went down the plains it became thinner.

On the 19th October, they crossed along fine downs, and passed four creeks running west and south; these were the last of the southern waters. The ground then began to rise very much, making a fine plateau of downs, beautiful in their fertile appearance. Altering their course more to the north, to make the gap already mentioned, three miles more of the plateau took them to it. It was the commencement of a fine river, but quite dry. It was a northern river, without doubt, and the scenery of the fine mountains around was of the most romantic character. The basaltic downs, like those of all the interior watersheds, were of the richest character, wanting only moisture to make them really perfect as an abode for man. Walker pushed on to find water for his horses. In crossing the western spurs of the range he met with the sources of other rivers, with small water-holes in their beds, but they were all drying up rapidly. Some natives were seen at one of them, who seemed so frightened, and escaped so hurriedly, that they left their tomahawks behind. These were iron, but much worn from use; Walker left others in place of them.

Want of water now began to tell very much upon the horses. Feeling sure of getting a better supply further north, they went out into the plain, in order to advance quicker. But the more they advanced, the more dry did the country become. The horses began to give in, one by one. After pushing along in almost every direction, the downs were found to decline towards the north. There were two high mountains near, named Castor and Pollux, which Walker ascended, in his anxiety to find some watercourse which would relieve his now suffering party. At the top of a gap between the two hills he got a fine view of the country to the north, and to his joy saw gum trees across the plain some five miles away. Descending from the downs towards this, and leaving horses behind at almost every mile, they reached a fine series of water-holes, in long reaches, evidently the backwater of some large river. Here their anxieties were ended for a time, and all the horses, except one, were recovered next day.

On the 23rd they crossed the river amid splendidly-grassed downs. It was a sandy channel, ninety yards wide, which was named the Barkly, after Sir Henry Barkly, K.C.B., then governor of Victoria. Five miles from their camp they crossed a large tributary, two-thirds the width of the first, and two miles more to the west of north brought them to the top of a basaltic ridge. These ridges seemed interminable; but the summit of this one showed that ranges would now have to be climbed. Walker thought at first to avoid them by keeping to the westward; but he soon found that he must cross if he wished to get north of his position. He rested one day before he made the attempt. There were many channels and small tributaries to the main stream hereabout. The Barkly was running north-west, and Walker, thinking that Leichhardt might have followed it, looked everywhere for his tracks, but this time without success. He supposed that the river was connected with Sturt's Eyre Creek in the desert, and that Burke had followed it up; but we have every reason now for believing that the Barkly was in reality the Flinders, and that if Walker had followed it he would have taken the shortest and best route for Carpentaria, and thus have anticipated the discoveries of Landsborough.

Now commenced the most important discoveries made by this expedition. When the party got to the top of the range, they found that they were on an extensive basaltic tableland. It was so elevated that the air was cool and bracing, and the aneroid barometer stood at 28° 9'. In the midst of the plain before them, a range with a peak (Mount Norman) rose still higher, and two high mountains were visible to the north-east. But however novel and romantic the scenery, the travelling was anything but pleasant. The basalt was so distressing to the horses that only very slow progress could be made. Stones, however, were not the only difficulties; at three and a half miles they were stopped by a deep ravine, with a large creek at the bottom. The ravine was lined with cliffs of basaltic columns, but a slope was found, down which they with difficulty descended. On reaching the foot of the cliff they ran down the creek for three miles to the westward, to a fine pool, where they camped. This was slow work. First on to the tableland, and then down it again, over spurs and into ravines, it seemed as if they were never to be extricated from the hills. The mountains seen to the north-east were named Mounts Mayne and Ward. The creek received the name of Jingle, after one of the native troopers.

The Jingle was followed to the westward on the 25th, until it joined the Barkly, which now ran to the west-south-west, turned by a spur of the basaltic range. There were open downs round it, and abundance of pigeons near a lagoon where they camped. From this an ineffectual attempt was made to proceed to the north-east; but the basaltic ridges again turned them back to a reach of water in the Barkly. Here they

met with natives, who told them that the river ran west-
south-west, and was joined by another from the north-
east, both flowing on to what they called Careegaree.
They also said that if the explorers went to the north-
west they would cross the north-eastern tributary, and
then reach a river flowing to the north coast. The
latter Walker hoped and believed was the Flinders.
What a pity that he did not know he was upon it.
The natives also indicated that they had seen a party
of white men before, probably either Leichhardt's or
Landsborough's. That evening an ascent of the range
was made by Walker, who saw that progress to the north
was impossible without crossing the basaltic tableland.

They set themselves to work on the 29th, and at
last, with great difficulty, crossed the mountain barrier
which had detained them so long. And now a great
change ensued in the character of the land they had to
explore. It was no longer rough basalt, with fine
grasses and rich soil, but rough sandstone, with a
heavy sandy soil, and plenty of the odious spinifex
grass. But it was by no means destitute of water.
There were little creeks and shallow lagoons, all pretty
well supplied, and on the 30th they came upon a river
with a course very little north of west. This was
named the Stawell. They disturbed a native digging
for water in the bed of the stream, and he evidently
gave the alarm to his companions, for shortly afterwards
they made a very determined attack upon the camp.
There could be no doubt as to their intentions, for their
language was the same as that of the native troopers,
and thus were their murderous projects distinctly understood. An encounter ensued, and no less than twelve
natives were killed; and all who showed themselves
were wounded. This result is surprising, and certainly
seems to have been unnecessary. Any one who has
read the preceding pages will easily see that milder
measures with more display, would as easily have dispersed them. It may be urged, in excuse for Walker,
that the native troopers in matters of this kind will
submit to no control, and in the presence of an enemy
he could not exert his authority. Besides, the number

killed showed that they would not, like any other blacks, run away at the first shot, or, like those who attacked Stuart, keep out of range at seeing a few of their companions fall. However, it must be said that this is the largest slaughter of natives recorded in the whole annals of exploration.

Not finding the Flinders as he had anticipated, Walker was doubtful whether he had as yet passed the main range. In order to ascertain this, two of the party were sent to the westward. They travelled about twelve miles over good downs, with a skirt of scrub on their right, and a river-line of trees upon their left. Turning at last to the latter they found a fine river coming from the north-east, and joining another further south, both running on to the Stawell. The course of that stream was then south-west, and it seemed to be a tributary of the Barkly. Owing to a fall of rain, and the loss of a horse, they did not move from their camp until the 5th November, when they went eighteen miles slightly west of north, to another tributary of the Stawell. They could find no water even by digging, so they tied up their horses and lay down supperless. During the night they found that the hole they had dug had filled, and they were able to supply all their wants. On the 6th they returned to their companions, who had in the meantime obtained all necessary supplies by digging in the bed of the Stawell.

For the next four days very little advance was made, as the country was so fearfully dry and heavy, and the weather oppressively hot. They were merely crossing the sandstone tableland, which supplies all the eastern tributaries of the Flinders. At times only they found a little water, so that in these few days they lost another horse. It was the greatest misfortune to Walker that he was looking for the Flinders to the north. It lay to the west of him; and while he was torturing himself and his companions by travelling amid the scanty eastern tributaries, a large and permanent supply of water lay at no great distance from his whole line of route. On the 10th, however, his difficulties were greatly mitigated by meeting a fine river, with plenty

of water. Its course was found to be west-north-
west, through heavy, sandy, scrubby ground, but
which afterwards became firmer and more open. It was
thought to be the Flinders, but in a very short time
Walker saw his mistake, and named it the Norman.
It had numerous arid branches and lagoons at intervals,
but none appeared at first of sufficient extent to be permanent.

The general character of the country was so heavy,
and the heat so great, that the party could only make
very short stages. This was the more annoying to
Walker, as he feared that the steamer would be gone
before he could reach the Gulf of Carpentaria. In
spite of his hurry he was obliged to rest a few days,
and after that the ground began to get better and
firmer. On the 20th they crossed the stream, the
course of which was now more easterly, and the
pools well stocked with fish. Pigeons, too, were
very numerous, but gunpowder had become so scarce
an article with the explorers, that they could not
get as much game as they wanted. They met with
natives, who were very friendly, and told them that the
river was north-west, over large plains, and that they
must avoid going to the west, as the country was bad,
and like the sandy soil they had seen in its upper
part. The land here appeared good, though subject to
inundation ; but the more Walker advanced, the more
puzzled he was as to the river he was upon. According to his calculations, he ought to have been near one of
Gregory's camps in 1856, and yet this did not agree
with the accounts given by the natives, nor what he
knew of Gregory's explorations. When his doubts and
anxieties were at their highest they were agreeably set
at rest by his finding that the Norman joined the
Flinders, and was marked in the maps as the Bynoe.
The main stream was reached on the 25th November.
They found it a beautiful and large river, with high
banks, and a delicious breeze blowing up from the sea.
There was abundance of game upon it—using the word,
of course, in the miscellaneous sense in which it is
applied by explorers.

At their camp, in lat. 18° 7', while they were still rejoicing on the success of their expedition, another great subject of congratulation was added. They found the well-defined trail of four camels and one horse, which had come down the stream. At once they knew them to be Burke's, and supposed he had gone down Leichhardt's track, intending probably to follow Gregory up the Albert. Next day Walker crossed the Flinders, having had to go up eight miles for a crossing-place, and then camped, as the horses were much distressed by the heavy ground. Here they found Burke's trail returning in a south-south-east direction, and Walker concluded that he had found the gulf, and then made his way back to the Barcoo.

All the energies of the party were now directed to reach the steamer as soon as possible, in order to follow up these tracks. They left the Flinders, and struck due west to reach the Albert River. By crossing the heads of the creeks near their origin they were able to avoid all the difficulties from the watercourses in the lower part of the Carpentaria Plains. On the 30th, they were only twenty-six miles from the Albert, and the excitement of the party became intense lest the steamer should have left. Rockets were sent up at night; but whether seen or not, they could not say, for they were not responded to. On the 1st December they were much delayed in having to trace up creeks for crossing-places, and in working their way over the numerous sandstone spurs. Towards evening the natives made an attack upon them. They advanced in a semicircle to surround the party, so that there was little alternative but to fire, and this led, of course, to some loss of life. All the natives were not, fortunately, equally hostile. Some were met with the day after the fight, who told them that there were white people on the Albert. It is rather singular that Walker's blacks could understand the language of Carpentaria, while the intermediate natives at the head of the Barcoo could not be understood.

On the 3rd December they reached the Albert. The water was not quite fresh where they came upon it,

so that they could be no great distance from the sea.
To relieve their anxieties they could hear that night
the distant booming of a gun. Next day, while Walker
and one of the troopers were looking for traces of the
steamer, they were attacked by natives. It was only
by the greatest exertions they escaped, as one of their
horses became so fatigued in the flight that he had to
be abandoned, almost in sight of their pursuers. They
could not return to the camp that night, but on reaching
their companions heard that they had found a bottle
with a note from Captain Norman, stating where the
depôt was to be found. Owing to the boggy nature of
the soil, the party did not reach the depôt until the
7th December, where their presence excited as much
joy as the news they brought. They had succeeded in
crossing the continent, and had found proofs that Burke
had reached the Gulf of Carpentaria, and then gone
back to the southward, where they hoped that he might
yet be found alive.

On arriving at the depôt, Walker informed Captain
Norman that he was sure that Burke had followed
down Eyre Creek to the Barkly, and that it was
possible he might return by the same route. He
thought it also probable that Howitt would be in those
latitudes about September and October, and having the
short rainy season in his favour, would probably have
met Burke, and supplied him with provisions. Walker
himself hoped to reach that part of the Barkly which
Burke struck about the dry season; and if his tracks
were found going south, there would be no necessity to
risk the lives of the party by following the arid region,
because it would be nearly certain that Burke had
reached the Barcoo in safety. He then proposed trying
to find the Careegaree Lake, spoken of by the natives,
by means of which he hoped to reach Adelaide.

Having refitted, and being supplied with all requirements, the party started on the 21st December, as
already mentioned. On the 30th, the Flinders was
reached, and Mr. Walker makes some remarks upon it
in his journal which are worthy of consideration. He
says that he never could agree with the opinion that

that river had a course of only one hundred or one hundred and fifty miles. He considered that three hundred miles at least must be the course of the stream. In proof of this he urged that the bed was three hundred yards in width, with flood-marks eighty feet above the ordinary level of the waters. He agreed with Gregory that the Flinders and Leichhardt must come from the interior tableland, but at a greater distance than was supposed. He adds, "The tableland, which is the continuation of the great Cordillera, south of the Gulf of Carpentaria, is, I believe, sixteen hundred feet high where I crossed it; and my belief is that further to the west it rises to a much greater height, and that there the Leichhardt takes its rise. The slope on the south side has in many places basaltic rocks, and the downs are formed of decomposed basalt. There is, therefore, every probability that these basaltic rocks in some places still exist, and at a great height. The great desert of the interior has been a great bugbear; if the discoveries made by Burke are preserved, it will be reduced to a small extent." After this, he adds that the available strip of country in Carpentaria was very small. It did not probably extend forty-five miles southward, and then red sandstone and spinifex country commenced.

These remarks of Walker very shrewdly anticipated the discoveries made shortly after by Landsborough and M'Kinlay. What he says about the Leichhardt and Flinders has turned out a prophecy. It is singular, however, that he never should have suspected that the latter and the Barkly were identical. The exact sources of the Leichhardt have not been ascertained; but there can be no doubt that its watershed is part of the same tableland which forms the sources of the Flinders, the M'Kinlay Ranges, and the Standish Ranges of Burke, the basaltic rocks at the head of the Gregory and Albert, and the volcanic hills at the head of the Victoria.

On the last day of the year Walker proceeded down the river to meet Norman. When he came to where they had seen the camel tracks, they searched in vain for signs of Burke's camp, and even the track itself disappeared upon a small sandstone range. While they were looking about, some natives came down, and prepared to attack them. A charge was made down upon them, and they immediately broke and fled. When they were flying at full speed, and were a long distance off, two were shot down, to show them, as Mr. Walker says, the terrible range of the Terry rifles. Let us hope that such a reason appeared a sufficient one to him for shedding their blood.

Many days were now spent in trying to make out the course of the camel tracks. It will be remembered that Burke left them all at one part of the river, while he and Wills went on to the sea with the horse. Of course, the camels feeding about for days at that wet season left many tracks behind. All sorts of surmises were made as to what the explorers had been doing. At first it was thought that the party had all been killed by natives, and the camels left to wander, because no footmarks were seen near their feeding ground. Then they found boot-marks, with naked feet following, which we should conclude to be signs that the natives were stealthily following Burke, but which Walker looked on as clear evidence that the camels had been abandoned, and the party were trying to make their way on foot.

On the 4th January they were upon the latitude where Captain Norman promised to meet them; but of course they could not get near the river, because of the salt-water inlets. The 5th was spent in an unsuccessful attempt to reach it, and then it was given up as hopeless, and the party returned. As they went up, they found other traces of Burke, and a tree marked B. cxix., and another S.S.E.¹⁴ Walker fancied that this was the 119th camp of Burke, and that the letters on the other meant, to dig fourteen feet south-south-east of the tree. They tried this, but the ground was hard, and had evidently never been opened before. The explanation probably was that it was either the fourteenth day or camp of the south-south-eastern route followed on their return. The search was renewed from this tree, but without being able to pick up the trail.   All that could be found were down-ward tracks, but no marks whatever of the return. This is the more singular, as we know that the weather was very wet when Burke set out on his return, and the tracks made ought to have been permanent.   The blacks were very numerous ; in fact, Walker says that he never saw a country so thickly populated with natives as this was.

A strange conclusion was now arrived at by Walker. He thought that Burke's party had never left this camp, and that the camels strayed back singly, leaving no defined trail; that while Burke left the camp on his foot expedition, the two men left behind were killed in his absence, and he shared their fate on his return. He admitted, however, that he might have missed the trail, as there was long grass on the plains to the south-ward which was too green for him to burn.   Having buried a bottle, his plan now was to run up to the Norman, and try to cut the trail of Burke on the red sandstone, where it would be like print.   Doubt-less many will smile at the perplexities and theories of Walker; but the sagacity with which the tracks had been followed hitherto reflects the greatest credit upon him.   It is not very easy at any time to distinguish tracks in red sand, especially to arrive at all the conclu-sions as to the horses, the foot expedition, and the camels, which were in the main correct.   If he could have burned the grass, the whole truth would have been plain to him, as by that simple means the faintest tracks become visible.

The party now moved up the stream, keeping some distance from it to avoid the bends.   In spite of this precaution, they had to turn very much about to follow its windings.   On the 15th, Burke's downward tracks were again seen, and on the same day their camp was near a creek which was not on the usual red sandstone, but a rock composed of layers of basalt, slate, and quartz.   The country became somewhat heavy, as the plains through which the river ran had evidently been recently flooded.   This accounted for the obliteration of Burke's track.   Natives were still numerous, and the water in the river was plentiful and permanent.   On the 20th they obtained some information from a native woman, whose language was partially understood by the guides.   She mentioned having seen Burke, but repeatedly denied that he had ever come up the river, after going down.   This was probably true, as he had turned off to Cloncurry Creek long before coming thus far.   As they went on, other natives confirmed her story.   From this Walker considered that it would be useless to continue following up the river.   Moreover, the continued heavy rains had made the plains very boggy, and he was afraid that the rainy season had set in three weeks earlier than usual.   He therefore determined to strike across to the Norman.

The road across the plains was dreadful for the horses, in consequence of the rain, which now fell continually in heavy showers.   The more they went to the westward, the less the signs they met of heavy rain, though they were occasionally visited by tropical squalls.   In the sandstone country, called by the natives Mangolā, the sand was much more firm, in consequence of the wet.   The natives were friendly and communicative, and all repeated the story of the man with the camels having gone down the river, but not returning.   To some presents were made, and in return they commenced to steal from the explorers.   This was resented by firing a gun over their heads.   As they retreated, a Terry rifle was fired into the bushes before them, and when the ball crashed through the branches, their screams of terror could be heard at the camp. After this, they did not trouble the party again ; but it is a matter of regret that such bloodless measures were not always adopted towards them.

On the 25th, they reached the Norman.   The day following, the river and an arid branch commenced to run, and the men had just time to pack up their baggage, when the water flooded their camp.   Shortly afterwards, the water was as high as the banks, and Walker congratulated himself on being away from the inundated plains of the Flinders, for there all travelling would have been stopped.   From this point, until the

31st January, they moved up the river upon their old
tracks. Walker then resolved to strike for Gregory's
tracks from the Victoria River, and then travel along
the Burdekin. Accordingly, on the 1st February, they
commenced a north-east course, over a gradually rising
sandstone country, very boggy in places. They camped
the first day on a very large river, named the Jardine.
It was an important stream, and joined a larger one,
forming a bed upwards of one hundred yards in width,
with a running stream half as wide in the bed. These
rivers, Walker considered, ran out to small channels, as
they got into the sandstone, and terminated in box flats,
subject to inundations, like most of the streams in
Australia.

Beyond these rivers they got a distant view of the
Gilbert River Ranges. They had been seen from the
top of a tree at the last camp, and from the tableland at
the head of the Flinders. They looked very formidable from a distance, being, in fact, a part of the great
Cordillera of the eastern coast, which runs from Bass's
Straits to Cape York. By crossing them thus early,
Walker hoped to reach a river bed which would be
more easy to follow to the settled districts, and more
secure for water than by trying to reach the head of
the Barcoo again. Such rugged mountain passes cannot, however, be passed very easily, and those who bear
in mind the sufferings of Kennedy, or the journey of
Oxley, narrated in the first volume, can foresee what
Walker would have to undergo. He ascended a considerable range on the 3rd. Other hills and ridges
were still before them, with conical summits, just like
the heads of basaltic columns. The scenery commenced
to be beautiful. There was a fine pastoral country in
advance, thinly timbered with small box trees, and
almost like downs ; but the ground was very trying for
the horses, being as stony as a newly macadamized
road. The downs terminated in a beautiful valley,
into which three large creeks were flowing. Beyond it
were the high Gilbert Ranges, and to the north-west a
splendid tract, extending as far as a telescope could
explore. To the northward was a tableland, with

numerous peaks dimly looming above the picturesque
horizon, very tropical in its character, and yet very fair
and fertile.   The highest part of the tableland was
named Mount Barry, after Sir Redmond Barry, judge,
and Chancellor of the University of Melbourne.   Towards this hill Walker was determined to proceed, but
he was detained in camp until the 10th, partly because
some horses were lost, and partly because the rainy
weather prevented his travelling.   His camp was
between the branches of a river which he supposed to
be the Carron of Leichhardt.

From Mount Barry he had a fine and extended view,
and could see the Carron running a long way to the
north-west, through fine pastoral country.   At an
immense distance southward, he saw the mountains
forming the head of the Flinders.   This he considered
confirmed his opinion that the tableland rose to a great
height to the westward, and probably from these
mountains were washed the specimens of basalt and
slate he had found on the banks of the Flinders, lower
down.   The route from Mount Barry was over very
broken, uneven country, and on the 12th they had to
go a little to the south of east.

And now commenced a terrible journey over the
mountain ranges.   Day by day the record of their travels was high ridges, deep and grassy valleys, precipitous rocks, and mountain streams.   The journey
throughout was very beautiful, and the scenery of the
most diversified description.   On the slopes of the hills
they met with sandstone, often covered with tropical
forest, and always with a dense brushwood.   On the
summits it alternated from granite to every kind of
trap rock.   There were the usual number of precipitous
cliffs and gorges, and even extinct volcanoes, with their
stony streams adding a new item to the picturesque
character of the scene.   It took, of course, a very long
time to travel over such ground, and delay was not the
only inconvenience from which they had to suffer.   The
land was as stony as a quarry.   At different times
they had to abandon fifteen horses, who were quite
unable to travel further.   Their provisions also were

very scanty, and they had no meat whatever except
what they could obtain by the use of their guns. A few
blacks could be seen, but no information could be
obtained from them. This was the more to be regretted,
as Walker was anxiously looking out for the Burdekin,
which, owing to some error in his reckoning, he expected
to have met long before. It was not seen until the 8th
March, and the party by that time were very considerably exhausted. Following the course of the stream
did not improve their position much. Its banks were a
rugged basalt, so distressing to the horses that they
could be traced along the stones by the tracks of blood
from their hoofs. Besides the rocks there was another
inconvenience : this was a high, rich grass growing on
the slaty portions of the channel. It was from six to
nine feet high, and covered with seeds, which worked
their way into the skin, and caused pain like the sting
of a wasp.*

On the 16th March, Walker made up his mind to
divide the party. Their sugar was nearly finished, and
the peas they had roasted for coffee were quite exhausted.
They had had no meat for a long time, so that with
every disposition to live upon rough fare, they had now
come to the end of all their contrivances. Four men
were sent on with seven of the best horses, and instructions to procure food wherever they could get it. The
remainder of the party camped for three days, and then
followed slowly. For twelve days they continued down
the river, making as rapid marches as the exhausted
state of both men and horses would allow. On the 4th
April they met the relief party on their return, and found
that they were close to a sheep station. Having obtained
the necessary supplies, Walker started back his native
troopers to recover the abandoned horses, and then proceeded through the settled districts to Rockhampton,

* On the south coast there is a grass seed which has similar properties.
The seeds are sharp and covered with fine barbs, and once they penetrate
the skin they will work their way onwards. They catch in the wool of sheep,
and in a short time reach the intestines. Very often I have been shown the
omentum of a dead sheep where the grass seeds were projecting like a pavement of pegs. The settlers call it spear-grass, and it is, I believe, a species of
Anthistiria.

where he arrived on the 5th June. He intended to
have continued his search for Burke and Wills when he
received supplies on the Burdekin, but he there heard
of their fate. In other respects the journey added little
to the knowledge of the physical features of the north
country between Rockhampton and Carpentaria.

CHAPTER XXVIII.

LANDSBOROUGH'S DISCOVERIES.

The Flinders River—Journey up the stream—Arrival at its sources—Walker's Table Mountain — The watershed — The Thompson — The Barcoo — Journey across the Warrego—The Maranoa—Completion of the journey across the continent.

WE return now to Landsborough, who was left starting from Carpentaria to follow up Burke's tracks. The party consisted of three white men and three blacks, and they left on the 8th February, carrying with them twelve hundred and seventy-nine pounds of provisions on horseback. In starting, no doubt, Landsborough's first care would be to try to follow up Burke's tracks, but if he failed in reaching them, he knew he could not fail to cross to the Barcoo. He knew also that if Walker did not follow up the Flinders, he could do so; and from the fact that Walker had found that river to the west of his course in coming to the coast, he could have no doubt that its sources were in the tableland passed close to the head of the Barkly. There was another reason why Landsborough could go into the interior without any fear of the result. He saw at once that the traces met by Walker were not Leichhardt's but his own. Just before starting on this expedition, he and another had been out exploring to the westward of Mount Narrien. Here he had met with a stream which he had named the Aramac Creek, but as the country was flooded and boggy he could not pursue his explorations further, and was obliged to turn northward where he had come in sight of Walker's tableland. He had no doubt now that he could reach the same place, and once there he

VOL. II. 2 H

could easily make his way to the Barcoo, along the creeks flowing to the southward.

The first duty was to reach the Flinders, which they did on the 19th February. They were glad to find that it had been recently flooded; probably by the very rain which had caused so much inconvenience to Walker upon the Norman. At first, a search for Burke's tracks was made. They were found, and Walker's also; but the rain had nearly obliterated both. It could be plainly seen that Walker had been making every search, so Landsborough kept straight up the stream. On the 25th he was on entirely new ground, and their camp was then near a hill, which was named Fort Bowen. It was only about two hundred feet high, but still it gave a fine view. Plains surrounded the hill on every side, those on the west bank of the river being the most thickly wooded. This was the character of the stream for many days subsequently. Sometimes a small hill was seen either to the right or the left, but in general the country was as level as the ocean, and as rich and beautifully grassed as any place Landsborough had seen in Australia.

On the 5th March they came upon the junction of a deep stream from the southward. This was in lat. 20° 23′. All the tributaries, as well as the main channel, were high at this time, for it was the season of the tropical rains, and no doubt could be entertained by the party that abundant supplies would be found until they reached the tableland. Whenever they wanted to cross the river they were obliged to swim the horses. The banks were a little boggy, but the country was still good; so good that Landsborough passes the following encomium upon it:—" Knowing that plains with just sufficient timber for firewood and shade have proved the best for pastoral purposes, this country delighted me; but I must say it would please me more if there were a few high hills in the distance. I was, however, charmed with the landscape round the camp this morning. In the foreground I saw fine box and other trees festooned with creepers; and beyond them the horses feeding on a fine grassy plain, extending to the north and east to distant blue mountains. As the day advanced this picture lost a portion of its beauty by the disappearance of anything like mountain."

The downs consisted for the most part of a loose brown loam, thickly covered with ironstone pebbles, but they were not always equally level, for sometimes they broke up into surface undulations, much like the Darling Downs. On one occasion some of the men went to the eastward of the stream for about twenty miles. The country was well watered even there, but the water was not permanent, and only lay in shallow clay-pans. On the 13th a range was seen for the first time to the southward. This was named the Bramston Range, and was found to be the first of a series of tablehills which confined the east bank of the river. There were a good many natives, who seemed to value the fresh-water mussels as much as the explorers had learned to do. They were a peaceable people, or else they were not numerous enough to attack the party. One of the principal articles of their diet appeared to be rats, of which their baskets were generally found to be filled. Landsborough ascended one of the hills of the Bramston Range. He saw that the country was rising, assuming a different character. Large fragments of basalt were met with here, and the grass was rapidly assuming that luxuriant character which is always found in volcanic soil.

On the 16th, Landsborough again ascended the range on the east bank of the river. It was a sandstone rock covered with volcanic soil, and from its summit the river could be seen to divide into many tributaries on the south-east. They all appeared to come from a high double range visible in the southwards, and this was, without doubt, the range which Walker had experienced so much trouble in crossing. It was called Walker's Table Mountain. Near it the native troopers found the old tracks of an expedition party. These were nearly obliterated by the rain, but they were making to the north-west, and there could be no doubt that they were Walker's. This settled the question of the Barkly River. It was no other than the Flinders River which Landsborough had thus traced up to near its sources.

2 H 2

The summit of the tableland was ascended on the 18th. Across a great part of the horizon there was nothing to be seen but plains which stretched away to the westward, just as Walker had seen them, but to the south-east there was a succession of mountains, rocky hills, and table ranges extending as far as they could see. The party did not think of trying to cross the mountain, but went round it. The land passed over was good, and the soil a rich reddish loam. The country consisted of downs luxuriantly covered with good grasses, except at intervals. These were occupied with a salsolaceous plant growing in the form of a ball several feet high. In the dry season it withers, and is easily broken off and rolled about by the winds, whence it is called roley-poley by the settlers. The downs were thinly wooded with Acacia. Walker's Table Mountain is of sandstone formation, covered at places with the abominable spinifex. At many places on the Flinders a most interesting vine was observed, which produced pods of a beautiful silky cotton. It is a *Cynanolium,* which extends into the desert region about Lake Torrens. The unripe milky pods are considered very delicate eating by the natives, and the party with Landsborough looked out for them as a most valuable addition to their rations.

Thus amid luxuriant plains and picturesque ranges, with abundance of food and water on the sides of the river, they gradually were crossing the continent in a most favourable and beautiful season. When we recall the dangers and difficulties, the trials and exertions of other explorers in neighbouring regions, such as those of Sturt and Leichhardt, one cannot help marvelling at the change which had taken place. Here was a small party, with small resources, doing what others would have trembled to do with four times the means, and the whole was done so easily, and with such a little sacrifice, that it seemed like a pleasure excursion.

On the 20th March, Landsborough at last left the Flinders. It was then a sandy channel, about one hundred and twenty yards across, with a shallow stream meandering through open plains of luxuriant herbage, surrounded by isolated ranges. The party followed up a tributary, named Gardner's Creek, flowing amid a beautiful valley. It was thickly grassed, open, and wooded with clumps of trees, but the ranges on the southern side were sandy and more barren than the rich basaltic soil which clothed the hills on the north. From Jardine Creek they crossed over the range to a very level country, overgrown with iron-bark trees and spinifex. In fact, it was a desert, only that there were patches of good soil, and here and there a creek with water. One of these watercourses they followed, but as yet they were not across the watershed. The stream contained abundance of water, but it did not lead in the direction they wanted to go. It brought them through a rocky, worthless country, near Bowen Downs, which had been discovered by Landsborough, in the journey to which allusion has been made. These downs were apparently occupied at that time, for the track of a cart was noticed. On both sides of the creek there were stony ridges grassed with spinifex. After leaving it, · they crossed many desert ridges of similar character, but in a short distance reached the outskirts of the Bowen Downs, where the soil was good, though run into by belts of scrub. Landsborough made to the southward, across the plains. The track was over rich undulating downs, slightly wooded with trees and well grassed. He recognised several hills and trees which he had visited on his former expedition, and at last reached the creek running to the southward, which he had named the Landsborough. This was on the 29th.

Thus he had crossed the watershed. The high downs covered with scrub and spinifex, must be considered a tableland of which Walker's Mountain is the northern boundary. The southern side gives rise to many tributaries to the Barcoo. One had been traced up by Walker, and it remained to be seen what was the creek down which Landsborough now commenced to conduct his party. After seeing the cart track, and subsequently the track of a single horse, he expected to meet a station at every mile, more especially as Mr. Buchanan, his former companion, had told him before leaving Brisbane that

he intended to form a station upon this watercourse.
Further on the explorers were confident that they were
on well-stocked country, because the grass was eaten
off very close.   But this had been done by grass-
hoppers, and the men soon found that no chance of a
station existed.   The country round the creek was a
rich soil, and wooded along the watercourses with box
trees and a few bushes.   Near the water the stream was
badly grassed, but further back the land was undulating and better.   The scenery was picturesque.   On
both sides rose table-ranges extending very far into the
back ground, while the horizon was coloured with all
the rich tints of the autumn atmosphere.

In a short distance the creek assumed the proportions of an Australian river.   It had been recently
flooded, so that the valley was clothed with very rich
verdure, with downs extending very far to the eastward.   Had Landsborough been able to tell his longitude, there is no doubt he could have seen at once now
that he was on the Thompson River, and that the plains
to the eastward were the low, open lands which Mitchell
had discovered lying between the Alice and the banks
of the Barcoo.   But he never could have known it from
the appearance of the country.   What with the reports
of Kennedy and Gregory, the Thompson was considered
to be a watercourse draining through one of the most
inhospitable regions in the world.   Nothing but barren
sandstone rocks bounded its valley, which was full of red
drift sand rising into hillocks, and utterly devoid of
grass.   But Landsborough found it picturesque and
verdant, and it was with no small interest he looked forward to the discovery of its exit.   On the 1st April, he
found the recent tracks of an exploring party, which
they followed for a short distance to the eastward.   It
was near an old camp of Landsborough, where there
was a tree marked L. LXIX, and might easily have
been mistaken for one of Leichhardt's.

Near this place some natives were met, who surrounded the party; but seemed very peaceable.   They
spoke of an exploring party, and told them that the
river was joined in about two days' journey by a large

one from the north-east. They said also that a long
way down the river the country was sandy and destitute
of grass, and that beyond the ranges in sight there were
no hills. They said further—this was very important—
that they did not know of any desert country to the
westward. On the next day's journey, Landsborough
believed that he had passed a tributary from that direction, for the stream was now quite unfordable, and about
twenty yards wide. The country, however, was not so
good; the grass was dry and brittle, and in the bed of
the stream low dense brushwood of polygonum began
to show; in fact, the characters were now approaching
to that dreary description which Kennedy found upon
the Barcoo. But still the valley was of rich soil, and
many tributaries were passed.

The natives all confirmed the account of the large
river coming from the south, so that Landsborough at
last thought it better to make at once for it, and thus
cut off the bends of the stream they were following.
On the 9th, he left the camp to go in search of water,
on the route he wanted to find. He went along the
plains on the left bank of the river, in a south and east
direction for eight miles. He expected to find in that
distance a well-watered stream, according to the
accounts obtained from the natives. But no river was
there. He then began to think he had been deceived,
and returned to the Thompson. After following it for
two miles, he met some natives who promised to bring
him to the main stream next day. Landsborough knew
all along that this river was a very important stream,
to which the river he had been following was only a
tributary; but he still never dreamed that it was the
Barcoo, because he was under the impression that
Gregory had been to the head of the Thompson in his
journey of 1858. He could not, however, lose any time
in trying to ascertain the fact, for the greater part
of his stores was used, and though the river seemed
flowing almost in the direction of Burke's starting-point
upon the Barcoo, he was resolved to leave it and make
for the settled districts.

He met the blacks next day according to their

arrangements. They were waiting for the explorers, and conducted the whole party to a good encampment. The day after, they went to show the road to the river. At first they walked, but afterwards Landsborough gave them a horse to ride alternately. The oldest of the two seemed to fancy that mode of progression very much, so he made his companion walk the whole of the way. They only went thirteen miles, for their guides stopped with a tribe of natives they met with. This made the day's journey very short, so that instead of two days they travelled four without seeing anything of the Barcoo. They passed, in the interim, a small range and a tributary creek, which had very extensive flood-marks in its channel, though the water-holes were empty. This was called Archer's Creek, after Mr. W. H. Archer, the registrar-general of Victoria, whose scientific acquirements have been so valuable to the colony in which he resides. After following this water-course for thirteen miles, they reached its junction, and thus at last they were upon the Barcoo. Its channel was full of water, and it had all those characters of a a fine river, which at the first sight had so captivated Mitchell. It was seen, however, to the best advantage. The rain had recently fallen upon its banks, and it was as yet under the influence of the floods which had come down the eastward. The grass was consequently long and verdant, and the sides were frequented by an incredible number of natives.

And thus Landsborough had completed that portion of his journey which was wanted to perfect the know-ledge of the interior which Burke had so ably com-menced. Had he known that at Burke's *cache* there was a depôt and party under Howitt, waiting to receive him, he would have gone there at once. But he was ignorant of all this — ignorant of Burke's fate, or the line he had chosen in going up to the Barcoo; and now that he was upon country previously explored, he was at a loss which way to turn. Many courses were open to him. He might go back east-ward to the settled districts along the Barcoo, or he might travel down it to the Adelaide district, as

Gregory had done before him. Fortunately, he chose a middle course, which—while it opened a new route to the Darling, better than Burke's—explored a new and vast tract of country of which nothing whatever was known.

On the 25th April, the party left the Barcoo, and journeyed south-east along a small creek which joined the river. This appeared to come from a range to which they crossed, and the other side was a level plain interrupted with belts of timber, like all the country round the northern tributaries of the Darling. It was through such a country that Mitchell tried to explore to the westward of the Maranoa, and through a similar tract Kennedy travelled across in making to the same river from the Warrego. Landsborough now, in making for the latter river, found no difficulty whatever from the land. A part of it was good soil, and a part was light clay; but the most of it was a loose sandy loam, sometimes poor and scrubby, but in part richly grassed. Looking at this territory as the lower part of the western slope of the tableland, one would not expect to find it well watered; but the party met with watercourses almost every day, and found no very great difficulty in advancing. Probably, in other seasons their progress would have been entirely stopped, and the country must not be regarded as quite so good at all times as Landsborough had the good fortune to find it; but it was better than any believed then to exist there, and he succeeded in bringing his party safe to a station on the Warrego, in lat. 27° 28', on the 20th. From thence to Menindee, the journey was through the settled districts, and by about the end of June the explorer was in Melbourne, to prove the success of his expedition, and the rapid manner in which he had crossed the continent.

Thus the expedition terminated. It was decidedly one of the most important ever made in Australia. It finally ascertained the division in the continent between the northern and southern waters, which Mitchell and Leichhardt had worked and explored so long in the hope of finding. No doubt, a part of Landsborough's success was owing to the previous discoveries of Walker, whose tableland is scarcely three hundred miles north of the junction of the Alice ; but to the former alone must be given the merit of having explored the whole of the route across the continent, and having determined that, so far as regards the eastern portion of it, there is no desert of any kind in the interior.

CHAPTER XXIX.

M'KINLAY'S JOURNEY ACROSS THE CONTINENT.

The lakes about the exit of the Barcoo—M'Kinlay sends back a party—
Explorations—Wills' grave—Dreadful heat of the weather—The Stony
Desert—Burke's Creek—Extraordinary floods—The Sandstone Tableland
—Numerous creeks and boggy plains—The Daly—The M'Kinlay Range—
Various large streams—The Leichhardt—Carpentaria—The journey to
the eastward—The Dividing Range—Port Denison.

WHEN we last left M'Kinlay and his party they were
at Lake Massacre, and had discovered what they
believed to be the graves of Burke and Wills who had
been murdered, as they thought, by the natives. Owing
partly to this conclusion, an unfortunate encounter with
the blacks had taken place. Subsequently, M'Kinlay,
though he had buried a record of his proceedings, had
despatched Mr. Hodgkinson, his second in command, to
the settled districts, in order to give tidings of the
missing party. The grave found was that of Gray.
Curiously enough, two bodies and graves were made out
of one, and it is very much to be regretted that certain
appearances about the body had been construed into
signs of death by violence. When it was known that
the natives had had nothing to do with Gray's death,
some malevolent dispositions, who would sacrifice anything for notoriety or a sensation, threw out dark
hints of foul play against Burke and Wills. It is an
insult to common-sense to go into any of the supposed
facts upon which such a mischievous extravagance was
grounded; but it is worth while to mention, that when
the body was found it had been more than six months
buried, and the flesh was entirely stripped from the
bones. The natives told M'Kinlay that the grave had
been violated, and the body eaten, after the departure of

the party, and certain marks upon the skull appear to
have been made, as they said, by the native swords, at
the same time.   This would account for all that was
seen if it ever needed accounting for; but it is useless to
pursue the matter further.

M'Kinlay started the party back to the settled districts on the 28th October.   During their absence, he
established a depôt in lat. 270° 41', long. 139° 30', and
from this he made several journeys to the east and west.
None of them, however, were very extensive, for he
did not like to be absent long from camp while the
number of his companions was so much reduced.   To
the east he found well grassed flats, with the beds of
dry lakes.   This was the character of the country to
the north, except that there were many hills of dry
sand, and, besides, some salt lagoons.   But there was
no fresh water.   Refraction, as in most parts of the
continent, was a constant phenomenon; and if the actual
character of the country was arid, the atmosphere made
up for it by converting the horizon into the most beautiful
lakes, as refreshing as the enchantment of distance
could make them.   There was scarcely any rain all the
time the explorers were at the depôt, making both the
air and the country as dry as a desert.   The climate
became in consequence unwholesome for men and
animals.   The feed was magnificent, but yet the horses
did not improve.   Not that it did not nourish them, but
they could not eat it.   The flies were such an incessant
torment to the poor animals that they would lie for
hours in the lake with nothing but their noses above
water, and even these plunged under every now and then.
Then the heat was almost incredible, and the changes
very sudden and extraordinary.   Thus the temperature,
at five in the morning, of November 15th, was 54°, and
at five in the evening, 100°.   For the three following
days it was successively 140°, 160°, and 146°, at noon, in
the sun, which, if the thermometer of M'Kinlay can be
depended upon, is a heat almost surpassing anything
hitherto recorded.   After a few days' hot weather it
would grow a little cooler, and seem to threaten rain,
but the clouds would always blow over.

Towards the end of the month, M'Kinlay became
alarmed lest some accident should have befallen Hodgkinson, for his prolonged absence seemed unaccount-
able; but on the 29th November he returned to the
depôt. He brought intelligence of the fate of Burke
and Wills, and the rescue of King by Howitt. M'Kinlay
now knew that he had been deceived about the graves,
but he was still of opinion that some affray had taken
place, for he had in the meantime gleaned a great deal
more information from the natives. They admitted
that only one of the whites had been killed on their
return from the northward, and that after the battle, in
which many natives had been killed and wounded, they
had buried their companion and marched southward.
They described all the waters they had passed, and
spoke of them returning from an attempt to reach
the Darling, and living for some time upon nardoo.
There is an odd mixture of truth and falsehood in these
stories, which can be accounted for by bearing in mind
that the information was conveyed by signs. M'Kinlay's sagacity must have been very great to make even
this much out of their gestures, but he was confident,
from what he saw, that some would be found still alive
upon the Barcoo. On hearing from Hodgkinson of
Burke's unsuccessful attempt to reach Mount Hopeless,
he remarks that had they only pushed further to the
westward they could easily have found water on a
route all the way to the Adelaide stations. Their error
was partly owing to Gregory's statement, that two-thirds
of the waters of the Barcoo emptied south by way of
Strzelecki's Creek. M'Kinlay was now convinced that
the greater portion of the river emptied to the northward of the latitude of his depôt.

Before leaving the camp, M'Kinlay intended to
explore to the east and west. He meant then to look
northward for waters spoken of by the natives. His
movements subsequently would be decided by the
appearance of the country. He was, however, under
no anxiety with regard to water. He had found that
it could be easily obtained by digging; in fact, a well of
good water had been obtained at less than ten feet from

the surface. But, in addition to this, the natives assured them that the Barcoo would soon be flooded, and that their camp would be uninhabitable.

His first journey was to the eastward. He passed through nothing but sand-hills at first, sometimes clothed with a little spinifex and scrub, but often as loose and barren as if they had been just drifted in from the ocean. When the red sand-hills ceased, clay plains succeeded, clothed as usual with gum trees and grass; and both plains and hills were interrupted by creeks and lagoons, the most of which were salt, and all of which were fast drying up. In short, the country was just what Sturt had found between Strzelecki's Creek and the Stony Desert, and it terminated here when M'Kinlay had reached the Barcoo. In journeying down the river he came upon the grave of poor Wills, as it had been left by Mr. Howitt, and then to that of Burke. At Howitt's camp, M'Kinlay left documents stating his future movements, and then returned to his companions.

The whole party were moved forward on the 17th, intending to reach Lake Massacre, and there wait for a change in the weather before moving onward. Many lakes and lagoons were passed as they travelled, showing how this country, even after the terribly dry season they had experienced, was still well provided with water. Into one of the lakes Mr. Hodgkinson swam out for three hundred yards, and found, with a plumb-line, that the depth was still over ten feet, while in other places it was considerably more, so that some might almost be expected to last through the whole summer. But there could be no doubt that they were rapidly evaporating, for the heat was so intense at the time that one of the bullocks died from the effects of it. The margins of these lagoons were verdant and picturesque, as all explorers have described them ; and what makes them more so, is the enormous flocks of parrots, pelicans, and pigeons, which seem to associate in the interior of Australia with a sort of alliterative instinct. The map of M'Kinlay's route shows that lakes on this part of his journey were beyond number, and his journal tells us that every one of them had myriads of birds upon its banks. This description in no way corresponds with our previous notions of the Australian interior. It is like going to face the Libyan Desert and finding oneself in the Valley of the Nile.

Among these lakes M'Kinlay passed the time until the rainy reason should set in. He was, in fact, detained, as Sturt had been, at the Barrier Ranges, but under far different circumstances, because there was plenty of water about, and he could retreat whenever he chose. The time went very slowly, and the delay was most tantalizing, especially as every cloud seemed to promise a shower. Nevertheless, the time was not lost: it was occupied in making a thorough examination of the neighbourhood; and any one who has inspected the chart, and seen the number of lakes there laid down, can form an idea of the extent of the survey. To attempt to give a list of them would be like an attempt to describe the chart. No two of them were alike. Some had been dry apparently for years; others, as above mentioned, were full of water. Some had a desert and sterile appearance, being surrounded by a jumble of sand-hills and flooded plains, covered with either the dank, unwholesome samphire, or the wiry, withered looking polygonum. Others had very rich feed around their banks. In journeying from one to another M'Kinlay would often be entangled among sand-hills, exactly like snow-drifts, with heath bushes protruding, though the prevailing character of the sand was a glaring red, dotted with coarse grass and shrubs. Creeks were very common in this sort of soil, and these not mere watercourses, but broad channels, with fish in their waters and mussels in their banks. All these probably formed tributaries to the Barcoo, and this is the clue to the physical character of the whole country around M'Kinlay's camp. Readers have seen how it is the character of Australian rivers to lose themselves in plains during some portion of their course, and, while running through numerous shallow channels, inundate the land. In no river is this more common than the Barcoo. Kennedy and Sturt both met with several

instances of this, and probably the principal one was in
the tract which M'Kinlay was now destined to explore.
It is the final overflow and spreading out of the waters
in one of the most level and probably depressed portions
of the interior: the ordinary inundations of the stream
probably go no further.

This tract was found by M'Kinlay to be very thickly
inhabited. The natives were living in crowds upon the
creeks, and supporting themselves upon the fish they
caught. Sturt had met with very few blacks, and these
he considered miserable and emaciated creatures; but
then Sturt viewed everything as mournful and gloomy,
under the influence the desert had produced upon him.
M'Kinlay thought them fine, tall, athletic fellows, who
might have been troublesome if they liked, but who
only once made an attempt to drive off the cattle, and
were easily dispersed. Often, indeed, they made themselves useful, and the explorers could always get one or
two to act as guides or to work in the camp. It can be
seen, also, that M'Kinlay was far from considering the
place a desert; and in this no one will differ from him.
Certainly many square miles of red, loose sand, clothed
only with useless, stunted vegetation, must be a great
drawback to any country, especially where such patches
are rather common. It would be very satisfactory to
learn what proportion they bear to the grassy plains.
If very large, the country would be no better than the
great Sahara, except in point of water; but if small, it
would be no worse than many parts of Australia on
which there are settlements.

Before leaving this territory, M'Kinlay had an
opportunity of comparing it with a desert about which
there could be no question. It rained all day on the
22nd January, 1862, and this enabled him to start out
to the north to examine the country before him. He
travelled over flats and sand-hills until he met with an
area of drifting sand, which he had to toil through for
longer than usual. Suddenly it terminated, like a sea
coast-line, with the Stony Desert at its base. He found
it to be just what Sturt described it. To the east and
south there was nothing but stones, while to the west

sand-hills interrupted the plains. He continued to the
north as far as he could, because he was anxious to find
a track for his party; but he returned unsuccessful.
His turning-point was amidst high sand-hills, without
any water, so that he was obliged to resign all hope of
going further in that direction. The country seemed
liable to floods at times, but was then quite impracticable. His track was to the east both of Burke's track
and Sturt's final attempt to reach the centre. There
can be no doubt that this is a desert in the true sense of
the word, equal to anything amid the scorching plains
of Arabia or the desolate sands of the Sahara. Of its
extent nothing is as yet certainly known, but no doubt
it exists in patches throughout a large portion of these
latitudes, amid which the Barcoo lakes may be considered as a sort of oasis.

After this experience, M'Kinlay was resolved to
wait for more rains or a rise of the waters of the Barcoo.
This, the natives assured him, was coming down, and
plainly intimated that unless the explorers moved away
they would be overwhelmed by the rush of waters. As,
however, they were much interested in getting the oxen
away from the water which they wanted for themselves,
M'Kinlay was resolved to risk the result. But not only
no floods came, but the waters around were so rapidly
drying up that it was questionable whether they would
not soon be obliged to beat a retreat. This state of
inaction was very distressing. Day by day went by
and nothing could be done, while the provisions were
getting exhausted and the men sickening very much
from the climate. On the 7th February, two of the
party were sent to examine the state of certain distant
lakes, towards which it was contemplated to remove.
While they were absent it rained heavily, with thunder
all round. This altered M'Kinlay's plans. As the
provisions were much exhausted, he reduced the rations
of the men, and moved at once to the northward. He
proposed to reach Eyre Creek, and then to follow it, if
it would permit him, towards Carpentaria.

Travelling was not easy at first. The rain had
made the sand-hills and flats very heavy, and the cattle

could only make short stages. They reached the Stony
Desert in due course, and camped upon it at twenty-
five miles. There was not a blade of grass near ; in fact,
the only sustenance for the horses was a little saltbush.
"It was," says M'Kinlay, "a most dismal looking
camp, with only a few isolated sand-hills all round."
Nine miles more, next day, however, brought them out
of it. As they left it, the rain came down heavily
again, and then the aspect of the desert was more dreary
than ever. The whole surface became covered with
glistening sheets of water, which made it look like an
interminable beach, from which the water had just
retired. Beyond the desert more sand-hills succeeded,
and then a plain, utterly destitute of any growth
except a few green shrubs in the watercourses. Of
these there were very many. The whole plain seemed
cut up with innumerable small streams, showing the
soft nature of the soil. Of course, there was no water,
even after the rain, but the country was very boggy.
They managed to advance twenty-three miles, and
encamped by the side of the creek. It was very large,
and lined with trees, with good water, in detached holes,
and plenty of ducks and fish. This was not Eyre
Creek, but the watercourse found by Burke and Wills,
after they had crossed the Stony Desert. It had been
named after poor Gray, and being a large channel, at
least ninety yards wide, it is perfectly incomprehensible
how Sturt managed to miss it. M'Kinlay's observations exactly tally with those of Wills. He described
its banks as precipitous, fifty or sixty feet high, with
numerous small creeks, and a junction of equal size,
close to the camp. I have already pointed out that this
river must join Lake Eyre, but where it comes from is
a matter of very interesting speculation.

In journeying up the river, which M'Kinlay now
named after Burke, they found the remains of a horse
and saddle, with numerous tracks of camels. This was
a portion of the disastrous expedition which last
explored these waters. It was not a very fortunate
locality, for the present explorer. M'Kinlay, was laid
up for several days with a severe attack of illness, and

several of the men were indisposed. One of the
bullocks died meanwhile, and then their native guide
deserted. Thus a great deal of time was lost, during
which only a very slight examination of the country
around could be made. But this was no great loss, for
there was absolutely nothing to see but the same old
series of flooded flats and sand-hills.

On the 25th they moved forward again, but could
only make a very short stage. The banks of the creek
bore as bad a character as any yet seen on an Australian
river. The sand-hills were almost impassable. They
were composed of pure drift sand, not gently sloping
like the hummocks in other portions of the desert, but
terminating in an abrupt cliff five or six feet high. To
get animals over these was a matter of great difficulty.
Even when the sand was shovelled down they slipped,
staggered, and floundered, as if they were in a morass.
After seven miles of such exertion, they formed a camp,
while one of the bullocks out of the four remaining was
killed. The place for the operation was not carefully
selected, and M'Kinlay had a very small suspicion of the
change that was about to take place in the nature of the
country. It rained heavily during the night, with all
the energy of a tropical shower. In the morning there
was no change in the weather, neither was there
throughout the day. For two whole days and nights
the rain came down heavily. At first, the creek began
to rise, and the ground grew muddy. On the second
day, the creek was much swollen, and the ground impassable. This was, be it remembered, upon the spot
where Sturt had noticed the ground was so soft, and,
suffering as he was for want of water, he dreaded to be
overtaken there by rain. M'Kinlay, however, had no
anxieties of the kind; as he had made up his mind to
attempt to reach the Gulf of Carpentaria, he was very
glad indeed to see such a supply of water. But when
the third day came, and then the fourth, and the rain
still poured down without intermission, matters began
to wear a very different aspect. At first, the waters rose
only at the rate of three and a half inches an hour, but
on the 1st March, the river began to rise much more

rapidly. But this was not the worst. The river was only receiving the drainage from the hills, while the plains were becoming rapidly inundated. The party were utterly unconscious of this, and only discovered it when they were nearly surrounded by water. There was not much time left for deliberation. With great difficulty the sheep and cattle were got over, and the stores were transported without much damage. Not a moment too soon. Towards evening a great portion of the flat was covered, and all was a perfect sea, dotted only by lines of trees and a few sand-hills. This sudden and unexpected change was like magic, but that it was not unusual in these latitudes was evident, for M'Kinlay noticed upon the trees flood-marks, which showed that water stood seven feet higher at times. This was the most extraordinary discovery made by M'Kinlay with reference to the interior, and he now understood what the blacks meant when they told him of an inundation which would drive him out of his camp.

The flood delayed the party until the 10th of March. The weather was at first very wet, but it cleared up at length, and became sultry. The time was occupied in shoeing the horses and jerking meat, while M'Kinlay made a little journey to some stony hills eastward. It was, unfortunately, too hazy to see from what quarter the river flowed. The country around was very thickly studded with hills, but from north, to nearly north-west, the heads of the trees were visible above the waters. The appearance of the dry land was very much changed. Even in that short space of time the rain had had a most favourable effect upon the vegetation. The rocks, which but a short time ago appeared bronzed and utterly barren, were now covered with luxuriant herbage, and the desert seemed to smile with verdure. One is reminded here of the effect a little moisture is said to have upon the sterile steppes of Arabia.

On the 10th, the explorers were in motion again. The journey was over stony hills and tributary creeks for sixteen miles. The camp was on the edge of a

flooded flat. There was a small movement in the
waters, which M'Kinlay supposed to be due to the
wind. But he soon found that the flood was still rising,
and the camp had to be removed further into the hills,
where the baggage was secured upon a pile of stones.
With other beasts of burden the party would have found
their position almost inextricable; but the camels
carried their loads over the stones with the utmost ease.
M'Kinlay gives it as his opinion that they were
undoubtedly the best of all animals for exploration in
Australia. They eat almost anything, from the gum
tree down to the smallest herbage, and then would lie
down round the camp, while horses and bullocks, if
feed was scarce, would ramble all over the country.
"With sheep and camels," says M'Kinlay, "one could
travel over any part of the continent, and keep them in
good condition."

The floods now made a great alteration in
M'Kinlay's course. With such a sea to the northward,
it was useless to try to travel in any direction except to
the east. This was taking him a good deal out of the
way he wished to go, but still there was nothing for it
but to try to skirt the inundation, travelling along a
table-range which lay upon their right. The soil was
a mere succession of sand-hills and stony plains, with
plenty of water and feed. On the 13th, they noticed a
gap in the range, which they crossed. On the further
side the country improved very much. There was
abundance of rich pasture and bamboo swamps, with
thousands of pigeons and teal, whose eggs furnished an
agreeable change of diet to the men. It was very easy
to travel through such land, except that the lagoons and
swamps were found rather heavy to cross. On the
15th, they came in sight of a splendid tier of table-
topped ranges. M'Kinlay rode to them over magnificent
pasture. From the summit of the hills, named Ella
Range, there was a fine view over the irregular tops of
hills around. These were, as usual, flat topped or
peaked, with innumerable creeks draining the country
to the west and north. It was impossible to say where
they terminated, but as far as M'Kinlay could see there

was no obstacle to his route, and then for many days
afterwards the journey was as uniform as most of the
explorations through central Australia have proved.
Readers will doubtless remember, that when Burke was
in these latitudes he had found a succession of grassy
plains, with creeks, and a few rocky hills. This was
about fifty miles to the west of where M'Kinlay now was,
and his experience was very similar. He was travelling
over the tableland which was rising towards the northward. The character of the sandstone plateau was not
more interesting here than elsewhere. It was the usual
stony plains, with sand-hills, Myall creeks, and well-
grassed gum flats, all either liable to inundation, or
having extensive sheets of water upon their surface.
One of the plains was very extensive, and almost a
complete morass, even though drained by many creeks,
joining a large watercourse, which they could not reach.
Beyond this the country was rather better for travelling,
in consequence of the fragments of sandstone which
strewed the ground. On the 30th March, there was
a little change in the scenery; mountains and rugged
peaks jutted out to the northward in all directions;
their red sandstone summits contrasted beautifully with
the green herbage upon their sides, looking all the more
remarkable as the soil, foliage, and grass about the
plains had the dull, brownish hue of Australian
landscapes. But the general aspect of the land ahead
of them was evidently of a difficult nature. It must
have rained heavily in this direction, for the ground had
the appearance of being almost ploughed up by the
surface drainage. M'Kinlay was of opinion that an
explorer caught by sudden rain in this locality would
never more be heard of.

But, in spite of creeks and quagmires, the party
were slowly working their way into the interior. Their
experience of the centre of Australia was very different
from what they had anticipated. Instead of a desert,
they were embarrassed by the waters. On the whole,
however, the country cannot be considered very available. These sand-hills were still of a desert character,
and from M'Kinlay's diary the vegetation appears to

have been more spinifex and Acacia than anything else.
The flooded plains were beautifully grassed, as they
always are; but the greater part of the ground was
not. On the 31st the explorers commenced journeying
up a creek, which came through a gorge in a sandstone
range. The gorge was fully three-quarters of a mile
wide, and for the whole of that space was either water
or bogs, with two limestone islands in the middle. On
the other side of the gap the land was rendered very
boggy by innumerable creeks from the eastward. It
was so soft that the men had great difficulty in ex-
tricating themselves. But the pasture on the banks
was magnificent. On the widest of the creeks the
natives had constructed a weir for catching the fish,
which were so abundant that the explorers could see
them splashing continually as they rose to the flies.
One cannot help speculating as to where all this
drainage came from. Large fish show a permanency
in the waters, which would argue some lofty range for
their sources; and it cannot be imagined that so many
channels can drain towards a salt lake without passing
into some very large main stream. At any rate, the
explorers found the country as difficult to travel over
as it could possibly be. Where it was not boggy it was
stony, and almost every day they found themselves
entangled in a new series of rocky gorges and table-
hills. The scenery was very beautiful at times, but the
country was almost a useless scrub, except on the banks
of the stream. On the 7th April they met with a fine
river some two hundred and fifty yards wide. Its
banks were forty or fifty feet high, lined with very
large trees. It had abundance of birds of every kind
upon its waters, and the grass was most luxuriant on
the plains of the surrounding country. It was named
after Dr. Mueller, the eminent Australian botanist.
This stream appeared to notify an important change in
the country, and the explorers hoped for better times
and easier travelling. Certainly they wanted both, for
they were now reduced to rations of meat, with as
much portulac as they could gather. But there was
no improvement. The banks were very bad travelling,

in consequence of the great number of stones upon the
surface, so the party had to keep to the northward
again. The usual creeks and flats succeeded. There
was no change in any respect, except that the rocks
became slaty. The creeks passed were all of a very
large size, and the travelling was miserable, in consequence of the stones. Three large streams were
named the Fletcher, the Cadell, and the Middleton.

The latter creek seemed to come from the north-
west—a direction which M'Kinlay was very anxious to
take. His intention was now to make for the Albert
River, and then to cross to Port Denison, for his provisions were too reduced to think of returning to Adelaide. He was within the tropics; the days were, in
consequence, very warm; but the evenings and morn-
ings were delightfully cool. Unfortunately, a new
difficulty beset them. The water, which had hitherto
been in excess, became scarce, and they were doubtful
whether the Middleton would contain sufficient to
enable them to reach its sources. But they were able
easily to cross the range from which it came, and found
other creeks upon the further side. These flowed
through flats of the richest possible description, though
bounded on the east by wretched sandstone hills, and
often crossed by ridges of the same description. They
flowed down from a noble range of mountains to the
westward. These mountains were different from anything the explorers had met with in the interior of the
continent. They formed a bold, picturesque range, or a
long chain of high and abrupt hills, extending beyond
the range of vision to the northward. It was not like
the flat, red sandstone summits, forming a castellated
outline of glaring colour, but blue slaty precipices, with
darkened ravines of thick forest. The spot was rendered very memorable to the explorers, in consequence
of their losing one of their party in its recesses for four
days. M'Kinlay showed his benevolence and good
feeling by making every possible effort for his recovery;
and so much did it affect him, that his journal is full of
nothing else for those few days but expressions of con-
dolence with the sufferer. The poor man was found at

last, and, of course, so much exhausted by his adventures that the party were obliged to remain encamped
a few days until he was somewhat restored. In the
meantime, M'Kinlay was enabled to make a thorough
examination of the country around. The range was
estimated to be three thousand feet above the plain.
There were many lesser spurs and parallel ranges near.
From all of them streams flowed to the northward, and
thus it appeared they had at last crossed to the watershed of Carpentaria. All the streams flowed considerably east of north, and probably they will be found to
be tributaries of the Flinders. One of them, certainly,
must be Cloncurry Creek, which was traced down by
Burke and Wills. It appears marked on the map as the
Williams. Though they were all of considerable size,
M'Kinlay did not like to follow any of them. They
turned too much to the eastward, and he was afraid they
had no outlet on the north coast. In this opinion he
was justified from appearances, because the widest
creek, though two hundred and fifty yards across, failed
completely when it was traced down, nor could its
further course be discovered. Possibly, the width of
the streams is no sure guide as to their length, for the
rain upon these tropical mountains would be sudden
and violent, and apt to hollow out wide channels, for a
fall of waters whose force would soon be spent. And
yet the number and magnitude of them was astonishing,
as the following epitome of the journal will enable
readers to perceive. On the 25th, the party started
northward for twenty-four miles along the east side of
the range, and in doing so struck a fine creek from the
hills, flowing in a bed three hundred yards wide. It
was seen to join another about a mile further on. The
main creek, the M'Kinlay, seemed to continue to the
eastward. Ten miles beyond the M'Kinlay there was
another creek, four hundred yards wide. and still
retaining immense sheets of water. This, I imagine,
was Burke's Cloncurry Creek. M'Kinlay seems to say
that the bed was trap-rock, but the range probably
differs from the more strictly volcanic emanations on the
watersheds all round Australia.

Leaving the Williams next day on a course nearly
north, they soon fell in with another fine stream, perhaps
a tributary of Cloncurry Creek. It had evidently been
recently subjected to extraordinary inundations, for in
its bed immense trees were strewn about, just as they were
torn from their roots. There were other large creeks
besides this one, and M'Kinlay could see that they
turned northward, and joined a large stream to the eastward; this was in all probability the Flinders. The
explorers thought that they could see its line of trees
extending for a long distance. In other respects the
country was an open, undulating plain. A few isolated
hills jutted out here and there, as well as some belts of
bushes. The grass was abundant, though rank. This
character of country continued until the 4th May, when
the party crossed high tableland, and commenced to
descend a creek flowing to the northward. In two
days it led to the Leichhardt. It was then a fine stream,
with plenty of water, but the banks too precipitous for
the animals to drink, and from a hundred and fifty to
a hundred and eighty yards wide. The country around
was an Acacia forest, or shrubby plain, and, as usual,
lined with the stately flooded gum trees.

Once upon the Leichhardt, M'Kinlay was no longer
exploring new country. He was upon the tracks of
others who had preceded him, and he knew now that his
expedition had succeeded. What made him more
sanguine in the result was, that he expected to find the
Victoria still anchored in Carpentaria, and that he should
be able to recruit his stores and supplies with her assistance. He followed down the Leichhardt, therefore, full
of hope. The river did not alter its character to any
great extent. It is true that it widened very much,
and tumbled down over steep rocky falls, and also that
during its course it ran through high basaltic rocks,
like all the rivers which flow down from the tableland,
but in most respects it was like all the others, except
that it was a wider, finer stream than any, except the
Flinders. M'Kinlay followed it to the sea, that is to
say, he traced it into salt marshes, but the dense forest
of mangroves prevented his reaching the beach. The

change from fine palm tree reaches to the coast scenery
was very great, and it was not without regret that they
bade adieu to the dense tropical foliage on the river side,
varied by lovely flowers, or graceful fan palms, which
threw such a beautiful shade on the still, clear reaches
of the river.

It need hardly be told, that M'Kinlay did not meet
with the *Victoria* steamer, as he had expected. It had
sailed nearly three months previously, so that the party
had no help to expect until they got back to the settled
districts. But which way they were to turn was the
question. Queensland was the nearest, but there were
the mountains to cross; Adelaide was further away,
but the route to it was well known. Unfortunately for
himself, M'Kinlay chose the former. It will be needless
to follow him along a route which has been so often
described. He started from the Leichhardt on the 30th
May, and soon was fairly among the ranges, steering
towards Port Denison. Those who remember the experience of Leichhardt, Kennedy, and Walker, will not
require to be told what M'Kinlay's troubles were. Like
Walker, too, his provisions were scanty, and he had to
eat first the cattle, then the horses, and then the camels,
for it was not until the 2nd of August that they arrived
at an out-station on the Burdekin.

Thus ended M'Kinlay's journey, which was as successful as any sent into the interior to search for Burke
and Wills. The peculiar incidents met with threw an
entirely new light upon the physical geography of some
parts of the desert; and in acknowledging this, one must
add, that for cool perseverance, and kind consideration
for his followers, for modesty, and yet for quiet daring,
M'Kinlay was unequalled as an explorer.

CHAPTER XXX.

SOME further particulars remain to be stated with
reference to the search for Burke and Wills. As soon
as the Governments of the various colonies had started
so many parties in different directions, it became necessary to provide a central depôt where any of them
might rendezvous for supplies. The camp on the
Barcoo was thought the best for the purpose; and soon
after his return, Mr. Howitt was despatched with
instructions to remain long enough to relieve any of
the exploring expeditions. On his return he was to
bring down the remains of Burke and Wills, that they
might be interred in a public manner near Melbourne.

The establishment of the depôt was an afterthought,
and none of the exploring parties were aware of its
existence except M'Kinlay. No doubt, the creditable
haste with which the expeditions were despatched prevented everything being thought of; but there was
certainly some little bungling in not giving Landsborough a hint of the relief at the Barcoo. Unfortunately,
though he was the only explorer to whom the depôt
could have been of valuable assistance, he passed within
comparatively few miles of it without knowing that
help was at hand.

When Mr. Howitt had reached the camp he made
a journey to Blanchewater, by way of Lake Hope, for
the purpose of sending despatches to Adelaide. This
was the track which Burke and Wills tried to reach.

Poor fellows! had they only kept a little further to the westward, their plans might have been easily accomplished. What Howitt said of the crossing-place of Lake Torrens is worth notice. The high, *white* sand-hills of Lake Eyre were visible all the day long upon his right, as he came down towards the Horseshoe Lake, where it ought to have been if the old maps had been correct. But the only indications of the basin at the crossing was a salt creek, connecting two boggy lakes. There was nothing else, for immediately afterwards the sand-hills ocurred again.

As he was returning to the depôt, Mr. Howitt learned from the natives that M'Kinlay's party were many days' journey to the north, beyond a flooded creek, which had cut them off from any communication with the country to the south, and that they were surrounded by water. This was perfectly true, and it reveals an interesting fact—M'Kinlay saw no natives around him while he was being flooded out; yet not only does it appear that they watched his movements, but that they transmitted the news to tribes at an immense distance. Howitt scarcely credited the intelligence, yet he admits that when he rode over the alternate sand-ridges, creeks, flats, and dry lakes, he could easily believe a party might be hemmed in completely were a flood to come down among them.

When Howitt's party reached the depôt, the men heard daily from the natives the story that the Barcoo was coming down and would soon flood the whole country. On the 8th April this was found to be true, for the river rose rapidly. The first water was quite undrinkable, being, of course, the rinsings of all the old holes of a river which brings heavy deposits of salt down into Lake Torrens. In a few days, however, it was quite fresh and sweet, and though the flood-water was by no means large in quantity, yet it had travelled seventy miles in six weeks, and soon gave the valley of the Barcoo a smiling, agreeable appearance.

On the 12th April, Howitt started to the north, with five men and thirteen horses. The result of this

journey was the discovery of some fine grassy land,
with creeks, very different from what was found in the
vicinity of the Barcoo.   Yet such spots were not extensive.   They were continuously interrupted by ridges of
sand, of a bright, fiery red—like red-hot iron, Howitt
says—with the horrid spinifex upon them.   Many creeks
were discovered; all, perhaps, channels by which the
Barcoo reaches Lake Eyre.   The natives had spoken a
good deal about a large creek, which Howitt searched
for, but it was found to be no more than a boggy watercourse, in red sand, lined with box trees.   Lat. 26° 46'
was the lowest reached in this journey.   Howitt would
also have explored to the eastward, but ever since
leaving the Barcoo he had had stony ridges and tableland in that direction; at first, twenty miles, but latterly
only eight miles distant.   On returning to the depôt,
May 13, the flood was found to have reached within
about four miles of the upper end of the water-hole
there.   The water was of a clear olive green, and came
down slowly, not, in fact, faster than two miles a week,
because of the many channels and backwaters it had to
fill.

   After another visit to Blanchewater, Howitt went
northward again in July, to search for M'Kinlay's
tracks; in the course of which he explored the part
between Sturt's furthest point (1845), and the route of
Burke and Wills.   In this expedition, of course, nothing
very new could be discovered, after the numerous
journeys of M'Kinlay.   There were the same old scenes
of desolation which Sturt's writings have immortalized;
the same sand-ridges, fiery and hot; the same plains
burnt up with drought; the same dull, dreary landscape;
where, in fine—if solitude and barrenness, aridity and
savage severity, can give grandeur—assuredly is to be
found the grandest and most awful scene in the world.
Only one feature was out of keeping with the rest, and
that was the constant occurrence of little lagoons, which
started out of the wilderness as if by magic.   It is
worth while describing the Stony Desert as it appeared
to Howitt, bearing in mind, at the same time, what
Sturt said years ago.   The former thus speaks of his

journey from Hope Plains. "For about ten miles we travelled across high ridges of loose sand, with an occasional large flat of sandstone gravel. Everything seemed perishing with drought, and was desolate in the extreme. The landscape could have been represented in Indian ink or sepia. After crossing red ridges, covered with spinifex, where every bush was dead, we came to the edge of the desert, the sand-hills running into it at various lengths. It was very much as I had expected to find it—extensive stony plains. We crossed about five miles of stones, not bad travelling, and camped on a sand-ridge; the stony plains extending northwards to the horizon, with scarcely any food for the horses—only the remains of the grass, which looked as if it owed its origin to the Deluge, and a few plants of portulac, which some light showers had freshened up. There were pools among the stones, with which the plains were covered, the latter densely packed together, like a pavement, or in some places large in size and loosely strewn on a spongy soil." This is Howitt's account, not so gloomy as Sturt's, we must admit, but still not an encouraging account of the interior of Australia. Altogether, Mr. Howitt was of opinion that these stony plains were very little different from large tracts of country which lie between the Flinders Range and Lake Torrens, in South Australia, except that the salsolaceous plants were wanting.

After this journey, Mr. Howitt again came down to Blanchewater with despatches, and then returned to the depôt. Up to this time, no tidings of any of the explorers had been obtained; and it seemed to be certain that there was no further chance of their calling at the depôt. Mr. Howitt buried four and a half bags of flour, and some clothes, according to instructions, and then collecting all the natives, informed them that the party were about to return to their own country. He distributed clothes and presents among them, with some engraved brass plates, setting forth the reasons the Victorian Government had for rewarding the natives of Barcoo. Having thus fulfilled all instructions, the depôt was finally removed, and, with the remains of Burke and Wills, the large train of horses, camels, baggage, &c. slowly wended its way back to the southward.

About the end of November the funeral train arrived in Adelaide. Nothing could have been more solemn than the arrangements for escorting the body into the city. All the colonists vied with each other in showing their sense of the noble self-devotion of the heroes, the wrecks of whose mortality were now first brought within the reach of civilized homes. From Adelaide the remains were carried to Melbourne, where nothing was spared to do honour to the memory of the departed. The public tribute of respect at this funeral will be remembered for many a year, and showed how the zeal and courage of the explorers were appreciated in the city which sent them forth. A beautiful monument has been erected over their remains. There is something touching in the thought that however sad and desolate the death-beds of those brave men, their graves are not now lonely, neither are they left unpitied in the desert, with none to mourn over the spot, or read the dreadful tale of their sufferings. At least, their bones are among friends who admire, while they regret and sorrow over a fate which nothing can now recall.

It may be easily guessed, that those who bore a part in these expeditions were liberally rewarded by the Government. Nearly all received grants of money, and their welcome home by the colonists was most enthusiastic. Probably, no explorer executed his task with more prudence than Mr. Howitt, and while accomplishing his instructions exactly, under circumstances of considerable difficulty, did so with less fuss and inconvenience to his followers than ever was seen in explorations before. He deserves the name of being a perfect type of an Australian bushman.

Before concluding this chapter, I must speak finally of the Australian Bight, which, after the encouraging explorations I have been recording, will seem very dreary.

It had been little disturbed from Eyre's time, but still discovery had not been idle even there. In 1862, Mr. Goyder, the surveyor-general, returned from a visit to the coast, north of Fowler's Bay. For a hundred miles inland he found nothing but a Myall and *Eucalyptus* scrub, with spinifex, a few herbs, and very little grass. A narrow strip of better land was seen to the westward, but there was no fresh water; in fact, the ground was incrusted with salt. Most of the country was a light brown sandy loam, free from stones, and sufficiently porous to absorb any quantity of rain. The natives were not numerous, and seem to subsist on water from the mallee roots, for these and two rock waters in granite were the only available supply.

In the same year, 1862, Capt. Delisser and Mr. Mackie, squatters, made an excursion into the same country. It was in July when they started, when the weather was cool, and the grass green and long. Their intention was to keep as far as possible from Warburton's tracks, and after passing the head of the Bight, to proceed as far west and north as they could.

Seventeen miles north-west, through dense scrub, brought them to a water-hole. Fifty miles further the same course led to no improvement in the country, or at least only a very slight one, so the explorers turned back to the sand-hills, in the south-west, for water. These sand-hills are very peculiar repositories of water, since that which is found by digging on the side nearest the sea is quite fresh, while that which is found on the north side is salt and undrinkable. They are also covered with white flints, and in other respects as desolate and as barren as can well be imagined.

Striking west from the sand-hills, Messrs. Delisser and Mackie soon came upon undulating plains of grass and saltbush. At first, there was a little scrub, but it soon disappeared, and they were upon the plain already discovered by Warburton, where not a tree nor a bush of any kind rose up to break the awful monotony of so vast a level. Though the ground was cracked and parched, and there were no signs of water at the most favourable season of a year remarkable for its rain, Capt. Delisser was very pleasingly impressed with the appearance of the country. He said he had seen nothing like it before. Major Warburton, Messrs. Komoll,

Kewson, and Shanahan had said too, that they had never seen anything like it before, but it was for aridity and desolation. I am afraid we must regard the latter as the most correct opinion. This is our latest intelligence from the singular plains at the head of the Bight, whose explorations were begun by Eyre. The matter has not progressed much in twenty-five years.*

* This tract, as already stated, has been settled upon, but under great difficulties in consequence of the want of water. Captain Delisser has publicly blamed me for having on another occasion adopted the opinions of Major Warburton as to this country in preference to his, but the results of Captain Delisser's settlement have not yet convinced me that I am wrong.

CHAPTER XXXI.

STUART'S LAST JOURNEY—CONCLUSION.

Stuart renews his attempt beyond Newcastle Water—Dense scrubs—King's Ponds—Various clay water-holes—The Strangways—The Roper—The Chambers—The Watershed—The Adelaide River—Reaches the coast—Return of the party—Dreadful sufferings of Stuart—Conclusion.

THE year 1862 was a remarkable one in the annals of exploration. Scarcely a month passed without bringing some new tidings of discovery made in remote parts of the continent. The colonies were so taken up with the search for Burke and Wills that no other expeditions were thought of. But when Walker, Landsborough, and, finally, M'Kinlay, had brought in their news, people began to think of Stuart, and to look forward to his return. He, too, was destined to complete the task he had so ably begun, and for so long a time had persevered in. We left him, at the close of his last expedition, returning baffled from his second attempt to cross the continent. In his first, the natives had driven him back when nearly two-thirds of his journey was over. In the second, he had got nearly as far as lat. 17°, but then was stopped by dense waterless scrubs, which surrounded him in every direction. Yet he did not consider them impassable. The reason why they had conquered him on that occasion was because his resources were nearly spent in searching for water before he reached so far. Under these circumstances, no sooner had he returned than the Government equipped a party to start with him again.

He left the settled districts early in January, 1862. With the early part of his journey the reader need not be troubled. It was much delayed for want of water,

2 K 2

and several very perilous advances had to be made.
On the 7th April he arrived at his furthest northern
point, from which he had turned back in May of the
preceding year. His plan now was to encamp the party
while he made a search for water in advance. He was
not very successful at first. He made a journey due
north, and then to the westward, but could not find any
watercourse. Some few ponds of water to the north-
west, of pretty considerable extent, enabled him to shift
his camp about twenty miles, but he could not get much
further for a long time. On the 25th he went about
thirty miles in a due north line. All but the last six
miles was fair travelling over plains, and then succeeded
a thick forest and scrub quite impassable, and without a
drop of water. For several days subsequently every
effort was made to pass through this forest. Stuart left
no direction untried, but ever with the same result.
The ironstone undulations of the plains always terminated in as thick a forest as had ever been seen in
that country. Every new defeat made a change in the
plans ; sometimes they would go towards the north, and
at others towards the Victoria River ; any way, in fact,
as long as they could get through. But the scrub forest,
haunted them in every direction ; and if, exasperated at
the delay, they made a desperate push into the thicket
it only resulted in prolonging their labours and in
tearing their equipage and clothes. In upwards of
fifty miles they did not see the least signs of a watercourse, and the grass seemed as dry as if it had grown
up years ago. But a change in their position came
at last.   To the north, How's Ponds were found,
and north of these some other sheets of water, named
after Mr. Auld. These were in a plain, to attain which
they crossed what seemed to be a sandy tableland,
covered with spinifex and gum trees. The latitude
was 16° 28'. Nor was this the end of the good luck.
Beyond Auld's Ponds, after a few belts or hedges
of scrub, the country opened into splendid lightly-
timbered, well-grassed plains. They then passed some
fine holes of water, and at five miles more they merged
into a broad deep creek of very important dimensions.

It soon terminated, and then another dry space ensued, but they had passed the scrub forest, and could afford to look hopefully on the country before them.

The large creek was named the Daly Waters, after the governor of the colony. It took a good time to get beyond it. The country to the north seemed a succession of swamps, if that name can be given to large alluvial flats, sometimes moist, but often so dry that the cracks and fissures were enough to engulf a man and horse. It is almost needless to add that the aspect of this country was very fertile. The grass was like a wheat-field, in open plains, lightly timbered with gum trees. The sheets of shallow water were covered with numerous wild-fowl.

Continuing over some well-timbered and grassy country, they reached Purdie's Ponds, and to these all the party were brought up on the 11th June. On the 13th, Stuart started again, and at seven miles crossed what seemed to be a watershed, with a very small creek running northwards. It gradually got larger, and at two miles there were a few small pools of water. Of course it was traced down. It wound and twisted very much. Twice it became very small, and Stuart was afraid he was going to lose it altogether, but it always opened again into a wide creek, while the general fall of the waters all round was to the northward. This was very encouraging. It was evident that they had passed the northern watershed, and they could now look confidently to the success of their undertaking, for this was certainly a tributary of the Roper. But it was not easy travelling. The further it was traced, the more rocky and precipitous its banks became, while the bed was occupied with large blocks of sandstone. There was no scarcity of water, however. The reaches were long and beautiful, containing many fish, and often fringed with dense brushwood or trees, which were quite new to the explorers. The river was named the Strangways.

It is needless to follow the daily journeys of the party down this stream. Its course was through the rocky gorges of the tableland. To the west the country was hilly, while to the east it was more level. On the

25th June they arrived at a large sheet of water in a
low swampy part of the country.   It looked like a
beautiful lake surrounded by a tropical vegetation of
palms, canes, and bamboos.   At the end of this was the
Roper River.   " The general character of the Strangways," says Mr. Waterhouse, the naturalist of the expedition, " is that of a deep narrow river, with steep banks
and a clayey soil.   The banks are well lined with large
trees, growing on rich alluvial ground, with tall and
good grass, although dry.   The fall is rapid, and much
drift was lodged in the branches of the trees high above
the banks."   The Roper was running, so they had to
follow it up for some distance to find a ford.   Stuart
said it was a splendid river, and the country around
really magnificent.   But it was very dry, and this was
the more unfortunate, as the natives, who were very
numerous, were setting it on fire, causing the party
great inconvenience.   Yet even in spite of its aridity
the banks were very boggy.   One of the horses became
hopelessly submerged, and in trying to get him out they
drowned him.   This was not such a great loss after all.
He was cut up, and his flesh formed a valuable addition
to their small rations.

On the 30th June they crossed to the north-east side.
At fifteen miles they came upon a large reedy swamp ;
and again at twenty miles the river was seen flowing
into the swamp from the north-north-west.   This was a
different branch to the one followed by Leichhardt, so it
was named the Chambers.   The scenery was still beautiful, and the soil covered with splendid grass ; all
around luxuriant plains, with scattered hills extended
beyond the range of vision, while here and there dark
lines of trees showed where tributary creeks flowed down
into the main stream.   Yet the aspect was not very
cheerful.   There was a lurid glare pervading the atmosphere, for the country was all on fire.   This was in
lat. 14° 47'.   Some natives visited their camp that
evening.   One was an extraordinary man, being no less
than seven feet high.   They had evidently seen whites
before, for they knew the use of fish-hooks, and were
very much frightened with the firearms.   They were

very peaceable, and kept at a respectful distance, but when they saw a pigeon shot they went away, and Stuart saw them more. In journeying up the Chambers, it was found not to be running, and it was thought that the current of the Roper must have come from a mass of springs in the bed of the swamp. The Chambers only supplied them with water for two days, and it then ran out into small watercourses coming from stony and poor, though high land. The valley was hemmed in by low sandstone ranges, supporting nothing but spinifex grass. It formed a great contrast to the Roper, and seemed like a change from an oasis to a desert. The last waterhole was in lat. 14° 25′. Beyond the sources of the Chambers a nice running creek was found, which Stuart at first thought was a tributary of the South Alligator or Adelaide. After following it for five miles he was very much disappointed to find that it ran through a stony gorge and went to the southward. He ascended one of the hills to see the country, but it was too thickly wooded for a very extensive prospect. The spaces between the trees, however, showed him that the country was a series of sandstone gorges of a desert character. Lonely and desolate, they rose one above another with all the dreary aspect of naked stones in a tropical climate. It was like the wilderness of Sinai, in Arabia, whose precipices would seem like human habitations but for the absence of anything like life around them. The similarity made it the more dreary. This was the tableland that so long had baffled Leichhardt. Stuart intended to cross it and descend to the sources of the Alligator, as his predecessor had done. For some distance his experience was precisely the same. There were many stony creeks, occasionally well-grassed valleys, more or less furnished with water.

At last, it appeared that the tableland was near its end. Basaltic rocks took the place of the sandstone, as they do on the edge of the whole northern plateau. A little beyond a small stream, named the Catherine, the basaltic country changed to slate and limestone, and the level descended slightly to a large swamp near some springs. These furnished water to several rivulets, all

so shrouded with the dense vegetation, combined with
graceful tropical ferns, that it was difficult to ascertain
their number. Further on, the country rose again ; it
was the last strip of the sandstone tableland. Like the
tract described by Grey, near the Glenelg River, it
would appear that the latter part of the plateau is a
succession of gorges separated by walls of sandstone
rock. Such intervening cracks are always of a desert
character, and Stuart was heartily tired of them, because
of the difficulty of finding water amid their sandy crevices. Yet they were not without a beauty of their
own. The diversity of colour alone gave a charm to
the scene that was not found elsewhere. The sun
glaring upon the red or yellow precipices made a beautiful contrast with the emerald verdure of the valleys
below; and then the diversity of foliage, from the
graceful palm which swung its feathered branches over
the top of the cliffs, to the stately forest of gum trees
which clustered in dignified masses on the edge of the
gorges, had altogether an effect which was handsome
and attractive. At thirteen miles this last wall terminated on a precipice which showed a lovely view
below. There was a valley thickly wooded, with a
creek running through it ; and there were other gorges,
but nothing seemed to bound the course of the stream
to the northward. With difficulty they descended to
it. It was running, and fringed with a forest of palm
trees, like plumes of green feathers. Stuart and his
party, of course, followed the creek, which led through
a precipitous valley, and on reading the description of
the tributaries and the gorges from which they came,
one is forcibly reminded of Grey's account of the
Glenelg.

Stuart now imagined that he was on the South
Alligator River, upon a branch which he called the
Mary. He subsequently found that it was a branch
of the Adelaide he had arrived at. In the first
volume it has been narrated that this stream was
found by Stokes. Stuart found, as he went down it,
that it bore just the same character that streams in the
tableland always have. Every tributary was difficult

to cross, because of the boggy nature of the soil, and the
country was so stony that his horses suffered severely.
On the 18th the party came to the Adelaide, that is to
say, the main channel. It was about eighty yards wide,
and so still that it was impossible to say which way the
current went.   The banks were thickly lined with
bamboo.   They were about twelve feet above the
water, and very steep, while the river itself seemed
extremely deep and free from fallen timber. On the
further side of the channel the glassy water was shaded
by a lofty range, whose shadowy gullies made a beautiful background to the scene. But if it was encouraging
to have reached this river, and if the scenery was beautiful, it was by no means pleasant to travel across. The
tributaries mostly flowed into marshes before joining
the river, and these were not only too boggy to cross,
but they were fringed by clumps of trees and bamboos
bound together by a climbing vine, through which it
was impossible to force a path. The marshes delayed
Stuart for a good many days, but at last he got clear of
them by skirting their edges and avoiding the river. At
the further side of them he met a dense forest of mangroves, and while forcing a way through it, came suddenly upon the sea.

Thus Stuart's task was accomplished, and he stood
gazing on the Indian Ocean with as much delight as
Bilboa when he crossed to the Pacific. He washed his
hands and dipped his feet into the water, to make his
actual crossing from sea to sea perfectly complete, and
having cut his initials upon a tree and hoisted a flag,
the party gave three cheers for the Queen and three for
the Prince of Wales. Beneath the tree he buried a
record of his visit, and having picked up a few shells,
he bade farewell to the north coast which he had visited,
close to Cape Hotham.

Of the triumph thus secured to Australian discovery
it is needless to speak. No man deserved his success
better than Stuart; no man had laboured so long and
so perseveringly to obtain it. It may be doubted,
indeed, whether the route thus opened will be always
practicable, except in its northern part. Indeed, we may

admit that the country between Lake Torrens and Newcastle Water is only one degree removed from a desert,
but the knowledge of this fact was invaluable to the
colony, all the more creditable to the explorer as it was
difficult to ascertain. It may be doubted also whether
the river which finally conducted to the coast was
really the Adelaide. It does not correspond with the
descriptions of either Stokes or Helpman, and was a
little east of the course laid down for that river. If,
however, it should be proved that it was a different
stream, so much the more important do Stuart's discoveries become. It is very sad to mention, in conclusion, that that this journey nearly cost the intrepid
traveller his life. He had been suffering from scurvy
before the coast was reached, and on his return he was
so bad that the horses were obliged to carry him upon a
rough litter. His sufferings were dreadful, and it is
pitiable to read his journal at that time. At one period
it was supposed that he could not reach Adelaide alive,
but he weathered through, and was enabled, happily, to
enjoy his triumph and the reward (£2,000) which the
Government bestowed upon him. The return journey
was marked throughout by a great scarcity of water.
Most of the holes upon which they had relied upon their
outward course were found perfectly dried up. On one
occasion the horses had to be pushed through one
hundred miles of country without finding water. Yet
notwithstanding such difficulties, the party sustained
few losses, and arrived on the out-stations early in
December, 1862.

After the arrival of Stuart's expedition, the colonies
rested from their great efforts to explore the continent,
and up to this time no formal exploring expedition has
been undertaken. But it is a subject which never rests,
and therefore new additions are daily made to our
knowledge. During Stuart's absence a portion of the
country north-west of the Great Australian Bight was
explored, by by several intending squatters. Their
observations confirmed what had been previously known
of this tract. They described the country as one vast
plain. Many parts have not a tree visible in any

direction, yet the grass was beautiful and green, for
rain had recently fallen. The result of the journeys was
the formation of a company, to sink wells and occupy
the land for pastoral purposes; the plan has not succeeded,
but the territory is occupied while these sheets are
passing through the press. Like Arabia, these tracts
will be characterised by their flocks and their wells;
but it remains to be seen whether such a country cannot
be made serviceable by an energetic and more enterprising race than the Arabians, with scientific improve-
ments to back them up, of which no Oriental ever dreamt.

In 1863, an expedition was sent out from Western
Australia to test the character of the country on the
tableland eastward from Swan River. Like every
exploration in that direction, it returned unsuccessful.
Mr. Lefroy, the leader, was of opinion that the country
discovered would be found fit for agricultural purposes;
but when he began to enumerate its qualities in his
report, they hardly bore out his opinion. He said that
it was utterly destitute of permanent surface water,
unless in a few native wells existing on the margins of
the bare rock. It is nearly destitute of valleys, which
could serve as channels, and though swept by thunderstorms in the summer season, the nature of the soil
did not permit it to retain water for any length of time.
There were few natives, and no game; yet Mr.
Lefroy considered that the rainfall was sufficient in the
whole year for all the necessities of stock, if means
could be taken to secure it. His furthest east was long.
121° 40', not very far north of the Dundas Hills, which
Roe had described as such an awful desert of scrub in
1848. The whole country was granitic, covered either
with a red sandy loam, or a thin crust of quartzite on
slaty rocks. There were no trap-rocks, such as basalt
or porphyry, and yet the soil was rich. From experiments made in other localities, Mr. Lefroy was confident that water would be found by sinking to a moderate depth; and on this, of course, depends his view as
to the availability of the land. If it were not so densely
covered with scrub in parts, one could believe in its
adaptability to the purposes of agriculture; but while

hoping for the best, past experience must prevent any
one being as sanguine in the matter as the explorers
themselves.

While these pages have been passing through the
press, exploration has still been going on in various
parts of the country. Western Australia has sent an
expedition to the River Glenelg, first explored by Grey.
It has found the mouth of the stream to be available
for the purposes of navigation, and the country round
quite as excellent as Grey had represented it. The
party also explored a great deal in the neighbourhood
of Camden Harbour, and the result of their report has
been that settlements are already commenced.

North Australia is now also about to be colonized.
A party has been sent from Adelaide to make the preliminary surveys. As yet little is known of its movements, beyond the fact that Adam Bay, near the mouth
of the Adelaide, has been selected as the site of the new
town. A fatal affray had taken place with the natives,
and some insubordination had been manifested by the
junior officers, but this is all that is known at present.

Another settlement has also been made by the
Queensland Government. In the early part of 1864,
H.M. steamship *Salamander* was put in commission,
under the command of the Hon. J. Carnegie, for the
purpose of proceeding to Port Albany. She arrived in
Sydney at the beginning of June, and after a stay of
about a fortnight left for Moreton Bay, where she
arrived on Sunday, the 26th June. While in Sydney,
the Hon. Captain Carnegie chartered the ship *Golden
Eagle*, for the purpose of conveying the necessary
stores and materials for the new settlement from
Brisbane to Point Somerset. This vessel sailed from
Sydney on the 25th June.

The last explorations which we have to chronicle,
are in South Australia and Queensland. In the former
colony, Mr. M'Farlane attempted to explore far into
those mysterious places at the head of the Australian
Bight. He proceeded in a northerly direction, over a
level, well-grassed country for fifty miles. This plain

appeared to be totally destitute of water, and in the whole distance there was not a single object except grass to break the monotony.

In Queensland, a small river named the Herbert was found at the back of Rockingham Bay, by Mr. Dalrymple. He was searching for a pass through the ranges, which, it will be remembered, caused such disastrous losses to Kennedy's party. At present there is a fine and flourishing settlement at Rockingham Bay. It is only sixteen years since Kennedy landed there as an explorer, and then the place was regarded with horror, as an irreclaimable wilderness. A pass has now been found through the mountains, and on the higher lands, on which such desperate struggles to advance were made by Kennedy and his party, large herds of sheep and cattle may now be seen quietly feeding. Thus it is that the tide of civilization rolls slowly onward after the explorer.

CONCLUSION.

IT was my intention to have concluded this history by a lengthened summary of the physical features of Australia, as far as they have been made known by the journeys and discoveries here recorded. But as the work progressed, the materials increased so rapidly that they became at last of such proportions that I could do justice to them only in a separate work. I have therefore abandoned my first intentions, and hope to be able soon to follow this work by a volume on the physical geography of Australia. I mean now only briefly to describe Australia as it is, or rather what our knowledge is, after all the explorations that have been made.

What we know of this vast continent does not go much beyond an acquaintance with the coast. One has only to look at the map to be convinced that we have as yet only obtained a very small glance into the interior. A little to the west of Central Mount Stuart, an immense blank occurs; and for twelve and a half degrees of latitude and longitude there is scarcely a mark to tell us what is contained therein. There are two small tracks on the edges, but, with these exceptions, nothing whatever is known of a tract of country nearly half a million square miles in area. Mr. A. Gregory described the north side of it as a desert. His brother characterized the north-west side in the same manner. Stuart on the west side was encountered by large tracts of spinifex grass and stately gum trees, apparently liable to occasional floods. Eyre, on the south side, and the explorers on the west, have been baffled by the same desert. It is, in fact, a sandy tableland, elevated on the west side, according to F. Gregory's observations, about three thousand feet above the level of the sea, and sloping down towards Lake Torrens, which is very little, if at all, raised above the surface of the ocean. From Lake Torrens and Lake Eyre it appears to rise again first in a range, and then in a series of terraces. This elevation terminates at last in the high, rugged Cordillera of the eastern coast. We may therefore regard the continent as tilted up on each side, and depressed in the centre to a kind of trough. The Gulf of Carpentaria would represent the northern portion, and the deep indented part of Spencer's Gulf the southern. Since, however, the northern coast is also tilted up, the trough or depression does not extend through the continent.

The eastern side of the tableland is the portion amid which the greater number of explorations across the continent have been made. It is decidedly better than the western half; a great deal of it is well watered, and probably, leaving out Australia Felix, nearly half of it may be considered fit for pastoral purposes. But there is much that must always be considered utterly useless to man. Apart from the arid nature of the climate, the soil is in places little better than a mere drift of red sand. This seems to come from a highly ferruginous tertiary sandstone, which prevails throughout all Australia. Its decomposition has left on the surface fragments more durable than the rest, and these strew the plains, making them most difficult to travel over. The exceptions to this rule are, the valleys of rivers, which are always fertile, and the neighbourhood of basaltic rocks. As the tilting of the great tableland has been accompanied by much volcanic action, trap-rocks and fertile country are found round the whole of its edges, and they are in reality the only true sources of large streams in Australia, and certainly the only exception to the sandy drifts in the interior.

It is on the western side of the central depression that the large blank occurs in our maps, through which Stuart's track seems like the winding of a small river. I am very far from believing that the interior of this is a desert, or should be considered as such, or that the glimpses obtained by two or three explorers are certain evidences of the nature of the whole. We have seen in the preceding pages how frequently explorers have been mistaken in their estimates. Oxley thought that the now populous districts of the Lachlan and Murrumbidgee would never be fit for the habitation of man. Sturt thought that the interior was a desert, because he visited in a dry season the most desolate portion of it.

The truth perhaps is, that the unexplored interior does not differ much from what has been hitherto discovered. There are most likely detached ranges of tablehills, granite peaks, watercourses, and even extensive creeks, emptying into well-grassed gum flats. There are, we may be sure, extensive rolling prairies of scrub, and many salt lakes, adding anything but a cheerful appearance to those torrid regions. There may even be rivers, and for this reason :—If the western edge of the tableland be on an average two thousand feet high, there must be a drainage to the interior nearly equal to that which causes so many rivers on the west coast. The watershed has never yet been crossed from the west side, but one cannot help remarking that wherever it has been crossed elsewhere good land has been found. It is no evidence against the existence of a river that none are found upon the south coast, especially in the

Australian Bight, where it would be most likely to appear. Many places in the interior of Australia have an extensive drainage, which never reaches the sea. The Barcoo drains into Lake Eyre, which is the receptacle of many other streams. A stream from the west coast might empty itself into Lake Gairdner. There must, at any rate, be some important drainage in connexion with that large sheet of water. Salt lakes always are, in Australia, the receptacles of many watercourses, and on the north-west side of Lake Gairdner, Stuart found a chain of such basins, which, in a more favourable season, might have been a fresh-water river. There may, however, be reasons why the rainfall in the interior should be less than on the coast, and therefore the character of the climate more arid. The rainy winds are from the north-west, and these must leave a great portion of their moisture on the high bluffs of the west coast, passing over the interior as a much drier wind.

With regard to the central depression or trough which runs from north to south, little need be said, for its character has often been described in the preceding pages. It is a series of salt lakes, sand drifts, and stony deserts. A great portion of it is redeemed, by the fact that it receives so much drainage from the east, by the various channels of the Barcoo, and from the west by waters which burst out in the form of immense thermal springs. The extent and number of the latter is almost incredible, and the depth from which they come is manifested by the great heat of their waters. Nothing could more clearly show the character of the central depression and the slow rate at which the tableland sinks down towards it, than the existence of these springs. Of the Sandy Desert, the greater portion is thickly covered with spinifex grass; but there are drifts of sand, with no vegetation whatever upon them, extending for several miles. This is probably drifted up into masses after the decomposition of the ferruginous sandstone. The siliceous fragments left behind form those shingle plains known as the Stony Desert: they exist over a far greater tract than that marked in the old maps of Australia as extending like an arm northwards from Lake Torrens. It would seem as if the decomposition of the rock here was owing in some measure to pressure, when the table-land on either side was uplifted.

Thus we see that after all the explorations have been made, we have adopted, with modification, the theory of the earlier colonists. It was thought in Oxley's time that the interior rivers must flow towards a central depression, and there form a kind of inland sea. Long after the abandonment of this theory we find it to be true, to a certain extent, and is realized in Lake Eyre, the extent of which is as yet undetermined. The inland lake theory was abandoned, after Sturt's discoveries, in favour of a central desert. This, it appears, is also true in a modified sense. Let us hope that there are such germs of truth in all the predictions about the future of Australia, and that it may realize the aspirations of those who look upon it as the seed of a vast and flourishing empire. If it does, it will be owing to the energy and activity of its sons, who may perchance be spurred to emulation by the deeds of daring their fathers have performed in obtaining the knowledge detailed in these volumes.

APPENDIX.

THE FATE OF LEICHHARDT'S PARTY.

I HAVE stated, in that part of the preceding pages which refers to Leichhardt's last expedition, that I should put together, in an Appendix, all the traces which have ever been found of the missing party. The question, which becomes more obscure and difficult as investigations proceed, as to what could have been the fate of the explorers, receives some light from the fact that the route is no longer in dispute. Traces of them have increased in number in the course of more recent explorations; and what was doubtful formerly, becomes almost a matter of certainty now. The first traces were those discovered by Mr. H. Hely's expedition. They consisted of certain relics among the natives, which could not be clearly referred to Leichhardt, unless in connection with a story which was so often varied and contradicted as to be quite untrustworthy. Besides the relics, there were two camps, evidently of an exploring party, and at each the trees were marked X V A, within a very rudely formed initial letter L. The L was reasonably supposed to stand for Leichhardt, for the trees could not have been marked by Mitchell for any purpose that one could guess, and there was no person in Mitchell's party whose christian name or surname began with the letter L. There was a person of the name of Luff with Kennedy, but it can hardly be supposed that he would have been allowed to mark two camps in succession with his initial, and that it should be the only mark left at the camps. Besides, we know from other evidence, that Kennedy's camps were marked E K. The X V A is very difficult of explanation. It could not refer to a date, because both camps would not have been marked alike; besides, Mr. W. B. Clarke has satisfactorily proved that Leichhardt could not have been at either of these camps by the 15th April, which is the only probable date to which they could be referred. But there is just a chance that the marks may have been made before Leichhardt's time. This surmise has some colour from the fact, that when the latter explorer went with Mr. Bunce to cross the tract between his former route and that of Mitchell, he found on the banks of the River Maranoa a tree marked with the letter L. The following entry in his diary has reference to these marks, and some others quite as inexplicable.

He writes: " Sept. 4.—We travelled about four miles south,
when we came to the place where we had first met the dray-
track of Sir Thomas Mitchell. A little further on we marked
a tree with L, and a *cross in the wood*. Sept. 8.—Mr. Bunce discovered very old horse-dung at the place where we camped.
We continued to follow up the river, and had scarcely gone
three miles when dray-tracks were observed, which were very
old and faint, and belonged to Mitchell's expedition. Fresh
horse-tracks were seen coming down the river, and apparently
turning up to the north-west of Mitchell's track, April 29, 1846.
These horse-tracks were observed all along our road, and at one
place an L was cut into a small water gum tree with a black
fellow's tomahawk."

So it appears that such a mark was there before Leichhardt's
time; but we must remember that this was at least two hundred miles from where Hely found the old camps. Altogether,
I think we must regard the camps as Leichhardt's, and whatever be the explanation of the V A, the X may be in some way
connected with the cross on the wood, italicized in the journal
as above.

After Hely's discovery comes that of Gregory, who found, in
1858, a camp, with a tree marked L, upon the Barcoo. This
single mark was considered unsatisfactory, until another camp
was found by Mr. Walker, about seven miles further down.
The question now was, to decide whither Leichhardt could have
steered after leaving the Barcoo. Was it along the Alice or
the Thompson Rivers. The former opinion seemed more probable, and it received apparent confirmation from the discoveries
of Walker. That gentleman found, at the head of the Flinders,
or near it, tracks of a large party going to the north-west.
Mr. Landsborough denied that these were Leichhardt's tracks.
He says, in a letter on the subject to the Rev. W. B. Clarke:
" In a journey in 1860, to search for runs, I went from Rockhampton to near the junction of what is now called the Bowen
with the Burdekin. As I could not proceed to the north-west,
owing to the flooded state of the country, I went to the southward until I reached Tower Hill, and thence on a southerly
course, about sixty-six miles to the junction of the Aramac
Creek with the Landsborough. I then followed the Aramac to
near its head, which was about sixty miles to the south-west,
then crossing a valley (probably the Alice), got to the watershed of the Belyando, and thence proceeded by Peak Range to
Rockhampton. In that expedition, we from time to time
marked trees L L. We always marked many trees thus at
our camps, as well as at every creek upon our route. You will
see by my journal that I think the main head of the Thompson
is to the west of the Landsborough. . . . Although continually

on the look-out for traces of Leichhardt in all my expeditions, and although I have often travelled on his route, the only tree I ever saw that was marked by him was one at the junction of Skull Creek with the Isaac River."

Walker's traces of Leichhardt must, I fear, be abandoned after this. Two things, however, should be noted. Though Walker said the tracks he saw were made in wet weather, and Landsborough states that the country was flooded at the time of his visit, yet Landsborough admits having seen some tracks on his homeward route (1862), which he could not account for. At one time he saw cart-tracks, and imagined that he was near a home station. He afterwards found that there was no station near. The country could hardly have been settled so early. Whose then were the cart-tracks? If they were recent (and unless they were, Landsborough could hardly have supposed them to have belonged to a recent settlement) there is an end to the idea of Leichhardt's party having formed them. On the Flinders also, Landsborough saw what he believed to be the tracks of Walker's party, while, according to the map, their routes never crossed. This fact may, however, be due to an error in their calculations, for the tracks were not very far off at the time. Lastly, Mr. Buchanan told Captain Norman that he had seen the tracks of Burke and Wills two hundred miles to the west of Mount Narrien. These were thought to be Burke's return tracks, but as we know that Burke returned by his outward route, and that near the place indicated would be on Walker's route, perhaps the latter gentleman was right after all; that is to say, of course, if Buchanan did not know which tracks were Landsborough's, which is hardly possible, as Buchanan, unless I am under a mistake, was out with Landsborough, or one of his former party.

With all these different rumours—with the marked trees and the story of Hely before one—it is very difficult to arrive at any conclusion with better claims for credence than the merest speculation. My own opinion, if of any value in a matter of such uncertainty, is, that if the party were not destroyed by the natives (a disaster which is hardly credible), they pushed on along the Barcoo, because that would be a good easy westerly course, with the certainty of water. As their difficulties would not really commence until they reached the western side of the centre, it was probably there they perished.

But in justice to the Rev. Mr. Clarke, I must here append his reasons for thinking that Leichhardt never went on to the Barcoo at all. In the face of the four L marked camps, the position is rather difficult to maintain, but I insert it as containing most interesting particulars about the unfortunate explorers, and his intentions before setting out on his fatal enterprise.

"Previous to his (Leichhardt's) last departure from Sydney," says Mr. Clarke, "he was on a visit to me, and we occupied some time in collecting information on the possibility of his overland journey to Swan River, and when I pointed out to him the great improbability that a direct route existed by means of oases in the desert, which was a favourite idea of his, he built very much upon a fact mentioned by Gregory or his brother, in his account of the country to the north-east of Perth, that a great accumulation of bones of supposed buffaloes had been met with. Leichhardt insisted that these were not the bones of buffaloes, but of *bullocks*, which had crossed the country from the western frontier of this colony. And he argued, that if cattle could get across it must have been by *oases*, where grass would be found, and that he could cross also.

"But after a great deal of consideration, he said it would be better to *skirt the desert*, and that, therefore, his final intention was to follow up the Burdekin to the river he named after myself, and proceed from the head of the Clarke, which he had not seen, to the westward, and so attempt to reach the country where the bones were found, by crossing the track along the north-west and west coast, which, so far as I believe, offers very little hope of success in any season.

"That this was always in the mind of Leichhardt may be inferred from what he himself published respecting his *second* expedition, from which he was driven back by fever:—'The object of the new expedition here alluded to is to explore the interior of Australia, to *discover the extent of Sturt's Desert, and the character of the western and north-western coast,* and to observe the gradual change in vegetation and animal life from one side of the continent to the other. Dr. Leichhardt does not expect to be able to accomplish this *overland journey to Swan River*' (i. e. by way of the bounds of Sturt's Desert, the west and north-west coasts) 'in less than two years and a half.' . . . (According to a letter written by him on the eve of his departure, December 6, 1846). . . . "He then purposed *to travel over his old route to Peak Range*, and then to shape his course westwards, but thought it not impossible, as his course depends on *water*, that he should be obliged to reach the Gulf of Carpentaria, and then follow up some river to its source.'— *Appendix to Journal*, p. 544.

"It is quite clear from this that he would never rashly venture into the desert, and it is not impossible that he might have been dead or dying nearer to the north-west Victoria,* from which Mr. Gregory started on the 21st June, 1856, than to the Victoria (Barcoo), where Mr. Gregory found the letter L in 1858.

    * North-west Victoria is that which Mr. Gregory visited in 1856.

"My impression therefore is, that Leichhardt never attempted to cross by way of Mitchell's Victoria.

"There is another reason why I think he would not. A great jealousy existed between the two explorers. Sir Thomas called Leichhardt (adding an expressive expletive) 'a —— *foreign coaster*'—alluding to his habit of keeping as near the sea as possible, and, under this impression, he removed one of Leichhardt's mountain ranges (Expedition Range) a *whole degree* of *longitude* out of the place to which he had assigned it. This may be seen on Sir Thomas's general map of his expedition up to the year 1850. A similar feeling would have kept Leichhardt from following Mitchell's tracks; and yet it is at the junction of the Alice and the Barcoo, where the united waters run south-west, that Gregory looked for traces of his outward-bound course. The letter L carved on a tree in long. 146° 6', is not likely to be Leichhardt's, because he was in the habit of marking all his camps, and only this has been found. It might, perhaps, have been the mark of Luff, who accompanied Kennedy. The spot is close to the camp of Sir Thomas Mitchell, of the 17th September, 1845, and of Kennedy's camp on the 29th July, 1847. Sir Thomas Mitchell repassed the locality the day he gave to the river its name. Kennedy himself does not appear to have marked his camp till his arrival at his furthest point, which was on the 9th September, and then his mark was $\frac{E\ K}{1847}$, the next camp upwards bearing K II. On looking over his journal, which I prepared for the press, I find Luff was frequently out with him.

"It is not impossible, however, that some stockmen may have been there. Expeditions of that kind are not uncommon; and the late Mr. Nelson Lawson told me that his stockmen at Fort Bourke, on the Darling, had been in this way across the country as far as what is now known as Mount Lyall, which was one of the points made by Sturt in his last expedition into Central Australia. No dependence then can, I think, be put on the solitary L, in long. 146°. And I am still of opinion that the remains of Leichhardt's expedition, seeing the cattle have not returned, will, if ever, be found far away to the north-westward of any search yet made.

"As conjectures can do harm, it may be further observed that Kennedy commenced his exploration of the unknown portion of the river on the 13th August, and he again reached his camp of 29th July (146° E.) on the 12th October, during which interval he remained ten days in camp at different places, making the locality in question the *fiftieth* of his camps. This might account for the L. But there is a fact mentioned by him, under date of 12th August, which seems to show that a

visitor had been on the Victoria since Sir T. Mitchell; for he
very far distant from his furthest point, and where he has
never been, in a spot too rough for pleasant riding, Kenn—
came upon *horse-dung* in two places near the river, and Mitch.
he says, as the charts also show, kept beside the river ther
for three days. Sir Thomas also says, that even there the
chief of the native tribe had possession of an 'iron tomahawk
with a very long handle to it.' This is on a river unknown
as he thought till then, to the white man! *According to*
Mitchell's account of the 'large permanent huts of the natives,' even the saplings, &c., seen by Mr. Gregory, *might be*
either the remains of a temporary hut, or of a native hut, as
well as of Leichhardt. At any rate, it is very unlikely that he
is living; and all the stories about his captivity appear to me
idle speculation. The parties who accompanied Leichhardt
were, perhaps, little capable of shifting for themselves *in* case
of any accident to the leader. The second in command, a
brother-in-law of Leichhardt, came from Germany to *join him*
just before starting, and *he* told me, when I asked him what
his qualifications for the journey were, that he had been *at sea*,
had suffered shipwrecks, and was therefore well able to endure
hardship. I do not know what his other qualifications were.
Leichhardt himself was of *weak sight*, afflicted with a troublesome complaint, and, if we are to believe the statements of
those who were with him, by no means a good bushman. *That*
under such circumstances he ever found his way through the
desert, where ophthalmia is so general an enemy, *is impro-*
bable; but knowing his ideas of exploration, and having con-
versed on the topic with him, I feel convinced he never attempted the desert where he has been looked for, and that
it is not improbable that some of his camps, which Mr. Gregory
found on his homeward journey from the north-west coast, are
likely to have been his camps on his third and last expedition.

"It is this problem which I hope will yet be solved; *and*
perhaps when the gold-fields, which will some day be discovered
about the Burdekin River, and its higher lands shall have
attracted population into that region, we shall know more of
the fate of my poor friend than we are likely to do from what
has hitherto been accomplished."

THE END.

LONDON: PRINTED BY WILLIAM CLOWES AND SONS, STAMFORD STREET AND CHARING CROSS.

www.ingramcontent.com/pod-product-compliance
Lightning Source LLC
LaVergne TN
LVHW012208040326
832903LV00003B/189

* 9 7 8 1 0 1 7 3 7 7 9 9 6 *